T0329653

The Business Ethics Twin-Track

The Business Ethics Twin-Track

Combining controls and culture to minimise reputational risk

STEVE GILES

WILEY

This edition first published 2015

© 2015 Steve Giles

Registered office
John Wiley and Sons Ltd, The Atrium, Southern Gate, Chichester, West Sussex, PO19 8SQ, United Kingdom

For details of our global editorial offices, for customer services and for information about how to apply for permission to reuse the copyright material in this book please see our website at www.wiley.com.

The right of the author to be identified as the author of this work has been asserted in accordance with the Copyright, Designs and Patents Act 1988.

All rights reserved. No part of this publication may be reproduced, stored in a retrieval system, or transmitted, in any form or by any means, electronic, mechanical, photocopying, recording or otherwise, except as permitted by the UK Copyright, Designs and Patents Act 1988, without the prior permission of the publisher.

Wiley publishes in a variety of print and electronic formats and by print-on-demand. Some material included with standard print versions of this book may not be included in e-books or in print-on-demand. If this book refers to media such as a CD or DVD that is not included in the version you purchased, you may download this material at http://booksupport.wiley.com. For more information about Wiley products, visit www.wiley.com.

Designations used by companies to distinguish their products are often claimed as trademarks. All brand names and product names used in this book and on its cover are trade names, service marks, trademark or registered trademarks of their respective owners. The publisher and the book are not associated with any product or vendor mentioned in this book. None of the companies referenced within the book have endorsed the book.

Limit of Liability/Disclaimer of Warranty: While the publisher and author have used their best efforts in preparing this book, they make no representations or warranties with the respect to the accuracy or completeness of the contents of this book and specifically disclaim any implied warranties of merchantability or fitness for a particular purpose. It is sold on the understanding that the publisher is not engaged in rendering professional services and neither the publisher nor the author shall be liable for damages arising herefrom. If professional advice or other expert assistance is required, the services of a competent professional should be sought.

Library of Congress Cataloging-in-Publication Data is Available

ISBN 978-1-118-78537-9 (hardback)
ISBN 978-1-118-78534-8 (epub)   ISBN 978-1-118-78536-2 (epdf)

Cover design: Wiley

Set in 9/12pt Photina MT Std by Laserwords Private Limited, Chennai, India
Printed in Great Britain by TJ International Ltd, Padstow, Cornwall, UK

To the three people without whom I could never have written this book: my parents, Hilda and Norman Giles; and my wife Val, the love of my life

Contents

Chapter 2: The business ethics framework

Chapter 3: Bribery, corruption and adequate procedures

Chapter 4: Reputation, risk and conduct

Chapter 5: The governance dimension

Chapter 6: Aspects of leadership: ethics, tone at the top and handling a crisis

Chapter 7: Risk, compliance and the controls framework

Chapter 8: The business ethics toolbox

Chapter 9: Whistle-blowing: encouraging a culture of openness

Acknowledgements

There are many people to whom I owe a sincere debt of gratitude for their time, ideas, insights, help and support during the writing of this book.

First and most importantly I want to thank my wife, Val Giles. I depend on Val totally and have done so ever since we were married. As with so much else that I have tried to do, I know that this book would never have been written without her steadfast support, advice and encouragement.

I also want to thank the various people at the publisher, John Wiley & Sons, who were instrumental in pulling this book together. The commissioning editors Stephen Mullaly and Gemma Valler helped to shape the initial concepts, whilst Wendy Alexander, business development manager, gave the project the go-ahead. I am particularly grateful to Gemma for her good advice and support throughout and for showing continued faith in me by agreeing to extend the original timescale to enable the book to be completed despite the pressures of work. My thanks also go to Wiley's marketing professionals, especially to Ben Hall for his positive attitude, understanding and gentle coaxing of promotional paragraphs out of me when required and to Jennie Kitchen for coordinating the artwork for the book cover with the design team.

Next, I would like to thank my interviewees – the business men and women who agreed to be interviewed by me as part of my research for this book and who gave up their valuable time in order to do so. They are drawn from different industry sectors and were chosen for their business experience and specialist expertise. These interviews provide important practical insights into some of the key issues discussed in the book and, from my point of view at least, they were great fun to conduct. So, I want to say a big 'thank you' to: Annabel Parsons, one of the partners at Heidrick & Struggles; Bernard Briggs and David Grew, respectively Managing Director and Finance Director of West Leigh Ltd; Cathy James, Chief Executive of the whistle-blowing charity Public Concern at Work; James Featherby, Chairman of the Church of England's investment advisory committee; Lis Batteson, ex-Managing Director of Quorum Training Ltd; Mike Meldrum, formerly of Cranfield School of Management and now an independent business leadership consultant; Peter Hanlon, senior executive at the Westpac banking group in Australia; Peter Jones, experienced businessman and chairman of the audit committees of the United Kingdom Atomic Energy Authority and the National Nuclear Laboratory; Peter Walshe, a director of Millward Brown, the brand consultancy; and Sandro Boeri, Managing Director of Risk Audit Professional Development Ltd.

Each of these 10 interviews lasted for between 45 minutes and 1 hour. I recorded them using a small digital voice recorder, a very efficient piece of technology but one that would have been no use to me for practical purposes had it not been for the time and effort put in by my friend and (for these purposes) audio typist, the splendid Julie Collins. I have been fortunate to know Julie for many years now. She agreed to type up all 10 of the interviews for me, which she did with her usual blend of patience and efficiency. This typing was all done in her spare time and doubtless took a significant number of hours to complete. Many, many thanks Julie – I am enormously grateful to you once again.

I wish to thank three individuals who each contributed to the book in different but significant ways. My thanks go to Charles Kingsmill, the business strategy consultant who helped me to pull various disparate thoughts and ideas together at the start of the writing process and for his friendship and encouragement throughout. Thanks also to Louise, the Ethics Officer at one of my clients. Louise did not wish to be identified in the book but she was kind enough to spend time with me discussing some of the day to day difficulties involved in trying to manage ethics and behaviour in the workplace. Many thanks also to Philip Weston, director at Kelso Place Asset Management Ltd, the London-based private equity firm, for providing his thoughts and insights into some of the important factors that have influenced his decision-making process when considering potential investment opportunities and when managing the companies subsequently acquired.

Finally, I want to thank the numerous business people who have assisted in the writing of this book, albeit unknowingly, through their contributions to the lectures, conference sessions, workshops and training courses that I have run. Almost every time that I speak at an event I learn something new from the various comments, questions, observations and stories of the people in the audience. I hope very much that all those who have listened to my talks have enjoyed them as much as I have enjoyed presenting and delivering them over the years.

Ultimately of course this book is my own. I take full responsibility for my writing – all of the judgements expressed, the recommendations put forward, the conclusions arrived at and the mistakes made are mine alone.

Prologue

 OPENING

Corporate values: an old story

'RICE'

In the mid 1990s a company in the United States attracted much acclaim for the innovative way that it talked about itself and what it stood for. This company developed a 'vision and values' platform to demonstrate to investors and employees (and also to third-party stakeholders such as customers, suppliers and the local communities where its operations were based) that it was committed to good business ethics. This commitment was most memorably summarised in the pithy and catchy acronym 'RICE'. Each letter in the acronym stood for one of the four core values that the organisation claimed underpinned its entire approach to business: respect, integrity, communication and excellence.

This was an impressive message, delivered in a highly innovative way. The company would respect everybody that it did business with. It would carry out all of its activities in the 'right' way, abiding by the law, keeping its word and meeting all of its obligations. The company would not only talk to people, it would listen to them too. And finally its people and the products and services that it provided could be relied upon because they were all underpinned by the highest level of technical competence and proficiency that guaranteed consistency of performance.

What was not to like about this? The so-called 'RICE model' was both smart (the acronym was put together by clever people to be 'catchy' so that everyone would remember it easily) and powerful – the underlying message was overwhelmingly positive. The model was designed to signpost those behaviours and actions that the company most valued and thereby to generate feelings of confidence and trust in anyone who had dealings with the business. It was an inspirational message, one that combined competence with a positive corporate culture – people could rely on this company.

So, how did it all turn out? What actually happened in practice?

Well, the story ended in the worst possible way with a dramatic corporate collapse. The cause was far removed from the values set out in the 'RICE model' – the collapse was brought about by accounting fraud perpetrated by some top executives and senior managers in the business. The company filed for bankruptcy in 2001, resulting in financial hardship and misery for thousands of employees who lost their jobs and many of them their life savings too. Investors lost billions of dollars. Numerous executives were indicted, mainly from the accounting or trading functions within the company, and many have spent time in jail. There was personal tragedy in the case too: the ex-chief strategy officer committed suicide and the ex-chairman died of a heart attack whilst awaiting sentencing.

The company's name was Enron.[1]

The 'say-do' gap

Enron included a summary of the values of the RICE model in its Annual Report of 1999.[2] The Enron case provides a classic example of the 'say-do' gap. This is an issue that I often encounter when discussing business ethics – people can become angry when they read corporate statements that are not supported by actions and behaviour. I understand this – it smacks of hypocrisy. It is a relatively easy matter for executives to compile a list of admirable qualities and behaviours and then to talk about these as comprising the 'core values' of their organisation. But it is sometimes more difficult in practice for those same executives to conduct business according to their stated values, especially when under pressure in terms of their organisation's results and performance. Failure to act in accordance with values has consequences, all of them negative: disillusionment and disregard for formal rules by managers and staff; and a loss of trust by third-party stakeholders, to name just two.

Turning again to the Enron example, the RICE model was promoted in a 1998 corporate video featuring Ken Lay, Enron's Chairman and CEO at the time, together with Jeffrey Skilling, the company's Chief Operating Officer, entitled 'Enron Vision and Values'. The footage is still available on YouTube and one section in particular is significant. It shows Mr Lay looking earnestly into the camera, nodding his head and saying: 'We treat everyone with absolute integrity. We stand by our word; we play by all the rules; we really concentrate on doing our job right.'[3] These words carry heavy irony today, knowing with the benefit of hindsight how Mr Lay and some at least of his people actually behaved in practice. Given much of what has been written about the Enron case, however, Mr Ley's words would no doubt have seemed hypocritical, self-serving and cheap to many at the time (not to all, however, and later in the book I recount a meeting I had with an ex-Enron manager that taught me the dangers of relying on simplistic assumptions).

This 'say-do' gap is something that people recognise very quickly and they don't like it. It is responsible for a lot of the cynicism and unease that I sense sometimes when I work with groups on business ethics, whether as part of an in-house project team or when delivering talks, workshops or courses. The gap helps to promote the idea that there are no ethics in business and that time and effort spent discussing values, culture and behaviour achieves nothing because all that matters in the cut-throat world of business is results – profits, dividends and maximising shareholder value. According to this thinking, business ethics is a piece of window dressing, at best useful for PR purposes but in reality not central to organisations or to the people who work in them.

I do not subscribe to this point of view. Indeed, I try to confront it head on by referring to the Enron case at the outset of any ethics session that I run and then drawing out the lessons in this example. My point is simple – there should be no 'say-do' gap. Nobody forces any organisation or any CEO to talk about their ethics or their values, what to say, what words to use. To the extent that they choose to do so, two things are vital in terms of the actual words that are used: first they must be authentic and be rooted in the culture of the organisation; and second they must be reflected in all the actions, behaviour and decision-making of those working in the organisation, both in good times and in bad. Consistency of performance is as critical here as it is in any other area of business. As always the key to this is leadership and tone at the top, two of the main themes of this book.

ABOUT THE BOOK

Original idea

The book has its origins in a meeting that I held with Gemma Valler and Stephen Mullaly of John Wiley & Sons in London in early 2013. Gemma was keen to publish a work around the themes of business ethics, reputation and corporate culture and she wanted to know whether this was some-thing that I might like to do. I was interested straight away. One reason was that I had spent the last 20 years or so working in precisely these areas in various capacities: as an investigator of fraud and financial crime; as an advisor to directors and senior managers on governance-related issues and operational risk; and as a lecturer and trainer on many connected topics – governance, risk and compliance, financial crime, audit and business ethics. I had written a book on corporate fraud two years previously and Gemma's proposal seemed like an extension of that which fitted very well with the way my own career had developed.

The other reason for my interest was simple – I felt that Gemma's suggestion was both important and highly topical. The global financial crisis of 2007–09 had seen sub-prime mortgage contagion spread from the USA to Europe and lead to a credit crunch and liquidity shortfalls. The result was the failure of a number of international financial institutions that either collapsed, such as Lehman Bros., or required bail-outs from governments in order to survive, like the Royal Bank of Scotland plc. Many economies in the Western world went into recession, with a wholesale loss of jobs, investment and confidence. Austerity became the political order of the day. Indicators like the 2012 Edelman Trust Barometer[4] pointed to a steep decline in trust in their governments by citizens and sharp drops in the credibility of political leaders. This was replicated by a credibility drop on the part of CEOs in business generally in a number of mature markets (e.g. the USA, the UK, France, Germany and South Korea).

These feelings were still very much alive at the beginning of 2013. The events of the previous year, rather than suggesting a re-building of trust, had if anything only increased the negativity. To me, an Englishman living in London, a number of events coalesced in the UK during 2012 that convinced me that this was a book that I wanted to write.

2012 effect

2012 was a remarkable year.

Most memorably from the UK perspective, 2102 was the year of the London Olympics. From the extraordinary opening ceremony of the Summer Olympic Games on 27 July, to the closing ceremony of the Paralympic Games on 9 September, the UK hosted a magnificent sporting spectacle that earned almost universal praise. There were stunning performances, most obviously from star athletes such as Usain Bolt, David Rudisha, Jessica Ennis, Michael Phelps, David Weir and Mo Farah but also from the many more medal winners and other competitors with 'personal bests' who took part in the Games. But the plaudits for the London Olympics were not reserved for the athletes alone. From the oversight of the planning and development of the Games carried out by the London Organising Committee of the Olympic and Paralympic Games, through to the construction of the new Games venues and infrastructure under the aegis of the Olympic Delivery Authority, to the people employed at the various stadia, to the 70,000 volunteers – people who committed to a minimum of 10 days volunteering – there was widespread recognition of jobs well done. The London Olympics generated intense interest and passionate support from the public, especially in the UK of course but also from people around the world. The Games were viewed as a huge success by virtually all stakeholders.

By way of complete contrast to the London Olympics, 2012 was also the year of corporate scandals and tarnished business reputations. Consider the following British organisations: Barclays Bank, the British Broadcasting Corporation (BBC), the Department for Transport, G4S, Royal Bank of Scotland, GlaxoSmithKline (GSK) and HSBC. Collectively, they attracted extremely negative head-lines and commentaries in the media at various times during 2012, sometimes because of gross errors and incompetence but more often as a result of poor and unethical behaviour. Indeed, some of the allegations pointed to possible criminal conduct. Nor were British businesses unique in this regard. For example, the reputations of these well-known international organisations were all damaged during 2012: News Corporation, Olympus, the Galleon family of hedge funds; the Stanford Group, UBS and JP Morgan.

I watched each of these stories develop during 2012 with a mixture of emotions. Like many people, no doubt, I was fascinated by the detail as each scandal unfolded, but I was also dismayed to learn of the inadequacies of often very highly paid senior managers, many of whom simply seemed not to be up to the job. I shared the sense of anger and outrage felt by large numbers of citizens all over the world at particularly egregious examples of greed, arrogance or complacency exhibited by people in positions of power. One emotion that I did not experience, however, was surprise – after all, there have been numerous examples of corporate scandals over the last 30 years, so why should 2012 be any different?

2012 did feel different somehow, however. To me this difference was expressed in another form of gap – this time a chasm in performance between those contributing to the success of the London Olympics and those who damaged the reputations of each of the organisations mentioned above through their actions and behaviours. This gap really caught my attention.

I also felt an enormous sense of frustration – people in business should know better and they should perform better. There is a template to promote the likelihood of successful outcomes, both on the athletics track and in the boardroom. This template is in two halves. First, the technical steps – the training schedules for the athletes, the systems, controls and procedures for directors and senior managers. These are necessary and must be calibrated correctly to suit each individual circumstance. They are not in themselves sufficient for success, however. The second component is critical and it involves personal commitment – hard work, consistency of performance and attitude, a focus on the long-term goals rather than on short term distractions. Both components are required for success, whether in sport or in business.

Something had clearly gone wrong with the business template in 2012. It is possible that some directors and senior managers were unaware of the series of policies and procedures developed in recent years that are designed to promote good business ethics, positive culture and consistent decision-making and thereby reduce the risk of reputational damage. Either that or else they were not prepared to contribute by setting the right example, the right tone at the top. Tone at the top is an often-quoted phrase today. It is easy to say but it is never easy to put into effect – effective tone at the top means that statements are translated into behaviour and actions. To do so involves the personal commitment of business leaders and the investment of time and resources over many years in order to embed a positive culture throughout their organisations. But it can be done.

My idea and objective was to articulate the template, or at least certain parts of it, in a way that would provide practical guidance for directors and managers on what they can do to make a difference in these areas. That was the key thought behind me writing this book.

Structure and methodology

Introduction

This is a business book, one that provides practical advice. It is not a theoretical treatise. So, I have written it based upon my own experience, supplemented throughout by three additional reference points: first, my research into some important headline scandals that I use from time to time to draw lessons from; second, the views of a number of experienced entrepreneurs and business men and women that I either know or have been introduced to, as expressed in interviews conducted for the purposes of the book; and third, the thoughts, opinions, concerns and suggestions that have been expressed to me during the course of my work over the years, whether in projects or in seminars or in workshops.

In order to facilitate the distillation of these ideas, I have written the book around a hypothetical project dealing with cultural change during which I advise a fictional client and facilitate a series of workshops with a senior executive project team. I describe this mechanism in more detail below, but before doing so I want to say a little about the interviews and the interviewees.

Interviews

I have included, at appropriate points throughout the book, extracts from 10 interviews that I carried out with business men and women to provide insights and comments based on their practical experience of the areas under discussion at the time. I am extremely grateful for their time and for enabling me to build this extra dimension into the book.

Taking them in the order in which they appear in the book (and with their positions stated as they appeared on the day of the interviews), the interviewees comprise: James Featherby, Chairman of the Ethical Advisory Group, which advises the Church of England on its investment portfolio; Bernard Briggs and David Grew, respectively the Managing Director and the Finance Director of West Leigh Ltd.; the leadership expert Mike Meldrum, formerly of Cranfield School of Management and now an independent consultant; Peter Walshe, Global Account Director at Millward Brown, the leading brand research consultancy firm; Annabel Parsons, a partner with Heidrick & Struggles, the worldwide executive search firm; Peter Hanlon, advisor to Gail Kelly the CEO of Westpac Banking Corporation, the first bank to be established in Australia; Peter Jones, experienced businessman and chairman of the audit committees of the United Kingdom Atomic Energy Authority and the National Nuclear Laboratory; Sandro Boeri, the founder of Risk Audit, a training firm specialising in running courses for internal auditors in the financial services industry; Lis Batteson, the ex-Managing Director of Quorum Training; and Cathy James, the Chief Executive of the whistle-blowing charity Public Concern at Work.

I want to extend a big 'thank you' to each of the interviewees.

The Stronach Group and workshops

When starting to write this book, I wanted it to be practical and relevant to those running organisations rather than simply a collection of theoretical essays. In order to promote this aim I decided to use a device, a mechanism that would enable me both to develop ideas and also to show how events might unfold in practice. This involved the creation of a fictional client whose chairman hires me to assist the organisation to develop a cultural change project through a series of workshops involving a small, high-powered executive team.

So, the ideas in the book, together with practical recommendations, are discussed and developed using the mechanism of a series of eight workshops that I facilitate on behalf of the fictional client, which I have chosen to call the Stronach Group. This Group is entirely made up, as are all the individuals and events that I describe in connection with it. Although necessarily artificial, the workshop mechanism enables me to connect the elements around the successful management of reputational risk (leadership and tone at the top, culture, behaviour and the modern business ethics toolkit) together in a logical way that also provides a sense of narrative flow.

The story begins in Chapter 1, which describes the sequence of events leading up to the meeting with the chairman of the Stronach Group and my subsequent hiring. Although these events are fictional they are not fanciful – I have obtained pieces of work through similar circumstances in the past. It is the same with the subsequent workshop programme. I have worked with organisations in this format before, although not in the structure that I have set out here in the book. One of the main differences is that, in reality, my workshops tend to be more discursive than those shown here with the Stronach characters. I am much more of a facilitator of discussion and a business advisor in real life than I am depicted in the workshop sections, where for the purposes of the book I am shown as taking the leading role throughout.

For the avoidance of doubt, it is important to state clearly that all the characters and events concerning the Stronach Group that feature in this book are fictitious. Any resemblance to real persons (whether living or dead) or to real corporations or to real events is entirely coincidental.

Workshop format and structure

For practicality and ease of use by the reader, each chapter after the first (which introduces the project) takes the form of a workshop and each workshop follows the same format. There are eight workshops in total and each has a three-part structure. The first part comprises a hypothetical discussion, with questions to and from the project team concerning the subject matter under discussion in that particular workshop. The second and major part of each workshop is then taken up with me addressing the subject matter itself, almost as a lecture and without reference back to the project team. The last stage sees the project team discussing the key lessons and learning points from the workshop and writing them up on a flipchart. In total there are over 40 of these 'key takeaways' spread throughout the book.

To conclude, I would say that this final part is something that I would always ask the participants to draw up at the end of a real-life workshop session. As well as being realistic, this method has an added benefit here. By having the fictional project team draw up their key takeaways at the end of each workshop, the reader is provided with a summary of the most important points arising – a series of practical recommendations that directors and senior managers can use to improve the business ethics framework in their own organisations.

 ## MY EXPERIENCE

Audit, risk and forensics

I am a chartered accountant by profession, qualifying in 1983 with the leading professional services firm Touche Ross (now known as Deloitte) in London. I started out as an auditor and in time became group manager of one of the firm's large audit departments before specialising in forensic accounting and risk management work. During the 1990s I worked for the firm on a number of high profile assignments, including the investigation of the collapse of the international conglomerate Polly Peck International and the activities of its then chairman and chief executive Mr Asil Nadir.

I left Touche Ross in 1997, initially to set up a forensic accounting business. Working with partners, colleagues and associates I was engaged primarily on financial crime risk management projects for the next six years or so, on an investigative and consultancy basis, helping directors and senior managers to obtain the best solutions to the various business problems that they faced. We advised some of the largest companies in the UK during this time and worked on a wide range of assignments in the UK, the USA and in various countries in Continental Europe.

Governance

Increasingly, during the early years of this century, my project work became focused on wider governance issues and providing advice to directors and senior managers, especially in the areas of compliance and risk management. I gained experience of working with multi-disciplinary teams, comprising at various times internal auditors, in-house lawyers and compliance officers, risk officers, human resources managers and information technology specialists. Reporting lines were to either main board committees (typically the audit committee) or to the board itself.

Over the last 10 years or so I have worked with directors and senior managers on a variety of projects and also in two specific arenas that have helped me to gain expertise in corporate governance. First, I have worked frequently with the London Stock Exchange. I run regular workshops for executive and non-executive directors in their offices in London. I also advise boards of directors on governance issues. This could be advice to foreign companies seeking to list on the London Stock Exchange or more general consultancy aimed at improving board performance. Second, I have worked with Heidrick & Struggles as part of their leadership team that carries out performance appraisals for the boards of their client organisations around the world. As a result, I have gained wide experience of interacting with directors and senior managers from many different backgrounds and jurisdictions. I have worked at board level with organisations as far afield as Trinidad and Tobago, the Bahamas, Nigeria, Egypt, the UAE, Mauritius, India, Kazakhstan and Mongolia (in addition to the UK, the USA and Europe).

Business ethics

Good business ethics provide the entire context within which corporate governance is set – without them, no organisation can pretend to be operating with good governance. Accordingly, business ethics has always been an integral part of my governance work. My first specific ethics assignment was in Trinidad and Tobago in 2006 when I worked with the leaders of a large financial services company to raise awareness of its ethics charter and related policies and help to embed the messages contained therein throughout the organisation. Since then, I have worked with a number of organisations seeking to develop their business ethics in various roles: sometimes as consultant, advising on the design and implementation of specific policies, procedures and controls; sometimes as workshop facilitator; sometimes in a training capacity, whether delivering face-to-face courses or helping to design online training modules.

As an observation, the attention paid by organisations in the UK to business ethics has increased noticeably over the last five years. This is no doubt partly a response to the global financial crisis and the concerns of citizens regarding the standards and conduct of people working in organisations in all business sectors, not only in financial services. But in my view the change is also in part a response to developing laws and regulations, for example the new requirements introduced by the Bribery Act 2010. As a result, all commercial organisations carrying on at least part of their business in the UK now have to put in place adequate procedures to prevent bribery and corruption from occurring anywhere in their operations. The need to comply with the Bribery Act 2010 has resulted in a considerable amount of work for myself (and no doubt for others specialising in this area) providing advice on the necessary policies, risk assessment, due diligence and training.

Speaking and writing

As will be apparent in the comments above, I have lectured in the UK and around the world on the broad subject area of governance, risk and compliance for many years now. I have worked with many different organisations to put on events, conferences and training courses and it has been an absolute pleasure for me to do so. I began in the UK by joining the lecturing panel at Quorum Training, whilst the first courses that I ran abroad were as part of the lecturing faculty at Euromoney Training and DC Gardiner. Since then, I have worked with a variety of other professional organisations including:

the London Stock Exchange, the Association of Certified Chartered Accountants (ACCA), the Institute of Chartered Accountants in England and Wales (ICAEW), Risk Audit, the Institute of Chartered Secretaries and Administrators (ICSA) and Lessons Learned Ltd. When working abroad I have often done so at the invitation of dedicated local trade associations and professional bodies, such as the Gibraltar Association of Compliance Officers (GACO) and the Malta Institute of Accountants (MIA).

A big part of the enjoyment for me in these lecturing assignments is that they provide the opportunity to meet and discuss business-related issues with people from all over the world. To take the broad European context first, business men and women from the Continent, notably from Russia, the Ukraine, France and Switzerland, attend my courses in the UK as delegates from time to time. I run courses regularly in the Isle of Man, the Channel Islands and Gibraltar. But I also work further afield and it has been a huge privilege for me to lecture and run courses in many different jurisdictions around the world. In Europe I have spoken at events in France, Germany, Spain, Luxembourg, Iceland and Malta. I have run in-house courses for Greek, Swedish and Danish banks and for a large pharmaceutical company based in Switzerland. I have worked in the Middle East in Egypt and in Kuwait. I have also lectured in jurisdictions further east, providing different experiences to those in Europe, specifically in Mauritius, Kazakhstan, Mongolia and Singapore. Finally, I have spent some time lecturing and working in the Americas: I have run a number of courses in the United States based in New York and Miami; I have participated in a variety of events (speaking at conferences, running public courses and giving in-house training for financial institutions and corporations in the energy sector) in the Caribbean island of Trinidad and Tobago and in the Bahamas; and I have run in-house training for a large Brazilian multinational energy group based in Rio de Janeiro.

I have also written about my business experiences, trying always to draw out practical advice and the lessons learned for use by directors and managers who run businesses. My first book called *Managing Fraud Risk* was published by John Wiley & Sons in 2012.

THE BOOK: KEY MESSAGES

Overarching principles

The two fundamental principles of this book are very simple: the first principle is that good business ethics is a necessary component of good business; and the second principle is always to remember that the first principle is important.

Taken together, these principles mean that all organisations that conduct business – from the large multinationals to small and medium sized owner-managed businesses and including the public sector, private sector, charities and voluntary bodies too – should devote time and effort to their values, their culture and their behaviour. Doing so offers the prospect of better engagement with customers and employees alike. Not doing so in my view simply increases risk, whether from the conduct of managers and staff or from association with an inappropriate third party or from adverse commentary in the media. Any or all of these will damage reputation and erode value.

Twin-track approach

Throughout the book I advocate that organisations take a twin-track approach to business ethics. To help readers visualise what I mean by this, I use two metaphors when describing this: the 'hardware' components and the 'software' components. Think of a computer or any piece of modern information technology. The visible part of any piece of IT (whether a PC, a laptop, a tablet or an iPhone) is its hardware – there is value in this of course, as demonstrated consistently by Apple with its innovative designs.

However, no piece of IT can function without the accompanying software. There is value in the software too – just ask Bill Gates. Hardware and software combined lead to a piece of IT that works.

It is the same with business ethics.

Business ethics hardware

Today, there is a well-established toolbox available to those directors and managers who wish to manage the culture and behaviours in their business. My concept of the ethical hardware equates to the tools in the box: value statements; ethics charters; codes of conduct and staff handbooks; policies and procedures; remuneration policies, especially around bonuses; whistle-blowing hotlines; a monitoring and review process (whether via compliance, audit or through hands-on review by managers).

This hardware kit is relatively straightforward. In the book I set out the main features of each tool and then provide directors and managers with practical tips on how to make the tools work more efficiently. The discussion on whistle-blowing hotlines in Chapter 9 is something of an exception here. It is more detailed and instructive because, despite being one of the most important tools in the toolbox, in my experience it is also one of the least well used.

In my view it is necessary for every organisation to have some at least of this hardware in place (proportionate always to the needs of the business) if it is to achieve even a basic level of assurance around behaviour and conduct.

Business ethics software

The ethical hardware will not be sufficient by itself, however, to enable an organisation to have assurance that it has good business ethics embedded throughout its operations so that its reputational risk is minimised. To achieve this, the hardware (the tools) must be combined with the software (the culture). This is where leadership and tone at the top are crucial, in particular the decisions that directors and managers make day after day. These decisions will vary depending on the type of organisation and the particular business sector. Here are just some of the many questions that business leaders have to answer regularly: who to hire, who to promote, who to sack; which prospective customers to accept and which to turn away; what level of due diligence of potential new suppliers should be carried out; what compromises to accept, if any, on the quality of the goods or services provided; and does the message from the top vary depending on the audience or on whether the news is good or bad, or does it remain consistent?

Business failures and scandals are caused more through software failures (poor behaviours) than through hardware failures (poor processes). It is more difficult to address software issues within an organisation. To do so successfully will require above all a hard-headed commitment from those at the top that leads to consistent decision-making based upon the values of the business.

I make use of examples in the book (both from my own experience and from headline cases) and extracts from the interviews to provide directors and managers with indicators of which actions and strategies are most likely to produce positive results in practice.

Role of compliance

Importance

I need to say a word at the outset about the role of compliance – the department and officers that ensure that first, external laws and regulations are being followed and second, internal policies and procedures are being followed too. This function is increasing in importance as legal and regulatory risk increases. Many organisations today, especially financial services institutions around the world, are investing heavily in compliance. Indeed at the time of writing in 2014 compliance officers have become amongst the most sought after professionals in the City of London. This is in direct response to tougher laws and regulations following the global financial crisis of 2007–09.

The first thing to say here is that I agree that the compliance function is important. It forms part of a broader control environment which is strengthened when an organisation builds up a working culture where compliance is embedded in the actions and decisions of all managers and staff. I also believe that it is right that if people in business break the law, if they contravene regulations, if they fail to follow the organisation's own rules and policies then there should be consequences.

Values and the integrated approach

However, I do not believe that compliance is the same thing as good business ethics. Good business ethics provides the context in which compliance is set. It is a broader concept too because it embraces values. It seems to me that those directors and senior managers who prefer to concentrate heavily on compliance and do little to promote values are failing to maximise the true potential of their business. So, I advocate an integrated approach throughout the book, with a respect for policies and procedures being combined with a deep understanding of the values of the organisation and a commitment to use those values consistently to direct decision-making.

Reference points

There are three crucial reference points for the business ethics framework that I use throughout the book. These are as follows.

Business resource

First, the business resource reference point. Everything that directors and senior managers do should be proportionate and appropriate to the unique circumstances of their own organisation. This applies equally to the ethical framework as it does to any other area of business. So, for example, it may not be appropriate for a medium-sized business, employing less than 100 staff, to have a large employee handbook, supported by scores of detailed policies and procedures. But this does not mean that the business should pay no attention to business ethics, rather it needs to do so in a different way – through the example set, through the actions taken, through the support and advice provided and through the decisions made every day by the leaders of the business.

Business time-span

Second, the business time-span reference point – short-term and long-term business drivers. For each of us the great majority of events in and around the workplace will seem to operate in the short term: meeting a deadline, landing a new contract, securing a promotion. Businesses too face a continual battle to hit their targets. For example, companies listed on a public stock exchange are generally required to report their results to the market more frequently than annually – quarterly reporting has become standard practice. This short-term focus creates pressure. Pressure is one of the key influencers of behaviour, it serves to accentuate short-term imperatives and so it can lead to longer-term goals being overlooked or disregarded.

Sustainability, achieving success over the long term, is often put forward as the ultimate objective of all organisations. I agree with that – values and good business ethics support the long-term view. However, in practice it is often difficult to turn away business, to lose a high-net worth individual as a client, to stop pursuing a deal that, whilst not in the best interests of the customer, will help a manager to hit targets at a time when his or her job is under threat.

Fundamentally, managing business time-span issues successfully is about leadership. It is about directors and senior managers communicating the need for their people to take decisions consistently that are in the long term interests of the organisation – and then supporting and rewarding them for doing so.

Business risk

Third, the business risk reference point. I believe that having good business ethics is beneficial to all organisations because it is the right thing to do. However, I also believe that it is in the best interests of all organisations to do so. While many organisations have developed sophisticated risk management processes, relatively few look at risk in their stakeholder base in a systematic way – what do their key stakeholders expect? This is a mistake.

Ultimately, when stripped down to its essentials, the job of a CEO comes down to two things: the allocation of capital and the management of risk. Failure to recognise and manage ethical risk is a failure of leadership.

 **SUMMARY**

Personal perspectives

I am a businessman, not a moral philosopher. I am not an environmentalist or a health and safety expert and my experience does not lie in areas such as logistics or quality control. I work with people and with procedures. To me business ethics equates to leadership and behaviour in the workplace. I have huge admiration for the great majority of directors and senior managers who run organisations in every sector of the economy. Their's is a tough job. My aim here is to help them by demonstrating ways for them to shape their organisations that will promote value and minimise the risk of reputational damage. To do so, I use the idea of the twin-track approach, the combination of controls and culture that I have seen work well in practice.

I firmly believe that the adoption of the twin-track approach has many benefits: the hardware components (the controls) provide rigour, discipline and assurance around compliance with the law and regulations; the software components (the culture) lead to a closer connection with stakeholders, in particular with staff and with customers. Taken together, they increase the likelihood that an organisation will maximise its potential and so be able to add value over the long term. The twin-track can be applied to all organisations, large and small, in the public and private sectors, though the precise calibration will vary according to the circumstances of each individual enterprise.

Results are always important of course – it is crucial for organisations and individuals alike to hit their targets consistently if success is to be achieved and sustained. However, I do not believe that results should be looked at in isolation or that the methods used to obtain them are irrelevant – I do not agree with Niccolo Machiavelli that the ends justify the means. On the contrary, I feel strongly that this type of thinking can lead sometimes to big problems. I find it remarkable how often poor results are combined with poor behaviour in headline crises and scandals – we will see exactly this in a number of the examples used in this book. In my view the two are often intertwined: profit short-falls lead to pressure to improve performance which in turn can often produce a short-term outlook that condones the bending of the rules. One obvious measure of leadership is in achieving impressive results. But the quality of that leadership is only truly tested when circumstances are tough. The acid test question for business leaders remains: 'How good are you at dealing with bad news?'

I am not naïve, however. I have not met any saints in business – on the contrary my experience in forensics has brought me into contact with a good many sinners! Malign intent, duplicity, self-serving actions, greed and entitlement, bullying and arrogant behaviour exist in every area of life including the workplace. But this has always been the reality – it is not unique to twenty-first-century business or to the world of sub-prime mortgage brokers and derivative traders. To take one example, Bernie Madoff is infamous today as the gigantic swindler of our times, a man who defrauded numer-ous investors and institutions over many years as part of his $65bn Ponzi scheme. Where Mr Madoff is unusual is in the size and longevity of his fraud, not in the fraud itself. The clue is in the descrip-tion. The term 'Ponzi scheme' originates in the activities of Charles Ponzi, an Italian businessman and fraudster who operated in the US and Canada in the 1920s when his bogus schemes cost those investing in them some $20m.

It is perhaps counter-intuitive to say so, given the outcry over the behaviours that caused the global financial crisis and that do not seem to have changed much since, but I have experienced vari-ous indicators that suggest to me that ethics in the workplace have improved in recent years at least in certain respects. The attitude of the authorities in the UK to bribery and corruption, to tax evasion and to insider dealing have all hardened in recent years, no doubt prompted by media exposures and the campaigns of pressure groups, but this has had a marked impact on behaviours.

To take a specific example relating to bribery and corruption, a friend of mine at my local golf club used to work as a sales executive for a large British company. He had responsibility for develop-ing business in various overseas markets during the 1970s and 1980s. He has long since retired but it is clear from the stories that he recounts of business life during this period that bribery was a rela-tively standard procedure to win contracts abroad, one used frequently by my friend's company and by their competitors – and not only in West Africa either. I simply do not come across this mindset when working with directors and managers today.

So, despite the frustrations of 2012, I see evidence of progress and believe that the twin-track approach can, if adopted, improve performance.

Before writing this book, I decided to road-test my ideas with various friends and colleagues from the business world, quite informally over lunch and coffee. The results were encouraging but there were some surprises too.

Road-test

Generally, people liked the idea of the twin-track approach. They could see the importance of both the hardware and the software components and they generally agreed that the latter would be more difficult to establish in practice.

Importance of trust

One of these discussions was held over lunch with Philip Weston, an ex-colleague of mine from Deloitte who now runs a private equity firm. I was interested in what are the main influences on his investment decisions – was it an analysis of the numbers or a judgement of the calibre of the people that counted most? Philip's answer was 'both' but he said that in practice he sometimes found the results a good deal easier to manage than the people. As we talked, it was clear to me that the biggest issue was often a breakdown of trust in the managers of the companies that his firm had taken over. From time to time these managers would seek to hide the true results from Phil and his partner, despite clear instructions to report everything to them, including any bad news. When the true position became clear, Phil felt that the only thing to do was to let the managers concerned go. I don't think that he had ever expressed these issues in terms of a loss of trust before, though he now saw very clearly that this was indeed the main problem in these cases.

Phil's comments are interesting because they demonstrate the overarching importance of business ethics in day-to-day situations in the workplace, even in what might be thought of as the cut-throat world of private equity.

Business ethics

Another point of interest arose from the other road-tests, where I was alerted to a number of issues that people had with the term 'business ethics', which surprised me. Broadly, three areas of concern were expressed to me, and these are summarised below.

First, there were those who felt that business ethics had little relevance to their jobs – it was not something that they thought about or had time for. Two managers said that they would feel uncomfortable talking to their staff about business ethics. However, as soon as I changed the words and focused on trust, honesty and telling the truth, people became more engaged. No one said that they would choose to do business with or to work with someone that they did not trust. So, I concluded from this that there might a problem with articulating ideas around the concept of business ethics, at least in the UK environment. I resolved to try to address this in the book.

Second, there were some objections raised at the idea of trying to manage business ethics in the workplace through traditional methods such as allocating responsibility to nominated individuals (the ethics officer for example) or running ethical training and development programmes for managers and staff. A number of my colleagues felt that this was all unnecessary, that managers should instinctively know what was right and what was not right. Their preference was to say less, rather than more, about ethics and behaviour to their staff. I have two issues with this point of view. First, pressure exists in the workplace and all of us need help, support and guidance from time to time to handle that pressure in the right way. Second, if the organisation's leaders choose to say little about ethics, then the managers and staff might conclude that ethics are not very important to them and react accordingly. Organisations in the USA have been using business processes to manage business ethics for decades now. They do not always succeed in ensuring that ethical behaviour happens in practice, but I think there are important benefits from this approach and I will make sure that I say so in the book.

Finally, I noticed that the same expression came up several times in the course of these conversations, which was that 'business is business'. Thinking about the discussions afterwards, there seemed to me to be two beliefs held by those who used this expression. The first I equate to pragmatism – a belief that organisations tend to act in their own self-interest. I do not have a problem with this and see it as being linked to a legal requirement in the UK – directors are required to use their best efforts to promote the success of their company. But it is important to note that, in so doing, they are also required to have regard to the interests of the stakeholders in addition to their shareholders and investors. The actions of an organisation must not simply be self-serving. The second belief is that the phrase is linked to an admiration for success – the feeling that successful directors and managers are smart people who are able both to understand and to exploit any advantages of size, skill or innovation that they might have in their organisation. Again I don't have a problem with this providing that it does not equate to gaining an edge through such actions as lying, stealing, bribing, bullying, cheating or deceiving the competition or their stakeholders. I checked to make sure that all my colleagues agreed with me on this point, which they all did.

'Simply the way we do things here'

I do not approach business ethics from a moralistic point of view, but from a risk perspective. I am not looking for flawlessness in directors and managers but for an understanding of the expectations of their respective stakeholders – knowledge of who the key stakeholders are and what their expectations are from the organisation. These expectations should be reflected in the values of the enterprise, which in turn should drive behaviour and decision-making. This is the most effective way of minimising reputational risk.

There are many reasons why an organisation should promote good business ethics: it is the right thing to do; lawyers and regulators require it; society demands it; and stakeholders deserve it. However, in my view good business ethics is simply best business practice. It can be promoted through the adoption of the twin-track approach. This enables directors and senior managers to embed their values throughout the organisation, demonstrated in the actions of their managers and staff day after day. In this situation good business ethics become unconscious behaviour – they are 'simply the way we do things here'.

 ## CLOSING

Value statements: a modern story

RISES

When looking at the Enron case at the beginning of the Prologue, I presented the 'RICE model' as a smart statement of corporate values largely because it carried a powerful message in a pithy form. The model attracted many imitators in the corporate world at the time and its influence can still be seen today in some of the ways that organisations choose to speak about themselves.

Consider the recent case of Barclays Bank plc (Barclays) for example.

In February 2013, Antony Jenkins, the bank's new CEO, delivered an important speech setting out his vision of the future for Barclays and a detailed roadmap of how to get there. Mr Jenkins' objective is to make Barclays the 'Go-To' bank for its stakeholders and he wants this to be known as his 'Transform' speech.[5] In it he puts forward a detailed plan to transform the fortunes of Barclays following the disastrous events of 2012, which saw the bank incur significant reputational damage and lose both its CEO and its chairman as a result of its involvement in the Libor rate-fixing scandal (other banks were involved in the Libor scandal too but Barclays was the first to reach a deal with the authorities in the UK, thereby attracting almost universal opprobrium and negative commentary).

I am a long-term customer of Barclays. So, as a stakeholder, I am very interested in what Mr Jenkins is trying to achieve at the bank. When I first read the Transform speech I did so with mixed emotions. These were my thoughts at the time.

There is a clear structure to the speech. Mr Jenkins sets out three elements to his transform agenda: first, 'turnaround' – the immediate task of stabilising the bank after the crisis of confidence in 2012; second, 'return acceptable numbers' – the changes and rationalisations to the business model required to make the bank's finances acceptable through the period to 2015; and third, 'sustain forward momentum' – how Barclays will embed a culture and a way of working that delivers the right outcomes, in the right way for all of its stakeholders.

His overall aim is to embed long-term change in the bank's culture in order to deliver long-term returns. Mr Jenkins describes the purpose of the bank as 'helping people achieve their ambitions in the right way' – by 'people' he means customers, clients and other stakeholders, including his colleagues who work for the bank. I like this framework.

One of the passages in this part of the speech catches my attention – the part where Mr Jenkins says that it is the customers who are always at the forefront of the bank's mind. I remember hearing something like this before, from one of his predecessors. I am a long-term customer of Barclays Bank and some years ago (eight, perhaps ten years ago?) I recall that Barclays tried to develop a new image based around the slogan that it was a 'customer-focused business'. I was not convinced at the time – nothing seemed to change in the way that Barclays treated me as a customer. With hindsight, having witnessed the mis-selling by Barclays (and other retail banks in the UK) of financial products such as payment protection insurance to huge numbers of their customers, I know that I was right – nothing did change, despite the catchy slogans. My view is that if Barclays and the other UK banks had a 'focus' at that time, it was around incentives and the size of the commissions that their staff could earn from hitting their sales targets rather than concerns about serving the interests of their customers.

So, set against this background, I start to be sceptical about the Transform speech.

Mr Jenkins then addresses the bank's values and he does so in a way that really does catch my eye. He chooses to use a catchy acronym to hang them from – the acronym is RISES. Each letter stands for one of the five core values that Barclays will now use to drive its business: respect, integrity, service, excellence and stewardship. I am very surprised. I immediately think of Enron's RICE model and with good reason – three of the values now espoused by Mr Jenkins (respect, integrity and excellence) are identical to those chosen by Mr Lay to describe the culture at Enron. It is not a happy comparison – has Barclays thought this through? I am feeling a good deal more sceptical now.

Then my feelings change. The follow-up passages in the speech impress me and I begin to feel more positive about the message. The reason is that Mr Jenkins is now talking with more passion. He is believable – I start to believe that these values really are important to him as both a person and a leader. As an example, he says that the values are not window dressing but 'they define the work we will do and the work we won't do'. Warming to his theme, he says that they 'define the way we hire, develop, promote and reward our people'. Again, he says: 'we will assess performance not just on what individuals deliver but also on how they deliver it' and ' we never want to be in a position again of rewarding people for activity that is inconsistent with our values'. Finally in this section he says that the great majority of Barclays' staff are already living these values day to day, but for those who have doubts 'it is time to move on'. This is a powerful statement of intent from the CEO.

Taken overall, I am impressed.

Of course, the crucial point of difference between the new, 'transformed' Barclays and the way that certain managers and staff at the bank have behaved in the recent past will not be seen in the words used by the new CEO but in the judgements and the actions that are taken by Mr Jenkins and his colleagues day after day in the future.

Will Barclays' values as stated in the speech actually become embedded in its corporate culture and therefore drive the company's future business behaviour? It is impossible to answer this question now, but in my view Mr Jenkins has made a good start. In his speech he combines a disciplined focus on generating strong and sustainable financial returns with an equally strong focus on values and culture. There will be challenges ahead, not least around the level of remuneration and bonuses that will be paid to Barclays' investment bankers. Also, it will be interesting to see whether Mr Jenkins is able to retain this twin-track focus or whether he is deflected by events, for example, if the bank's financial performance should come under sustained pressure.

Mr Jenkins deserves to succeed and if he is able to stay the course he may well do so. I wish him luck.

CHAPTER ONE

The ethics project

 THE OPPORTUNITY

Initial contact

Introduction

Much of my work since the global financial crisis of 2007–09 has been contingent in its nature. Times have changed. Scheduled bookings on courses and speaking engagements are no longer guaranteed to go ahead and pressure on fees is intense. Business opportunities still exist of course, but in my experience since the crisis they often appear unexpectedly and quickly, requiring an immediate response or else they are lost. They always demand thorough preparation and yet are almost never confirmed until the last minute. In other words, business opportunities are now time-critical and difficult to convert into paid work. The Stronach project came about in just this way.

Looking back, the project seems to be the result of a number of lucky breaks: the initial discussion that went so well; before that there was the presentation – both unusual and highly enjoyable; even before that, there was the successful one-on-one coaching session on governance; and to kick-start the whole process, there was the initial telephone enquiry where it all began. I was fortunate indeed to have the time available because it was only this that enabled me to respond positively and quickly at every stage in the process. Downtime does occasionally have its advantages!

The sequence of events that I describe below confirms two things for me. The first is that there is much truth in the old saying, attributed apparently to the Roman philosopher Seneca, that luck is what happens when preparation meets opportunity. The second is that the most important marketing tool in business today remains a good contacts book.

The call

I pick up a call on my mobile in late November 2012. It is from a contact of mine in the business consulting field, a lady called Margaret. After exchanging pleasantries, she quickly comes to the point of her call: a friend of hers is looking for some coaching, some training and/or assistance (the precise requirement is not clear) around the subject of corporate governance. This is not Margaret's area of expertise at all but she knows that it is something that I cover – might I be interested? There is only one snag, the help, in whatever form it eventually takes, must be provided in the first week of December – so, almost immediately. Am I able to help? As it happens (and this is where I really do get my lucky break) I do have time available in the next week or so and I say that I would be delighted to help – the assignment sounds interesting.

As a result, the call concludes positively: Margaret passes her friend's contact details on to me; I say a big 'thank you' to her for thinking of me; and we arrange to meet in the New Year to catch up properly.

Coaching session

Establishing the parameters

Margaret's contact turns out to be Veronica, a senior executive in a professional services firm based in London. I try to call her straight away, get through to her personal assistant Stephanie, make my introductions and we set up a call with Veronica for the next day, first thing in the morning.

The following day I spend 20 minutes talking to Veronica. She has recently been promoted to partner in the UK practice and has been given an additional area of responsibility – to develop and grow the part of the business that offers board evaluation and performance reviews to corporate clients. Veronica thinks there are good opportunities here and is determined to make a success of her new remit. These board appraisal projects will normally result in a board evaluation report setting out observations and recommendations for improvements in the performance of the board itself, the main board committees and the individual directors. Veronica is looking to improve her knowledge of corporate governance standards both in the UK and around the world (her firm receives a number of enquiries each year from foreign companies looking to improve their board performance) and to gain a better awareness of current governance themes and hot topics.

After listening to Veronica's requirements, I say that I am confident that I can help and would be delighted to do so. I take her through my experience of working with boards of directors and also outline the contents of the regular corporate governance workshops that I run for directors and others at the London Stock Exchange. We decide that a one-day coaching session would be the best option for her and arrange a mutually convenient time for this session, which will be held in Veronica's offices the following week.

Coaching

The offices are located near Oxford Street in the heart of the West End of London. I arrive and am met by Stephanie who takes me to the boardroom, where I start to set up. Five minutes later, Stephanie returns with Veronica – she makes the introductions and then leaves us to get on with other things. Veronica and I have coffee, exchange pleasantries and then get down to work.

I have my laptop and slide deck with me. I use the slides periodically during the day to take Veronica through a classic modern corporate governance presentation including: different governance regimes around the world; directors' duties; agency risk; committee structures; leadership;

the role of non-executive directors; board processes and behaviours; and the benefits and business drivers of strong corporate governance.

The slides provide a useful framework, but this is not a lecture and we spend most of the time talking. At various stages I take Veronica through some of the headline scandals and corporate failures of recent years to help illustrate the key points: the Enron saga in the USA; the Satyam fraud in India; and the banking failures at Northern Rock and the Royal Bank of Scotland in the UK. We discuss the importance of understanding and managing risk, including the crucial area of 'people risk' arising from malign or negligent actions. As part of this we talk about some of the behavioural issues at the top of organisations that often underlie many of the problems in business: arrogance and greed; the failure to challenge effectively around the boardroom table; a lack of cognitive diversity in the approach to problems by directors and senior managers. We agree that good corporate governance is an essential component of a good business and that, without it, reputations can be damaged quickly, both for individuals and for organisations alike.

The day goes well. The coaching has worked and I can see that Veronica is pleased. For my part, I have really enjoyed working with Veronica. Walking out into Berkeley Square and then on to Oxford Street with its Christmas lights and thousands of shoppers I think that there is a good chance that we will work together again in the future.

As it happens, such an opportunity came about much faster than I thought.

An unexpected request

Follow up

It is now the third week of January 2013 – it is cold here in the UK, snow is on the ground and, as is normal for this time of year, it is a quiet period for me business-wise.

Then one day, out of the blue, I get a call from Veronica: 'Lovely to speak to you, did you have a good time over the festivities, how is business?' Veronica comes quickly to the point: 'How is your diary looking for the second week in February? I am hosting a networking event for a group of leading business ladies, about 20 in total. We will start with drinks before dinner, during which there will be talk around a topical subject, followed by a discussion. I need a speaker and I thought of you – might you be interested?'

I know straight away that the timing is not good – my wife and I have a holiday planned for that week, we are going to stay at a place on the Norfolk coast, some 120 miles north east of London. However, it occurs to me that this might not be impossible – I could drive back to London after lunch on the day, attend Veronica's event in the evening and then return to Norfolk early the next morning. My wife is always brilliant and totally supportive when business opportunities come up. So, following some rapid calculations I take a deep breath and reply: 'Yes, absolutely – what do you have in mind?'

The briefing

It turns out that what Veronica has in mind is a 20–30 minute talk based loosely around the themes of damage to corporate reputation caused by poor behaviour and what the board and senior managers can do to minimise this risk. She thinks that a number of examples of business scandals and failures, similar to those we discussed at the coaching session before Christmas, together with practical tips and recommendations, will go down very well with the audience and provide a good platform for subsequent discussion.

We talk through some of the detail and Veronica tells me a little of what I might expect: I should aim to arrive at her offices by 7.00 pm; the talk will take place at some stage during dinner, probably whilst the guests are eating their main course; it will be difficult in the circumstances to have a projector and screen in the room, so forget the slide-deck; and there will be time for discussion and debate over coffee afterwards. Veronica ends by saying: 'Everything will be finished by 9.30 pm. – what do you think?'

'Yes ... Great, I look forward to it, see you there.'

Hot talk, cold chicken

Setting the scene

I am sitting at a long dinner table set up in the boardroom of Veronica's firm, totally transformed from the last time that I was there. Veronica is not present – she has had to travel to Dubai on urgent business – so one of her fellow partners is hosting the event and is looking after me. I have been introduced to the guests – a mix of business leaders both from the public and private sectors, high-flying accountants and lawyers, academics and authors, all strong achievers in their respective fields and interesting to talk to. As an example, I spend some time talking to an American executive who tells me that she has recently spent time in China and written a book on Western business practices and etiquette for Chinese business people.[1] It is currently the best-selling business book in China – now that is a smart idea! The American impresses me hugely.

Veronica's colleague introduces me to Rachel Gordon, another American, who is chairing the discussion this evening. Rachel is tall and elegantly dressed, perhaps in her late 50s. She tells me a little about her business background: after graduating with an engineering degree, she changed direction and started her career in financial services where she flourished, eventually reaching main board level. She married an Englishman and has been living in the UK for the last 20 years, holding a number of non-executive director positions. She briefly mentions her new role – six months ago she was appointed as the non-executive chairman of a large FTSE 250 engineering group.

Rachel has had a distinguished career but I am also struck by how down to earth she is – I like her.

Dinner

I am the only male in the room, but this is not what is bothering me. We are now sitting around the table, the dinner is well under way and everyone has finished their starters. Rachel opened by asking us all to introduce ourselves when we first sat down and she is now speaking again, preparing the ground for my talk. I am suddenly very aware that the waitresses are beginning to serve the main course. Rachel and I are sitting at the head of the table, so they start with us.

The result is that I am served with the main course, a chicken dish, on a large plate just at the exact moment when Rachel introduces me and invites me to begin my talk. I stand up and the waitress looks straight at me – she is not quite sure what to do and neither am I. It is slightly comical and the result is predictable. Nothing is done so the plate remains on the table in front of me – it stays there for the next 20 minutes, with the chicken untouched and going cold, before the waitress finally takes it away prior to serving dessert.

This is a new challenge for me – the first time that I have ever made a presentation with my dinner sitting there on a plate, right under my nose, staring up at me so to speak, untouched and untouchable.

The talk

Unlikely as it sounds, given the double distractions of the untouched chicken and the waitresses clanking about as they serve the other guests with their food, the presentation seems to go well enough. The title is 'Reputation and People Risk in Business Today' and I focus throughout on one simple idea – more problems are caused by malign or negligent behaviour than through failings of processes. This is something that I firmly believe to be true – the human factor is the root cause of many scandals and failures.

I take the ladies through a number of examples, both headline cases and those from my own experience. I include two 'killer statistics': the first is about dishonesty in the workplace (no more than 10% of workers are totally honest[2]); and the second concerns the lack of employee engagement (50% of workers sleep-walk through the day[3]). I then give them my best summary of the key motives behind occupational fraud that cause managers and staff to act on opportunities in the workplace presented by weaknesses in systems and controls – financial pressure and/or job dissatisfaction.[4] I discuss the consequences of this in the form of a risk analysis – reputational risk brought about by an organisation's failure to meet the expectations of its stakeholders. To finish, I give a brief description of how best to handle the ensuing crisis.

My two conclusions are straightforward. First of all, the best way to manage reputational risk is actually by doing business well, so that good business ethics is simply good business. Second, that conduct and reputation are crucially important and that they demand the attention of directors and senior managers. A twin-track approach works best: having the necessary policies and procedures in place to promote compliance combined with an ethical culture and positive tone from the top throughout, based on the organisation's values.

Discussion and debate

During the discussion over dessert and coffee I am asked to say a little more about certain aspects of the talk: what organisations can do to manage crisis situations, including the threats from social media today; and also for my recommendations on how to make reporting hotlines as effective as possible.

But it is the idea of the twin-track approach that interests the guests most. There is some debate amongst themselves about whether behaving well is not something that should just happen – perhaps the key is simply for managers to do their jobs properly. However, there is an understanding in the room that in practice things can and do go wrong. So what are the main features of the twin-track approach?

I encourage them to think in terms of ethical hardware and ethical software. The hardware takes the form of an ethical tool-box. They will all be familiar with the tools: the assortment of codes, charters, remuneration policies, training programmes, hotlines and compliance monitors that organisations have available to them today. I say that it is necessary for organisations to take some at least of these tools out of the box and actually use them – the precise combination will depend on their individual circumstances. But the tools will never be sufficient in themselves to minimise reputational risk. To do so requires the crucial addition of the software: in particular, leadership and tone at the top, with the right people taking decisions consistently in line with the values of the organisation. By doing so, values become embedded in culture and are translated into actions.

I end by repeating my belief that the twin-track approach – this combination of ethical hardware and software –provides the best prospect of minimising people risk and protecting reputation.

Conclusion

It is approaching 9.30 pm and Rachel draws the discussion to a close. As we all prepare to leave, I thank her for looking after me and she tells me how much she enjoyed my talk and the subsequent discussion. She seems to be very interested in the twin-track approach.

We exchange business cards and she says that she will call me – there is something that I might be able to help her with. Her company is about to start a review of ethics and behaviour – it is clear that Rachel has instigated this review and is also coordinating it. I say that I will be delighted to help if I can. We agree to speak again at 8.30 am tomorrow on the telephone with a view to arranging a meeting at Rachel's offices in the near future.

Walking out onto Oxford Street, still full of people and traffic at 9.30 pm, I take a proper look at Rachel's business card. I see that she is chairman of The Stronach Group plc. I have not had any dealings with this group in the past but I am aware of them. They are engineers. There is something else – a problem, an issue, something to do with India perhaps, in the last year or so. I cannot quite recall the details. I need to do a little research first thing tomorrow before I speak to Rachel again.

 ## THE STRONACH GROUP PLC

Background research

Company history

It turns out that the Stronach Group plc (Stronach) is a FTSE 250 engineering consultancy business based in the UK. A quick review of the information available online shows the following highlights in its history and development as a business over the last 70 years or so.

- The original company, Stronach Engineering, was established in 1935 as an engineering consultancy with its offices in Surrey, UK. The founder, Walter Stronach, was a renowned civil and structural engineer. Design and consultancy work in these areas provided the core of the company's business throughout the 1930s.
- The company rapidly expanded in the years following the end of World War II when it was successful in winning a succession of large and lucrative government contracts. As a result it developed expertise and specialist services in a number of related disciplines: engineering sciences, town planning, architecture and project management.
- During the 1970s and 1980s the company grew both organically and through a series of mergers and acquisitions of specialist consultancies in the UK. As a result, Stronach added infrastructure and building services, the design and construction of marinas and independent property asset management services to its skills portfolio.
- The 1990s saw Stronach expanding abroad into Europe (Spain and Ireland plus a major bridge building contract in Bulgaria), Australia and, at the end of that decade, into the US market. The group launched its environmental business strategy at this time and developed a strong reputation for innovation, corporate social responsibility and for its ethical business practices generally.
- In 1995, the company was floated on the London Stock Exchange and subsequently traded under the name The Stronach Group plc. Using the money it raised from the flotation to sustain its growth and development, Stronach thereafter became firmly established as a FTSE 250 company.
- Embracing the new environmental challenges and combining them with its traditional business expertise under the corporate slogan 'Making the World of Difference by Solving Problems',

Stronach continued to grow in the early years of the twenty-first century before the onset of the global financial crisis in 2007. One highlight was the opening of a fledgling office in India in 2005. This office grew significantly in a short period of time and management took the highly innovative step, given the recent history of relations on the Asian sub-continent, of setting up a branch in Pakistan.

So, by 2012 Stronach was firmly established as one of the world's leading design and engineering consultancies. It had built up an excellent reputation based on technical expertise and good business practices. Despite the downturn experienced in Western economies over recent years, it appears to be well placed to take advantage of opportunities in developing markets and any upturn in its traditional UK and Continental European base.

Recent trading results

From the Stronach website I quickly review the 2011 Report and Accounts, together with other pieces of information available there for investors. I also read the recent press releases. Key pieces of information are as follows:

- Group revenues were £1.2 billion in 2011, with a split of 60% coming from the UK and 40% from overseas markets. Sales have been under pressure as a result of the global economic downturn and in 2010 they fell by 7% on the previous year; 2011 saw a slight recovery but trading was still 5% below 2009 levels. Turnover has been largely stagnant in the UK since 2008, with public sector contracts proving to be a particular problem. The accounts show that some 62% of all UK business is with the public sector.
- Profits after tax from operations were approximately £50 million in 2011. As might be expected they have been adversely affected by the financial crisis too, with profits down in each of the last three years. Profits are now running at almost 15% below 2008 levels.
- Total assets on the balance sheet in 2011 were just over £1 billion. Goodwill and trade receivables were important components of this, but so too were cash and cash equivalents. Cash amounted to over 25% of total assets.
- Total shareholders' funds stood at £15 million in the 2011 Report and Accounts.
- Stronach employs some 15,000 people worldwide. The technical expertise of managers and staff are critical to the Group's multi-skill, local-market focus strategy of problem solving and excellence and there is a clear commitment to the ongoing training and development of staff throughout its operations.

Stronach's reputation

Given the context of last night's presentation, I am particularly interested in how Stronach promotes itself in terms of its ethics and values – how it describes itself and what it claims to stand for. In common with most listed companies today, Stronach does indeed have much to say about the corporate ethos: it has published on its website and in its media advertising campaigns a series of statements emphasising the importance it places on three things: the excellence and high quality of its work; corporate social responsibility, with the emphasis on a health and safety culture and on environmentally friendly designs; and impeccable business ethics in the conduct of all of its business. I make a note of the following quotations:

- 'Our core values are: trust; respect for the individual; encouraging diversity; pride in the company and its achievements; and responsibility.'

- 'We intend to sustain a culture of excellence that will motivate our staff always to give of their best instilling in our clients a confidence that we will deliver solutions of the very highest quality.'
- 'The public trust is our most valuable asset. We aim to earn this every day through our focus on the principles of integrity and fairness to all our stakeholders.'
- 'We are always mindful of our legal obligations. We aim to comply with both the law and with all relevant regulations in every jurisdiction in which we operate.'

I ask myself a question: these are all fine-sounding statements but are they backed up by actions?

Corruption allegations

Introduction

My brief research confirms something that I was already aware of, if only vaguely, namely that Stronach has been the subject of rumours concerning the activities of its subsidiary company in India. I see that these allegations originally centred on Duncan Stronach OBE, son of Walter and the Group's longstanding Chairman and CEO. There are media stories alleging corruption of local politicians, close ties with an Indian businessman and an ongoing police investigation.

Then there was tragedy – almost a year ago now Mr Stronach's wife and only son died in a car accident. This dreadful event clearly hit Mr Stronach hard – he immediately announced his resignation and simply walked away from the business and all of his other commitments. His retirement has been absolute. One consequence of this tragedy and resignation was that it seems to have taken the sting out of the media allegations, although they have not gone away completely.

Mr Stronach was replaced as Chairman by Rachel Gordon and as CEO by an insider, John Holt, who was promoted to the senior executive role at the very young age of 38.

Is it this corruption probe that Rachel wants to talk to me about? I do some more online digging.

Events in India

The rumours of corruption began on social media sites in India and in local gossip columns over a year ago now. They concern Stronach's relations with the Super-Blue Marina Corporation ('Super-Blue'), an Indian company based in Goa, specialising in the design and management of marina waterfront properties. Last year Stronach invested £50 million in Super-Blue. The deal includes an option whereby Stronach can achieve a full takeover of Super-Blue within the next seven years at a price to be determined by the middle of three external valuations.

Apparently, the opportunity to invest came about through contacts developed by Stronach's Indian subsidiary, where the head of operations is the brother-in-law of one of Super-Blue's top salesmen. In addition, a number of local media stories have highlighted the close friendship and personal business dealings between Duncan Stronach, the Group's former Chairman and CEO and the Chairman of Super-Blue.

Super-Blue

There appear to be sound business reasons for Stronach to invest in Super-Blue. It has been recognised by analysts for some time that India's economic upturn and the growing affluence of its middle classes present huge opportunities in the leisure sector. India's developing economy has seen rising yacht sales, which, in turn, have created a demand for marinas that need to be available as soon as possible because there is a shortage of docking facilities at present. It is thought that the high-end leisure boating market will be worth at least $1 billion over the next five years.

However, the marine leisure industry in India remains in its early stages and so far demand has outstripped supply. The key to success in this sector is for an organisation to secure planning permission for the construction of marinas. Before the tie-up with Stronach it was thought that Super-Blue lacked both the finances and the international reputation required to take advantage of the opportunities offered. It struggled to obtain planning permission.

Rumours

It was a surprise, therefore, when Super-Blue announced in May 2012 that it had received permission to build four extensive marina projects, two in Goa, and one in each of the cities of Chennai and Kochi. All four projects were granted planning permission shortly before Stronach's investment in Super-Blue. The rumours started almost immediately, with allegations that Super-Blue paid bribes to local government officials to secure permission to build the marinas. Some went further and implicated the new investor, Stronach. They suggested that senior managers at Stronach were either aware of the bribes and chose to turn a blind eye to them or else they were complicit in the corruption scheme itself and might even have assisted in the payment of the bribes.

Within 48 hours of the first rumours circulating, Twitter, Facebook and other social media sites in India became inundated with rumours that Super-Blue acquired planning permission for its four marina projects by paying bribes to local government officials. The stories quickly became laced with sensational details. Apparently, the close ties between Super-Blue and Stronach were cemented following a series of lavish parties and valuable gifts made by the head of Stronach's Indian subsidiary to a number of executives of Super-Blue. In addition, it was alleged that the payment of bribes to local government officials was sanctioned by the chairmen of both Stronach and Super-Blue as a secret part of the investment deal negotiated between themselves.

These rumours were picked up by Western media agencies also and they began to gain a degree of traction outside the Indian sub-continent. Examples that I can see on the Internet are: a piece in the UK magazine *Private Eye* that touched on the Stronach operations in India, together with a particularly unflattering photograph of Duncan Stronach; a paragraph in one of the investment reports for the industry referring to mysterious 'clouds' hanging over the Stronach business interests in India; and rumours that the BBC's Panorama programme is going to feature Stronach in a forthcoming series about 'the secret life of corporations' asking questions about whether bribery and corruption is still a necessary factor when trying to conclude business deals successfully in certain parts of the world, including India.

This is all rumour, of course, nothing has been proved. I note that the stories have cooled down since the death of Mr Stronach's wife and son, especially in the Western media. Nevertheless, they remain a concern and I can't help wondering in passing whether the Serious Fraud Office has opened a file on Stronach.

Recent trading difficulties

As is clear from the 2011 Report and Accounts, the Group has been facing difficult trading conditions since the onset of the global financial crisis in 2007. In particular, the downturn in the USA and in Europe has put pressure on revenues and profits alike. The UK market has traditionally accounted for the majority of the Group's business with a significant proportion of that coming from contracts in the public sector.

Stronach's new CEO, John Holt, has made it clear in recent interviews with the press that he has initiated a major strategic review of the group's operations. There are a number of alternative options available and he has hinted that Stronach might well look to position itself differently in the future, so that it responds to changing markets by becoming less reliant on business in its traditional European markets and on contracts from the public sector in the UK in particular.

The results of the strategic review are due to be revealed shortly, as part of the announcement to the markets of the Group's next set of quarterly results.

The board of directors

Recent changes

As I am now aware, the most significant change at the top of the company, perhaps in the whole history of Stronach, occurred only nine months ago when Mr Stronach OBE, the Chairman and CEO of the company, stepped down following the death of his wife and son.

Mr Stronach is the son of the company's founder, Walter Stronach. He had been the CEO for the last 20 years, taking over the additional role of Chairman in 2009 and combining the two offices from that time. Mr Stronach had a long and distinguished career. Having achieved a First Class degree in Engineering at Cambridge University, he became a Chartered Engineer and worked for more than 30 years in the industry, during which time he held many positions and won a variety of prestigious awards. As examples: he is chairman of the UK Engineering Skills Advisory Board; he is a director of the Industry Forum; he was awarded an OBE in the Queen's New Year's Honours list in 2009; and he is a fellow of the Royal Academy of Engineering. Mr Stronach's influence on the Group has been immense, taking it from what was essentially a family-run firm of engineers based in the UK and transforming it into an international business group operating in many countries around the world and listed on the London Stock Exchange.

I have a question here. I ask myself to what extent has the culture at Stronach changed during this time – has it remained essentially a family-run business despite its stock exchange flotation and global business success?

Current board composition

The Stronach board now comprises seven directors in total: Rachel Gordon, the non-executive Chairman; two executive directors – the CEO, John Holt and the Group Finance Director, Malcolm Mainwaring; and four independent non-executive directors.

I know a little bit about Rachel Gordon's background from our meeting and I am interested to read the short biographies of each of her fellow directors contained on the Stronach website, which have the following descriptions:

John Holt: Chief Executive Officer.

'John Holt was promoted to CEO following the resignation of Duncan Stronach in 2012 at the age of 38. He studied engineering at Imperial College London, where he graduated with a First Class degree. He joined Stronach straight from university and has worked in the Group ever since. A talented all-round businessman with a pragmatic approach and excellent marketing skills to complement his technical competence, he quickly rose through the ranks of the business. In particular, he gained much experience of developing the companies' operations in overseas markets by leading the expansion of business in the USA and Australia. He is the driving force behind the expansion and success of the overseas strategy as a whole.

John Holt was the obvious man to succeed Duncan Stronach as CEO in 2012.'

Malcolm Mainwaring: Group Finance Director.

'Malcolm Mainwaring was appointed finance director when he joined Stronach in 1989. A graduate in Modern Languages from Balliol College, Oxford, he began his accountancy career at Deloitte Haskins & Sells where he qualified as a chartered accountant. He soon left the accountancy profession to pursue a career in business, holding a variety of senior finance, treasury and cash management positions before joining Stronach, most notably at General Electric Company Plc where he worked in the finance department under Lord Weinstock.'

Lord Harris of Cockfosters: Non-executive Director.

'Lord Harris was appointed a non-executive director in November 2005. Following a successful career in the rail industry and with London Underground, he was elected to Parliament where he served as a Junior Minister in the Department for Transport and also in the Department for Energy before standing down from Parliament at the 2005 general election. In 2006 he was appointed to the board of the Olympic Delivery Authority. He was elevated to the peerage in 2010. He is the senior independent director and is a member of the Remuneration and Nomination Committees.'

Ashley Corbett: Non-executive Director.

'Ashley Corbett was appointed a non-executive director in February 2007. He is a chartered accountant and has a broad range of international experience as a senior finance executive in a number of large organisations working in the property and construction fields and also in the logistics sector. He has worked in the UK, Australia and in the USA. He is chairman of the Audit Committee and is a member of the Nomination Committee.'

Neville Ponting: Non-executive Director.

'Neville Ponting was appointed a non-executive director in September 2007. He held several senior positions at EMAC plc, the global engineering and project management group, before becoming its chief executive, a position he held until 2006. He is a fellow of the Royal Academy of Engineering and is also a member of the Advisory Board of the Centre of Business Research at Cambridge University. He is chairman of the Remuneration Committee and is a member of the Audit Committee.'

Richard Williams: Non-executive Director.

'Richard Williams was appointed a non-executive director in March 2010. He graduated in mathematics from Trinity College Cambridge and qualified as a barrister in 1983. He then specialised in corporate finance, working for major institutions in the financial services sector both in the UK, in various countries in Continental Europe and in the USA. He is a member of the Audit and Remuneration Committees.'

Initial observation

My initial view is that this is a technocratic board of directors undergoing pretty radical change. Previously, it had been all-male, Caucasian, similar backgrounds – consequently there was in the past very little to suggest a diversity of views and opinions around the boardroom table. I am more than ever struck by the thought that the appointment of Rachel Gordon, an American businesswoman, as Chairman must have been a radical step for this most traditional of organisations to take. That, combined with the appointment of John Holt at 38 to be the new CEO of the Group, has transformed the appearance of the board of directors. I take this to be a very good sign.

I am more intrigued than ever to find out what Rachel wants to talk to me about.

 ## AN OFFER FROM THE CHAIRMAN

The meeting

Introduction

It is 8.30 in the morning and I am sitting in the Chairman's office on the top floor of an office block with excellent views over Berkeley Square in central London. I am drinking coffee and listening as Rachel Gordon tells me what she wants to cover in our meeting today.

I am here as a follow-up to our initial meeting. As agreed, I telephoned Rachel the next day and we had a very constructive discussion: she outlined her requirements; I set out my background with examples of the type of advisory work that I had done with other clients; we briefly discussed fees; and then we arranged to meet at her offices the following week. In the meantime I agreed to send her my CV.

Rachel's agenda for today's meeting is to brief me about current developments at Stronach. She wants to tell me a little more about her appointment as Chairman by way of background. Then she will outline for me the two key initiatives currently being worked on at board level in the company: first, a major strategic review, which is being overseen by John Holt and his senior executive team; and second, a high-profile ethics project looking at the whole area of values, culture and behaviour in the business.

Rachel tells me that she is taking the lead on the ethics project herself. She is personally committed to its success, partly because of her disquiet at the rumours in India but also partly because of concerns of her own about certain aspects of the Group culture. She feels strongly that the ethics review is an essential step if Stronach is to continue to develop successfully in the future. The project is in its very early stages and she has not made much progress so far. Having heard what I had to say the other night, she wants to discuss whether I can help, perhaps by being a facilitator – what ideas do I have, how might I go about the review?

Rachel lets me think about this for a while and proceeds to take me through the other two areas on her agenda.

Appointment as Chairman

Rachel's appointment had, as I suspected, been driven by Stronach's investors. Not that she was known personally to any of them – there had been a proper selection process in place. But it was pressure from the investors that led the company to look, for the first time, outside of the Group for a chairman who would be truly independent. They felt that the combination of poor results and the rumours coming out of India meant that it was time for an objective perspective and a fresh approach. I ask Rachel what had attracted her to the role and she explains that the chance to go back to her engineering roots, plus the inherent challenges of the job, had been very attractive.

It seems that the job is indeed proving to be challenging. Although everyone is 'very nice', Rachel finds Stronach to be surprisingly insular in many ways, with an unusual combination of rigid hierarchies, poor communication and technical excellence. The influence of the Stronach family is still being felt – 'because we have always done things this way' is a standard response when she questions a procedure. The board agenda and the board meetings themselves illustrate her concerns – she thinks that the template probably had not changed for 50 years before she came along!

I ask her about the board. Her reply is interesting: charming people; they seem to get on well together; experienced and knowledgeable; little challenge or scrutiny; perfunctory board appraisals; an absence of diversity. When I hear the last point I smile: 'Apart from you,' I point out. She laughs: 'Yes, apart from me and there is now the chance to develop this further because we are in the process of appointing a new non-executive director.' She tells me that they are looking at a short-list of three candidates compiled by an executive search firm. The candidates are all very different. The first is a woman from another industry sector altogether (the media) – tough, self-made, successful. The second is a more traditional candidate – a British professor of engineering, brilliant, now retired. The third is a Malaysian businessman with a strong engineering background – a successful entrepreneur with extensive contacts around the world. Some of the directors are pushing for the second candidate, the 'safe' candidate. But interestingly not all of them – so that at least is progress! The Nominations Committee will make its formal recommendation to the main board shortly.

The most progressive director in her view is John Holt, the new CEO. Rachel is really enjoying working with him and is convinced that, together, they can transform the business. John is an engineer by training and qualification and so from a technical standpoint he is a highly competent individual. But he is also commercial and strategically aware, communicates well and is focused on the management of risk. Rachel clearly has confidence in him and trusts him implicitly. She thinks that I will enjoy working with him too.

Strategic review

Initial decision on strategic direction

John Holt is leading the current review of strategy. The broad strategic direction of the company over the next five years was agreed at the last board meeting and has already been announced to the public, but Rachel takes me quickly through the decision-making process for information purposes.

John presented his revised strategy proposal at the board meeting. The paper set out clearly the changing market conditions that the Group is facing, which led to an acknowledgement by the board that Stronach faces a clear strategic choice in terms of its positioning.

One option would be to stay as it is, remaining largely focused on business in the UK and in Europe. This is clearly where the company's expertise and experience lies and this strategy would play to its strengths. In addition, these markets will not disappear and might well grow again at some point in the future. However, given the likelihood of years of austerity measures in Europe to come and the certainty of ongoing cut-backs in the UK's public sector, at least in the short to medium term, this option is not an attractive one. There is little prospect of organic growth and profitability is likely to be difficult for a few years to come.

The alternative is for Stronach to expand its business overseas. It already has an established business presence in the USA, in Australia and in India. One option here would be to seek expansion in these markets and elsewhere in Europe by taking over local businesses. Another would be to venture into new markets such as China and the developing economies in South East Asia. South America is another possibility.

John provided a thorough and balanced strategic appraisal but his recommendation was clear and it seems that his fellow directors were prepared to support him. After discussion, the Board decided to commit to changing the Group's business portfolio so that it will be less reliant in future on the UK market. As a consequence, it decided to set a new target for Stronach of reversing the present split of work between domestic and overseas markets over the next five years. In other words, the current 60:40 split between UK and overseas business will become a 40:60 split by 2017.

Opportunities for a strategic acquisition

The decision to make a broad strategic pivot away from dependence on Stronach's traditional UK markets was announced to the market after the board meeting. The reaction from investors was positive and the share price rose by 6% as a result.

John Holt's more detailed strategy underpinning this pivot is to build a balanced portfolio of construction and development projects by growing Stronach's presence in emerging economies, complemented always by a continued presence (and hopefully growth) in markets in which the company already has a presence. The board's initial thoughts are that Eastern Europe and Australia should be prime targets with South America and South East Asia forming the new markets for investment.

In order to kick-start this process and to provide a symbol of the new regime running Stronach, John and his team have been looking at a number of different possibilities that exist for the Group to make a strategic acquisition in the near future. Despite having no specific remit to do so, the non-executive directors are also keen to help by tapping into their network of contacts and John has gone along with this. As a result, three opportunities for strategic acquisitions have been developed. All have merit and it will be for the board to decide which option offers the best prospect of helping Stronach to meet its revised strategic objectives.

Rachel quickly takes me through the main features of each of these three opportunities.

Option 1: Joint venture to develop ski resorts in Bulgaria

- Stronach's European Division has identified an opportunity to enter into a joint venture with a local Bulgarian company to develop, construct and manage three ski resorts in Bulgaria. The aim will be to take advantage of relaxed planning regulations by the Bulgarian Government following the country's entry into the EU.
- Bulgaria has turned into a highly desirable ski location, with some of the best value skiing and après-ski available in Europe. Stronach's prospective joint venture partner has identified the sites and has obtained planning permission to build three new resorts, one in each of the country's main ski centres. These are at: Bansko, the most developed of the resorts; Borovets, the largest resort; and Vitosha, set in a national park and overlooking the capital city of Sofia. The opportunities look good.
- The prospective joint venture partner is now looking for capital investment and expertise in construction and asset management in particular. The Group has a good track record of building ski resorts in Scotland and also in Canada. Coincidentally, Richard Williams has worked with one of the Bulgarian company's senior executives in the past when each was a corporate lawyer at a major European financial institution and has endorsed his capability. The investment required would be in the order of £75 million, in return for which Stronach would obtain a controlling 51% stake in the joint venture.

Option 2: An engineering construction consultancy in Argentina

- John has been working with Lord Harris on the opportunity to buy a construction consultancy in Argentina, a country in which Stronach currently has no presence. The board briefing paper for this option shows that the Argentinean economy is booming but that the country is suffering from a chronic shortage of both housing and power facilities. It is estimated that Argentina needs 2.5 million new homes and that a lack of good housing is affecting nearly 25% of the population. In addition, there is a need for improved hydro-electricity facilities to cope with what have been described as 'chronic power shortages'. Argentina is now a net importer of natural gas, oil and fuel oil, with demand and applications continuously increasing. Government funding is expected to provide a boost to both of these areas of activity.

▪ Lord Harris has been told that a recent trade mission sponsored by the UK Government's Trade & Investment Department was approached by a representative of an Argentinean consultancy looking for a partner or, alternatively, a purchaser for the business. The representative explained that the expertise of the consultancy was in civil engineering but that the country is suffering from a shortage of architects and other skilled construction related professions, which has limited the development of projects that they can bid for. Cash flow is a big problem, so that the consultancy either needs to start to lay off staff soon or else find a partner to help it take advantage of the impending upsurge in housing and power activity. The consultancy recognises that if it reduces staff headcount now it is unlikely to be able to rehire them when the projects start to come through.

▪ Lord Harris feels that this represents a golden opportunity to establish a foothold in a fast growing economy. The consultancy's turnover is attractive at £25 million and Lord Harris's contact, who was part of the trade mission, thinks that it is well positioned to take advantage of the expected growth in these two sectors. The consultancy's founder is a charismatic entrepreneur, known locally to be a campaigner for Madres de Plaza de Mayo, a charity with strong public support because it is seeking information and redress on behalf of Argentina's 'missing thousands' from the late 1970s and 1980s. Lord Harris's government contact would also be able to help broker the deal if Stronach was interested. He also reported that in spite of the political risks, there was considerable interest from other UK consultancies and so had advised Lord Harris that a quick response was needed.

Option 3: The acquisition of a rival company in the UK

▪ Neville Ponting has approached John with a different proposition. He has learned through very reliable industry sources that one of Stronach's rivals is in trading difficulties and that, according to his contacts, there is a 'once in a lifetime' takeover opportunity here. Given the present state of the UK economy, with little prospect of significant growth in the medium term, Mr Ponting feels strongly that there 'is not room for all of us' in the UK marketplace. This provides Stronach with a chance to buy up capacity in the industry and to consolidate its position in readiness for the eventual upturn. In the short term this takeover would be expected to yield significant economies of scale.

▪ Mr Ponting understands that, despite a marked downturn in parts of its operations plus concerns over its UK public sector business (especially the PFI initiatives), the rival retains a number of premium contracts in its portfolio. He believes that, very conservatively, the deal would provide an immediate boost to Stronach's revenues of over £100 million pa. It is hoped that the purchase price could generate 15% profitability over the next five years, so that the return on investment promises to be very healthy.

Rachel is smiling as she completes this summary of the current state of the strategic review. She can see from my reactions that I understand that Stronach's celebrated strategic pivot into new markets still has some way to go before it gains widespread acceptance in the company, not least around the boardroom table! Still, this has been a very helpful overview because the new strategic direction will have an impact on the culture and attitudes within the Group. Equally, the culture and attitudes of the business will have an impact on the success or otherwise of the new strategy.

The ethics project

Ideas

Rachel now gets to the main point of her agenda. She asks me for my comments and ideas regarding the ethics project – would I still like to help and, if so, how would I propose going about it?

I thank her and say straight away that, yes I would very much like to be part of this project. Then, I set out some ground rules for my involvement. As already indicated, I see my role very much as that of advisor and facilitator – Rachel and her colleagues will take all decisions, they will agree and put to the board for approval any changes that they wish to implement arising out of the recommendations of the review. It is for Stronach – not for me – to set its own course in terms of how it conducts business, the values it wishes to promote, the behaviours and culture it wants to encourage amongst its people.

I now take Rachel through my ideas.

I explain that I can add most value by working alongside a small high-profile team from Stronach, rather than as a full-time consultant. I see this project as being ideally suited to a workshop setting, where I would act as facilitator to a small group (comprising no more than five people) that meets regularly, perhaps once a month, to discuss issues and develop action plans.

Rachel's response is positive – she likes the suggested approach and asks who should be on the team? I say that one member must be herself and that she should head up the team. She nods. Next, if at all possible John Holt should be on the team too. In my experience, if the CEO is known to be involved with and supporting an initiative like this one, then there is a chance that managers and staff in the organisation concerned will get behind any changes that result – there is no guarantee of ultimate success of course, but there is a chance nevertheless. If the CEO is not part of the project and is known to be (or thought to be) ambivalent towards it, then it has virtually no prospect of success. Rachel agrees – she has discussed the ethics project with John and he gives it his full backing. It might be tough to get the necessary time in his diary but she will see what she can do.

Finally, it would be ideal if we can include in the team the leaders of the two areas in the Group that are crucial to the success of this project – money and people. The individual controlling the money is easy to identify – the Group Finance Director, who is Malcolm Mainwaring. As for the people angle, it is less clear to me who the right person might be – the Board does not include a human resources director. Rachel tells me that the head of personnel is David Hurley, although his job title is HR Manager. She does not know him very well, he is really a middle-manager and she is a little concerned that he might be out of his depth. But I convince her to take a chance – we will need his input on any initiatives concerning the development of Stronach's people. So, we agree on a team of four, as discussed, with myself making five in total.

Workshops

Regarding the workshops, my view is that they should be held every four weeks or so and that each should last for around two hours – some might be longer, some shorter. Rachel asks if I will need any facilities for showing slides or videos. I shake my head. The only essentials are something to drink and a flipchart with pens available in the room – I won't be using the flipchart much myself, it is there for use by the project team to note down those action points arising from each workshop that they wish to take forward.

How many workshops might be needed? Longevity is always difficult to assess at the outset of a project like this, so I list my ideas for the subjects that might be covered in each workshop: an initial overview, definitions and so on; risk analysis; leadership and tone at the top; what might be termed the ethical toolkit; reputation; perhaps two or three specific topics (for example, whistle-blowing hot-lines and crisis management). So, there would be perhaps eight workshops in total, meaning that the project might last for around eight months – certainly it should be no longer than one year in duration.

Rachel is enthusiastic and agrees in principle to this approach. She asks me to put together a written proposal. She will speak to the individuals we discussed as possible team members as soon as possible and will aim to set up the first workshop in the near future. Obviously, she cannot commit at this stage to the whole project, it will depend to a certain extent on how successful that first workshop turns out to be. Rachel herself is supportive but some of her colleagues might be more sceptical – she is hopeful however. My fees (discussed earlier) are not a problem.

As I walk out of the offices and into Berkeley Square I sense that this project will be quite a challenge. There is no doubt that the prospect is exciting, however. Indeed, I am looking forward to working with Rachel and to meeting her colleagues at the first workshop. I already have some key takeaways to suggest from this introductory meeting and I will include them in the proposal document I send to Rachel later.

Key takeaways

As mentioned, I will be looking for the project team to identify their key takeaways at the end of every workshop. My initial discussion with Rachel has laid the foundations for the project but that is not to say that there are no learning points to come out of it. On the contrary, there are three. In many ways these are amongst the most important recommendations in the book and they are as follows:

✓ **Be proactive on business ethics**. The ethics project at Stronach takes place as the result of a reaction to events (in this case, a corruption scare) and I see this happening all the time in reality too. Organisations may aspire to be proactive in everything they do but most remain essentially reactive. All organisations should commit to a periodic review of their ethical framework and to making improvements where necessary as a result.

✓ **Engage the right people at the top**. The commitment and engagement of people at the top of the organisation, especially the CEO, is crucial to success for initiatives around business ethics. Also, small, high-calibre teams are often the best means of achieving results quickly – the Stronach Group plans to use a project team of five people, considered by some to be an optimal number for these purposes. Core components of the team should reflect the requirements of the project. Often this means that representatives of the finance department (money) and the HR department (people) should be on the project team.

✓ **Understand that working on business ethics takes both time and effort in order to bring about change in culture and behaviour**. So make the commitment of both resources and, perhaps more importantly, of 'political will' to improve over the long term. Success will not be achieved quickly or easily. The Stronach project envisages an eight-month to one-year timetable. In reality, this timescale might prove to be too short.

DISCLAIMER

I need to make it clear at this point that all of the characters and events described in the book in connection with the Stronach Group are fictitious.

The events of this chapter leading up to my introduction to Stronach are a mixture of actual events and artificial details. The names of the individuals mentioned have been changed, as have the details of my evening presentation. Essentially though, these events did take place and I refer to them because they provide a good example of the contingent nature of business today, requiring flexibility and speed of response.

For the avoidance of any doubt, everything that I have written concerning the Stronach Group and its operations, whether mentioned in this chapter or in subsequent chapters, has been entirely made up by me for the purposes of this book. The 'Stronach story', if I might describe it so, is completely fictitious – this includes all of the individuals, all of the organisations and all of the events referred to in whatever way in connection with the Stronach Group. As they say in the movies, any resemblance to real persons (whether living or dead) or to real corporations or to real events is entirely coincidental.

The Stronach story is included to provide a narrative flow to the book and an added layer of interest too. The workshop setting enables me to 'top and tail' the core content of the book with discussion, questions and answers relating to some of the key practical issues that directors and senior managers ask me about in real life. This combination of distilling theory and applying it to situations that arise in practice mirrors what I try to achieve with all my clients, whether on projects or in classrooms.

CHAPTER TWO

The business ethics framework

  THE ETHICS PROJECT: FIRST WORKSHOP

Opening

Introductions

It is 8.30 am on a Tuesday morning in March 2013 and I am sitting in the boardroom in the head office of the Stronach Group just off Berkeley Square in central London. This is the first meeting of the ethics project team. In the room with me are Rachel Gordon, the Chairman; John Holt, the CEO; Malcolm Mainwaring, Group Finance Director; and David Hurley, HR Manager. So, it is clear that Rachel has been successful in assembling all the individuals for the project that we discussed the last time we met.

Before formally introducing me to her colleagues, Rachel breaks the ice with an observation – a joke almost. She asks whether anybody else has noticed the digital sign outside the boardroom door (this sign is updated daily and is used to inform managers and staff about whether the boardroom has been booked and is in use). Today it is signifying, correctly, that the room has been booked for three hours by Rachel Gordon but the purpose of the booking is described on the sign as 'Essex Project' – rather than, of course 'Ethics Project' as it should be. Rachel laughs and says: 'So much for my famous communication skills!' Everyone is smiling now, it is an amusing mistake and Rachel's self-deprecating humour helps to relieve a certain tension in the room.

Rachel now makes the formal introductions. As we each say 'hello' and give a few brief remarks about ourselves, I have the following initial observations about the team members: Rachel is energetic and totally committed to the project – she is the sponsor but it is obvious that she is passionate about it too; John Holt is a northerner, heavily built, very business-like who appears fully engaged; in contrast, Malcolm Mainwaring seems to me to be indifferent, he is distracted, irritable almost – he is in his mid 50s, well-spoken but his body language suggests that he would rather be somewhere else;

the final member of the team, David Hurley, is younger than his colleagues (early 30s perhaps) and, although he seems to be a pleasant enough fellow he also appears to be nervous and ill at ease. I think to myself that my initial thoughts are confirmed – given the mix of personalities and experience in the room, this is likely to prove to be a challenging project indeed.

The ground rules

Workshop approach

I begin by thanking everyone for giving me the opportunity of being part of the ethics project – I am pleased to meet the team and am looking forward to working with them all very much. The purpose of the planned series of workshops is threefold: first of all, to enable the team members to discuss all aspects of the Group's approach to business ethics in an open, collaborative, but challenging way; second, to recommend ways to improve the effectiveness of this approach where required; and third to assess whether the values of the business are truly embedded in its corporate culture in terms of how the managers and staff actually behave day to day. The overarching objective is to minimise reputational risk to the Group.

My role is to facilitate the discussions and to provide guidance and suggestions based upon my experiences. I will try always to make the recommendations as practical as possible and to do so I will be drawing on my observations of what works best in other organisations. My objective will always be the same – to add value to Stronach's business. I explain that my style is not didactic but I will look to use examples and stories wherever I can do so, whether these are headline cases to highlight the reasons for organisational failure or scandal or situations that I have either encountered myself or been told about by my business associates.

Workshop mechanics

Although the room is booked for three hours, we have a two-hour timeframe to work with today and Rachel confirms this. I say that we should aim to keep the workshops to the same length in all subsequent meetings, though some flexibility might be required from time to time.

Each workshop will begin with a series of questions, either from me to the team or from the team to me. I will then devote the bulk of the workshop to presenting and illustrating my ideas on the subject matter at hand. In order to make best use of the available time, I suggest that in general the team should keep their questions until the end, when we will have time to discuss them fully.

At the conclusion of each workshop, including today's, I will ask the team to set out on the flipchart the main takeaways and key action points arising out of the session – those ideas and recommendations that they believe will, if implemented, contribute to improved performance in the Stronach Group in the future. The aim will be for one member of the team to take responsibility for each action point. Finally, of course, it will be for the team both individually and collectively to make sure that the action points are indeed implemented subsequent to the meeting, within agreed timescales that are stretching but realistic.

Personal approach to business ethics

Introduction

Before moving on to today's agenda, I set out briefly my own approach to business ethics. I begin with two core principles. The first principle is that good business ethics is an essential component of good business. The second principle is that the first principle is important – with the consequence that it demands and deserves the time and attention of directors and senior managers.

I am well aware that not everyone shares this view. First of all, there are the rogues, cheats and fraudsters that exist in every business sector – largely motivated by greed and/or competency shortfalls in their work: business ethics is an irrelevant concept to them. We will address this group and the threats that they pose in a subsequent workshop on behaviour and conduct risk. Second, there is a wider group of individuals, including many directors and senior managers, who seem surprisingly ambivalent to business ethics for various reasons. Some are instinctively uncomfortable with the term 'ethics' being applied in a business context and so do not wish to engage with it. Others consider that results are all that matter in business – how those results are achieved is largely irrelevant providing crucially that everything is done within the law. Yet another set of senior managers choose instead to pay lip-service to business ethics. They are happy enough to use words such as 'integrity' and 'trust' when describing their organisation's values, but they are not prepared either to invest the necessary resources in embedding ethics throughout their business or to take tough decisions based on those same values that might damage results in some way.

I say that, in my view, the danger with all these approaches is that they are essentially short term, they offer little in the way of inspirational leadership and they provide no assurance against reputational damage.

There is an alternative, which is to view good business ethics as an integral part of good business – this is why we are all here today, of course. If directors and senior managers are prepared to take the lead, to commit their time and allocate resources to these areas, then progress can be made. There are well-established tools and techniques for managing business ethics. It is frustrating for me whenever I learn that organisations are not using these tools. It is equally frustrating when the tools are used but they are ineffective because of a lack of commitment from the top. I am delighted to see evidence of this commitment here at the Stronach Group – this is the first essential step in managing business ethics successfully.

Twin-track approach

I introduce the team to the twin-track approach. This is the practical framework that I like to work with when discussing business ethics because it incorporates the elements that are both necessary and sufficient for effective management in these areas. I will refer frequently to the twin-track approach during the workshops, most often in references to ethical hardware and software. I will also be advocating an integrated approach to behaviour that balances both compliance-driven and value-driven actions.

I explain that I am not the originator of the expressions 'ethical hardware' and 'ethical software'. I was introduced to them by a business associate of mine.[1] I immediately saw their attraction and so I have adopted and developed them, especially in conjunction with a consideration of the differences between necessary and sufficient conditions. They lend themselves naturally to the twin-track approach and enable ideas around business ethics to become both understandable and relevant to different audiences. Rachel confirms that she herself had been particularly struck by the twin-track approach when she first heard me mention it during the talk.

I explain a little more. The ethical hardware equates to the various policies and procedures that are available to organisations today. It includes: ethics charters, codes of conduct, value statements, staff handbooks, remuneration policies, due diligence procedures, training programmes, whistle-blower hotlines, and management review processes. I call this the ethical toolbox. It will be necessary for organisations to have some combination of these hardware tools in place, calibrated to the needs of each individual enterprise, in order to gain assurance around business ethics.

These tools alone will not be sufficient to achieve assurance, however, because there is no guarantee that the messages will 'stick' and influence behaviour. This requires the addition of the crucial ethical software: leadership and tone at the top; consistency of judgement and decision-making based on values; using those values as the basis for decisions in the key areas of hiring, remunerating and promoting managers and staff; and a good understanding of the organisation's ethical risks – what the expectations of its investors, customers, employees, suppliers and other stakeholders really are. Awareness of ethical risk is important because if it is not well understood and managed it could result in serious reputational damage.

I spend a little time talking about the second area where a twin-track approach is beneficial – the importance of taking an integrated, balanced approach to compliance and values. It is necessary to comply with the law and relevant regulations, so there must be systems and controls in place to provide directors and senior managers with assurance that their organisation is doing so. Discipline is an important part of the compliance process – there must be consequences for individuals who transgress the rules no matter what their seniority or past track record of business success might be. However, it is equally important to combine a compliance focus with one that looks at the organisation's values and how these are used to direct decision-making. To ignore these values is for directors and senior managers to fail to maximise the potential of their organisation.

Finally, I say to the team that I will be referring to the business timespan as a crucial reference point from time to time. It is important to understand always the benefits of taking a long-term approach that promotes the idea of sustainable success, rather than to indulge in short-termism, however tempting. Organisations need to be prepared, sometimes, to take decisions that are detrimental to their results in the short term in order to secure their reputation and long-term success.

Agenda

The purpose of this first workshop is to set out and understand the broad business ethics framework. We will use it to explore and articulate a number of the key themes and ideas that underpin the framework and also to discuss any issues and questions that team members may have.

Specifically, the workshop will cover three areas as follows:

- An overview of the business ethics framework including: exploring the purpose of business organisations, why they exist, what they are for; reviewing mission statements and value statements; and considering the duties and responsibilities of directors and others at the top of organisations.
- Articulating the meaning of a number of key terms used in this area such as business ethics, integrity, trust, corporate culture and compliance.
- Providing examples that show how the decisions and behaviour of individuals can be better understood, assessed and developed through the use of dilemma-based scenarios.

Key questions

Before I begin the presentation, I ask each member of the team to consider the issues for today's workshop from their own personal perspective and to come up with a question that they wish to be addressed. I will then make sure that the presentation addresses these issues and they are picked up in the subsequent discussion.

After some minutes of thought the team produces the following set of questions, each team member contributing one:

- 'People are all different and we all have different standards and beliefs. So whose ethics are we talking about here?' This question comes from David Hurley, the HR Manager, who is concerned about how well any changes decided on by the project team will be accepted by the thousands of people who work for the Group.
- 'Stronach is a listed company, so as directors we clearly need to look after the interests of our shareholders – do we have to do anything more than that?' This one comes from the Group Finance Director Malcolm Mainwaring. Malcolm is still giving the impression of being somewhat ambivalent towards the project. He appears to be sceptical, cynical even – I am not sure what to make of him just yet. He adds a cryptic comment to his question by muttering almost under his breath: 'We don't always appear to have the time to think about the niceties of business ethics here at Stronach.'
- John Holt, the CEO asks: 'What is the difference between a business that behaves ethically and one that complies with the law?' John has clearly had dealings with lawyers in the past and he is keen to understand where exactly the boundaries might lie here.
- 'How can we improve our decision-making process, especially when the circumstances are unclear and difficult as they sometimes are in practice?' Rachel Gordon, as Chairman, wants to know more about the ethical decision-making process and how she and the organisation can be confident that everyone is making consistently good choices.

I thank everyone for their questions. Having listened carefully to them, I am confident that each will be addressed during my talk. However, I am conscious of the time so I say that I am going to begin the presentation now with some general comments and observations around business ethics generally.

THE BUSINESS ETHICS FRAMEWORK

Overview

Background

Following the global financial crisis of 2007–09 there has been much focus (by the authorities, politicians, the media, business associations and the public alike) on the importance of business ethics, corporate culture and the way individuals behave in the workplace. Much of this has been directed towards the financial services industry and the behaviour of bankers in particular. Indeed, as a result of the fallout from the crisis, the UK has established a new regulatory regime. One of the new regulatory bodies is the Financial Conduct Authority (FCA). The overall objective of the FCA is to ensure that financial markets work well so that consumers get a fair deal.[2] In order to achieve this, it needs to consider, among other things, all aspects of behaviour. Implicit in the new regulator's name is the concept of conduct risk, which we will discuss in more detail later.

The emphasis on good business ethics and integrity is not confined to people working in financial services, however. It applies necessarily and equally to all business sectors and to all organisations regardless of size. Set out below is a typical overview, provided by my own professional institute, the Institute of Chartered Accountants in England and Wales ('ICAEW') in the introduction to a paper entitled 'Instilling Integrity in Organisations':[3]

Ethical behaviour is fundamental to an organisation's reputation, trustworthiness and long term performance. Integrity is at the heart of ethical behaviour.

This seems straightforward – most of the directors and senior managers that I work with would not disagree with the sentiments expressed. However, the terms used are not defined in the ICAEW's paper and I know from experience that many organisations struggle to set out clearly what they mean by words such as integrity and trust. An important corollary is that it is not straightforward for any business to embed the principles of integrity and trust throughout its corporate culture – in fairness to the ICAEW this is made clear in its paper.

Articulation

Directors and senior managers are business people, they are not moral philosophers. I know from my workshops that the great majority have not been able to devote any significant amount of time to studying business ethics or to thinking deeply about ethical issues. They are practical men and women who are paid to deliver results against agreed business objectives and performance targets.

I include below a summary of and commentary on some of the key terms and concepts that are often used when discussing business ethics: the ethics concept itself; the golden rule of reciprocity; integrity and trust; the law and compliance; and corporate culture. In my view, this summary provides a useful framework within which organisations may develop their ethical hardware in terms of codes, handbooks, detailed policies and procedures and so on.

However, before looking at these key terms, I want to take a step back to first principles and consider what the fundamental purpose of an organisation actually is, regardless of business sector or size of operation. Most business men and women are above all else pragmatic in the workplace, so I will look at this idea of the purpose of organisations in conjunction with the introduction of some initial ideas around corporate values and the responsibilities of directors. Taken together, these areas provide the important foundations on which a solid business ethics framework can be built.

Purpose

Why do organisations exist, what are they there to do? Set out below are a number of observations.

First key question for directors: Why does your organisation exist?

I have run corporate governance workshops at the London Stock Exchange three times a year in each of the last 10 years. The delegates attending vary in terms of their backgrounds of course but typically include: directors (both executives and non-executives) of companies listed on the main market in London, or on the UK's Alternative Investment Market (AIM); representatives of companies based overseas (again mainly directors) that are either looking to list in London in the near future or have already achieved a listing; company secretaries and legal representatives; and other interested business professionals. So, it is predominantly a private sector, corporate environment, with larger rather than smaller businesses represented in the room, as might be expected given the venue.

I like to begin these workshops by asking the delegates a series of questions. These questions are designed to be straightforward and thereby to encourage discussion and debate at the start of the day. One of them is perhaps the most basic question that I could ask anyone who works for a living. It is simply this: 'Why does your organisation exist, what is it here to achieve?' Despite its simplicity, this question always creates a certain amount of surprise – delegates sometimes appear as though it makes them feel uncomfortable, which is perhaps an interesting observation in itself. I ask the questions in open forum and the first answer that I receive is almost always the same – a delegate will call out something along the lines of: 'to make money' or 'to make a profit'. This points to the maximisation of shareholder value as the purpose of business and looks back to the Chicago School of Economics of the 1970s, when its leader, the American economist Milton Friedman, famously said that the only social duty of a company is to make a profit.[4]

Now, just to be clear, I do not consider this to be a 'wrong' answer at all and I make sure that all the delegates understand this. In a free market economy it is absolutely necessary that an organisation operating in the private sector does indeed make a profit – if it fails to do so for any extended period then it is unlikely to have a future, certainly not in the long term. However, if not a wrong answer, this seems to be a limited answer – making money, making a profit always represents the baseline for a business in my view. It is the minimum requirement – the starting point, not the end point. I do not wish to suggest that it is easy to make profits and I understand that in some years it may well be impossible to do so. However, profitability over the long term is a necessary condition for success in a private sector business.

But is it a sufficient condition? Some delegates will almost always pick up the concerns behind this supplemental question as the discussion develops. For example, one interesting pre-cursor to sufficiency is the answer that I have heard a number of times which is: 'to make profits ... to pay my employees', rather than simply paying dividends to shareholders. So the discussion will then typically move on to consider the concept of the value that a business generates. As soon as we do this, the comments of delegates broaden from a focus on profits and the interests of shareholders to views that include other groups that are affected by the business – the employees, customers, suppliers and other interested parties, known collectively as stakeholders.

This enables me to bring the discussion on this seemingly simple question to a conclusion by saying that, in my view, the purpose of a company should be to maximise value to its stakeholders over the long term. The delegates are almost always content with this. The interesting thing to me is that it often takes a little time to get them there.

So, it seems to me important that directors and senior managers should from time to time pause, consider and remind themselves perhaps of what the true purpose of their organisation actually is.

Business fundamentals

The need for such reflection was highlighted to me by James Featherby during our interview for this book. James had a successful career as a lawyer in a major law firm in the City of London. When we met he was Chairman of the Ethical Investment Advisory Group, the committee that advises the Church of England on its investment portfolio – not only on where not to invest, but also on how best to engage with those companies in which the Church is investing in order to improve their environmental and social governance performance.

We were discussing culture and values at one point during our interview when James requested that we pause, re-wind and consider first the question of business purpose. This is what he had to say in this context.

> *I think one of the most significant factors in this is for a business to decide what its purpose is. I don't mean a kind of six line mission statement that gets pinned up on the wall, but a serious reflection on the fundamentals: 'why are we in business, what is it we are trying to do?' I think there needs to be a level of honesty about this, so that these questions are answered truthfully rather than from a PR perspective.*

If the truth is simply that you are in business to make money and for no other reason, then you are in trouble because the ends quite quickly start justifying the means. If on the other hand you are in business because you like, say, making bricks or you like running a chemist shop or you like being an accountant and that you therefore have a sense of fulfilment of public purpose and contribution to society from what you are doing, then I think that sets a completely different environment in which ethics start to make much more sense. Because rather than having just 'making money' as the main motivation – which one might say is a selfish motivation – if my motivation is to serve society then that gives rise to a whole series of different behaviours and values and things that back those up.

So I think this issue of purpose is absolutely fundamental.

We were talking briefly before you turned the tape on about the situation at Barclays. I think Antony Jenkins is absolutely right to focus on customer benefit because without that I don't think they have a hope. Now that is a really difficult and rigorous thing that he is trying to do there – to drive that through and make it stick in a big organisation. But you know for small or medium sized businesses it's not quite so difficult perhaps. In all organisations you then have to start embedding that in all sorts of processes and procedures to make it work. But you also have to keep on beating out the overall message that this is why we are in business.

I think that James makes a powerful point here that applies to all organisations – an honest assessment of purpose is the starting point for long-term success, or at least it should be.

Public sector viewpoint

My focus when working at the London Stock Exchange is on the private sector. But this fundamental question of purpose applies equally to all business sectors. I have seen this myself in the context of the public sector in the UK.

As an example, I worked on a project with a local authority in London in 2007 to assist in improving the authority's risk management, internal controls and processes at exactly the time when the public sector's 'Good Governance in Local Government' best practices framework received a significant update.[5] Although no doubt most people in the authority were unaware of it, this update created quite an impression amongst the audit and risk teams that I was working with at the time. The revised framework is built around six core principles of good governance. It is significant that Principle 1, the overarching principle, directs the senior management team to focus on what the purpose of the authority actually is and what are the desirable outcomes for the community (the citizens and users of the authority's services) in order to create and implement a vision for the local area.

Mission statements and value statements

Introduction

Picking up on a comment made by James in passing during the interview extract quoted above, mission statements and value statements are a modern business phenomenon that can attract a good deal of scepticism, cynicism even. They are intended to be general statements of the guiding beliefs of an organisation and are meant to connect with employees and external stakeholders alike. Much work and attention goes into drafting these statements, many are well constructed, some have real depth, yet often they have little impact.

Why is this so? Well, it seems to me that the main cause is likely to be that the ethical software (as I have described it) is missing. The actual words used in the statements matter far less than how they are brought to life, in particular by the actions of those at the top who commissioned and signed off on the statements in the first place.

This brings us back to the 'say-do' gap that was discussed in the Prologue. If the leaders of a business are seen to be or are perceived to be behaving in ways that are contrary to their own core values, then those values become hollow words and will be viewed simply as 'window-dressing' or worse. The drafting of mission statements and value statements always takes effort and an allocation of resources. But the real investment by an organisation, in terms of time and emotional commitment, comes later – in the ongoing efforts, day after day, to match the words in the statements with the actions of everyone working in the business.

Equality under the twin-track approach

There is one other thing to say here and hopefully it is clear. Mission statements and values statements must be underpinned by the ethical hardware that we discussed earlier if they are to be implemented successfully – the systems and controls, the policies, procedures, codes of conduct and so on.

The ethical software is important too, of course, because these policies and procedures need always to be enforced by management if they are to have any traction or influence within the organisation. So, if individuals transgress and behave in a way that is inconsistent with the values then there should be consequences, no matter who the transgressor happens to be – whatever position he or she holds within the organisation, whatever the level of business they generate, whatever success they have had in the past should be irrelevant here. Everyone in the business needs to be treated equally when it comes to breaking the organisation's own rules if the ethical hardware that we have talked about is to have general respect and credibility.

Benefits

If the true purpose of an organisation can indeed be distilled into a short mission statement, then there are tangible benefits to the organisation in the form of an enhanced reputation with outside stakeholders and also the creation of positive engagement and passion from the employees. I have seen this latter effect myself from time to time. For example, I did some work a number of years ago with a large housing association in the UK. Among their services was the provision of social housing to some of the poorest and neediest people in the country, men and women who were often suffering from chronic health problems in addition to their poverty. Providing for these people was a tough job and the managers and staff that I worked with on this assignment had my sincere admiration.

The housing association had a very simple mission statement at the time I was working there which was both striking and short. Their mission was: 'Making the difference for people in need.' This statement encapsulated perfectly the purpose of the housing association and it used language that everyone working there could relate to directly. All the managers and staff that I worked with on the assignment were aware of the mission statement, they connected with it and they were proud to work for the association.

Responsibilities of directors

Those working at the top of all organisations carry significant responsibilities. This section focuses on the responsibilities of company directors.

Second key question for directors: Is a director's primary duty to the shareholders?

There is another question that I ask delegates attending my workshops at the London Stock Exchange that is particularly relevant here. This one concerns the duties of directors and is based on a simple statement as follows: 'A director's primary duty is to the shareholders.' The question is, do the delegates agree with it?

Again, this question is straightforward but I am often surprised by how poorly it is answered. I like to address it in the first instance to those delegates in the room who are not lawyers by training – it is actually a question about company law. In my experience, the majority by far of the non-lawyers to whom I address this question say that they do agree with the statement. They are not correct to do so.

Under UK law, a company is a separate legal entity. As a result, a director owes his or her primary duty to the company itself and not to any individual shareholder or group of shareholders. I always check this with any lawyers present in the workshops – and they always confirm that my understanding is correct.

I ask this question about directors' duties not to score cheap points or to embarrass any of the delegates but rather to try to gauge the level of awareness that people in the room have about this important aspect of company law and corporate governance. I now have quite an extensive set of data, drawn from delegates' answers over 10 years. Unfortunately, the conclusion that I am forced to draw is that a high proportion of people working in senior positions in business today (those who are not from a legal background at least) are unaware of this basic duty of directors to act always in what they consider to be the best interests of their company. Included in this are people sitting on the boards of some of the largest companies in the UK.

This is both a surprising and a concerning conclusion. It shows a common deficiency in knowledge by directors about the very job that they are being paid to do. There is a key recommendation for individuals and organisations alike arising from this – namely that ongoing training and development of staff at all levels is essential if gaps in skills, knowledge and experience are to be addressed.

Directors' duties: the Companies Act 2006

The duties of directors in the UK are now set out in statute. The Companies Act 2006[6] introduces for the first time in the UK a codification of the principal duties that directors owe to their companies. Like the common law duties they replace, these statutory duties are owed by a director to the company.

According to the Act all directors are required to do as follows: act within the powers of the company; promote the success of the company; exercise independent judgement; exercise reasonable skill, care and diligence; avoid conflicts of interest; refrain from accepting benefits from third parties; and declare any interest in a proposed transaction or arrangement.

None of these duties are exceptional. But the wording of the second of them – the duty to promote the success of the company – as set out in the legislation is significant because it points the way to understanding, through the duties of directors, what the purpose of a company might be considered to be according to the law. It provides an official signpost, so to speak.

Stakeholders

Section 172 of the Companies Act 2006 states that directors must act in a way in which they consider, in good faith, would be most likely to promote the success of the company for the benefit of its members as a whole (the term 'members' here refers to the shareholders).

Section 172 goes on to say that in doing so directors 'must have regard to' a number of other factors. These other factors are described as follows: the likely long-term consequences of their decisions; the interests of employees; the need to foster business relationships with suppliers, customers and others; the impact on the community and on the environment; the desirability of maintaining a reputation for high standards of business conduct; and acting fairly as between members of the company.

What can we learn from this? First, Section 172 provides confirmation of the principle, long established under common law in the UK and referred to above, that directors must look after the interests of the company for the benefit of the shareholders as a whole. So, enhancing shareholder value is indeed a fundamental purpose of every company.

But is this the only purpose? Not according to Section 172, because the directors cannot now consider shareholders in isolation but must have regard to other interested parties whenever they take important decisions: employees, suppliers and customers, and the local community. In other words, they must consider all those who have a stake in the business. The final point to make here is that directors are required to have regard to the long-term consequences of their actions, so that something much more than short-termism (a focus purely on the immediate results and outcomes of a decision) is looked for now under the law.

- Having reviewed the legal duties of directors, I say to the team that we can now look to answer Malcolm's question at the start of the workshop. He asked whether the directors of Stronach, a listed company, needed to do anything more than look after the interests of the company's investors and shareholders. My answer to this is 'yes', absolutely, but with one important caveat – generating profit is an essential requirement of the job. The interests of shareholders must be protected – commercial success increases the value of the shareholders' investment and it enables returns to be made to them in the form of dividends. However, in my view, profit should be regarded as the starting point rather than the only point of being a director. Although the directors are accountable to the shareholders, their prime duty is owed to the company itself and their efforts should be directed towards promoting its long-term success. To achieve this, they need to take into account the interests of their key stakeholders also, for example, the employees, suppliers, customers and citizens in the local community. Their ultimate objective, like that of the company itself, is sustainable success – maximising value to the stakeholders over the long term.

Pragmatic approach

Introduction

The discussion about directors' duties and the separate legal identity of companies leads to another important dimension, which is that many directors and senior managers in business take an essentially pragmatic approach to their work and to the workplace. This tends to short-circuit into a mindset whereby the interests of the company must be protected at all costs. For certain individuals this will always be the case, but it is perhaps particularly apparent in times of tough trading conditions.

The economic downturn in the USA and in Continental Europe following the global financial crisis has meant that the recent past has seen tough trading conditions indeed: many businesses have been forced to close; many managers and employees in both the private and the public sectors have lost their jobs; and many investors and creditors have lost their money. The natural response in these circumstances has been for employees to keep their heads down, to get on with their work and to try to hold onto their jobs, whilst for directors and managers it has been to do whatever is needed to keep the business going. Many in this situation no doubt question the relevance of business ethics to the realities of the workplace – what they have to do day after day to generate income, to control costs and to earn a living by doing (and keeping) their jobs.

Pragmatic approach in action

This attitude was encapsulated in the interview I carried out with two long-term business associates of mine, Bernard Briggs and David Grew. Bernard is the managing director and owner of West Leigh Ltd, a specialist steel window manufacturer based in Bermondsey, South London, and David is the finance director. They also run another business, the Cotswold Casement Company based in Gloucestershire. They employ 60 staff, rising to 100 when their sub-contractors are included. So, they are a classic medium-sized manufacturing business operating in the UK.

Bernard began the interview by saying that he feels that many organisations might like to talk about their good business ethics, but that this fine talk can quickly disappear in practice, especially when times are hard and there is a continual struggle to win new work. This is what he said at the start of the interview:

> *If there's a contract up for grabs and you are tight on work, you are not going to bother with any business ethics. They just aren't going to exist. Business ethics are convenient; it's nice to have them. It's a bit like having good manners – I think it is nice to have good manners and we all try to have good manners but sometimes good manners aren't always there. And I think business ethics is something similar in so much that you purport to have them but when push comes to shove I'm not sure that they are really still around.*

Business realities and responsibilities

During the course of the interview, Bernard and David outlined their own approach to business ethics. Despite the comments above about business ethics being a 'nice to have', I interpret what they told me as confirmation of what I already suspected – that they have always run their business according to certain principles and values. For example, Bernard used the phrase 'business is business' and I thought for a moment that he was going to say that anything goes in business. In fact, what he went on to say during the course of the interview was something quite different.

Both Bernard and David made it clear that they will not conduct business with anybody that they do not trust, the only possible exception being if they were to be paid in full in advance of the work being carried out, so that their commercial interests are fully protected. They both have a practical, 'hands-on' management style and are deeply involved in the day-to-day workings of the business. So, they set the tone at the company in a very direct way and are well aware of the responsibilities that running a business brings. Bernard summed this up very succinctly:

> *It all comes back to being a responsible company and a responsible employer and to acting legally.*

Bernard and David then went on to give me their perspective of what these responsibilities mean in practice at various stages of the interview, beginning with responsibilities to their customers:

> *Take our customers for example. As a company, obviously we sell windows. Windows leak but we, as far as I know, have never failed to return and help a customer who has got a problem. It's very easy once you have been paid in full to think 'we've finished the job, we've been paid, that's it all completed'. But we won't allow our people to walk away from anything. If a customer has a problem – obviously we've had a lot of storms recently, windows have been leaking, they might*

well have an issue – we would still go back and help them because that's the way we want the business to be run. Whether it's Mr Smith or whether it's ICI, it doesn't make any difference to us, we would still do it. This comes back now to reputation and this is the reputation that we want to portray ... that we will always respond. You measure companies by how they respond when things are going wrong.

The point that Bernard and David make here about judging companies by how they perform when things go wrong is very important and perceptive I think and we will return to it later.

Then, Bernard and David tell me about responsibilities to their employees and other stakeholders:

I think business ethics goes further than just customers. You've got to take the way that you behave as a business, your attitude towards individuals within your business, particularly your attitude and your approach towards employees. So business ethics expands. You know we were talking just now about dealing with customers, people we can trust, but ethics goes a lot further than that in companies. A lot of other things come into play particularly with your employees. You need to try and be straightforward with them, deal with them straightforwardly and consistently and to create hopefully trust between you and them. So, it's about doing things right, it's the way you behave as a company not just to your customers, but to your suppliers and probably most importantly to your employees.

Again, the points made about being straightforward with employees and about doing things right are fundamental and we will come back to both later in the book.

Next, they discuss their responsibilities to ensure the health and safety of their employees. These are referred to only in passing because of the context of the interview, but it is clear from what Bernard says that he takes the health and safety of his workers very seriously:

The same applies with health and safety which has often been a problem in a lot of companies. We are really adamant that we do not scrimp or scrape on anything to do with health and safety.

Finally, Bernard and David mention their responsibilities to make sure that all of their employees, their sub-contractors and their suppliers have complete assurance about getting paid for work done:

Picking up on that ... Paying people. We have always paid our sub-contractors on time – they are paid on the last day of every month. Another thing is meeting your payroll liabilities – it is very, very important that your employees know they are going to be paid at the same time every month – all this is part of the trust and honesty we try to build up. It is the same with our suppliers – our suppliers know that they are going to get paid. Ok there are going to be times, like in all companies, we might be a bit slow sometimes, we might just drag it out slightly, but they never feel that they are not going to get paid – I can't remember the last time anybody tried to take action against us for non-payment. At times we forget or things slip through the net, we are a business, we are not perfect, but by and large our customers and our suppliers trust us.

Comments

It seems to me that what Bernard and David describe during our interview reflects an approach to running their business that combines pragmatism with strong underlying values and principles. They are aware of their responsibilities to their stakeholders (employees, customers, suppliers) and they try their best, day after day, to discharge them. But Bernard and David are also aware of risk and of the over-riding need to ensure that their companies are able to continue trading. In difficult times this means that they have to manage key areas of the business carefully: for example, cash management is probably the most critical area of all, so, as they mention, sometimes payment to suppliers is slower than at other times, but the key point from their perspective is that their suppliers are always paid.

I think Bernard and David's comments here are typical of the approach taken by thousands of business men and women who manage small and medium-sized businesses every day. Not all of them, of course – there are plenty of unscrupulous people in business – but most of them. Managing a business is a tough thing to do and in difficult trading conditions it must seem to directors and managers that the concept of business ethics is far removed from the daily grind of making sure that the organisation survives. Like Bernard and David, many will not choose to talk about their organisation's ethics or values explicitly in statements printed on the pages of staff handbooks or posted on the company website. But these ethics and values do exist, they are ingrained and they are implicitly held. Employees, customers and suppliers will certainly be aware of them, not so much through what they might read but through the actions and decisions taken every day by the owners and managers of those businesses.

 KEY TERMS

Set out below are observations around some of the key terms used when considering business ethics, culture and reputational risks arising from the actions and behaviours of people. This is important because in practice many directors and managers struggle to articulate what these terms mean. We start by looking at the concept of ethics itself.

Ethics

Definition

The *Encyclopaedia Britannica* defines ethics as: 'the branch of philosophy concerned with the nature of ultimate value and the standards by which human actions can be judged right or wrong'. Ethics concerns moral principles and values. It also concerns actions, with a focus on how individuals behave or groups conduct themselves. In my view, this concept has a clear application in the business world so that ethics becomes an extension of good management.

The word ethics is derived from the Greek and it means character or manners. Ethics asks fundamental questions of us all about what we should and should not do, about what principles should guide our behaviour and about what values we should live by. Ultimately, ethics asks us what is the purpose and meaning of life? Our individual choices affect both our own lives and those of others around us – whether we like it or not, how we view the world and how we behave and conduct ourselves matter.

Development of ethical theory

Ethical theory was developed by philosophers in ancient Greece such as Plato, Aristotle and Socrates. They set out to address issues concerning morality – questions about right and wrong, good and evil, justice and crime. Out of their work ethics, or moral philosophy, has developed a set of principles of right conduct, a theory or a system of moral values, in the Western philosophical tradition through the efforts of deep thinkers such as Machiavelli, Kant, Bentham, Mill and Nietzsche.

The other great influence on morality is of course religion. Each of the three great 'religions of the Book' (Judaism, Christianity and Islam) claims that morality is based on divine authority. Religious morality, like religion itself, is a matter not of reason or logic but of faith. As a personal maxim, I always try to avoid discussing either faith or politics in a business setting. So, when I work with directors and managers from various parts of the world (whether on business ethics or on other subjects) I am always careful to steer clear of entering into debate around the merits of the various religious beliefs or political views that might be represented in the room on any given day.

Business ethics

Introduction

When required, I try to direct all discussions on ethics away from the theoretical and towards the practical – in particular, towards how people at all levels behave in business situations, how they conduct themselves at work, how judgements are formed and how decisions are taken. For me, this is the crucial component of business ethics.

There is much evidence to support the view that our conduct is always heavily influenced by our environment. So, in the workplace context, my view is that it is management's responsibility to provide some form of guidance for their staff on conduct, whether in policies or by personal example. I would class failure to do so as poor management and little short of negligence. It also may give staff the impression that issues to do with the law, with conduct and behaviour and with values, are not important, which is entirely the wrong message to send out.

Definitions

Building on the definition of ethics set out above, the term 'business ethics' may be seen as the study of business situations, activities and decisions where issues of right and wrong are addressed.

There are many definitions of business ethics, but no universal standard. As an example, here is the working definition provided by the Canadian Chris MacDonald on his website BusinessEthics.ca:

> *Business ethics can be defined as the critical, structured examination of how people and institutions should behave in the world of commerce. In particular, it involves examining appropriate constraints on the pursuit of self-interest, or (for firms) profits, when the actions of individuals or firms affects others.*

Personally, I like the managerial approach taken by Linda Trevino and Katherine Nelson in their book *Managing Business Ethics*.[7] Trevino and Nelson define ethics as: 'the principles, norms and standards of conduct governing an individual or group'.[8] This focuses on conduct and the authors have a clear expectation that employers should establish guidelines for work-related conduct. Building on this they define ethical behaviour in business as: 'behaviour that is consistent with the principles, norms and standards of business practice that have been agreed upon by society'.[9] They say that many of the standards have been codified into the law, while others can be found in industry codes of conduct, international trade agreements and indeed in company codes. Of course, sometimes what is viewed as acceptable standards of business behaviour can change – as an example we discuss the changing attitudes to tax avoidance schemes below.

Trevino and Nelson treat the decisions of people in work organisations as being influenced by both the characteristics of individuals and the culture of the organisations themselves. I think that this is an instructive approach and we look at these influences on workplace conduct in the paragraphs below.

The drivers of conduct at work

Ethical business behaviour is determined by the interaction of many factors. Examples of the most important drivers of conduct in the workplace are: the law; government regulations; industry practices; professional codes and standards; corporate culture; cultural and social mores; and one's own internal moral code. In practice, some of these factors are more important than others.

When I ask delegates in my workshops to nominate just one out of the list that they consider to be the most important driver of behaviour, almost all of them choose the same factor – one's own internal moral code. They are not wrong to do so because our own personal standards, beliefs and biases can be very influential in the decision-making process at work. For some individuals, their own morals and ethics will over-ride anything else in terms of how they behave in the workplace.

An important recent example of this is provided by the case of Edward Snowden,[10] the security contractor who contrived to download a huge quantity of classified information concerning the activities of the National Security Agency in the USA and then proceeded to disclose that information, via media outlets, to the public. It appears that Mr Snowden did not do this for any monetary gain but rather because of his strongly held belief that government agencies in the USA were grossly abusing their surveillance powers, in breach of the law and to the detriment of citizens around the world. He became determined to expose this and he succeeded in doing so. Mr Snowden provides a good illustration of ethical risk, a factor that all organisations need to be aware of today. We will return to this case later in the book.

Not everyone feels so strongly about issues in the workplace as Mr Snowden, however. Although no doubt we would all like to believe that our own moral compass will always determine how we act and behave when at work, the evidence suggests that corporate culture has a bigger influence on how people actually conduct themselves day to day. Corporate culture is often the key driver of behaviour in the workplace – we consider it in more detail later in this chapter and elsewhere in the book.

Corporate culture needs to be properly aligned with the other factors listed above: the law and regulations, professional standards and the cultural and social mores of the societies in which we live. This often creates challenges, notably for global businesses where cultural norms and standards of behaviour vary in different parts of the world. In addition, from time to time business sectors or individual organisations develop practices that, when reported in the media, give rise to anger or offence among the wider public. These practices may not break the law, but they can lead to reputational damage. The payment of very substantial bonuses to investment bankers is probably the most obvious example of this at the present time.

Another aspect of this challenge is that the public perception of certain business practices can change over time, sometimes very quickly. As an example, consider the issues of tax avoidance. The use of tax avoidance schemes by corporations trading internationally in order to reduce their tax bills has been a part of sound corporate planning for decades. Such tax planning is perfectly legal but, since the global financial crisis, tax avoidance has attracted much public opprobrium, certainly in the UK and in many other countries too. We will look at these cultural challenges in more detail when we examine the components of conduct risk later in the book.

As an aside, it is interesting to note that the Institute of Business Ethics (IBE) was established in London in 1986. One of its main founding purposes is to encourage high standards of business behaviour based on ethical values.[11] In doing so, the IBE recognises that business is a part of society and that business people need to conduct themselves in a way that is consistent with the principles, norms and standards that have been agreed upon by society.

The golden rule

Introduction

There have been many ethical principles and beliefs developed since the time of Aristotle and Plato, stimulating much intellectual dispute and not a little disagreement among moral philosophers over the centuries. The issues under debate include: freedom and the harm principle; the golden rule; the concept of ends and means; the principle of double effect; utilitarianism; free will; the social contract; and nihilism. Each of these ethical ideas has merit, of course, and their development over time has had a big influence on the way that we think today. However, most of them are not helpful to me when I am trying to develop practical advice aimed at improving performance for directors and managers working in the business environment.

The exception is the ethical principle that has come to be known as the golden rule or, more fully, the golden rule of reciprocity. Put simply, the golden rule states that:

We should treat others in exactly the same way that we want others to treat us.

Reciprocity

It seems that the underlying principle of reciprocity, sometimes thought of as 'do as you would be done by' appears, in some guise or other, in almost every ethical code or system, both religious and secular, and in both the Western and the Eastern philosophical traditions. The imperative of returning a favour or a benefit received is therefore one of our most fundamental moral instincts.

I refer to the ethic of reciprocity in many of my courses because I believe that it can be applied directly to the business world. Indeed, reciprocity is one of the most fundamental principles of business itself, encapsulating positive behaviours like fairness and honesty, responsiveness and a willingness to admit to and to correct mistakes made. Or at least it should be. We all know that things do not always work out quite so well in reality.

Ultimately, it is the law rather than the ideal of reciprocal treatment that provides the essential conditions and the necessary safeguards for business to thrive. Contracts entered into by two or more parties, whether in writing or given verbally, need to be honoured. Contract law underpins this principle and provides a means of redress for an injured party. Any organisation seeking a short-term advantage by reneging on a deal will always face the possibility of being sued in the courts. An organisation that fails to honour its commitments, however, also risks losing its reputation for integrity and thereby forfeiting the trust of its business counterparties in the future – something that is often more damaging than the cost of any civil remedies that the courts might impose.

'My word is my bond'

We will discuss aspects of integrity, trust and the law further in the paragraphs below, but before we do so there is one idea that it is important to mention at this stage. The principle of reciprocity is closely connected in the commercial world with the maxim 'my word is my bond'. This maxim is sometimes viewed with nostalgia as we look back on earlier times when a handshake, rather than a detailed legal contract, was all that was required to ensure that a business deal, once agreed upon, would indeed be carried out.

In reality, as we all know, there never was such a time of unbridled honesty and fair dealing. There have been rogues in business as long as there has been business itself and certainly long before the recent global financial crisis. So it is interesting to note in this context that the IBE was originally founded in the UK in November 1986 on the day after 'Big Bang' came into effect. Big Bang effectively ended the traditional way that stocks and shares were traded in the City of London, through the use of separate firms of brokers and jobbers. The IBE was formed by business leaders as an organisation to support business people by trying to maintain the very principle of 'my word is my bond'. Clearly, the founders of the IBE felt that the principle was under threat from the changes introduced by Big Bang and perhaps they were right – certainly the financial services industry in the UK has never been the same since.

Despite Big Bang, the golden rule of reciprocity continues to be an important principle that underpins business success. It is a prompt towards consistency in performance and behaviour, so it is a vital component of sustainability and of taking the long-term view. But there is also a sense of empathy, of personal engagement in business implicit in the concept of reciprocity – it moves us away from figures and calculations and pushes us towards personal relationships. It is closely connected to trust.

A business paradox

Here is another extract from my interview with James Featherby. It is particularly insightful because it provides us with a bridge that connects the two ideas of reciprocity and trust. As stated earlier, James used to be a successful lawyer and spent many years as a partner in a large London legal practice, so he is well-versed in the protections provided by the law. But his observations on business paradoxes and the differences between a legal contract and the concept of trust are not those of a typical lawyer; they are all the more interesting for it.

> *I think that one of the problems with economics or with economic theory is that it doesn't do paradox very well – it tends to think in almost 'Newtonian physics' terms. It seems to me that one of the great paradoxes of life – and it is very evident in business as well – is that you have to give before you receive. That is really true in business. You have to make the sale before you can enjoy the profits; it isn't the other way round.*

> *I believe that there is, staying with paradoxes, a sort of strange connection between generosity and business. Let me try and explain what I mean, talking about trust. Suppose that you and I have a contract between us: if I do something then you will do something in return and we both fulfil that contract. Now, that isn't really trust at all, that's just what we are legally obliged to do – we might well go to prison if we don't. So, it's not really trust at all.*

> *Where trust exists is where we have agreed to do something together and you do more than I'm expecting, more than the contract requires you to do because you value my goodwill and my repeat business. So there is an element almost of generosity here – certainly it is going beyond the contractual requirement in terms of the relationship between us.*

> *So if we look at an energy company, for example. It could have a customer service department that is focused on simply swatting away customer complaints as quickly as possible and minimising all possible downsides. Or it could have a customer service department that says: 'Yes, we do mess up on a fairly regular basis but how can we sort this problem out for you? We may not be contractually required to do this for you, but we'll do it anyway.' Now, that's how you build up goodwill in my view.*

James makes an important point here. Trust is an elusive concept, it is difficult to define adequately but the sense of giving, of doing the best that one can for the other participants in the transaction, of empathising with them, is a key aspect. This personal component is what makes trust such a powerful concept and it is something that is also picked up by Mike Meldrum, another business associate of mine, as will be seen in the extracts from my interview with him that are quoted below.

But before we consider trust, we need to discuss another important concept in business ethics: that of integrity.

Integrity

Introduction

Integrity is a word that will feature in the statements that many organisations make about themselves on their websites, whether these statements are about 'mission' or 'values and principles' or 'core beliefs'. This is hardly a new phenomenon. We looked at the Enron example in the Prologue; the comments made by Ken Lay, the ex-Chairman, during a video made during the 1990s to promote the company's vision and values are a classic example of what is known as the 'say-do' gap. He stated that:

> Enron is a company that deals with everyone with absolute integrity. We play by all the rules; we stand by our word; we mean what we say; we say what we mean. We want people to leave a transaction with Enron thinking that they have been dealt with in the highest possible way as far as integrity, truthfulness, really doing our business right.[12]

The problem here, of course, was that these fine-sounding words were not matched by the actions of Mr Lay and a number of his colleagues at the top of Enron. Integrity is not compatible with accounting fraud. Following Enron's bankruptcy in 2001, over 20 executives, accounting officers and traders either pleaded guilty or were found guilty of fraud by the US courts. Mr Lay himself was found guilty on all counts of securities fraud, wire fraud and making false and misleading statements. He died of a heart attack before the appeals process was exhausted so his conviction was abated.

There is much scepticism today towards the statements made by business leaders (and by political leaders too). To be credible, organisations need to back up their words by actions, and nowhere is this more applicable than in the financial services sector. Banking has been one of the most challenged industries regarding the integrity and conduct of its people, at all levels, in recent years. There are many current initiatives to try to close the 'say-do' gap in banking, of which the two described below are good examples.

■ At the national level, the UK established a new regulator, the FCA, in 2013 in recognition of the fact that consumers and investors alike had lost confidence in the industry following the scandals and failures of the global financial crisis. The FCA has three operational objectives: protecting consumers, ensuring market integrity, and promoting effective competition. As a good conduct regulator, encouraging and upholding business ethics throughout the financial services industry in the UK is at the heart of what it was set up to do. To help to achieve this, the FCA has set out 11 Principles for Business. These are general business statements of the main regulatory obligations that apply to every authorised firm in the UK. The first of these principles could not be more straightforward or direct: 'A firm must conduct its business with integrity.'[13]

■ At the organisational level, I work from time to time with Tim Parkman and his company Lessons Learned Ltd on various ethical training and development programmes that he runs for large International Financial Institutions (IFIs). One of these programmes is called 'Integrity Matters', which Tim delivers regularly to staff joining the European Bank for Reconstruction and Development (EBRD), based in London. The EBRD provides project financing for banks, industries and businesses in over 30 countries. Its mission is to help foster the transition to open and democratic market economies in developing countries in Central and Eastern Europe, central Asia and the southern and eastern Mediterranean. It is owned by 64 countries, by the European Union and by the European Investment Bank, so it is essentially taxpayer funded. Being able to demonstrate integrity, accountability and anti-corruption is essential to its reputation, therefore. Tim works with the bank's compliance department on training initiatives to ensure that the highest standards of integrity are applied to all aspects of the bank's activities. A central part of this effort is the bank's flagship integrity induction programme. It is a highly interactive half-day course that is mandatory for all new hires at the bank. It provides discussion, debate and hands-on experience for the delegates of using the bank's policies and code of conduct to answer a number of practical scenario-based case studies. The messages contained in 'Integrity Matters' are re-inforced and supplemented by additional ongoing training. It provides a good example of the commitment of time and resources that many banks are now making in order to embed a culture of ethics and integrity throughout their operations.

Meaning

It is clear that integrity is a necessary component of good business ethics but what are its essential features?

According to the *Oxford English Dictionary*, the word integrity means moral uprightness and honesty. Being seen to uphold and represent generally accepted moral standards, such as being fair and telling the truth, is therefore one key aspect of acting with integrity. Other definitions associate integrity with incorruptibility, transparency, accountability, loyalty and trust. So, being straightforward with nothing to hide, avoiding conflicts between workplace and personal interests and activities, having regard to other people's interests and views and being prepared to admit to mistakes made are also important components of integrity.

One essential feature of integrity is being law-abiding. Our attitudes to the law are not as straightforward as might at first be thought and we will look at this in more detail below. But it remains true that being convicted of a criminal offence, especially one involving theft, fraud or corruption, will make it difficult indeed for an individual (or an organisation) to claim to act with integrity.

When applied to the actions of an organisation, I personally associate the word integrity above all with a commitment to try to do things right, first time and every time and to do so always in accordance with the law.

So there are two essential components of business integrity for me. First of all, it is about consistency of performance – integrity is not about just being honest and fair when it suits you to act in this way. It is about behaving honestly and fairly at all times, even when such actions might be thought likely to harm your own interests in some way, at least in the short term. Second, integrity is about compliance with the law. By this I do not mean simply complying with the letter of the law but with the spirit of the law too.

Letter and spirit of the law

The law establishes rules that govern our behaviour. Obeying the law as it applies to us is a duty on each of us as citizens, whether individuals or organisations. The law actually represents minimum standards of behaviour so, when an organisation claims to operate with 'absolute integrity' or states that 'integrity is the cornerstone of our business' – which are actually not uncommon statements – I expect to see evidence of something more from it than compliance with the letter of the law. For example, when I read reports in the media that a CEO, in response to a regulatory probe or a journalist's inquiry into the conduct of his or her organisation, replies along the lines of 'well, none of my people have broken the law', my response is to think 'well, so what?' I expect the law to be complied with. If compliance with the strict letter of the law is all that an organisation is striving for, then much of the talk about integrity in corporate statements becomes banal and meaningless. In order to be impressed by claims of integrity, I always look for signs of compliance with the spirit (or intention) of the law also.

Example: General Electric

A good example of what I mean by an abiding focus on the spirit and not just the letter of the law is provided by General Electric Corporation (GE). Here, the long-term Chairman and CEO, Jeffrey Immelt, has shown a strong personal commitment to high standards of business ethics within the company ever since he succeeded Jack Welsh in 2000. In June 2005, he signed off on GE's Statement of Integrity and launched the company's overarching business principles. Two aspects of this are particularly noteworthy for me. First, GE has a striking motto on the cover of this document, which is: 'Always with unyielding integrity.' I like this phrase as it carries the promise of consistent performance, no matter what the circumstances. Mr Immelt has made frequent use of it subsequently. Second and most importantly, the document itself is titled: 'The Spirit and The Letter: guiding the way we do business.'[14] GE's integrity policy is summarised in a short one-page statement as follows:

> *Every day, everyone at GE has the power to influence our company's reputation everywhere we do business. The Spirit and the Letter helps to ensure that, after more than 125 years, we all conduct our affairs with unyielding integrity.*
>
> *For well over a century, GE employees have worked hard to uphold the highest standards of ethical business conduct. We seek to go beyond simply obeying the law – we embrace the spirit of integrity.*
>
> *GE's Code of Conduct articulates that spirit by setting out general principles of conduct everywhere, every day and by every GE employee.*

Every GE employee signs a pledge promising to adhere to this integrity policy when they join the company.

These statements and pledges represent powerful and classic pieces of ethical hardware. By themselves they offer no assurance that the principles in them will be followed, of course. However, it seems clear that GE has the required ethical software in place also, in terms of tone and commitment from the top. I have never worked for GE myself but I have been impressed by the comments of a number of delegates attending my courses over the years who had been employed by GE in the past. In discussion, each of these delegates confirmed a number of things that I had read about: that Mr Immelt's personal commitment to The Spirit and The Letter is clear to all managers and employees – he does indeed begin and end each annual meeting with an affirmation of the company's integrity principles, as is often reported; that individual performance around these principles feeds directly into GE's appraisal and remuneration systems; and that there are constant reminders of the need for all managers and staff to act with integrity in terms of training programmes, messages on notice boards, screen-savers, bulletin boards and so on.

GE provides a good example of tone at the top in action – of statements being translated into action. Employees can access the Spirit and the Letter in an interactive eBook with access to additional resources including a database of frequently asked questions, videos and links to online training. There are compliance drivers too. A commitment to perform with integrity is instilled in every employee as a non-negotiable expectation of behaviour.

Personal experience

I have some experience of working with organisations where the focus is on the spirit not only the letter of the law. One good example of this is provided by my time working on a project for the Gambling Commission in the UK in 2007. This project involved reviewing all aspects of compliance and enforcement of the law and regulations of the gaming industry in the UK in response to the changes introduced by the Gambling Act 2005.

One of the Gambling Commission's three licensing objectives at the time was to protect children and other vulnerable persons from being harmed or exploited by gambling. The legal age for gambling in the UK is 18. However, right from the outset the Gambling Commission encouraged all operators in the industry to, as the Commission termed it, 'Think 21'. That is to say, employees working in the industry were instructed to check the IDs of anyone entering their premises that appeared to be under the age of 21, rather than focusing their time on checking people who looked to be younger than the legal minimum age of 18. By doing this, the Commission felt that it would be far more difficult for a 16 or 17 year old youth to be able to gamble.

Although controversial within the industry when first introduced, this move was designed to assure the public that casinos and betting shops were acting responsibly by looking to follow the intention of the law and so better protecting young people, rather than simply adhering to the letter of the law around strict age limits. It is replicated today in the approach taken by many public houses in the UK. Before serving young people with alcoholic drinks, the bar staff are encouraged to 'Think 21' and where there is any doubt, they will then ask the young person to show some official document confirming his or her age. Failure to do so will mean that alcohol will not be served to them.

Trust

Meaning

Trust is a crucial concept but sometimes one that is difficult to pin down. The *Oxford English Dictionary* defines the word trust as: 'A firm belief in the reliability or truth or strength of a person or thing.'

Writing in a paper for The Institute of Business Ethics,[15] Dietz and Gillespie define trust as being: 'A judgement of confident reliance in either a person or an organisation.' They set out in the paper a very helpful model of trust, according to which we tend to judge the other party's trustworthiness along three dimensions as follows:

- their ability (technical competence);
- their benevolence (motives and interests); and
- their integrity (honesty and fair treatment).

If the overall judgement is positive, this increases our willingness to take a risk in our dealings with that individual or organisation. Put simply, we are inclined to trust them (for example, by buying an organisation's products or services, or by investing in its stock or by signing on as an employee). But a deficiency or abuse of any of these attributes, in the form of a scandal or failure, can result in this trust evaporating very quickly.

Trust is an essential component of ethics, reputation and long-term success. In my view it is the critical 'x-factor' in every relationship that an organisation has with its stakeholders because it introduces a personal dimension and connection into the business equation. Trust comes from being honest and keeping to commitments made.

Trust is also connected to values. If the values of an organisation are closely aligned with our own, then we will be more inclined to like that organisation and therefore to do business with it. This can be seen most clearly today in the branding of individual products (we look at the importance of brands in Chapter 4 when we look at reputation). Conversely, many individuals will choose not to do business with organisations on moral grounds if they operate in certain industries (for example, the traditional 'sin sectors' of tobacco, armaments and pornography). However, for most of us it is not necessary to like an organisation in order to transact with it.

As with integrity, a necessary ingredient of trust in my view is consistency of performance and standards that meets or exceeds expectations. Such consistency implies competence. A number of factors might be involved in our judgement of competency including: academic and professional qualifications; assessments and certification from third parties; and referrals from family, friends or others whose judgement we hold in high regard.

Most important, however, in our assessment of both performance and standards will be our personal experience – have our own expectations been met or exceeded not only once but time after time? To take an everyday example, customers will shop regularly at their favourite supermarket because of factors such as price and convenience but above all because they know from their personal experience that it is reliable – they have confidence that the supermarket will provide them with food, drink and other products to a consistent standard every time they do their shopping at the store (we examine in Chapter 4 what can happen when such confidence is brought into question by looking at a recent food scandal in the UK and the steps that supermarkets then had to take in order to rebuild trust with their customers).

I have heard trust described as 'the residue of promises fulfilled' and I think that this is an interesting perspective. Keeping promises, in whatever form, promotes loyalty and loyalty is an important by-product of trust. Building up a 'trust reserve' will also better equip an organisation to deal with future mistakes and failures.

Personal ingredient

In the interview extract quoted above, James Featherby spoke about the important role of relationships in business and he gave me his view that trust is not at all the same thing as a legal contract. This personal ingredient that he refers to is something that Mike Meldrum also spoke about when I interviewed him for the book, illustrating his comments with examples from his own personal experience.

Mike held a research post at the Cranfield School of Management in the UK for many years, moving from a marketing background into general management and leadership studies. He ran business leadership programmes for five years, which were Cranfield's most senior offering at the time. Mike currently works as an independent consultant. This is what he had to say to me during our interview about trust, about its close linkage with integrity and about how it is for him closely tied to his own personal feelings about a transaction or a relationship.

Ok, so for me, if you take trust back down to its essentials, effectively if I am going to have trust, to trust you, to trust the organisation, that means that I am prepared to make myself vulnerable to you. So that by purchasing your product or doing business with you or whatever it is – giving my money to you, whatever it is – then I am effectively saying: 'If you do not fulfil your promise, if you show yourself not to have the integrity that I have assumed through placing my trust in you then I will suffer.' And of course the bigger the risk the more important it is to have that trust. One of the key issues, therefore, is integrity – it is doing what you say you are going to do. And another is appearing to be interested and concerned about me. So if you can give me indications that you are actually interested in me then I may trust you.

First Direct would be quite a good example for me as a corporate, one that comes out relatively near the top of my personal 'trust league'. There are two sides to that which I will tell you about. First of all, First Direct was the first organisation to offer telephone banking successfully in the UK. Why were they successful? There were two key reasons why they were more successful than previous attempts. One was that they went for the 24 hour service and they were always there, they always manned the telephones – I don't know how many people phoned them on Christmas Day to make sure that they were actually living up to their promise! And secondly they didn't employ bankers to be on the other end of the telephone because bankers couldn't work in the way that First Direct wanted them to work – which was all about engagement with the individuals. So, the impression First Direct creates ... well, anybody who has got an account will tell you that they are always very friendly, they are very personable. They have always demonstrated an interest in me. So they will try to sell me things but the moment I say I'm not interested they pull back, they accommodate me, they provide lots of indications that they are interested in my opinion, they live up to their promises etc. etc. So they do really well in terms of building up trust with me.

So part of it is integrity, part of it is because my personal experience of interaction with them is that they are actually interested in me. As an example, when I get a £25 fine for an unauthorised overdraft, I phone them up and say: 'Damn, this was a real oversight, my mistake, a real shame – is there anything you can do?' They will say 'We'll withdraw the fine, just don't do it again.' Again, there is a lot of empathy and sympathy from them – and consequently lots of trust from me.

The essential ingredients of trust are the same for Mike and James: consistent performance; concern to do everything possible (over and above the strict letter of the legal contract) to satisfy the needs of the other party in the transaction; and engagement and empathy with that other party.

Fairness

Mike also had some interesting things to say about fairness. It is necessary for organisations to treat their employees fairly and with respect if they are to engender trust in the workplace. There are a number of fundamentals that must be in place if this is to happen: equal opportunities; no discrimination, intimidation or harassment; and a commitment to a safe and healthy working environment. These are the baselines and we will return to them later in the book when discussing the ethical toolbox.

Mike does not equate treating people fairly with being kind or understanding, however. He told me in the interview that it is not necessary for organisations always to treat people kindly in order to gain their loyalty and respect. The key factor in his view is that people know where they stand and are treated consistently. Mike used the example of the Hanson Trust plc (Hanson), the old British-based industrial conglomerate set up in 1964 by James Hanson (later Lord Hanson) and Gordon White (later Baron White of Hull) to illustrate his point. Hanson's success was based upon the business model of purchasing under-performing assets and then turning them around through efficient management. This is what Mike had to say:

It depends on what sort of business you are going to build. Hanson was a classic example wasn't it? Run by two people; massive empire; very successful; and run entirely through a dozen metrics.

They bought the business, cleared out the old guard, all the people who had been frustrated for a long time by the old guard were promoted into the new business, given the metrics. And then it was more or less: 'off you go, sink or swim'. This was fair because it was all down to the metrics, harsh because it was sink or swim – very appropriate for a capitalist society. On the downside, if you failed you suffered but on the upside if you succeeded you did very well. So it seemed to be fair – draconian but admired because of their success.

Would you want to work for them? Actually the employees had quite a clear choice: yes I am prepared to live by that; or no I'm not because my fate is not always in my hands. What is the extent to which Hanson and White will interfere or not interfere? Well, they developed a reputation for not interfering – unless the numbers were suffering at which point they did get involved and there would be consequences. So it was all very clear.

Authenticity

How authentic are the statements made by business leaders about trust and integrity? If they are not genuine then organisations run the risk of charges of hypocrisy which, if taken up by the media (and especially today by social media sites), might result in widespread damage to their reputation.

Of course, the words must be backed up by actions. Whether this happens or not will depend crucially on two factors:

- First, whether everyone who works for the organisation is aware of the statements made by their leaders and understands their importance – are these principles at the forefront of their minds when doing business? In other words, it is crucial that core principles and values are repeated and re-inforced by the organisation at every opportunity – in meetings and presentations, in training programmes, on screensavers, on notice-boards and so on. This is not an easy process, nor can results be achieved quickly in practice – it requires an ongoing commitment from the top.
- Second, the words must be backed up by the actions of all employees, starting with the conduct and decision-making of the directors and senior managers at the top of the organisation. This must apply both in good times and in bad – there must be no 'say-do' gap. The acid test here is to observe how well an organisation and its leaders are able to deal with bad news.

The law

Meaning

The law comprises a set of rules governing behaviour that has evolved over time. Each country will have its own set of laws and its own legal system. In each jurisdiction there will be an important distinction between criminal law and civil law. Criminal law deals with crimes and their punishment. Crimes can be committed by individuals (for example: murder; drug trafficking; or theft) and by organisations (for example: fraud, bribery and corruption; or tax evasion). Civil law involves individuals and organisations seeking to resolve non-criminal disputes through the courts. Civil disputes can occur at a personal level in such circumstances as neighbours arguing over late-night noise or access to a shared driveway and with organisations as when customers do not pay their bills or companies fail to deliver a service to an agreed level.

Criminal offences are generally regarded as more serious than civil offences, especially in terms of their impact on perceptions of integrity.

Criminal offence – example: Arthur Andersen

In 2002, Arthur Andersen (Andersen)[16] became the first and so far the only professional services firm to be convicted of a criminal offence when it was found guilty by a court in Houston, Texas of one count of obstruction of justice by shredding documents relating to its client, Enron. On one level, this criminal conviction meant that the firm could no longer provide auditing services to publicly quoted companies in the USA. On another level, it meant that Andersen had lost its reputation for integrity and professionalism. Not surprisingly, it very quickly lost its clients too. Despite a successful appeal of the judgement subsequently, Andersen's business never recovered and its audit, tax and consulting practices were subsequently separated and sold to various competitor firms.

Civil offence – example: JP Morgan Chase

Contrast the Andersen case with the more recent experience of the US bank JP Morgan Chase (JP Morgan).[17] In 2013 the bank announced that it had set aside total provisions of $23bn to cover fines, settlements and other legal expenses as it worked through a number of investigations into aspects of its past conduct by regulators in the USA and abroad. It quickly started to use up much of this contingency fund. As an example, in November 2013 JP Morgan agreed to a record $13bn settlement with US authorities for misleading investors over mortgaged-backed securities during the downturn in the US housing market in 2006–07. The bank acknowledged that it had made 'serious misrepresentations to the public' but said that it did not violate US laws.

It should be noted that a large proportion of the mortgages under investigation in this case were not originated by JP Morgan itself, but were transferred when it acquired the troubled banks Bear Stearns and Washington Mutual at the height of the global financial crisis. However, it is striking that the bank's investors, while no doubt concerned at the scale of the fines being levied, appear above all to be relieved that a civil settlement had been reached and uncertainty removed. At the time of writing in 2014, JP Morgan remains profitable, the share price has held up well and Jamie Dimon, the bank's long-term Chairman and CEO, is still in post.

Attitudes to the law: general

The law binds all of us in society and it is recognised as enjoining or prohibiting certain actions, enforced by the imposition of penalties. The law actually represents minimum acceptable standards of behaviour. All of us, both individuals and organisations alike, should conduct ourselves so that we comply with these minimum standards at all times. This appears to be an obvious statement, but what actually happens in the realities of day-to-day life? Non-compliance with the law does happen, more regularly than many of us might like to admit.

As individuals, most of us like to believe that we are law-abiding citizens. In practice, many of us will break the law on a reasonably regular basis. As an example, consider those adults in the UK who drive motor cars. Most of us will exceed the designated speed limits from time to time, despite the fact that those speed limits exist to reduce the risk of accidents. A smaller number (but still a significant minority) will use their hand-held mobile phones when driving for communication purposes, either phone calls or text messaging. Both speeding and the use of a hand-held mobile phone whilst driving are criminal offences in the UK.

So, how law-abiding are we in reality?

Attitudes to the law in the workplace

When I work with organisations around the subject of business ethics, I like to test the attitudes to the law of some of the managers and staff who work in those organisations by means of a series of questions and short case studies. This is always a fascinating exercise. Tim Parkman likes to use anonymous voting technology here because he feels that the anonymity may well encourage greater candour and therefore produces more genuine and interesting results.

Whatever method is used to conduct these exercises, there are always a number of people in the group who are prepared to admit that they have taken office pens and stationary for private purposes – they consider this to be either a minor misdemeanour or no misdemeanour at all. Another group, generally a smaller number, will acknowledge that from time to time they may have used unlicensed software or illegally downloaded music either at home or on their work computers. According to Tim, very few individuals will ever admit to submitting false expense claims or to lying on an insurance claim in order to gain a financial advantage, even though we all know that neither of these behaviours is unheard of in reality. There are limits to gaining a true understanding of attitudes to the law, even with anonymous voting technology.

Observations

So, what is going on here? Well, it seems clear that most people bend the rules in some shape or form both in their private lives and also when at work. In most cases, there are limits to this, of course, depending upon an individual's perception first of what he or she considers to be 'right or wrong' and second when he or she considers that the risks of detection become too great. This illustrates the importance of having robust systems and controls in place, with consequences for transgressions, in all organisations.

When working with organisations, whatever method is used, the consistent conclusion coming out of these exercises is that there are almost always significant differences in the answers given among members of the group. This is an intuitive finding – we are all individuals after all, we have different beliefs and values, we will behave differently and have different attitudes to the law from time to time. This may seem fairly obvious. However, this conclusion, obvious though it might be, has potentially significant consequences for organisations if these differences surface in the workplace environment. Organisations need assurance around consistency of behaviour among their people. So directors and senior managers need to put in place systems and controls (the ethical hardware that we have talked about) in order to provide this consistent framework and thereby minimise reputational risk.

■ I pause here and say that this might be a good time to address the question posed by David Hurley at the beginning of the workshop, which was: People are all different, we all have our individual standards and beliefs, so whose ethics are we talking about here? As we have seen, David is quite right when he says that different people have different views about ethics and integrity. This observation has important consequences for all organisations, especially in view of the need for consistency in performance and decision-making that has already been highlighted. So, my answer is that we are talking about the ethics of the organisation as a whole – common standards, shared values and behaviour that matches these standards and values. It is necessary for directors and senior management to establish these. All organisations, especially those operating in many different countries around the world, need to have clear signposts around their values and ethics in order to protect their reputation.

Compliance

Meaning

Compliance means conforming to a law, rule, policy or standard. These may be set externally or internally. It is crucial that an organisation is able to demonstrate that it complies with all external laws and regulations that are applicable to it. We discussed aspects of the law above. The word 'regulation' in this sense generally refers to a set of binding rules issued by a private or a public body which has the necessary authority to supervise compliance with them and apply sanctions in response to violations of them – a national government for example.

It is essential that every organisation takes steps to ensure that it is both aware of and compliant with all applicable laws and regulations. This is not easy because of the increasingly complex compliance landscape. For example, there are a huge number of different regulations in place today. This is certainly the case in the UK, where there is the extra layer of Directives from the European Union and where various business sectors are policed by different bodies – as examples, the FCA, the Environment Agency and the Competition and Markets Authority. In the USA, regulation tends to be set out in statute, for example in pieces of legislation like the Sarbanes–Oxley Act and the Dodd–Frank Act.

The importance of the compliance function

Given the complexity of the law and regulations today, any inconsistencies in behaviour and judgement by managers and staff are dangerous for all organisations, whatever their size and whatever business sector they are operating in. In order to meet these challenges, compliance needs to operate effectively at two levels. First, at the external level: as we have seen, it is crucial that an organisation, if it is to build trust with its stakeholders, operates within the law and complies with all applicable regulations. Second, at the internal level: managers and staff must act in a consistent way that is in line with the organisation's own policies and values.

In order to obtain assurance around compliance issues, many organisations look to install an effective compliance programme. This applies in particular to firms operating in the financial services industry, where an independent compliance function will have specific responsibility for the organisation of legal and regulatory compliance. Almost always, this function will be headed up by a Chief Compliance Officer, whose fundamental duty is to identify and manage regulatory risk. Since the global financial crisis, compliance professionals have been in great demand with banks and other large financial institutions now looking to recruit heavily in this area in response to more robust scrutiny by the regulators.

We will look at compliance in more detail in Chapter 7, but there is one important point to make at this stage. It is neither appropriate nor affordable for small- and medium-sized businesses to hire an army of compliance officers. Nor do they need to do so. What they do require in practice as an absolute necessity is for their CEO or managing director to be vigilant and hands-on in terms of the management of the business, to ask questions, to be personally engaged and committed to the need for the organisation to comply with all applicable laws and regulations. A similar approach at the very top is most effective in larger organisations too, although here the CEO will have an extensive team of managers and assistants to provide support and carry out most of the work.

So, counter-intuitive though it may sound, the most effective compliance officer in all organisations, large and small, is in my view the CEO.

Relationship between compliance and business ethics

This brings us to John Holt's question at the beginning of the workshop about the differences, if any, between ethical business behaviour and compliance with the law. It is an important question that requires some context.

The first thing to say is that a compliance programme should not be confused with an ethics programme. There is some overlap between the two of course – an organisation that breaks the law will struggle to describe itself with credibility as an ethical organisation – but the focus of each is different. Compliance programmes will focus on the rules, both external and internal, that the organisation is subject to. In contrast, ethics programmes will focus on values. One of the challenges for managers is to ensure that the behaviour of their people matches the values of their business, something that should be demonstrated in the decisions made and in the actions taken every day.

The area of overlap between business ethics and compliance concerns working always within the letter of the law and applicable regulations. This is necessary and should be clearly stated in every organisation. But ethics and compliance are not the same thing. A good example of the difference between the two can be seen in one of the most talked-about outcomes of the global financial crisis. At the time of writing, some five years after the end of the crisis, it remains true that there have been very few prosecutions of individuals for actions that broke the law at that time in any of the most affected jurisdictions. Contrast this with the widespread condemnation of the unethical conduct of a number of bankers (in particular on trading desks) who were prepared on occasion to take huge risks with other people's money while being paid substantial bonuses for doing so. This was not a compliance problem, but it has certainly now become an ethical one.

The integrated approach

I advocate taking an integrated approach here, one that balances values and rules. Organisations should promote ethical behaviour but without tolerating unethical conduct. Zero tolerance of violations is a concept that we will discuss in Chapter 3 when we look at the implications of pieces of legislation like the Bribery Act 2010, but it is important that there are consequences if rules are broken and that these consequences are consistently applied. The real imperative for directors and senior managers is to be able to ground compliance explicitly in the values and ideals of their business.

In summary, directors and senior managers must understand that the baseline requirement of their organisation is to comply with the law and regulations. A compliance programme, appropriate to the circumstances of the organisation, is needed to give reasonable assurance that this is happening. However, compliance alone will not be sufficient to build trust with or to demonstrate integrity to stakeholders. To succeed in this, compliance needs to be combined with a business ethics programme, so that there is a commitment to behave in accordance with the organisation's values, with enforcement structures in place to back this up.

▪ This is an appropriate time to address John Holt's question at the start of the workshop, which was: What is the difference between ethical behaviour and compliance with the law? My answer to this is that business ethics represents 'the law plus'. Compliance with the law is the essential baseline for all organisations but many of the most interesting questions concerning business ethics arise at the point where the law ends, in the so-called 'grey zone' where values might be in conflict. Complying with the letter of the law means meeting minimum standards of behaviour and this is necessary for any organisation claiming to operate ethically. In my view it is not sufficient, however. Ethical behaviour includes this but goes beyond it. Business ethics is about matching the values of the business with the actions of its people and enables an organisation to comply both with the letter of the law and with the spirit of the law too.

Corporate culture

Meaning

Anthropologists view culture as a body of learned beliefs, tradition and guides for behaviour shared among members of a group. Building on this, the culture of an organisation expresses shared assumptions, values and beliefs and it provides an important indicator of how that organisation might conduct itself in practice. Corporate culture is therefore an important concept, but what does the phrase actually mean? The *Financial Times* online Business Lexicon has a useful description of corporate culture as follows:

> *Corporate culture is seen in an organisation's behaviour and its structure. A hierarchical company may have individual offices, a formal environment and intricate rules regarding travel allowances and dress code. It used to be said, for example, that you could recognise IBM employees when travelling for business because of their formal dark suits and ties.*

> *Companies emphasising equality and innovation will demonstrate these values visibly too, for instance, Apple is famous for its casual dress and elegant product design. At Intel, which is known for its culture of face-to-face open discussions, everyone, including the top executives, works in the same size office cubicle and even senior managers fly economy class. Such symbols send powerful messages about a company's culture.*

I use the following as a simple working definition of corporate culture on my courses:

> *The culture of an organisation may be taken to mean the combined set of individual and corporate values, attitudes, competencies and behaviour that determine an organisation's commitment and style.*

Importance of organisational culture

Each organisation has its own unique culture. This will be manifested in many ways – from policies and systems to norms of behaviour, including modes of dress, working hours and so on. The most important influences that shape culture will come from the style, actions and decision-making of those senior managers at the top of the organisation. The tone is always set at the top. Senior managers need to be aware of this and the fact that everything they do in their actions day to day will have an impact on the culture of their organisation. They should be looking to create the conditions for a positive culture where behaviour is openly assessed, challenged, developed and rewarded.

It has always been my view that the really interesting and challenging aspects of business ethics start where the law ends and focus on the culture of an organisation and the behaviour of its people, especially when under pressure. These situations can sometimes give rise to dilemmas, where choices have to be made but where there are no easy solutions. Simple compliance with the law is both a legal and an ethical duty – there are no dilemmas here.

So, for me, the acid-test of an organisation's ethics occurs in those 'grey areas' of business where values often come into conflict. For example, situations where short-term commercial drivers – especially the need to hit monthly or quarterly targets, either as an individual or as an organisation

– produce intense pressure to achieve results at all costs. Many of the questions posed here are equivocal or controversial. Studying and paying attention to business ethics, especially when using dilemma scenarios, will help an organisation to make better decisions, although not unequivocally right decisions. We look at this below.

 ## BUSINESS DILEMMAS

Setting the scene

Introduction

- I say that it is now time to address Rachel Gordon's question at the outset of the workshop, which was to ask for my recommendations on ways to improve the ethical decision-making process. My answer is that I would advise the use of business dilemma scenarios, ideally in workshop settings, as the best way of developing the thinking of managers and staff. Scenario-based case studies are practical and interactive and each organisation can develop examples that address situations of special relevance to its own circumstances. I like to use these types of exercises for training purposes as a way of developing delegates' thinking – the delegates work through examples of a number of difficult situations, discussing the various options available to resolve the dilemmas presented, with the objective of reaching the optimal decision available.

Rachel is interested in this and so are the other team members. Can I give them some examples of what I mean by business dilemma-based scenarios now? I reply that yes, this is possible, and suggest that we might spend the remainder of the time in the workshop looking at a number of different scenarios before concluding. They are all in agreement with this.

Dilemma-based scenarios

Dilemma-based scenarios are, as the name implies, situations where decisions have to be taken but where there is no obviously right or wrong answer to the dilemma. For maximum effect, the cases should be constructed so that a number of the organisation's values are in conflict, meaning that there are no easy solutions – difficult choices have to be made. The benefit to an organisation of having its senior managers discuss dilemmas among themselves as part of their development is that these exercises promote constructive debate, which can be directed towards those outcomes that are most in line with the organisation's own standards and values. In other words, dilemma-based discussions encourage consistency of thinking at the top of an organisation and so they are likely to promote consistently better decision-making – not always unarguably 'right' decisions as these are not always possible in the business context.

I propose that we look first at some classical ethical dilemmas before moving on to considering business-focused dilemma situations. I say that I have one topical scenario in mind, something that is particularly 'hot' in terms of its media coverage at the moment – after reviewing the ethical dilemmas we could work through this case. What do they think? They all agree to this. I make the point that, if they like the dilemma concept, then they may choose to adopt it internally and use it to examine how their people might approach different situations, each one being tailored to Stronach's own operations and circumstances. In my own mind, I am convinced that, if they agree, the use of dilemma-based scenarios will be of great benefit to Stronach in the future at various levels: the board of directors, the senior management team, middle managers and to the Group generally.

Ethical dilemmas

Example 1

So, I begin by giving the team an example of a basic ethical dilemma, as follows:

> *Imagine that you are walking past a building that is on fire. You see that there are three people in one of the rooms and what looks like a single individual in another room on the opposite side of the building. The problem is that you can tell from the energy of the fire that you do not have time to rescue everyone. You will only be able to reach one of the two rooms in time – who do you choose to save?*

Not surprisingly, all members of the team choose to save the three people, rather than the single individual. This is a clear example of utilitarian thinking – considering the consequences of actions and basing decisions on which course of action will be likely to result in the greatest general wellbeing or utility.

One of the most useful characteristics of ethical dilemmas is that they can be modified relatively easily but to great effect. In the simple example above, the answer in practice might depend on certain practicalities (for example, which of the two rooms is the easier to access) or on instinct. Utilitarian thinking would indeed suggest that the team is right to want to save three people rather than one – contributing to the greater good, all other things being equal. In real-life situations, things are rarely so simple, however. I ask the team to consider the following simple adjustment: Suppose that the single individual in one of the two rooms is your own brother – would this change your choice of action? This immediately becomes a more difficult choice. As an alternative, suppose that you can now see that the single individual is in fact a child – again, would this new fact alter your decision?

Example 2

Rather than allow them to debate these and other possible amendments to the dilemma for any length of time, after a short discussion I ask the team members to consider another situation. This time I give them what is known as the 'trolley problem'. This ethical dilemma was first posed by the British philosopher Philippa Foot in an article in 1967[18] and since then has been much used when debating the moral doctrine of the double effect. The doctrine of the double effect attempts to draw a morally significant distinction between the good and bad consequences (the 'double effect') of an action. It is morally permissible, it is claimed, for a person to carry out an action if he or she intends to bring about the good consequences and merely foresees the bad one. In other words, it may be acceptable to perform a good act in the knowledge that bad consequences will follow, but it is always wrong to carry out a bad act as a means to achieve some good outcome.

I take the team through the original trolley problem, described as follows:

> *There is a runaway tram hurtling down the track, heading straight towards five men working on the line. You are sitting in a control room. Next to you there is a lever which, if pulled, will divert the tram onto a side track. You notice that there is unfortunately one person on the side track. If you do nothing the five people on the main track will be killed; if you pull the lever the tram will be diverted, saving the five but killing the person on the side track. What should you do?*

Once again, the view of the team is unanimous – all of them would pull the lever in such a situation. Again, this is a classic utilitarian response. The intention is admirable – saving the five people on the main track. You foresee, with regret, that the unfortunate person on the side track will die. The death is not part of your intention, however – it is a foreseeable but unintended side effect. To utilitarians (in this example all of the team members), sacrificing one life in order to save five produces a net gain in utility and so it is morally permissible. However, in reality there will be others in society (sometimes referred to as moral absolutists), who will argue that, as it is always wrong to kill, it is wrong here to kill the person on the side track. So they would advocate simply doing nothing, not choosing to intervene in this situation.

Example 3

I then provide the team with a final moral dilemma situation, actually a modification to the original trolley problem, this time devised by American philosopher Judith Thomson in 1976.[19] Does this new version produce any change in the team's views of what is the best action to take?

> As before, the tram is running out of control and is heading towards five men working further ahead on the line. But this time you are standing on a railway footbridge over the track watching events from above. Next to you is standing a 20-stone man. A quick calculation of his size tells you that if you were to push him off the bridge and into the path of the trolley, his massive body will get in the way of the tram, stopping it before it can reach the five people on the line. If you do nothing, the five workmen will be hit by the tram and killed; if you push the man off the bridge, he will be killed but the five will be saved. What should you do?

This time, there are hesitations and some reservations – it is much more difficult to reach agreement. After much discussion and debate, the majority of the team remain consistent and say that they would go ahead and push the man off the bridge, the deciding factor being the same as before – the calculation of one life lost in order to save five. Three of the team conclude that it is the right thing to do to push the man off the bridge, but they are less sure than previously. One of them, David Hurley, strongly disagrees. He does not want to push the man off the bridge; he simply feels that it is wrong to bring about his death in this way, regardless of the possible beneficial consequences.

This result to some extent reflects what research has shown, namely that this example tends to reverse the common intuition of Example 2 – our gut feeling in Example 3 may well be that it is wrong to kill someone deliberately in these circumstances.

The doctrine of the double effect provides an explanation for this feeling. In this case the death of the fat man is actually required: the harm done to him is not merely foreseen but it is intended as the means of saving the workmen and therefore the action is (according to the double effect doctrine) morally impermissible.

I say to the team that, faced with these scenarios, the majority of people from a wide range of cultures around the world say that they could not push the fat man off the bridge in Example 3, but they would pull the lever in Example 2. Clearly some factor other than a utilitarian calculation (in this case the totality of death) influences our moral judgement.

Business dilemmas

Example 1

I say to the team that we now need to move on. As promised, I want them to consider a different type of dilemma, this time one specifically focused on a realistic and topical business situation. I ask them to listen to the following scenario and then discuss what actions they might take if a similar situation was to arise in the Stronach Group in the future.

I begin by setting out some background information, as follows:

Imagine that you are the finance director of a large company listed on the London Stock Exchange. You were appointed to the position in January 2012 and were delighted to learn of your successful application – your new company is an international group with trading operations and subsidiaries around the world and this represents a big step up on the career ladder for you personally. So, it is an excellent opportunity, made all the more attractive because you share wholeheartedly in the company's values and ethos. The company motto is: 'Integrity is the cornerstone of our business and we always uphold the spirit as well as the letter of the law.'

Since you took up post, trading conditions have continued to be challenging, especially for the European operations. The company is struggling to achieve its strategic objectives of developing more business in Continental Europe, increasing dividends to shareholders through improved profit margins and achieving best value in the purchase of all goods and services.

Despite the challenges, however, you remain highly motivated to help the company to succeed in delivering these objectives.

How would you react in the following situation?

It is September 2013 and you are coming towards the end of your first full year as finance director. The finance department has performed well during the year and you are confident that your inclusive leadership style, coupled with a willingness to listen and your consistent encouragement of innovation has motivated your staff to perform at their best. In fact, you have been so successful that some of your fellow directors and senior management team are starting to refer to the finance department as the group's new 'profit centre'!

You have a meeting with your Number Two, the financial controller, during which you learn from her about a new opportunity to reduce the company's corporation tax bill that she is very excited about. Working with tax experts from your auditors, she has put together a proposal that has the potential to cut dramatically the company's corporation tax liabilities, starting in the current year and ongoing into the future. The proposed mechanism is simple: sales of technology products in the UK will in future be completed in Eire, thereby attracting significantly lower tax rates than apply in the UK. The Financial Controller assures you that the tax advisors from your 'Big Four' professional services firm have confirmed that the scheme is perfectly legal. She is now looking to you to obtain the approval for the necessary changes by the company directors and senior management at the forthcoming round of board and committee meetings in September.

So, my question for the project team is how would they proceed on this proposed new tax initiative if they were in the position of the finance director?

At the outset of the discussion, everyone looks to Malcolm Mainwaring to provide his thoughts, for obvious reasons – he is the Group Finance Director after all.

Malcolm obliges and is, in my view, quite measured in his comments – I am impressed. He begins by summing up the central dilemma in the question very succinctly: on the one hand, the proposed tax scheme appears to be highly beneficial for the company's finances, so the finance director has a duty to look at it carefully; on the other hand, the company might incur reputational damage if the scheme is reported in the media as yet another example of an unethical tax avoidance scheme by a large corporation, with the result that the British taxpayer has once again been 'ripped off'. Malcolm goes on to say that he would himself take two important steps: first, praise the financial controller for her initiative and go through the proposed scheme carefully with her in detail, so that he fully understands the mechanics of the scheme himself; and second ask for confirmation in writing from the tax advisors that the proposed scheme does indeed comply with the law. Malcolm concludes by saying that he would then inform his fellow directors about the proposal, together with his own conclusions as to its legality and desirability.

John Holt thanks Malcolm for his observations and now adds something from his perspective. As CEO he is always wary of lawyers and other experts telling him what is 'strictly legal', by which they mean that the proposal under review is legal because it falls within the strict letter of the law. John's concern is always that this might be an arguable position and therefore be vulnerable to scrutiny by aggressive journalists and tax inspectors alike. So he would look at the extent to which the proposal is artificial, a device to take advantage of a loophole in tax law but not something that is a genuine reflection of business transactions or trading. John is clearly sceptical about the proposal.

David Hurley concurs with his CEO. He says that as this is a technical financial issue, he cannot add much to the discussion. But he reads the newspapers. Personally, he would feel extremely uncomfortable if the company was to enter into a tax scheme that was branded unethical even if it was 'strictly legal'. David said that he thought such an approach would be contrary to the company's motto and leave it open to charges of hypocrisy or worse.

Rachel Gordon thanks everyone for their comments. She says that, in fact, she does have experience of a similar situation recently at another company where she is a non-executive director. On that occasion, the finance director recommended a scheme designed to reduce tax – this scheme had also been signed off by the tax advisers as being legal – and it was discussed at a subsequent meeting of the board of directors. After some challenging questions from the non-executives, it was decided not to go ahead with the recommendation because reputational risk was felt to be too high in this case. Rachel feels that the same approach to the board of directors should be taken here. Directors have a legal duty to take decisions that are most likely to promote the success of the business over the long term, so this is a proper issue for board discussion and debate.

I draw the discussion to a conclusion at this point, thanking everyone for their contributions and saying that I think that they covered all the major points. I mention David's contribution, particularly his comment that he felt very uncomfortable about the proposal, despite his lack of technical knowledge. In my view, these emotional reactions should always be factored into the assessment and never simply ignored – it is always important to 'check the gut feel'.

All the members of the team say that they have enjoyed the discussion and have appreciated the dilemma exercises. I conclude by saying that I will make sure that they have the opportunity to look at other business scenarios in some of the forthcoming workshops.

 ## WORKSHOP CONCLUSION

Closing

I start to draw the workshop to a close by asking for feedback. I am looking for both general comments on what the team thinks about the workshop and also specific feedback in two areas: first of all, what are the most important insights and lessons that the participants have gained from the session – or to use the consultancy jargon, what are their key takeaways from the session; and second, what are their thoughts and views on topics for the next workshop.

The general comments on the workshop are favourable and encouraging. Everyone seems to like the format with the only caveat being that my idea of dealing with their questions at various times during the presentation had the effect of interrupting its flow somewhat. We agree that in future workshops I will deliver the presentation in its entirety and then take questions at the end.

Key takeaways

Now turning to their key takeaways from the workshop, I ask the team first to discuss these and then to write up on the flipchart the five ideas, recommendations or insights coming out of the workshop that they will look to incorporate into Stronach's operations in the future. Rachel Gordon takes the lead in the subsequent discussion and this is what she writes down on the chart:

✓ **Building the twin-track ethical framework**. Rachel says that she was impressed by this idea when she first heard me articulate it. She feels that the combination of the necessary hardware (policies and procedures etc.) and adding to them the cultural software (tone at the top, consistent decision-making etc.) to provide sufficiency is both thoughtful and snappy. She is sure that the managers and staff at Stronach will be able to relate to it and everyone agrees with her.

✓ **Purpose = profits plus**. Malcolm Mainwaring puts this forward. He sees this as another snappy idea but one that could be used widely around the Group because, to him, it encapsulates what Stronach is all about. The Group needs to make profits to satisfy its shareholders but the culture here is focused on creating value and delivering excellence through everyone being professional and good at their jobs. The team fully endorses this view.

✓ **The integrated approach to business ethics**. David Hurley, the HR Manager, likes the idea of integrating values with compliance to drive behaviour and performance in the business. He says that all too often, not only in the Stronach Group but in the other organisations that he has worked for, people seem to be directed by rules. He says that rules are needed of course, but if they are uninformed by values then it is like working to a checklist, to tick a box – working blind somehow. He checks to make sure that everyone is with him on this – I can tell by their reactions that they most certainly are.

✓ **The CEO is the most important compliance officer in the organisation**. John Holt, the CEO of the Stronach Group is particularly taken with this phrase. He does not see himself as walking around with a checklist or trying to catch people out – far from it. He interprets the phrase as meaning the CEO needs to be involved and engaged in issues of legal and ethical compliance, to ask questions and to listen to the answers. He makes a commitment to be visible and to lead on these issues in the future.

✓ **Using dilemma-based scenarios in future management development programmes**. Rachel in particular is convinced that the use of dilemma exercises will lead to improved decision-making throughout the Group. She asks David Hurley if he can look to develop some appropriate scenarios, ones that address the issues of importance to Stronach, and incorporate them into future training and development exercises. Rachel says that she would be happy to contribute to this process.

Looking at the flipchart, I am impressed by these takeaways and say so. All of the team seem committed to putting these points into practice – for example John Holt, who has clearly taken on board the idea that the CEO has a key role to play in promoting good business ethics throughout the organisation. But I am pleasantly surprised to see Malcolm Mainwaring being so positive also – I had feared a rather different reaction from him.

Next workshop

Everyone is of the view that the workshop has been valuable and they all quickly agree to hold another session in the near future, ideally sometime in the next month subject to diary availability. Rachel agrees to organise this.

There is some discussion around possible subject matter and it is John who comes up with a suggestion that soon has everyone's support. He says that there have been a lot of ideas put forward today and it would be extremely helpful if next time I could demonstrate how they all fit together in practice. Could I take them through an example of the type of framework that I recommend (the twin-track approach, including the hardware and software elements) that demonstrates how it might actually work? I nod and, after a few moments thought, I suggest as a working title for the session: 'Business ethics in action'. Everyone likes this idea and it is quickly agreed.

Reflections

Walking out of Stronach's offices and into Berkeley Square, I reflect on the first workshop. Overall it has gone well – better than I expected in fact. All the team members contributed well to the discussion, including David Hurley, who I think will only increase in confidence as the project develops. I am not quite sure what to make of Malcolm Mainwaring just yet as he seemed to send out contradictory signals at various points during the workshop. However, I know that Rachel is fully committed to the project and I feel that John Holt is too. In my experience, if the chairman and the CEO both support a project then it has a pretty good chance of success.

As I am walking, I spot Malcolm rushing off somewhere in the opposite direction – we acknowledge each other with a brief wave. This triggers a slight concern. I have an idea to make bribery and corruption the broad topic of the next workshop, focusing on the procedures that organisations need to have in place to prevent it as the 'business ethics in action' theme. However, seeing Malcolm I decide that it would be better for me to talk this through with Rachel first to gauge her reaction before I start to prepare anything. Malcolm has worked here for many years and I don't want to embarrass him or anyone else by raising a subject that might be considered controversial, given the recent history of the Stronach Group in India.

CHAPTER THREE

Bribery, corruption and adequate procedures

 BUSINESS ETHICS IN ACTION: SECOND WORKSHOP

Opening

Introduction

The team is assembled again for our second workshop, four weeks after the first. As agreed last time, the subject is to be an example of business ethics in action so that everyone has a template of what best practice looks like in this area that they can try to emulate in the Stronach Group.

My idea for this workshop is a little unusual. It is not based on any particular example of best practice that I have seen myself in one of my clients, neither is it derived from anything that I have read about in reports of a particularly admired company or business leader. Instead, I am going to talk about bribery and corruption and, specifically, about the procedures that organisations should adopt if they want to prevent it from happening in their business. When doing so I will be recommending that the team follows the approach set out in guidance from the UK Government that accompanies a recent piece of legislation, the Bribery Act 2010 (UKBA). This guidance represents, in my view, a classic example of the twin-track approach to a workplace situation.

I contacted the Chairman, Rachel Gordon, shortly after the conclusion of the first workshop because I wanted to sound her out about my choice of subject matter for today on two counts. First of all, the UKBA is regarded with scepticism in some quarters of the business world because it is thought to be burdensome and harmful to enterprise. An Ernst & Young survey in 2012[1] found that nearly 25% of 1000 middle managers that it surveyed thought that the UKBA was harming the UK's competitiveness, either because some foreign competitors were not yet subject to the same anti-bribery restrictions or because of high costs of complying with the Act. Second, the Stronach Group was itself the subject of corruption rumours in connection with its operations in India. I did not wish to cause any embarrassment, whether to Malcolm Mainwaring, the long-term Group Finance Director, or to anyone else.

I should not have worried because it turns out that Rachel likes the idea. Given the Group's experiences in India, she feels that bribery and corruption is actually a very important piece of the ethics project. In addition, she is keen that Stronach reviews and updates its response to the UKBA in any event, so my proposals for the next workshop will be very helpful from that perspective too.

Agenda

I introduce the workshop by saying that today we will look at bribery and corruption, with an emphasis on what organisations should be doing to manage the risk of bribery occurring in their operations. Our main reference point will be the 'adequate procedures' guidance accompanying the UKBA, which in my view is an excellent example of business ethics in action because it advocates not only strong controls but also the need for an anti-bribery culture to underpin them if they are to be effective. So, the official guidance puts forward exactly the twin-track approach that I advocated in the last workshop.

We will look specifically at the following areas today:

- The international context. We will review the evolving responses of the authorities around the world to the threats posed by bribery and corruption, in particular the corruption of government officials and employees. I make the observation that sometimes, when working with directors and managers, I get the impression that they think that the tough approach of the UKBA has come out of a clear blue sky somehow – that it is unnecessary and burdensome and interferes with business. Nothing could be further from the truth in my view.
- The Siemens corruption case of 2006–08. The scandal was shocking in its size, breadth and nature and it provides the essential background to all recent anti-corruption initiatives. We will analyse the causes of the scandal and its consequences for Siemens before returning to the case in the next workshop to understand how Siemens has been able to re-build trust with its stakeholders and therefore to re-establish its good business reputation subsequently.
- The prime focus of the workshop will be a review of the UKBA. I say that I view the UKBA as an important signpost showing the way that the authorities are thinking in terms of combating financial crime – it points the way to a powerful template for organisations to follow covering both compliance frameworks and business ethics. In particular, the legislation introduces a brand new offence of failing to prevent bribery by either employees or by third parties acting on behalf of the organisation concerned. In my view, this is a major commitment to ethical corporate culture. The UK Government has issued guidance on the 'adequate procedures' that organisations need to have in place in order to have a defence against a charge of failing to prevent bribery. These adequate procedures are built around six guiding principles. Taken together, this guidance provides an excellent example of how measures designed to promote and strengthen a positive culture can be combined with traditional controls and procedures to man-age bribery and corruption risk. It is an excellent example of the twin-track approach, therefore.
- Finally, I will take the team through examples drawn from my own experience, which show how two very different organisations have each adapted the government guidance to suit their own individual circumstances to good effect.

A business dilemma

I have my presentation on bribery and corruption prepared. Before starting, I ask whether there are any questions. No, everyone seems content with the workshop outline. David Hurley, the HR

Manager, tells me that Stronach did provide training for staff on the UKBA – like many organisations, it embarked on a flurry of activity in 2011 when the legislation first came into effect. He also says, with a quick glance towards his CEO, that little if anything has been done since.

So, I am all set to go but before I start Malcolm Mainwaring, the Finance Director, has a point to make – not so much a question, he says, more a business dilemma of the type that we were discussing during the last workshop. He is interested in hearing my views on the issues raised by it. Apparently, he had attended a conference some months ago at which the impact of the UKBA was discussed. During one of the plenary sessions, a delegate had put forward the following scenario in support of his contention that the Act is generally unhelpful to business:

> *Imagine that you are the finance director of a large international trading group. You are based in London. You are sitting in your office one day in August – the chairman and all the company's senior executives apart from yourself are currently on vacation or are otherwise unavailable. Shortly before lunch an urgent telephone call is put through to you. The call is from the Captain of one of the ships carrying your cargo around the world. He has a problem. He is trying to sail the ship into port in order to unload the cargo but the harbour master is demanding a $1000 cash payment before he will allow the ship to dock. The Captain is aware that, if he was to make the payment, it would constitute bribery under the law in the UK. He also knows that your company has an anti-bribery policy that sets out the company's commitment to zero-tolerance of all bribes and any other form of corrupt payments. However, he tells you that some of the cargo that his ship is carrying is perishable and that any delay will put these perishable goods at risk. He estimates that every day that he is prevented from entering the port will cost your company $1 million. The Captain is asking you to tell him what he should do.*
>
> *What would be your instructions to the Captain in this situation?*

I listen to the scenario, nod to Malcolm and thank him for raising it. This is the type of question that is designed to show that in certain circumstances the UKBA is impractical and indeed harmful to business – I have heard similar scenarios before.

I suggest to the team that we should leave the analysis for now and return to discuss it at the end of the workshop. Everybody is happy with this approach, including Malcolm. I make the comment in passing that we should be able to work through it pretty quickly and that, despite appearances, there is not too much of a dilemma in this scenario. The team members look a little surprised at this comment, apart from Malcolm, who is nodding in agreement. Interesting – what would Malcolm do in this situation I wonder? We will find out at the end of the workshop.

 ## BRIBERY AND CORRUPTION

Overview

Background

Bribery and corruption is today one of the biggest obstacles to economic and social development around the world. The sheer scale is astonishing: the World Bank estimates that the global cost of bribery and corruption is some $1 trillion each year, much of it in poor and developing countries. It causes significant harm, not least because bribery and corruption affect the poorest and most vulnerable people the most. It distorts markets, stifles economic growth, undermines democracy and the rule of law and creates an uneven playing field in the international conduct of business. On the ethical level, bribery and corruption reduce public trust and belief in the fair and transparent operation of business and public services.

There has been a growing international anti-corruption movement since the 1970s and this has gained momentum in the new millennium. It is often seen as focusing primarily on the actions of politicians and with good reason. It has long been known that some political leaders in developing countries have been able to abuse their power to enrich themselves, their families, their cronies and associates by embezzling public funds and stealing state assets. The Suharto, Marcos and Abacha regimes in Indonesia, the Philippines and Nigeria respectively are three of the most notorious examples of this, but there are others. Certainly, political corruption stories continue to be reported in the media. For example, the year 2014 opened with reports of corruption-inspired tensions in Turkey[2] (with a corruption inquiry looking into alleged bribery involving public tenders), continued with stories of a concerted anti-corruption drive by the authorities in China[3] and even contained headlines implicating royalty, with news that the Spanish Infanta (the youngest daughter of King Juan Carlos King) has been named as a suspect in a long-running corruption probe in Spain.[4]

It is not only corruption by political leaders that causes outrage. The widespread 'graft' payments that have to be handed over to local public officials by ordinary citizens every day in order to access basic services in many parts of the world can provoke anger too. Take the recent initiatives against bribery and corruption in India, for example; 2011 saw the development of a widespread anti-corruption movement throughout the country, led by the activist Anna Hazare, with the aim of alleviating endemic corruption in public life through forcing the Indian parliament to enact tougher legislation. More recently, the local government in Delhi when under Arvind Kejriwal's short term as leader (28 December 2013–14 February 2014) set up an anti-corruption helpline providing tips to members of the public on how to expose the public officials who seek bribes when they issue documents such as driving licenses and marriage and death certificates. The helpline received more than 4000 calls in the first few hours of its launch.[5]

The anti-corruption drive has been extended in recent years from a focus on politicians and the public sector to the conduct of organisations and individuals in the private sector also. Modern legislation, including the UKBA, looks to deal robustly with person-to-person and business-to-business bribery in addition to public sector corruption.

Corruption

The word 'corruption' is traditionally associated with payments made to public officials, whether the individuals are heads of state or government ministers (and thereby hold positions of political power) or they are state employees. So, a functional definition of corruption is: 'the use of public office for private gain'. Transparency International (see below) defines corruption as: 'the abuse of entrusted power for private gain'.

There are a number of related activities that are closely associated with corruption:

- kickbacks (a proportion of the value of a contract demanded as a bribe in return for securing the contract);
- extortion (demanding money or goods with the threat of harm if the demand is not met);
- conflicts of interest (where an employee has an economic or personal interest in a transaction); and
- bribery.

Bribery

In contrast to corruption, bribes are more closely associated with the private sector rather than the public sector. The term 'bribery' may be defined as the giving or receiving of something of value in order to influence a transaction.

Note that a bribe is defined as 'something of value'. In practice, bribes are often paid in cash but this is not always the case. For example, expensive gifts or lavish entertainment might constitute bribes if they are given with the intention to influence a transaction.

The term includes bribes made to individuals in both the public sector and the private sector.

Transparency International

The fight against political corruption around the world has been led since its formation in 1993 by Transparency International (TI).[6] TI is the global civil-society pressure group, based in Berlin, whose mission is to create change towards the goal of a world free of corruption. TI says that corruption 'hurts everyone who depends on the integrity of people in a position of authority'. Together with organisations like the World Bank it has drawn attention to the devastating impact of bribery and corruption, especially on the poor and vulnerable people in developing countries where incomes are depressed and child mortality rates increase as a result.

Many business people that I work with have never heard of TI, or if they have heard of it they have only a vague idea of what the organisation stands for. This is slightly surprising but it could also be dangerous because authorities in many countries regard TI's work as being an important indicator of risk in terms of public sector corruption around the world. Organisations that seek to take advantage of globalisation by trading in emerging or developing jurisdictions need to be aware of the risks that this entails. Indeed, so far as bribery and corruption risk is concerned, the authorities will expect these organisations to be aware of TI's work and its findings – it is important to remember always that ignorance is no defence before the law.

A key indicator of bribery and corruption risk is the Corruption Perceptions Index (CPI).[7] TI compiles this every year and it measures the level of public sector corruption perceived to exist around the world. Almost every country and territory in the world is included in the index, which ranks these against each other in a 'league table' of corruption. The CPI draws on the results of 13 independent surveys and assesses expert perceptions of public sector corruption. In 2013 the CPI included assessments of 177 countries and territories and listed them in order, from the country with the best perceived public sector (ranked number 1) to that with the worst (ranked number 177). It ranked Denmark, New Zealand, Finland and Sweden as the least corrupt countries in the world and Somalia, North Korea, Afghanistan and Sudan as the most corrupt.

While there is nothing too surprising in those nations appearing at the top and bottom of the list, organisations need to be aware of the rankings of the countries in which they do business, or in which their key business partners are based. This is particularly the case when the overseas business is in one or more of the fast-developing markets. One reason is that working with new business partners combined with a lack of familiarity with the trading conditions on the ground in new markets will increase risk generally. Another is that developing markets often create tensions between two important business goals, namely profit and compliance.

As examples, consider first the TI CPI rankings in 2013 of the most important developing countries, the so-called BRIC nations (this acronym was originally coined by Jim O'Neill of Goldman Sachs in 2001): Brazil is at number 72, Russia is 127, India is 94 and China is 80. Then consider the ranking of some of the new emerging global trading powers, collectively described more recently as the MINT countries by Boston-based asset management firm Fidelity Investments: Mexico is at number 106, Indonesia is 114, Nigeria is 144 and Turkey is 53. Generally, the risk of public sector corruption is perceived to be high in these countries (in some, for example Russia and Nigeria, it is perceived to be very high) and any organisation looking to develop business in one or more of them needs to have strong controls and procedures in place to mitigate this risk.

Bribery and corruption in business

Introduction

Concerns are not only centred on corrupt politicians of course – they have long extended into the corporate world. There have been a number of headline corporate corruption allegations over the last 30 years, amongst them persistent rumours of bribes being paid to secure arms contracts between BAE Systems and Saudi Arabia and the Siemens case involving the payment of bribes to government officials in many countries around the world by the German engineering group in order to obtain or retain business contracts. We will look at the Siemens case in detail later in this chapter.

Insider trading and the Galleon case

Since the global financial crisis of 2007–09 there has been much attention on improper practices in the financial services industry. Stories of price and rate fixing by traders and of the mis-selling of financial products to the public by retail bankers have made headline news in the UK since 2011, while in the USA there has been a notable clampdown by the authorities on market abuse.

The Galleon case[8] is particularly important as an example of the crackdown by authorities in the USA on market abuse. The founder of the Galleon hedge funds group, Raj Rajaratnam, was found guilty in July 2011 of insider trading and sentenced to 11 years in prison, the longest ever sentence at the time for insider trading. The core of the allegations made was that Mr Rajaratnam was passed secret, price-sensitive information about certain listed securities by a network of informants (which included a number of very successful and high profile business men and women), enabling him to make significant and illegal profits on future trading in those securities. This conviction was upheld on appeal in 2013.

The Galleon scandal is usually portrayed as an insider dealing and conflicts of interest case, which of course it is. However, in my view it is also a case that has exposed business corruption on Wall Street. Those involved have been prosecuted through the criminal courts and, where found guilty, have received tough sentences. In this sense the case is part of a much wider crackdown on corrupt practices generally. This includes various robust pieces of legislation and regulations against economic crime, money laundering and the financing of terrorist movements around the world. Our focus here is on corruption, but all companies in the financial services industry in particular will be familiar with the far-reaching requirements of anti-money laundering legislation such as the USA PATRIOT Act and the Proceeds of Crime Act in the UK.

Common elements of business corruption

All individual cases will differ in their details, but there are often a number of common elements in business corruption schemes. Examples of these are as follows:

▪ The first thing to say is that bribery and corruption schemes will always be secret arrangements involving two or more people. This is obvious, of course, but it does have one important

consequence – a corruption scheme will be very difficult to detect. Specific controls, in particular whistle-blowing hotlines (which we discuss in detail later in Chapter 9 of the book), will be required to uncover them.

▪ Second, these schemes will often involve paying out a financial inducement from company funds (for example, to a public official) in return for the award of a contract. One probable consequence of this will be false accounting carried out in the books of the company paying the bribes. The corrupt payment will have to be recorded somewhere and it will have to be mis-described if it is to avoid instant detection, for example, as 'commission' or as 'after-sales tax'. I have spent over 30 years as a chartered accountant and I have seen many nominal ledgers in my time, but I have yet to come across a nominal ledger with a 'bribery and corruption' account in it!

▪ There is often an overseas element involved as businesses chase contracts all over the world in a highly competitive marketplace. Payments to foreign public officials may be required to win a contract or to retain a lucrative business deal – or that might be the perception of the organisation concerned in any event. These payments could be made directly to the official but they often involve making use of a third-party agent, somebody who is based in the country where the work will take place to pay the bribes.

▪ Finally, the payments themselves are often circuitous, being routed through various companies or bank accounts in different jurisdictions before they reach the recipient– the aim here being to disguise the audit trail surrounding these transactions.

Allegations of corruption in business continue to make press headlines. For example, the year 2013 closed with the UK's Serious Fraud Office announcing that it was launching an investigation into Rolls Royce, the world's second largest engine manufacturer, over concerns of bribery and corruption in its overseas markets such as China and Indonesia.[9] Some of the allegations date back over 10 years.

Examples of anti-corruption laws and conventions

Introduction

It is the gradually strengthening laws and conventions around the world against business corruption, however, started in the USA in the 1970s, that has made the compliance requirements in this area so important for commercial organisations today. Set out below is a brief overview of two of the key pieces of anti-corruption legislation and convention in the USA and under the auspices of the United Nations, before we look in detail at the UKBA. Directors and managers need to be aware of the key points in these and similar legislation in other countries because their effect has been to increase significantly the risk for those individuals and commercial organisations alike that continue to use bribery as a sales technique in order to win business and to retain business around the world. Bribes are no longer regarded as a 'normal part of doing business' in most parts of the world, fewer people are prepared to turn a blind eye to them and the authorities are increasingly vigorous in prosecuting those who break the law in this area.

This process has been led by the authorities in the USA and we review below the first major piece of anti-corruption legislation anywhere in the world, the Foreign Corrupt Practices Act.

The US position: the Foreign Corrupt Practices Act (FCPA)

The FCPA[10] was passed in the USA as far back as 1977 and it was a ground-breaking piece of legislation at the time. It has influenced many subsequent anti-corruption laws, including the

UKBA as we will see below. The overriding purpose of the FCPA is to crackdown on the bribery of foreign public officials by corporations. There are a number of key aspects to it, summarised below.

- **The anti-bribery provisions**. The FCPA prohibits US companies and citizens, foreign companies listed on a US stock exchange, or any person acting while in the United States from corruptly paying or offering to pay, directly or indirectly, money or anything of value to a foreign official in order to obtain or retain business.
- **The books and records and internal control provisions**. The FCPA requires any companies (including foreign companies) with securities traded on a US exchange (or which are required to file reports with the Securities and Exchange Commission) to keep books and records that accurately reflect business transactions and also to maintain effective internal controls.
- **Fines and penalties**. Violations of the FCPA can result in significant fines against individuals and corporations, as well as the imprisonment of those implicated (including company executives) for up to five years. In addition, there are harsh collateral sanctions available, including termination of government licenses and debarment from government contracts.
- **Extra-territorial jurisdiction**. The reach of the FCPA is extensive. No US territorial nexus is required for the FCPA to be invoked against US companies and citizens. FCPA violations can, and often do, occur even if the prohibited activity takes place entirely outside of the United States. The activities of foreign companies listed on a US exchange anywhere around the world also come within the ambit of the FCPA, as do any acts of bribery and corruption that take place in the United States itself.
- **Exceptions**. The one significant exception under the FCPA is where a payment is made to a foreign official in order to expedite or secure the performance of a routine governmental action. These are generally referred to as facilitation payments, sometimes known as 'grease' payments. The exception is not as significant as it is sometimes made out to be, however, as it has limited application. Generally it only applies to non-discretionary actions by a foreign official (such as processing paperwork) and providing routine government services (such as allowing entry into the country for passengers with valid travel documents and permitting cargo to be unloaded from ships to a port).

The United Nations' position: the UN Convention against Corruption (UNCAC)

The UNCAC (2005)[11] is the first legally binding international anti-corruption instrument and it has been signed by over 140 countries. The UNCAC is the culmination of a series of developments in which experts and politicians have tried to establish effective measures against corruption at both the domestic and the international level. The Inter-American Convention against Corruption (1996), the OECD Anti-Bribery Convention (1997), and the African Union Convention on Preventing and Combatting Corruption (2003) are all examples of efforts made by organisations around the world under this initiative. Following extensive negotiations, the text of the UN Convention was presented for approval by the United Nations General Assembly in 2003 and came into force in December 2005. With the passing of the UNCAC, international action against corruption has finally progressed from general considerations and declarative statements to legally binding agreements.

The UNCAC obliges all signatory countries to implement a wide and detailed range of anti-corruption measures affecting their laws, institutions and practices. These measures aim to promote the prevention and detection of corruption, as well as international cooperation between signatory powers on these matters. Some of the most important and far reaching features of the UNCAC are as follows:

- It includes offences relating both to public sector corruption, including a broad definition of the term public official but importantly also to private sector (business-to-business) corruption.
- It provides an international cooperation framework that aims to improve mutual law enforcement assistance, notably in the extradition of individuals to face charges in foreign jurisdictions and in the conduct of investigations.
- It sets out, for the first time, an asset recovery framework on a global basis covering countries in both the northern and the southern hemispheres.

The third significant piece of legislation that we will look at is the UKBA. In my view, it is a highly significant development because it introduces, for the first time, a corporate offence of failing to prevent bribery. The effect is far reaching as we shall see. But before we consider the implications of the UKBA, we need to review the most important corruption scandal of recent times because it provides the essential background to the UKBA. This is the case of the German electronics giant, Siemens.

 CASE STUDY

The Siemens corruption case part 1: scandal and penalties

Introduction

The company Siemens AG (Siemens) was formed in Germany in 1847. Today, it is headquartered in Munich and is Europe's largest engineering conglomerate with a diverse range of products and services including: transportation, telecommunications, medical devices, power plants and oil refineries. According to its website:

> *Siemens is a globally operating technology company with core activities in the fields of energy, healthcare, industry and infrastructure. On a continuing basis, we have around 362,000 employees, as of September 30th 2013 and business activities in nearly all countries of the world and reported consolidated revenue of Euro 75,882 billion in fiscal 2013. We operate in excess of 290 major production and manufacturing plants worldwide. In addition, we have office buildings, warehouses, research and development facilities or sales offices in almost every country in the world.[12]*

During the period 2006–08, Siemens was embroiled in a developing corruption scandal involving revelations of widespread and longstanding bribery of officials in many countries around the world in order to win new contracts and to retain existing contracts. Hundreds of employees were involved. The key aspects of the scandal, together with a summary of the subsequent enforcement actions taken by authorities in the USA and in Germany and other consequences for Siemens, are set out below. The efforts of Siemens thereafter to recover and re-build the trust of its stakeholders in its business are discussed in the second part of this case study in Chapter 4 on reputational risk.

Development of corrupt practices

Siemens prides itself on being a truly global business with operations in every part of the world. Although the company's trading outside of Germany started as early as 1853, when it was commissioned to work on expanding the Russian telegraph network, Siemens began a concerted search for business in less developed countries in the years after the end of World War II. The reason for this was simple: the war had shattered the company's infrastructure and Siemens turned to markets outside of Europe in order to compete. Bribery became a reliable sales technique and certainly by the mid 1990s Siemens had developed a practice of making improper payments to foreign public officials when competing for business. So, bribery became part of the culture at Siemens; it was not regarded as wrong or extraordinary, rather it was simply how business was done in certain parts of the world.[13]

It is important to note, however, that these types of payments were not illegal under German law at the time and it is also likely that other companies were making them too. Before 1999, bribes were deductible as business expenses under the German tax code and the act of paying off a foreign official was not a criminal offence.

Changes in legal risk

Two significant changes to the legal framework as it affected Siemens happened at the start of the twenty-first century. These changes exposed Siemens to significantly greater legal risk, but the company's management failed to respond appropriately, either quickly or at all.

First, as noted above, the law in Germany changed in 1999, so that the payment of bribes to foreign public officials became a criminal offence.

Second, in 2001 Siemens achieved a listing on the New York Stock Exchange. Siemens had long been a public listed company – it first listed on the Frankfurt Stock Exchange as far back as 1899. However, the listing in New York meant that the company now became subject to the provisions of the FCPA under which, as we have seen, the payment of bribes to foreign public officials is illegal.

Business as usual

Despite these changes in the law as it applied to them, Siemens' management and employees did not change what had become its standard business practice of making bribes when competing for business in many countries overseas. Astonishingly, the only noticeable effect of the new legal conditions was that managers and staff tried to hide the corrupt payments by disguising them. The corporate culture remained the same. Siemens failed to react appropriately to these changes in the law with either a strong compliance programme and tougher internal controls or a concerted effort to focus on values and business ethics. Instead, the payments to foreign public officials, now illegal in Germany and also subject to the provisions of the FCPA, continued to be made. It was business as usual.

Business as usual ended for Siemens on 15 November 2006 with a series of dawn raids on the head office in Munich and on the homes of various officers and senior managers by German law enforcement as part of an investigation into suspected embezzlement. After only a very short period of initial bluster, Siemens responded quickly and positively, setting up its own rigorous internal enquiry run by an American law firm to investigate the allegations. The company also cooperated fully with the authorities, with voluntary disclosure of its past conduct to the German law enforcement agencies and also to the Department of Justice (DOJ) and the Securities and Exchange Commission (SEC) in the USA. The result was the uncovering of systematic and wide-spread corruption.

Examples of the improper payments made by Siemens

The numbers involved in the Siemens corruption scandal are truly eye-watering.

Between 21 March 2001 and 30 December 2007 Siemens and its subsidiary companies used a variety of methods of bribes and kickbacks to make some 4283 illegal payments either to public officials or to 'consultants' in order to win government contracts or retain existing contracts that came up for renewal. Managers and staff created off-the-books slush funds, used middlemen posing as consultants, and delivered suitcases filled with cash to bribe officials. The total amount of the improper payments was estimated to be approximately $1.4bn.[14]

It was not only the scale of the corruption that was unprecedented but also its geographic reach. Bribes were paid to government officials in Asia, Africa, Europe, the Middle East and Latin America. Set out below are five examples of the improper payments made, which illustrate both the worldwide spread of the corruption and the variety of businesses that were involved.

- From 2000–02 four Siemens subsidiaries were awarded 42 contracts valued at more than $80 million with the Ministries of Electricity and Oil in Iraq under the United Nations Oil for Food (OFP) programme. These contracts were secured by paying over $1.7 million in kickbacks to the Iraq Government. The company netted over $38 million in profits. As with other OFP cases the contract price was inflated prior to the submission of the contract to the UN for approval. The payments were improperly recorded in the books and records of the subsidiaries. It should be noted here that Siemens was only one of a number of contractors embroiled in the OFP scandal.
- Siemens' subsidiaries in Latin America also violated the FCPA. From 1998–2007 Siemens Argentina made over $31 million of corrupt payments to various Argentinean officials. These transactions were improperly recorded in the books and records as 'legal fees', 'consulting fees' and other similar mis-descriptions designed to make them appear to be legitimate. The payments were made to obtain favourable business treatment in connection with a $1 billion national identity card project for the Argentinean Government.
- Siemens Venezuela also made corrupt payments, in this case beginning in the year 2001. In total, this subsidiary made over $18 million of corrupt payments to various Venezuelan officials to obtain favourable treatment in connection with two major metropolitan mass transit projects. Again the payments were not properly recorded in the books and accounts.
- Siemens Bangladesh admitted that from 2001–06 it made corrupt payments of over $5.3 million. The payments were made to obtain favourable treatment during the bidding process on a government-sponsored nationwide mobile telephone network project.
- In May 2007 a German court convicted two former executives of paying $6 million in bribes from 1999–2002 to help Siemens to win natural gas turbine supply contracts with Enel, an Italian energy company. The contracts were valued at $450 million.

The above are illustrative examples – the overall corruption of government officials was much more extensive. In addition to these examples, documents filed by the authorities during the hearings show significant bribes being paid by Siemens to officials in Russia, China, Israel, Mexico, Nigeria, Greece and Vietnam.

In summary, Siemens routinely used bribes paid out of slush funds in order to secure huge public works contracts around the world. The comments of Joseph Persichini Jr, the then-head of the Washington office of the Federal Bureau of Investigation, following the settlement of the case in December 2008, show very well the systematic and institutionalised nature of the corruption at Siemens during the years leading up to detection in November 2006:

> *Their actions were not an anomaly. They were standard operating procedures for corporate*
> *executives who viewed bribery as a business strategy.*[15]

Reasons why the corrupt payments were made

There appear to be two overarching reasons that explain why Siemens was using bribery almost as a standard business practice when competing for work around the world at the outset of the twenty-first century.

The first reason was fear. Siemens' managers were terrified that if they did not pay the bribes then they would lose a lot of their business in many of their overseas markets. So, there were underlying concerns about how robust the company's business model actually was in practice. It was thought to be vulnerable to competition from business rivals, so that if the bidding process was not corrupted and tenders were not rigged Siemens would lose contracts to its rivals. So, Siemens was not interested in a level playing field here – not at all. It needed an uneven playing field on which to compete. Here, business economics was an important driver of poor business behaviour.

The second reason was self-serving justification. There was a belief within the company, strongly held by some no doubt, that it was simply necessary to pay bribes in certain countries in the world in order to win business – public officials in these countries 'expected to be paid'. Linked to this was the view that their competitors were paying bribes too. It is no doubt true that some other international companies were paying bribes in the early years of this century in order to win contracts in developing countries. However, the Siemens case is notable above all for three things: the sheer breadth of the bribery; the sums of money involved; and how entrenched and systematic the mechanics of the bribe paying processes used by the company to win and retain business had become within the corporate culture.

It seems that the managers and staff involved in paying the bribes to government officials were in no doubt that, by doing so, they were breaking the law. In December 2008, the *New York Times* carried extracts of an interview with Reinhard Siekaczek, a former mid-level accounts executive in the Siemens subsidiary that sold telecommunications equipment overseas.[16] His was one of the homes raided by the German police in November 2006. In the newspaper interview, Herr Siekaczek recounts how, on opening his front door to the police, he spoke to them straight away in the following terms: 'I know what this is about, I have been expecting you.'[17] In his position as accountant he oversaw an annual bribery budget in the region of $40–50 million and he himself made the arrangements that enabled the payments to be made. In the interview, he says these payments were vital to maintaining the competitiveness of Siemens business overseas:

> *It was about keeping the business unit alive and not jeopardising thousands of jobs overnight ...*
> *It had nothing to do with being law-abiding, because we all knew that what we did was unlawful.*
> *We thought we had to do it, otherwise we'd ruin the company.*[18]

Herr Siekaczek was sentenced in Germany to two years' probation and a $150,000 fine. This was only one of many penalties imposed on Siemens and a number of its ex-managers as a result of the investigations.

Penalties and costs

On 15 December 2008 Siemens settled charges with the DOJ, the SEC and the Munich Public Prosecutor's Office with the payment of $1.6 billion in total in fines and penalties. The fine would have been much higher had it not been for the extensive cooperation of Siemens with the authorities, but it remains the largest monetary sanction ever imposed in an anti-corruption case.

Significantly, the company pleaded guilty to many charges of accounting violations but it avoided either a guilty plea or a conviction for bribery. The US authorities allowed Siemens to plead to accounting violations only because the company had cooperated fully throughout the investigation and its directors and senior managers had shown themselves to be committed to changing corporate practices and culture in the future. Pleading to bribery allegations could have excluded Siemens from bidding on public procurement contracts in the USA and elsewhere. Siemens did not dispute the authorities' account of its actions.

So, despite the record size of the settlement, it might be thought that the deal represented a partial victory at least for Siemens. However, this was by no means the end of the consequences of the corruption scandal. There were a number of other significant costs and consequences for the company resulting from the case, including:

- Siemens had to reach a settlement with the World Bank because one of the allegations concerned the corruption of a World Bank project in Russia by the Siemens' Russian subsidiary. The settlement was announced in July 2009. In addition to Siemens agreeing to pay $100 million over the next 15 years to support anti-corruption work, it included a four-year debarment from bidding for World Bank business for Siemens' Russian subsidiary and a two-year debarment on World Bank contracts worldwide for Siemens generally.[19]
- The scandal impacted on Siemens' investors, of course. The Siemens share price came under significant pressure as a result of the scandal – it fell by over 50% at various times during the investigation.
- The two leaders of the company at the time were forced out as a result of the scandal. In April 2007, first the Siemens Chairman (and former CEO) Heinrich von Pierer and then just days later the Chief Executive, Klaus Kleinfeld, announced their resignations. Both denied any wrongdoing.
- The scandal was the trigger for wide-ranging management changes. The new CEO Peter Loscher was the first outsider (and indeed the first non-German) to lead Siemens in its history. He used the sense of urgency created by the scandal as an opportunity to take a hard look both at the organisational structure of the business and the people holding positions at various levels of management. In an interview shortly after becoming CEO, Mr Loscher stated that 'The management culture failed. And that's something we will address ... all of it. 470 executives have already been sanctioned and we have parted ways with 130. It is important that every Siemens employee knows that rules and laws must be observed. Anyone who fails to comply can expect the most serious of consequences.'[20]
- The scandal imposed heavy additional costs on the company. For example, the money spent on the in-house investigation was significant in respect of fees paid to lawyers, accountants and consultants and amounted to over $850 million in total.

Reputational damage

Perhaps the most significant impact of the scandal, at least in the short term, was that it cost Siemens, hitherto a symbol both of German engineering excellence and also of corporate probity, its good reputation. The comments of Acting Assistant Attorney General Frederich at the press conference following the court settlement in 2008 make this clear:

> *Today's filings make clear that for its business operations overseas, bribery was nothing less than standard operating procedure for Siemens.*[21]

He went on to note that Siemens' executives had the use of off-the-books slush funds, employed shell corporations to funnel payments and at times used 'suitcases filled with cash' to facilitate the payments.

Not that the after-shocks from the scandal ended in 2008: despite the settlements mentioned above, Siemens continues to be investigated for these events in a number of countries. There are also enforcement actions ongoing against some of its former senior managers who are facing both criminal and civil charges.

However, the company has put great effort into its re-vamped compliance programme and other activities designed to repair the trust breakdown with its stakeholders and to rebuild its reputation. We will look at how successful Siemens has been in this regard in the second part of this case study in Chapter 4.

 ## THE BRIBERY ACT 2010 (UKBA)

Background

The first prosecution under the UKBA

This was a case that attracted a lot of media attention considering the insignificant sums involved. It was bound to do so, of course, because it was a case that made legal history in the UK.

In October 2011 a young man of 22, who had been working as a clerk for the Magistrates Court in Redbridge on the southern outskirts of London at the time of the offence (and was therefore an employee of the Ministry of Justice), pleaded guilty at his trial to one count of bribery. This involved him soliciting and then accepting a £500 bribe as the price for him agreeing not to add the details of an individual's traffic summons onto the court's database. Following a tip-off, journalists from a national newspaper in the UK had filmed him arranging the bribe. He was sentenced to three years imprisonment for bribery and six years in jail for misconduct in a public office (later reduced to four years on appeal).[22]

Thus, Munir Patel entered history as the first person to be convicted under the UKBA.

Background

Bribery and corruption have been crimes in the UK for hundreds of years. The UKBA replaces all existing statutory and common law offences. It serves to consolidate the various different pieces of legislation into one act and to bring everything up to date. Under the UKBA bribery is, of course, a criminal offence.

The UKBA[23] was enacted by Parliament in April 2010 and came into effect on 1 July 2011. It is not a retrospective piece of legislation and so it can be applied only to actions and events from that date.

The UKBA is rooted firmly in the principles that underpin both the FCPA and the UNCAC, but it has attracted some controversy and adverse comment amongst business people in the UK. This is primarily for two reasons. First, it is widely regarded as the toughest piece of anti-corruption legislation anywhere in the world, going further than the FCPA in a number of respects. Second, and linked to the tough approach, the UKBA adopts an extremely robust attitude to private-to-private sector bribery and corruption, as part of which it places a new legal duty on commercial organisations to prevent bribery from happening anywhere in their business.

As a result, it can appear that the UKBA places an unfair burden on UK companies, especially those looking to compete for business in overseas markets against competitors from jurisdictions that do not take such a tough approach to bribery and corruption. Some directors and managers are concerned that it may lead to both the loss of some existing contracts and the failure to win new ones. This is arguable, but in my view it is a short-term concern. I believe that any disadvantage that does exist will be temporary because authorities around the world are increasingly clamping down on bribery and corruption and are looking to put in place their own legislation similar to the UKBA.

Comparison with the FCPA

For many years, the FCPA has led the way in terms of international anti-corruption law and certainly in terms of its enforcement by the US authorities. The UKBA is part of the more recent and broader international trend targeting both public and private sector corruption, as exemplified by the UNCAC.

There are a number of similarities between the FCPA and the UKBA: both laws have extensive extra-territorial application; both have provisions making it an offence to bribe foreign officials; and both have severe sanctions, though the UKBA is even tougher here with unlimited fines and/or a maximum of 10 years imprisonment for anyone found guilty of bribery – double the maximum custodial sentence under the FCPA.

There are also a number of important differences, however, as follows:

- The FCPA deals with bribing foreign officials, not with private-to-private bribery.
- The FCPA only covers active bribery, that is to say the offering or paying of a bribe. The UKBA prohibits both active and passive bribery, where passive bribery is the flip-side of active bribery – agreeing to be bribed, 'taking the money'.
- The FCPA creates an exception for facilitation payments. There are no such exemptions or exceptions in the UKBA – it is truly a 'zero tolerance' piece of legislation. This means that all facilitation payments are deemed to be bribes (although the UK authorities have indicated that they will exercise discretion in deciding whether to prosecute in these cases, providing always that the payments are not systemic).
- The UKBA creates the new corporate offence of failing to prevent bribery, which does not appear under the FCPA. The corporate offence extends to the actions of 'associated persons', which term means anyone who performs services for or on behalf of the commercial organisation in question. So, in addition to employees, the corporate offence extends to the activities of associates such as agents, brokers, intermediaries and subsidiary companies also.

Summary of the UKBA offences

The UKBA is a relatively straightforward piece of legislation in terms of its drafting. It contains three main offences and, in addition, the new and unique corporate offence of failing to prevent bribery. The relevant sections are as follows:

Section 1 and Section 2

These are the general bribery offences of: active bribery (Section 1); and passive bribery (Section 2).

Active bribery is the offering, promising or giving of a bribe to another person. It is important to note here that the bribe does not actually have to be paid – simply making the offer is sufficient to trigger the offence.

Passive bribery is the reverse or flipside of active bribery. In other words passive bribery is where someone either requests, agrees to receive or accepts a bribe.

A bribe is described in the legislation as: 'a financial or other advantage'. So, it does not have to be a payment in cash.

Bribery is defined in Sections 1 and 2 in terms of an intention to use a financial or other advantage to encourage or induce 'improper performance' by any person in breach of any duty or expectation of trust or impartiality. Improper performance occurs when there is a failure to perform one's duties in line with a 'relevant expectation'. In other words, it will be deemed to be improper performance if it is intended that, by paying the bribe, the recipient of the bribe would be expected to act otherwise than: in good faith; in an impartial manner; or in accordance with a position of trust.

As an example: a manager running a tender process for a company would be expected to award the contract to the bidder who comes in with the lowest price or the best value proposal (or whatever other criteria is appropriate under the terms of the tender document). If in fact the manager awards the contract to the bidder who offers to pay him the biggest bribe, then this would be improper performance because the manager has failed to perform his duties in line with a relevant expectation.

Section 6

This section introduces a new standalone offence in UK law of bribing a foreign public official. Here an offence is triggered if the bribe is given with the intention to influence a foreign public official in the performance of his or her duties and thereby to obtain or retain business or an advantage in the conduct of business.

There is an important distinction here with the general bribery offences described above. Where bribery of a foreign public official is concerned the consideration of improper performance in the Section 1 and Section 2 offences does not apply. Instead, the test used in Section 6 is 'intention to influence'.

It should be noted that no offence arises if there is a local 'written' law permitting or requiring the official to be influenced by the advantage. However, local customs or unofficial practices that may appear to permit these kinds of payment in certain parts of the world will be deemed to be irrelevant by a UK court.

There are two important points to make regarding Section 6. First of all, the category 'foreign public officials' in practice comprises a large set of people, including as it does not only elected or appointed government officials but also employees and officers in state-owned enterprises. As examples: the police, border guards and also employees at ports and airports where these are owned by the state (as is often the case) are considered to be foreign public officials. Second, because the test of 'intention to influence' is considered to be easier to trigger than the improper performance test in Sections 1 and 2, all transactions with foreign public officials should be treated as high risk for the purposes of the UKBA. As a result, they should always be entered into with extra care. All dealings with foreign public officials should be subject to strong controls and procedures in order to mitigate the higher risks arising.

Section 7

Section 7 represents a highly significant legal development. It contains a new offence under UK law – the failure of relevant commercial organisations to prevent bribery. Because of this, Section 7 is sometimes referred to as the 'corporate offence'. It imposes for the first time a requirement on commercial organisations to take adequate steps to prevent bribery from occurring anywhere in their operations. In my view it represents a major commitment by the authorities in the UK to ethical corporate culture.

Section 7 applies as follows: a relevant commercial organisation (C) is guilty of an offence if a person (A) associated with C bribes another person intending to obtain or retain business or an advantage in the conduct of business for C. For the purposes of Section 7, A bribes another person if and only if A is or would be guilty of an offence under Sections 1 or 6 (whether or not A has been prosecuted for such an offence).

A 'relevant commercial organisation' means a company or partnership that is either incorporated or formed in the UK (and carries on a business either in the UK or abroad) or a foreign company or partnership that carries on a business or part of a business in the UK. The effect of this is to give the Section 7 offence broad scope. In addition to UK organisations it also applies to entities formed outside the UK provided that at least part of their business is conducted in the UK.

Under Section 7, a person is classified as an associate if they perform services for or on behalf of C. This is an important point. It means that the category 'associate' applies not only to C's employees but also includes certain third parties who perform services for C. Examples of these third parties include: agents, brokers, intermediaries, subsidiary companies and main contractual counter-parties. Bribery by any associate can render C liable to the Section 7 offence. It is essential, therefore, that all associates, both internal and external, are made aware of C's policies and commit to abide by them.

There are a number of unusual features about the Section 7 offence as follows:

- It is a strict liability offence. In other words, absolute legal responsibility for damages or injury can be imposed on the wrongdoer without proof of fault or negligence. The only defence available is for C to prove that, despite a particular case of bribery, it nevertheless had 'adequate procedures' in place (see below) designed to prevent persons associated with it from carrying out bribery.
- The bribe can be paid without the knowledge, authorisation or involvement of anyone else in the organisation. Knowledge of the offence is irrelevant.
- A case can be brought to trial on an information-only basis.
- It does not matter if the bribe took place in a foreign jurisdiction where bribery is considered to be 'accepted business practice'.

So, it is a compliance imperative that organisations have the appropriate adequate procedures in place to prevent bribery in any part of their operations.

The other main provisions

Other significant aspects of the UKBA include the following.

Extra-territorial jurisdiction

The Act has wide jurisdictional reach in three areas.

- First, it covers all bribery offences committed in the UK, no matter who commits them.
- Second, the UKBA applies to bribes paid by UK companies and partnerships and also to individuals committing one of the main offences who are British nationals or who are ordinarily resident in the UK wherever the bribery offence is committed – there is no territorial limitation.
- Third, the Section 7 corporate offence applies (in addition to the above) to all non-UK commercial organisations where they carry on a business or part of a business in the UK. This means that a foreign company can be prosecuted under the UKBA for bribery offences in relation to conduct in a foreign country that is not connected with its UK business at all so long as it has a demonstrable business presence in the UK. The aim is to create a level playing field for all commercial organisations trying to win contracts around the world. Here the UKBA has adopted the same principle of extra-territoriality in matters relating to financial crime that we saw is included in the FCPA.

Penalties

The penalties for non-compliance with the UKBA are severe and deliberately so – they are designed to act as a deterrent to corrupt behaviour.

Individuals found guilty under Sections 1, 2 or 6 can be imprisoned for up to 10 years (twice the maximum prison term of the FCPA) and/or receive an unlimited fine. Commercial organisations found guilty of any of the four offences can receive an unlimited fine. The proceeds of any bribery can be confiscated also.

Prosecution of senior officers

The UKBA makes it easier for the authorities to prosecute the senior officers of an organisation if it can be shown that bribery was committed with their 'consent or connivance'.

If any commercial organisation is found guilty under Sections 1, 2 or 6 then a senior corporate officer of that organisation (defined as a director, manager, company secretary or similar officer) can also be convicted if he or she is deemed to have given their 'consent or connivance' to the offence. An offence could be given by the 'passive acquiescence' of a director or senior manager (as indicated by, for example, a failure to put in place adequate procedures) if in practice that amounted to consent to bribery. As a result, directors and managers cannot afford to turn a blind eye to potential bribery in their organisations.

Facilitation payments

The UKBA takes a zero-tolerance approach to all bribery and corruption. All actions that fall under the Act's definition of bribery are illegal, no matter how small the payments might be. Accordingly, all facilitation payments are prohibited, unlike the position taken in the USA under the FCPA.

Adequate procedures

Introduction

The phrase 'adequate procedures' introduced by Section 7 of the UKBA sounds innocuous, prosaic and even a little dull perhaps. I don't see it this way, not at all – it is highly significant. In my view, the phrase provides an important signpost to the effective management of business ethics and behaviour within organisations that goes beyond the immediate subject matter here of bribery and corruption. I believe that organisations should be looking to have adequate procedures in place throughout their operations, rather than constructing a separate silo within which they place their anti-bribery measures.

The key word here is adequate. What is meant by this is that controls and systems need to exist, they need to be appropriate and they need to be proportionate, with the key reference point for considerations of proportionality being risk. In other words, an organisation's procedures need to be proportionate to the risks that the organisation faces, which is a simple and powerful message.

The other interesting thing to me about the official guidance (see below) on how best to prevent bribery is that it does not focus simply on the existence of a number of designated procedures – those procedures must actually work in practice, time after time, day after day. This fundamental point is emphasised throughout in the guidance. So, in order for the procedures to be adequate, they need to be embedded in the culture of the organisation. The guidance sets out a number of ways that this might be achieved including: the absolute commitment of directors and senior managers to bribery prevention; effective communication of the message, both internally and externally; a programme of training that is ongoing and not a one-off event; and the monitoring of progress over time.

In short, this is a classic twin-track approach. It is applied here to the specific issue of bribery and corruption but, in my view, it has the potential for wider application. It is an approach that could be adapted by organisations to many other areas of their operations with advantage.

Importance of adequate procedures

It is essential that the directors and managers of any commercial organisation that is carrying on a business or a part of a business in the UK are aware of the Section 7 offence of failing to prevent bribery. As mentioned above, it is a strict liability offence. In practice, this means that, if information is received by the authorities which is cogent and persuades a court that an associate (either an employee or a third party service provider) has paid a bribe intending thereby to obtain or retain business or a business advantage for an organisation, then it will follow that the organisation in question will be guilty of the Section 7 offence. It makes no difference if the organisation was unaware that the bribery had taken place. As we have seen, a Section 7 offence is punishable with an unlimited fine.

There is only one defence available: the organisation must be able to show that, despite the particular act of bribery, it nevertheless had put in place 'adequate procedures' designed to prevent and deter bribery from taking place.

My own interpretation is that this is actually a piece of classic risk management and controls theory applied to the legal process. There are no certainties in business, we all know this. Even the strongest of controls cannot be guaranteed to work all the time – controls are designed to provide reasonable assurance, never certainty. This key point has been recognised by the authorities in the UKBA. Commercial organisations are not expected to be perfect. Instead, any organisation will have a full defence if it can show that, despite a particular case of bribery, it nevertheless had adequate procedures in place to prevent persons associated with it from bribing.

There is no description of what the phrase 'adequate procedures' means in the UKBA itself. Instead, this can be found in official guidance from the UK Government in the form of two papers produced by the Ministry of Justice (MOJ).

- The first is called: 'The Bribery Act 2010: Guidance about procedures which relevant commercial organisations can put in place to prevent persons associated with them from bribing (section 9 of the Bribery Act 2010)'.[24]
- The second is a condensed version of this and is called simply 'The Bribery Act 2010: Quick Start Guide'.[25]

Official guidance on adequate procedures

A principles-based approach

The official guidance is formulated around six guiding principles. It is important to note that these are principles and not rules and so they are not prescriptive – the guidance is not a checklist that must be followed. Rather, the six principles are intended to be flexible and outcomes-based. Their application will depend upon the individual circumstances of each commercial organisation. Also, it should be remembered that although these principles have been drawn up by the UK Government, they still represent guidance only – ultimately, the facts will be decided by the courts in individual cases (at the time of writing in 2014, no prosecutions have been brought under Section 7, so there is no legal precedent to refer to as yet).

Whatever the courts ultimately decide, the six guiding principles will remain a most useful signpost for all organisations. The six principles are: proportionality; top-level commitment; risk assessment; due diligence; communication (including training); and monitoring and review.

Each of them is reviewed and discussed briefly below.

Principle 1: proportionate procedures

The first principle concerns the importance of organisations taking a proportionate approach. The guidance notes describe this as the overarching principle and as such it is worth setting it out in full:

> *A commercial organisation's procedures to prevent bribery by persons associated with it are proportionate to the bribery risks it faces and to the nature, scale and complexity of the commercial organisation's activities. They are also clear, practical, accessible, effectively implemented and enforced.*

There are two important points to make by way of commentary on this principle.

First of all, the key measure of proportionality is not size – rather it is risk. While it is both intuitive and correct to think that large multinational organisations will be expected to have detailed procedures and strong controls in place to prevent bribery, it does not follow that smaller organisations need do very little about bribery prevention. The controls required depend crucially on the extent of the bribery risks that the organization faces. Where risk is low, then procedures might indeed be modest. But where bribery risk is high, even in small organisations, then strong systems and controls need to be not only in place but also working correctly in order to prevent bribery from occurring.

Second, bribery prevention policies are necessary but they are not in themselves sufficient for compliance with the guidance – the policies must also be implemented effectively. For example, it is essential, in the context of the UKBA, that an organisation has a specific anti-bribery policy in place. By itself this policy is not sufficient to comply with the Act, however. In order to be compliant, all of the organisation's associates (both the employees, all the subsidiary companies and the third-party service providers) must be made aware of the policy and understand that they need to comply with it at all times, which means that an investment in training and communication will be required. This is where Principle 2 is important, that of top-level commitment.

Before we look at Principle 2, however, it is perhaps useful to pause for a moment and to look briefly at the anti-bribery policy itself. The policy is signed off by the board, of course. What message should an organisation send out in order to comply with the UKBA? Set out below is an example of the type of statement that should be set out clearly at the beginning of the anti-bribery policy (in terms of the policy document itself, the organisation should include additional paragraphs covering aspects such as scope, definitions and responsibilities):

> *XYZ's policy is to conduct all of its business in an honest and ethical manner. The company takes a zero-tolerance approach to bribery and corruption. It is committed to acting fairly, professionally and with integrity in all its business dealings and relationships wherever it operates and to implementing and enforcing effective systems to prevent and deter bribery.*

> *The company will uphold all laws relevant to countering bribery and corruption in all jurisdictions in which it operates. However, it remains bound by the laws of the UK, including the Bribery Act 2010, in respect of its conduct both at home and abroad.*

Principle 2: top-level commitment

Principle 2 is powerful and straightforward and it addresses culture directly. It states that the top-level management of the organisation (whether that is a board of directors, the owners or any other equivalent body or person) should be committed to preventing bribery. Directors and managers should foster a culture in which bribery is never acceptable.

This principle recognises that tone at the top is the key influence on the culture of any organisation. Directors and senior managers are responsible for developing the values of the business and for promoting them throughout the organisation. In order to comply with the UKBA, one of these values must be a commitment to conduct business fairly and with a zero tolerance of any form of bribery. Principle 2 encourages the involvement of top-level management in the decision-making process regarding designing appropriate bribery prevention procedures and also in managing bribery risk. The evidence of such involvement will be seen in the communication of the organisation's anti-bribery stance (both to employees within the organisation and to outside stakeholders) and in the development and sign-off of bribery prevention policies.

The guidance notes highlight two practical ways for organisations to demonstrate that top-level commitment to preventing bribery does indeed exist. The first is that directors and senior managers encourage and provide the funding for an ongoing programme of anti-bribery awareness training for employees and associates. The second is that they take part in the anti-bribery training themselves.

Principle 3: risk assessment

Principle 3 states that a commercial organisation needs to assess the nature and extent of its exposure to potential risks of bribery, including both external and internal risks. The guidance goes on to say that the risk assessment should be periodic, informed and documented.

Implicit in this principle is that all organisations should take a risk-based approach to bribery prevention. Principle 3 promotes the adoption of a proportionate risk assessment procedure, which could be a part of the organisation's general risk management process or else it could be a specific, standalone bribery risk assessment. The crucial point here is that bribery risk needs to be properly considered by the appropriate people in the organisation, who pull together the results in a bribery risk assessment document (which may be termed variously a register, a profile or a matrix) that is reviewed and updated periodically.

In practice, I find that many organisations, smaller ones in particular, are still not documenting their risk assessments. As an example, following any presentation that I make on the UKBA there will typically be a number of people in the audience who wish to speak to me afterwards on specific aspects of the talk. Typically, some will spend several minutes taking me through their business and the risks facing it before asking me what I think that they need to do in order to comply with the Act. My reply is always the same: first I ask them whether what they have just told me is documented – have they written it down somewhere. Then, in response to the usual answer of 'no' I say that they must find the time to do so. They have just demonstrated to me that they are well aware of the bribery risks facing their organisation, but to comply with the guidance this knowledge must be documented rather than remaining intuitive. Finally, I say that once that is done, they should base their organisation's compliance with the UKBA on a proportionate response to the bribery risks in the business. But the first step is always to think about risk and document the conclusions. Without a documented risk assessment, there can be no risk-based approach.

The guidance notes include indicators of risk, both external and internal, building on the work of TI and others. External risk factors include: the geographical areas or countries in which trade is carried out; the business sector concerned (bribery threats in the extractive industries and in large-scale infrastructure projects are highlighted); and the type of transactions entered into, with particular emphasis placed on deals involving foreign public officials, which might include taking part in public procurement tenders, paying for licenses and permits or making donations to political parties.

The guidance notes make clear that internal risks are important considerations also. The internal risk factors referred to are: deficiencies in employee training, skills and knowledge; a bonus culture that rewards excessive risk-taking; lack of clear financial controls; the absence of a clear anti-bribery message coming from the top; and a lack of clarity in policies around high risk areas such as gifts and hospitality, promotional expenses, political donations and so on.

Principle 4: due diligence

Principle 4 states that the organisation should apply due diligence procedures, taking a proportionate and risk-based approach, in respect of persons who perform or will perform services for or on behalf of the organisation. The aim is to mitigate identified bribery risks and so this principle is closely connected with the risk-based approach set out in Principle 3.

Due diligence is part of a broader framework of good corporate governance. All organisations need to know about the extent of their business relationships and they should always understand the risks that a particular business opportunity raises. Organisations need to 'know about' the companies and individuals that they do business with in order to protect themselves. Due diligence has traditionally taken the form of various legal and financial checks including: verifying the legal constitution of the company (for example, the memorandum and articles of association); reviewing the annual report and accounts; and checking the credit rating of the company.

By taking a risk-based approach, an organisation commits to a robust due diligence process. The type of due diligence checks themselves will vary according to risk. Today, given the global nature of business, it is crucial that, in situations where bribery risk is high, traditional due diligence is supplemented by carrying out extra checks, in particular on the reputation of the individuals who control the company that the organisation is thinking about doing business with.

This process is known as integrity due diligence. It may be carried out either internally (primarily through desk-top research and searches of the Internet), or by using external firms of risk consultants. For example, financial services companies have for many years chosen to outsource the checks that they are required to make of their customers to various official lists: lists of terrorists and proscribed organisations; lists of 'politically exposed persons'; and sanctions lists for the purposes of compliance with anti-money laundering and counter-terrorist financing regulations. The purpose of conducting integrity due diligence work is to enable an organisation to feel confident that the business relationships that it has entered into (perhaps with a new supplier or with an agent to facilitate trade in a part of the world that it has never done business in before) are transparent, legal and ethical.

Principle 5: communication (including training)

Principle 5 states that the organisation should seek to ensure that its bribery prevention policies are embedded and understood throughout the organisation through internal and external communication, including training, that are proportionate to the risks it faces. Communication and training help to deter bribery by raising awareness and understanding not only of the organisation's procedures but also of its commitment to their proper application. Making information available assists in more effective monitoring, evaluations and review of bribery prevention procedures.

Communication should be both internal and external. Internal communication is a combination of specific policies (for example, an anti-bribery policy, a gifts and hospitality policy etc.) and the tone and culture of the organisation. Particularly important in this context is for organisations to encourage a culture of openness – internal reporting and tip-offs are the most common way by far that bribery and corruption schemes are detected in practice. Here, the guidance notes refer to 'speak-up' procedures, which are sometimes known as whistle-blowing hotlines – we look at whistle-blowing in detail later in Chapter 9 of the book.

In addition, organisations should make sure that all of their existing and potential business associates are aware of their anti-bribery commitment. This can be achieved through a mixture of actions, such as putting suitable statements up on the organisations' website and also inserting appropriate anti-bribery clauses in contracts with third parties and in terms and conditions of trade (this may well necessitate changes to existing contracts).

Training is a critical component of communicating an organisation's anti-bribery message. A thorough training programme is needed to establish firmly an anti-bribery culture. This is emphasised in the guidance notes, which state that the anti-bribery training programme should be mandatory and ongoing. So, compliance with the UKBA necessitates commitment to a substantial investment, in terms of both money and time, in training over the long term. The reason is clear: training is needed to provide relevant staff (and associated third-party service providers also) with the knowledge and skills needed to operate procedures and to deal with any bribery related problems that might arise.

Principle 6: monitoring and review

Principle 6 represents a classic piece of controls theory. It states that the organisation should monitor and review procedures designed to prevent bribery and make improvements where necessary. Monitoring is always a feature of well-controlled organisations because they understand that situations and circumstances change over time. This is no different when looking at bribery risk than to considering risks in any other part of the business.

There are two important components of Principle 6. First, the bribery risks facing an organisation may change over time so the procedures needed to mitigate the risks may also change. It follows that regular monitoring is needed. Second, a review may be required in order to respond appropriately to actual events (as examples: a change of government in the country of a trading partner may increase risk; a specific incident of bribery may be discovered involving an agent in some way; and there may be negative comments concerning a business associate in the media).

There are a variety of traditional monitoring controls that may be used for this purpose: financial control mechanisms; staff surveys; periodic reports for senior management; internal audit and/or compliance reviews; and some form of external assurance. It is important to build an element of independence into any review process in order to gain maximum assurance from it. This is why I am a strong advocate of anti-bribery reviews forming part of an internal audit department's work plans. In addition, an organisation might also ask its external auditors to look at any areas of high risk.

As a best-practice maxim, controls need to be sensitive to changes in bribery risk and updated regularly.

Adequate procedures: summary

The MOJ's guidance to the UKBA points to a series of controls and procedures that help to prevent bribery. These include: regular and documented assessments of bribery risks; a clear anti-bribery policy, together with policies in high risk areas such as gifts and entertainment, political donations and tendering processes, all signed off by the board; whistle-blowing hotlines (or, as they are referred to in the official guidance, 'speak-up procedures'); comprehensive training for all relevant associates (both internal and external) that is mandatory and ongoing; due diligence processes for agents and other third parties; reference to the organisation's anti-bribery stance in its contracts and its terms and conditions of trade; and a regular monitoring and review process.

These controls and procedures represent the ethical hardware. There is no requirement for any organisation to have all of them in place; rather each organisation must do what is proportionate according to its own unique risk profile. However, it is pretty clear that, should an organisation fail to put in place any of these procedures, then it is unlikely to be compliant with the official guidance and will therefore be potentially exposed to the Section 7 charge of failing to prevent bribery. So, it is necessary for some, at least, of the procedures set out in the official guidance to be in place in order to comply with the UKBA.

The guidance notes make it clear, however, that it is not sufficient for an organisation simply to document a series of controls and procedures in order to prevent bribery – the controls must actually work in practice. More than that, they must be seen to work – seen by employees, by external service providers and by contractual counter-parties alike.

In order to achieve this, there needs to be a clear and powerful anti-bribery culture in place throughout the organisation. Simply put, this means no bribery, whatever the circumstances. So, even when trading conditions are tough or when contracts are being negotiated in parts of the world where corruption is thought to be endemic, there is no thought, no temptation, to use bribery to gain an advantage.

Whether this works in practice or not will depend crucially on the culture and values embedded in each individual organisation. The tone is always set at the top. Senior managers must be committed to the principle of anti-bribery in everything that they say and do. Putting a statement of zero tolerance of bribery on the website is a powerful symbol and a good start, but it is only a start. It must be backed up consistently, every day, in the decisions made and in the actions taken by everybody associated with the organisation. This is the crucial ethical software.

Caution: beware of paying lip-service

Introduction

As we have seen, in October 2011 Mr Patel received a six-year jail sentence for taking a £500 bribe. Of course, the fact that he was an employee of the Ministry of Justice and accepted the bribe in order to corrupt the judicial process, thereby displaying a major breach of trust, meant that he was always likely to receive a severe sentence. Neither was this a case involving the corporate offence of failing to prevent bribery. Nevertheless, I believe that this case sends a clear message that bribery will be dealt with severely by the courts when proven in future. No organisation (and certainly no director) wants to be the first to be convicted under the UKBA's Section 7 corporate offence. To avoid this, adequate procedures to prevent bribery must be in place.

Attitude of the authorities

The UKBA came into force on 1 July 2011, some three years before the writing of this book. There is no doubt that many commercial organisations will have failed to implement anything by way of adequate procedures to prevent bribery since that time. I consider this to be negligent management – these organisations are clearly exposed and I would urge the directors and managers concerned to correct this omission as soon as possible.

Organisations that are negligent are not my only concern here, however. In addition, there is a risk that normally conscientious directors and managers might begin to lose focus on the Act and become complacent because of the small number of prosecutions brought by the authorities to date. The UKBA came onto the statute book and became effective in July 2011 with much fanfare and publicity. Since then, nothing much appears to have happened and the costs of continuing compliance (in terms of ongoing training, due diligence enquiries and, in some cases no doubt, the turning down of business opportunities because bribery risk is considered to be too high) might start to attract sceptical scrutiny from senior managers looking to improve results.

At the time of writing, in 2014, there have only been three convictions in the UK for bribery under the UKBA. All three cases concern the actions of individuals, of which the Patel case was the first. As a result, there is a real danger that commercial organisations begin to think that the authorities are not pursuing bribery and corruption vigorously and so start to question the level of money and resource commitment needed for installing, refreshing, updating and reviewing the adequate procedures that the UKBA requires. If the authorities are not serious about prosecuting offences, then some directors and managers might think that there is an opportunity to reduce significantly the costs of compliance in this area by paying lip-service only to the UKBA.

In my opinion, this is mistaken and dangerous thinking, and for two reasons. The first is that the Act is not retrospective and so it can only be applied to bribery events that take place after 1 July 2011. What we are witnessing is a fairly standard time-lag working here – financial crime cases involving organisations always take many months to develop and bring to court. As an example, the FCPA is today the most enforced anti-corruption law in the world, yet relatively few cases were brought under its auspices during the first 10 years after it was passed in 1977. The second reason is that the authorities in the UK are indeed investigating cases. The Serious Fraud Office (SFO) brought its first prosecution under the UKBA in September 2013 – the trial is continuing at the time of writing.

David Green, appointed as the new Director in charge of the SFO in April 2012, has made it clear in speeches and interviews since then that he will use the powers under the Act to prosecute offenders. He has stated that the SFO: is ramping up its intelligence capacity; is taking a more proactive approach around 'sweeps' of the key bribery risk sectors of public contracts and construction, utilities, real estate and legal services, oil and gas, and mining; and would never decline to investigate an allegation on the grounds of cost. In particular, Mr Green has changed the SFO's approach to self-reporting of problems by organisations. Under his regime, whilst the SFO will continue to encourage corporate self-reporting it offers no guarantee that a prosecution will not follow in these cases.

Mr Green has put all commercial organisations on notice that the SFO is committed to tackling bribery and corruption. During his speech to the Cambridge International Symposium on Economic Crime in 2013 he said: 'We are investigators and prosecutors ... we are not a regulator, a deal-maker or a confessor.'[26]

 PERSONAL EXPERIENCES

Introduction

Background

Over the last three years a number of clients have asked for my help on various aspects of compliance with the UKBA. I set out below a description of the consultancy process involved in two of these assignments, working through from the issues confronting each organisation when I was first commissioned, to the recommendations for changes, to the procedures that were subsequently agreed to and acted upon. An element of cultural change was present in both assignments. Results in this area are difficult to see immediately, however – it will require time to assess whether or not they have become embedded in each respective organisation.

The companies in the two examples are very different. The first is the UK subsidiary of a large multinational energy group with its headquarters in Paris. The second is a medium-sized UK business that manufactures high-technology components in its factory in the Midlands and sells them to companies operating in the defence industry around the world. It is part of a larger German group.

General observations

Each of these companies took a positive and proactive stance towards complying with the UKBA – they approached me soon after the Act went live in July 2011 and I was impressed by the commitment of each of them. Their reasons for contacting me were different and each illustrates an important point concerning compliance and cultural change, as follows:

- The UK subsidiary of the global energy group was looking to use compliance with the Act as a catalyst to kick-start changes to its existing procedures and style of operation that senior managers wanted to make in order to improve their business in the future. The message here is very powerful: organisations can use the basic requirement of needing to comply with the law to bring about fundamental change.
- The medium-sized UK manufacturer operating in the defence sector quickly adopted a number of the extra controls and procedures to comply with the UKBA that I recommended to them. I was impressed by this and also slightly surprised, at least at first. I soon realised, however, that there was one fundamental reason why the company was acting in this way – the changes were all driven through actively and personally by the managing director. This is one of the best examples I have seen of the effect of 'tone at the top' and how it can change the culture of an organisation.

Compliance questionnaires, ripple effects and card games

Responses to any piece of legislation vary and not all of my clients have been as proactive in complying with the UKBA as these two. A number have contacted me and asked for help as a matter of urgency because of what I call the Act's ripple effect. These clients almost always need help in one of two areas (sometimes in both): the drafting of an anti-bribery policy and the provision of training for staff. While I am generally able to satisfy these requests, there is little appetite displayed by these clients to do more than the minimum required for compliance with the UKBA. I think that this is almost always a missed opportunity.

Why do these organisations come to me needing help so urgently? The reason is almost always the same. Typically, one of their major customers has written, asking them to complete a compliance questionnaire within a short time period – usually one month. The questionnaire requires, amongst other things, copies of the firm's anti-bribery policy document and details of the anti-bribery training programme that it has provided for its staff, together with any other relevant measures it has put in place to comply with the UKBA.

This is classic compliance ripple-effect caused by a major piece of legislation. It provides evidence that many large organisations are now seeking actively to manage the risk of bribery and corruption in their supply chains.

I often refer in my talks to this practice of sending out compliance questionnaires as an example of modern business coming increasingly to resemble the rules of a card game such as whist or bridge, wherein all players must be able to reply to a card in the same suit. What I mean by this is that today those commercial organisations that are protective of their reputations are looking to work only with third parties that are able to replicate their own business standards. To the extent that a third party is unable to do so, then the commercial organisation is taking on increased risk if it decides to go ahead with the contract. Often it will decide not to do so because the increased risk of reputational damage is deemed to be unacceptable.

Example 1: UK subsidiary of a global energy group

Issues

The following issues became apparent during my first meetings with this client:

- My main point of contact in the London office was the UK ethics officer – actually the subsidiary's in-house lawyer who had been appointed to this post as an additional responsibility, rather than it being her full time role. Ordinarily, I am sceptical about how effective such a dual role will turn out to be in practice and I am always concerned that this type of arrangement does not demonstrate full commitment by senior management to the challenge of improving ethics and culture. However, this lady proved to be an excellent colleague during the course of the project, always working hard to cover both roles.
- The Group had an Ethics Charter in place, one that had been issued relatively recently. The Charter was put together in consultation with the Group's 130,000 staff worldwide – for example, the four values of the Group, as set out in the Charter, came out of the consultation exercise. One issue, however, was that the Charter seemed to have little traction with the employees in the UK subsidiary.
- In addition to this last point, the policy framework in the UK subsidiary, together with the code of conduct, was in the process of being reviewed and updated. This added to a sense of uncertainty, of a state of flux in the UK business.
- Set against this background, the UKBA was seen as providing an opportunity for change. One of the Group's core ethical principles is that employees always act in accordance with the law and regulations so there was a strong commitment to do everything necessary to comply with the

Act as soon as it became law. As a result, an extensive review into a number of areas of policy and culture that were impacted by the UKBA was being carried out: gifts and hospitality, which could on occasion be lavish and extensive (for example the hospitality extended to those managers and employees, suppliers and contractors who were invited to attend the annual England–France rugby union international, either in London or Paris at the company's expense); risk assessment (there had been no bribery risk assessments carried out and there was little awareness generally amongst managers and staff of financial crime risk); whistle-blowing hotlines; and the wording used in contracts and agreements with third parties.

Actions

The project resulted in substantial changes to policies and procedures as well as prompting a degree of cultural change within the UK subsidiary. The most important features of these changes are set out below:

▪ A new code of business ethics was developed, with particular application to the UK operation. It made use of the principle of subsidiarity that the Group adhered to, whereby this code fitted under the umbrella of the Group Ethics Charter, but the tone and language of the code were now much more relevant to the employees in the UK business. As a result, the new code had more impact with those working in the UK subsidiary.

▪ A working group was set up to review the risks of bribery and corruption in the business. As a result, a threat assessment was discussed by relevant managers, documented and made available to the business.

▪ Building on the new code of business ethics, the existing gifts and hospitality policy was substantially revised and re-written whilst at the same time a new whistle-blowing policy was developed and introduced.

▪ The new gifts and hospitality policy reflected a substantial review of corporate entertainment within the UK business. As an example, the managing director asked for a summary of the past spending incurred on entertaining suppliers, consultants and staff at the annual England–France rugby international referred to above. This spend would include paying for such items as flights, hotel accommodation, food and drink, tickets for the matches and so on. I was never told the exact amount other than it all added up to a 'significant' amount of money. Having reviewed the information, the managing director decided to cancel the Group's attendance at the forthcoming international match, giving two reasons: first, he felt that the cost was inappropriate in the difficult economic conditions that existed at the time; and second, he did not wish to embarrass those contractors and suppliers who might have felt under some pressure to attend so as not to give any offence. One result of this new policy and the focus given to it by the managing director was a noticeably more considered and prudent attitude to gifts, hospitality and corporate entertainment generally by all those working for the UK subsidiary subsequently.

▪ The new code and policies were communicated formally to staff and third-party consultants during a series of one-day ethics training courses that I delivered for managers, staff and contractors. These courses emphasised throughout the importance placed by both the Group and senior management in the UK on good business ethics. They contained a significant piece on the UKBA but also aimed to raise awareness of the various risks from corrupt business practices generally. The courses covered the revised ethics code and policy framework, spending time in particular on the new whistle-blowing policy, with exercises designed to show how the new policies would work in practice. Being part of a French group, it was not possible to make this training 'mandatory' but it was given widespread publicity and everyone in the organisation (plus the consultants) knew that they were expected to attend one of the sessions. Certainly, all members of the senior management team did attend. It was planned to supplement this face-to-face training programme by computer-based training on business ethics and the UKBA, which was to be rolled out in subsequent years to all managers, staff and consultants.

- The ethics officer used her legal knowledge to carry out a comprehensive review of contracts and agreements, so that each was amended and re-issued to suppliers and contractors for signature with appropriate anti-bribery clauses now included. The company's zero tolerance of bribery was thereby made clear to all of its service providers.

Example 2: medium-sized UK business in the defence industry

Introduction

I gave a talk in London on the UKBA in 2011, at the end of which I was approached by one of the attendees asking for help. It turned out that this lady was the finance director of a company manufacturing high-technology products and selling them to companies in the defence industry. She told me that her managing director was determined to ensure that their company was fully compliant with the UKBA – could I help?

I was impressed from the outset by the commitment to comply with the Act and I was very pleased to assist.

Set out below is a summary of the main issues facing this company in terms of full compliance with the UKBA. In many ways they are typical of the problems that many small- and medium-sized businesses experience when faced with new legal requirements. Like them, no doubt, my client here is operating with stretched resources, working often under severe time pressures with tight staffing levels and is faced with the business reality of winning or retaining contracts in order to survive. This example shows what can be done when the drive to make necessary changes comes from the very top.

Issues

The following issues were present when I started working with this client:

- The company had few formal policies and procedures in place around business ethics and no specific anti-bribery controls – there was no ethics charter, no gifts and hospitality policy, no risk assessment, no whistle-blowing hotline. It had a small number of administrative support members of staff – the majority of employees were involved in the production process or else worked in sales and marketing. It was an operational business, not a bureaucratic one. Other than in the area of health and safety issues (which were taken very seriously), this was not a controls-conscious operation.
- There were no documented risk assessments in place. However, like all successful organisations, the managers knew their business thoroughly and so were in fact well aware of the major threats, including the threats of bribery and corruption. The company traded overseas to a significant extent, in countries such as India, Italy and Israel. It made use of agents to win business and to retain business in these jurisdictions but it knew very little about the backgrounds or reputation of the agents themselves. Little if any due diligence had been carried out on these

agents. The managers understood very well that this represented an exposure in terms of bribery and corruption risk.

- The company had formal legal contracts and standard terms and conditions of trade with its major counter-parties, including with the overseas agents. These contracts were longstanding, generic documents, however, and they did not refer specifically to the UKBA.

- The company had what might be described as a 'traditional' approach to gifts and hospitality – by that I mean that little in the way of corporate entertainment was provided by the company, but there was no prohibition on managers and staff accepting offers from customers and suppliers. Clearly, there was not a culture of lavish entertainment in this company – typically the type of corporate entertainment received would be invitations to suppliers' golf days held at local golf clubs and similar events.

Actions

This project resulted in significant change both to the policies and procedures of the organisation and perhaps to its culture too. The major points of change are set out below:

- The crucial factor in the success of the project in enabling full compliance with the UKBA was the support and engagement of the managing director. His commitment was obvious from the outset – he spent over one hour with me during my initial briefing visit and he always made time to see me when I visited subsequently (providing he was on the premises of course). I told him that our objective should be to come up with an approach that was appropriate to the circumstances of his business, in particular one that was proportionate to the risks faced. We discussed the options, I then made some recommendations and I was delighted to see that generally he was fully supportive of them. Because of this, change happened and it happened quickly. As an example, within 24 hours of that first meeting the managing director had posted a statement on the company website declaring the company's commitment to integrity and a zero tolerance of bribery, exactly as I had suggested. No one at the company viewed this as a cosmetic exercise or as lip-service to the Act. Because the statement was made by the managing director who was known to be personally committed to full compliance with the UKBA everyone took the changes seriously.

- Next, the managing director demonstrated this commitment by spending money on implementing two of my key recommendations. First, he hired a specialist lawyer to re-draft the company's contracts and terms and conditions of trade in order to make them compliant with the UKBA. Second, he took the significant step of hiring an external firm of risk consultants to carry out due diligence work on the small number of agents that the company used to source business overseas, thereby mitigating the company's most significant area of bribery risk exposure.

- The training obligations implicit in the UKBA were also addressed. Very soon after the project began, the managing director arranged for me to run two half-day workshops on the Act for company managers and accounts staff, one of which he attended himself. He backed this up by undertaking personally to raise awareness of the UKBA amongst the remainder of his staff and to make them aware of their personal responsibilities under the Act – he carried this out subsequently in a series of 20-minute briefings.

- The company also addressed the issue of putting an appropriate policy framework in place. It was not thought appropriate to try to develop an ethics charter but a suitable gifts and entertainment policy was drawn up and included in the staff handbook. Likewise, it was thought unnecessary to set up a whistle-blowing hotline, but a process to document, review and keep updated the assessment of bribery risk was put in place.

WORKSHOP CONCLUSION

Closing: bribery dilemma

Before concluding the workshop, I say that we need to return to the bribery dilemma put forward by Malcolm Mainwaring at the beginning of the session, namely: what instructions to give to the Captain who has been asked by the harbour master for a $1000 bribe in order to allow his ship to enter the port and unload the cargo, always remembering that each day that the ship is delayed will cost the company $1 million.

I begin by observing that facilitation payments such as these are illegal under the UKBA. If this particular company was in the habit of making them on a regular basis then there would certainly be a problem. Is this likely, however? What do people think?

David Hurley takes the lead here. I have been struck by how engaged David has been through-out the presentation – bribery and corruption is clearly an issue that he feels strongly about. He makes the point that the scenario is artificial because in reality a company that trades interna-tionally is unlikely to be confronted by a situation such as this where these actions of the harbour master are so completely unexpected. The company's aim should be to create a reputation whereby no one asks it for bribes. This means being proactive, committing to a period of working hard on the ground, during which the company and its local managers take the time to get to know the officials (including in this case the harbour master) and make it clear to them that the company has an anti-bribery policy and simply does not pay bribes. All requests for them will be refused and referred to the authorities. I am genuinely impressed by this and say so – this is an excellent sum-mary and David clearly has a good insight into what is required to make an anti-bribery policy work in practice.

Just to explore this a little deeper, I ask what would they do if this scenario really did happen – for example, if this was the first time that one of the company's ships had tried to dock at this particular port. John Holt, the CEO, is concerned about the significant loss that might result from a refusal to pay the bribe. He is clearly tempted to instruct the Captain to pay the $1000, although in this case he would also instruct the Captain to make it clear to the harbour master and to the local authorities that this is a one-off payment that would not be made again. He has heard about the guidance from the UK authorities regarding facilitation payments: these are classified as bribes but the authorities are much more tolerant of one-off payments than they are of any ongoing arrangements, which they are likely to regard as systemic bribery. So, this might be a pragmatic solution, but John is clearly unsure and uneasy.

Rachel Gordon, the Chairman, agrees with John's last point but thinks it is a technical one and she is very uncomfortable with the idea of paying the bribe.

Clarity is brought by Malcolm himself. Malcolm says that, if it were up to him he would instruct the Captain not to pay the bribe but to look for other solutions – perhaps speaking to the local author-ities, perhaps unloading the cargo in another port. He is not sure of the precise details. He is sure of one thing, however – Stronach's zero tolerance of bribery would be compromised if the payment were to be made. Malcolm adds the comment that this would be going back to some of the practices of the past when the previous chairman and CEO was able to do whatever he liked, providing that it made money. His was a short-term view and, as everyone in the room knows very well, it had almost backfired during the negotiations in India when Stronach barely escaped serious reputational dam-age. John Holt is nodding his head, acknowledging the point. I am both surprised and impressed to hear this from Malcolm. I had not realised until now quite how frustrated he had been under the old regime at Stronach – I had simply assumed that he had been an integral part of it.

I draw the debate to a close by thanking everyone for their contributions and thanking Malcolm for raising the question in the first place – to me this discussion has shown very well the value of dilemma-based scenario analysis, a view that all the team members are in agreement with.

Key takeaways

By way of a conclusion to the workshop, I have a question for the team and I introduce it by making an observation: there seemed to be a lot of note-taking going on by everyone when I was talking about the UKBA and, in particular, when I was going through the issues faced and the subsequent actions taken by two of my clients in this regard. This suggests that there might be some unease about Stronach's current position, so I ask each one of them to note down on the flipchart the priority issue around compliance with the UKBA from their own individual perspective. This is what they came up with:

✓ **The quality of the risk assessment process**. This is the issue of most concern to the CEO, John Holt. John says that the key to adequate procedures under the UKBA is sound assessment of both internal and external bribery risks, but he is unsure how adequate this particular procedure is at Stronach. He has some questions that he does not know the answer to and this makes him nervous: Who has responsibility for oversight of this at board level; how well is the bribery risk profile communicated around the business; and how often and how rigorously is it updated? John has been impressed by the example I gave of the medium-sized business where, because the managing director there had taken the lead, full compliance with the UKBA was implemented quickly. He now makes a commitment to personal oversight of the bribery risk assessment process at Stronach in the future.

✓ **The nature and rigour of the training programme**. This point comes from David Hurley, the HR Manager. Like many organisations, Stronach rolled out a compliance training programme to its managers and staff in the summer of 2011 when the UKBA first come into effect. David is concerned that, apart from the addition of an anti-bribery component in the induction training for all new hires, little more has been done. He feels that the company is not meeting in full the requirements of the official guidance, which he now understands to be demanding and to go much further than a one-off training course. He says that he will take it upon himself to review the position, including researching the most effective way to deliver ongoing anti-bribery training to Stronach's workforce. David says that he will also look at the effectiveness of the current ethical training and development provided by the Group. Rachel, the Chairman, is very supportive of this and asks to be briefed by David on the results, with a view to presenting a proposal at the next but one board meeting.

✓ **The adequacy of due diligence processes**. The Group Finance Director, Malcolm Mainwaring, is concerned that Stronach's knowledge of some of its suppliers and business partners is not as good as it could be, especially in its operations overseas. He fears that a risk-based approach is not in reality always taken. This makes him feel uncomfortable – there are no specific cases that cause him concern, it is more a general sense of unease. He says that he will review the procedures and will also commission the internal audit department to carry out some work in this area. Malcolm then asks me if I can put him in touch with one of the specialist risk consultancies that I mentioned – he wishes to gain additional assurance on some of the third parties used in operations in countries with a significant bribery risk, such as India. I say that I will be happy to do so of course.

✓ **The effectiveness of whistle-blower arrangements**. Rachel Gordon, the Chairman, expresses her concern that the company's reporting hotline is not working effectively. She is not aware of any reports being made via the hotline during her time at Stronach – the other members of the team confirm that disclosure levels have always been low since the whistle-blowing procedure was established three years ago. Rachel asks what can be done to gain a better understanding of whether or not the process is effective. She feels that this is a critical area, not only for compliance with the UKBA but also for the ethics project generally. I agree completely with this view and make the point that, in my experience, there are two broad questions that need to be answered before the effectiveness of whistle-blower arrangements can be assessed: First, do the employees know about the hotline; and second, do they trust it? This is an important subject and quite a complex one too. So, rather than spending time now discussing it, I recommend that we allocate one of the subsequent workshops to the whistle-blowing question. Everyone agrees with this suggestion.

Next workshop

A date has already been agreed for the next workshop, again in four weeks' time. The team is keen to pick up and discuss further one of the principles surrounding the UKBA, namely that of top-level commitment. Specifically: How can directors and senior managers best demonstrate ethical leadership and what actions can they themselves take to improve the Group's performance in this area? I am also asked whether I can provide good examples of how that well-known phrase 'tone at the top' actually works in practice? Can we address these issues in the next workshop?

I say that we can indeed do this, but before we agree to do so there is an observation that I want the team to consider first. In my view, risk is the key driver of many aspects of business today and this is true in the areas of reputation and business ethics also. My preference would be to use the next workshop to look at various aspects of risk, especially reputational risk and how issues such as the conduct of senior managers and staff can impact upon it. This would provide a strong foundation on which to examine the topics of governance and leadership subsequently. Once the risks to corporate reputation have been discussed and understood, then we will be in a better position to consider the various structures and controls (of which governance is one) that are required to manage these risks during the later workshops. What does everyone think?

After only a brief discussion the team members are in agreement. The subject of the next workshop will be reputation and the risks surrounding it, with particular focus on the damage that can be caused to an organisation by the actions and behaviour of its people. I observe that there will be much to discuss so we might need more time. Rachel says that she will try to coordinate diaries with a view to having a three-hour workshop next time.

I thank Rachel and the team for their agreement to this and also for their participation during the workshop.

Reflections

As I enter the lift to leave the building at the conclusion of the workshop, I am joined by an out of breath Malcolm Mainwaring who tells me that he is running late for a meeting in the City with Stronach's bankers. As I begin to apologise for the 10-minute overrun on the workshop, Malcolm interrupts: 'Don't you worry about that at all. The Chairman believes that the ethics project is important for the future of our business and I happen to agree with her. And Steve, I am enjoying these workshops of yours ... great fun and very refreshing to be able to talk about all these things. It's a big change from the old days – for the better, mostly.' With that, the lift reaches the ground floor, we shake hands and say our goodbyes.

I walk out of the building and into Berkeley Square, reflecting on how, sometimes, first impressions can be misleading. When I first met Malcolm, I had not warmed to him at all – he seemed impatient, irritable and with little time for or engagement with the project. I knew that he was part of the 'old guard' at Stronach and, although as Group Finance Director I wanted him to be part of the team, I suspected that he might prove to be an obstacle to the smooth running of the workshops. How wrong I turned out to be!

CHAPTER FOUR

Reputation, risk and conduct

 REPUTATIONAL RISK: THIRD WORKSHOP

Opening

I arrive early for this morning's workshop, the third in the series as part of Stronach's ethics project. Today we will be looking at aspects of reputation and in particular how corporate reputation can be affected by the ways managers and staff behave and conduct themselves. These are important subjects – by analysing them, my aim is to help the ethics team to improve Stronach's existing compliance and controls framework so that the board has greater assurance that reputational risk is being managed in the most appropriate way for their business.

Agenda

I welcome everyone as they come in. We have a lot to cover today and so I quickly take the team through the agenda over coffee. The workshop will be divided broadly into four sections, as follows:

- First of all we will look at corporate reputation, including the components that are most important to the idea of a 'brand' and focus, through examples, on the reasons for reputational damage.
- We will then re-visit the Siemens example. This time we will change the focus and look at the measures that Siemens had to put in place in order to repair the damage to its reputation brought about by the corruption scandal that we looked at in the previous workshop.
- Third, we will consider behaviour. Specifically, the various threats from what I term 'people risk' – those attitudes, actions and behaviours of people within an organisation that can cause harm to others, either to the organisation itself or to its stakeholders. Included in the discussion will be reference to the concept of conduct risk, the new focus of regulatory attention in the financial services industry. My overarching aim will be to demonstrate that it is the actions and

judgements of people rather than process failures that bring organisations into disrepute. It is operational risk and specifically the human factors of operational risk that can cause most damage to corporate reputation.

▪ Finally, we will look at the area of ethical risk. Because of digitisation and social media, this is a more important area of risk today than it has ever been before. I will use a series of examples including a review of the Edward Snowden case. Every organisation needs to identify where ethical risk lies in its own stakeholder base and take steps to manage and mitigate it.

Risk

But I want to begin the workshop with a brief overview of the concept of risk and to explore, in particular, what risk management means to the members of the team and to the Stronach Group as a whole.

I start by saying that, while the effective management of risk has always been a feature of successful businesses, risk management has developed over the last 30 years or so into a formalised process, the main components of which have been taken up by organisations of all sizes and in all sectors. I explain that it is not my purpose today to review the business discipline of risk management – the processes used today to identify, assess, prioritise, manage, mitigate, communicate and report on risk. Rather we will concentrate on one particular aspect that is central to the ethics project, that of reputational risk.

I know already from my discussions with Rachel Gordon, the Chairman, that Stronach has a well-established risk management system in place, comprising policies, registers and risk professionals, together with a training component and a reporting process. But I want to get a feel today for what these four executives operating right at the top of the organisation really think about risk, what their particular focus is and to what extent they have been successful in embedding a risk-aware culture throughout the Stronach Group. I propose to do so by means of a Risk Awareness Quiz, something that I have used to good effect in the past with many different groups.

Risk awareness quiz

I walk over to the flipchart. On the chart I have already written down five key questions to do with risk that I want the team to consider, as follows:

▪ What is risk?
▪ Who is responsible for managing risk in the Stronach Group?
▪ Are you looking to minimise risk at Stronach?
▪ How is risk measured?
▪ What are the two key questions that must be asked when assessing the strength of the internal controls framework that is in place at Stronach to manage the risks?

I do not begin with the first question, however, but instead point to question number three on the chart.

Are you looking to minimise risk at Stronach?

I ask for those who think that the answer to this question is 'yes' to raise their hand: David Hurley, the HR Manager, immediately puts his hand up; Malcolm Mainwaring, the Finance Director starts to raise his hand but then thinks better of it; neither Rachel nor John Holt, the CEO, make any movement. So, I ask John what he is doing, as CEO, if he is not seeking to minimise risk throughout the Stronach Group. Straight away he replies: 'My job is to manage risk.' This is an excellent answer and I say so. I am impressed – every organisation needs to take some measure of risk in order to achieve its objectives and this risk must be managed.

Before setting out how I might respond to this question, I apologise to David Hurley for having ambushed him like this so early in the morning – if I had given him more time to think, he would no doubt have responded differently. David smiles a little sheepishly – seeing this, I am actually not so sure. No matter.

I have a particular point to make and I use my own situation as a freelance consultant to illustrate what I mean. I say that if it was my intention to minimise my own risk then I would not be here with them all today facilitating this workshop – absolutely not. There are various good reasons to think this: in order to reach Stronach's offices, I have to drive my car on one of the most dangerous roads in the country; and then get on board a crowded underground train; before putting my professional reputation on the line in front of such a tough group of senior managers! So, if my objective is simply to minimise my risk, I would have stayed at home, no doubt enjoyed a nice breakfast, read the newspaper and generally had a relaxing and stress-free day. However, from a business perspective, choosing to stay at home would give me two problems: first, I would not get paid; and second I would not achieve one of my main aims in business, which is to work with organisations to improve their performance.

Everyone understands the point. To conclude on this question I say that I always encourage organisations to go a stage further than John has indicated in his answer. We have agreed that organisations today should not be thinking of minimising risk. However, if they really want to add value, then they should be aiming not only at managing risk but also at optimising the level of risk that they are operating with at any point in time. Here the crucial reference point will be each organisation's unique risk appetite – broadly, how much the organisation is prepared to put at risk in the pursuit of value. As with individuals, risk appetite varies from organisation to organisation.

Again, the team members nod in agreement. John in particular is enthusiastic – he says that he will use the idea of optimising risk as a way of promoting a risk-aware culture. He feels that it will help to change people's perception of risk management around the Group, so that it becomes more of a motivational tool and less of an irritating form-filling exercise that is seen to take up valuable time for little purpose.

This is encouraging and leads naturally to my next question, which is the first one listed on the flipchart.

What is risk?

I ask the team to call out those words or phrases that are most meaningful to them when thinking about the term 'risk' – I will note them all down on the flipchart. After a short period of rapid-fire answers, these are the words that I have written down on the chart: 'threats'; impact and probability'; 'events that stop us achieving our objectives'; 'things that go wrong'; 'unexpected'; 'harmful'; 'managing the unknown' and 'contingencies'.

I stop them there to make an observation: most of these answers focus on downside risk – threats, harm, things that can go wrong. I say that I understand very well the importance of managing threats – I am an English chartered accountant after all and in many ways I am one of the most naturally risk-averse of people. However, the effect of concentrating on threats and harm is sometimes to lose sight of the other side of the risk equation, which is opportunity. Where people and organisations are prepared to dare, to take a chance in the pursuit of their objectives, they are often rewarded with success. I stress that I am not advocating gambling or taking a reckless approach here, not at all. Rather, I am talking about taking action when opportunities present themselves based on a careful assessment of all the circumstances. This is an integral part of what risk management is all about.

For me, risk means uncertainty, in particular uncertainty of outcome – if we could only know for sure what is going to happen to us in the future then there would be no risk and we could all prepare for tomorrow with absolute assurance. This is impossible of course, we cannot foresee the future. The future will always be uncertain and in an uncertain world, two things can happen: there is the threat of loss (indeed there are many and varied threats that need to be assessed and managed); but there will also be opportunities. Success comes from managing both sides of the risk equation effectively.

So, this leads to a simple and powerful definition of risk management: 'a discipline for managing uncertainty'. Organisations need to be aware always of both opportunities and threats when setting strategy and in their decision-making.

Who is responsible for managing risk in the Stronach Group?

This next question about responsibility is important. When I work with any organisation for the first time I like to understand how the directors and senior managers answer it as soon as I can because the answers will provide me with a strong indicator of that organisation's understanding of and approach to the management of risk.

So, what is the answer here at Stronach? Rachel Gordon very quickly gives me the one-word response: 'everyone'. The others all nod to signify their agreement. This is a powerful answer and I say so. I have an observation to make, however: this answer was rare when I first started asking the responsibility question some 15 years ago, but now I hear it all the time. I am a little sceptical, therefore, and have a supplemental question for them: If I was to ask the same question of four other people in the Stronach Group, this time selected at random from amongst the managers and staff, are they confident that I would receive the same answer? They are hesitant, not so confident now. I reassure them that this is a common response to the supplemental question. It indicates to me that more attention could be given to the training and awareness-raising of all staff around risk and risk management. This training should start at induction and be ongoing thereafter. I give them another observation: in my experience if employees, especially junior staff, do not receive any training in these areas, they are likely to assume that risk management is concerned simply with health and safety risk assessments – an important part of risk management, but only a part.

I then phrase the question in a slightly different way: Who has ultimate responsibility at Stronach for managing risk? Again, the reply is swift, this time coming from John Holt who answers: 'The board of directors, particularly me.' I feel like clapping! This is absolutely the right answer and demonstrates good awareness from the CEO. Ultimate responsibility for the management of risk resides at the top of an organisation, always.

Just to check, I ask if anyone has anything else to add by way of an answer to the responsibility question. Malcolm mentions the risk coordination manager. Now, this officer clearly will have a number of job-specific responsibilities for managing risk, but he or she will not work in isolation.

I suggest that organisations should be looking to the broad category of their business managers to manage risk. In my view it is the departmental heads, the line managers, the team leaders who manage risk on the ground, day to day, in every department and in every operation. A fundamental principle of modern risk management is that risk devolves to the line. Is this happening at Stronach? From the responses given by the team, it appears to me that it is not happening or, to be fair, it is not happening consistently throughout the business.

To conclude on this question, I say that what we have been discussing here is a powerful responsibility framework for risk management that I recommend to all organisations regardless of size or business sector. Risk management should be devolved throughout an organisation: the board of directors will have ultimate responsibility; this should be delegated to management, in particular to line managers and team leaders; and to make it all work, everyone in the organisation should be aware of his or her responsibilities in terms of managing risk as part of meeting their personal objectives.

It is important that this responsibility framework is working at each of these three levels. I say that we will be looking for evidence that this is the case in Stronach throughout this ethics project. As examples of the areas that we will cover:

- The Stronach board is clearly taking responsibility for risk management, but is it always asking the right questions and considering the key risks? We will look at some aspects of this concerning reputation and conduct risk later on during this workshop.
- I am always interested in the goals and targets that managers are set each year. For example, if I do not see the word 'risk' featuring in the managers' objectives then I will remain sceptical about whether those managers are really focused on their risk management responsibilities. We will consider the design of performance assessment and remuneration packages later in the project.
- Training and development programmes provide one of the most important controls in any area of business, not least in risk management. Without training in risk management, it is unlikely that all managers and staff will understand their individual responsibilities to manage risk. We will look at the whole area when we review the review the ethical toolbox – in my view training is one of the most important tools in the box.

How is risk measured?

This question is straightforward and all the team members know the 'correct' answer to it. There are two key metrics that are most commonly used to measure risk: impact (or severity) and probability (or frequency). Impact is the measure of the severity of an event should it materialise. Probability is the likelihood of an event materialising during a certain period of time.

I briefly describe to them two recent and related developments in risk management: first, the greater involvement of those at board level in overseeing strategic risks; and second, the focus on high-impact events, especially those hidden or underestimated risks that can cause serious damage to an organisation. Examples include: fraud, corruption and information theft; cyber-crime; brand damage (increased through the speed and potential reach of attacks on social media); IT failures; and problems arising from the actions of third parties in the supply chain, where the root cause is often inadequate due diligence processes.

There is a lot of interest in the room around these high-impact risks that I have briefly listed – clearly, a number of them at least have special relevance to the circumstances at Stronach. I point out that the common factor that links them all together is reputation, which is of course the subject of this current workshop. This means that we will be picking up some of these threats today. Indeed, we will be looking at aspects of all of them at some stage during the course of the ethics project.

What are the two key questions that must be addressed when assessing internal controls?

Malcolm, being the accountant, takes the lead in answering this question about internal controls. His actual answer is very concise: 'We need to ensure that the controls are efficient and effective.' Again, this is an excellent answer and during the subsequent discussion it becomes clear that Malcolm's ideas are absolutely aligned with my own on the subject of internal controls.

I thank Malcolm and say that I like his answer very much. I want to develop it slightly. Of the two questions, the first should be directed towards the design of the control. Malcolm nods and says that this is exactly what he meant by the word 'efficient' – the control design should always be aligned with and proportionate to the associated risk. I give him a 'thumbs up' gesture – exactly so. Risk drives controls, not the other way around. I make the observation that this first question is often overlooked in practice (whether by line managers, internal auditors or compliance officers) with the result that control gaps can arise. While risk is dynamic and can change very quickly, the controls in place to manage risk can sometimes remain largely static, so that they can seem to be almost anchored in the past. If risk increases and controls remain the same, then control gaps are created. There is real danger for organisations if these control gaps are allowed to widen over time because they will create exposures. As an example, the risk of fraud increased significantly during the recent global financial crisis at a time when many organisations were reducing their staffing levels, especially in middle-manager positions. As a result, certain anti-fraud controls, such as segregation of duties, were reduced at precisely the least appropriate time for this to happen.

The second key question that needs to be asked is whether or not the control is working in practice in accordance with the control design. Everyone in business knows that simply having a control documented in a procedures' manual is no guarantee that the control is working as it should be. I just check to make sure that this is what Malcolm had in mind when he used the word 'efficient' in his answer. He nods his head and gives me a 'thumbs up' gesture in return.

I conclude the quiz by thanking all of the team for their participation in the discussion – it has given me a good insight into the awareness and understanding of risk among the team members. The quiz has also provided a good introduction to today's session on reputation and people risk.

With that, I begin the presentation.

REPUTATION

Reputation and brand

Introduction

The threat of damage to reputation, whether personal or corporate, is one of the biggest risks of the twenty-first century. Reputation itself has various components. First, it is based around competence and ability – the precise technical skills and craftsmanship vary from business sector to business sector of course, but competency is a baseline requirement for all organisations. Other important aspects of reputation include: consistency (past performance is an indicator of likely future outcomes); innovation and style; comparison with competitors; fair treatment; and how matters are handled and communicated when mistakes are made.

There is a close connection here with the concepts and components of business ethics that we have already considered. For example, it is consistency of performance that establishes an organisation's track record; it is the track record that produces confidence that the organisation is doing things right and this in turn is the foundation of trust, the 'x-factor' that organisations are looking to engender in their stakeholders. Trust combined with respect (arising out of successful performance) produces positive public perception. All of these factors combine to bring about the prospect of sustainability and long-term success.

For an organisation these components provide the essential building blocks on which positive corporate branding and image can be built. For individuals, they provide the essence of our character, of our personal brand if you will.

Each of us, as individuals and as part of organisations in our working lives, should think carefully about our actions and the possible implications of them on our reputation. As the legendary investor Warren Buffett puts it in one of his most frequently quoted remarks: 'It takes 20 years to build a reputation and five minutes to ruin it. If you think about that you'll do things differently.'[1]

The concept of the brand

In order to learn more about brands and corporate reputation, I spoke to Peter Walshe, an expert in this area. Peter is a global account director at Millward Brown, the leading brand, media and communications market research consultancy firm. Aside from the vast experience he has gained from working in this field for over 25 years, Peter is the man who, in 1998, invented the study known as 'Brand Z'. He has run it every year since then on behalf of the WPP Group. The 'Brand Z' study now incorporates an extensive piece of research covering some 10,000 brands in over 30 countries, which has resulted in a huge database of information. Since 2006, Millward Brown has built on this to compile a valuation of brands, which it puts together in a league table each year. This valuation is a combination of two things: the corporation's financial results multiplied by the 'brand contribution'. So, if anyone understands brands and what makes those brands tick, it is Peter Walshe.

I began the interview with Peter by asking him to describe the key components of a brand that would differentiate one from another. This is what he had to say:

> There are three key metrics if you like that drive the success of a brand and we know that because we validate all our data against actual market performance.
>
> The first of these is being meaningful. If the associations that you as a consumer have about the brand are relatively meaningful that means that you think that the brand meets your needs for the category. So in a sense that could be rational, but it's not entirely a rational process because there is the factor of the brand's appeal and whether you 'love it'. So meaningfulness is a mixture of the emotional and the rational – the brand stands out to you as a consumer because it is unique in that sense.
>
> The second thing is differentiation. Is the brand unique in a positive way? The key factor underpinning this is whether the brand is setting the trend or whether it is perceived to be setting the trend. In other words it's doing good things for you as a consumer so you feel you are going to get a good deal from it.
>
> And the third area is saliency. So, as a consumer, when you think of your needs or when you go to buy a product and have a choice to make, does this particular brand come ahead of its competitors spontaneously in terms of meeting your individual needs.
>
> So we have the three factors: meaningful, different and salient. These factors combine to produce a brand which: first of all will sell more so it will have a greater volume share; secondly it will have the ability to command a greater premium because it is more meaningful, different and salient; and thirdly it will have potential for the future. If all three exist the consequence is that it is almost set up as if you have a pre-disposition to purchase this brand ahead of all its competitors. It all sounds a bit technical but it is not – in essence it is the relationship that each consumer has got with the brand.

The linkage between brands and corporate reputation

The focus of Peter's work on brands is of course primarily on the consumer, both individuals and business-to-business. However, he went on to make the important point that the data he collects is increasingly showing the merging of the brand with corporate reputation – it is becoming much harder to distinguish what the corporation is doing from the brand that it owns. Because of this, Peter has developed a parallel measure looking at the corporation rather than the brand. This is how he described the findings:

> We ask a series of quite simple questions, again being validated, and we can summarise the answers into four areas.
>
> The first and the most important area is leadership. This then links back directly to the sales for that brand. Leadership is really about a perception of being successful and a perception of leading the way and often of being innovative. So, it's almost a mix of the brand factors we discussed before of being meaningful and different.
>
> The second area is what we call fairness. Fairness is the whole mix involved in the perception that I – whether that is 'me' as an individual consumer or 'me' as the b-2-b man dealing with IBM or whoever it is – am getting a good deal. It's not just money and cost, it's actually value in a much more rounded sense. There is also a component of whether the corporation is perceived as treating its employees and suppliers fairly. So, there is a big wrap around in terms of fairness which goes right the way through from what happens inside the company to how it deals with outsiders. What the perception is, regarding fairness, is very important – it's quite a hard measure.
>
> In fact leadership and fairness are the two things that between them comprise about two thirds of the effect of the corporate reputation that is driving sales.
>
> The other one third is split between two things. The first is responsibility. So this is more traditionally what people would think of as corporate responsibility. Traditionally this sits somewhere in the corporate responsibility department, but actually it is increasingly very much a part of a much bigger thing. In my view it should not be dealt with separately at all. You know that there are different aspects of responsibility: obviously to treat the earth responsibly, so environmental responsibility; also being a responsible corporate citizen; and treating other people fairly.
>
> And the final area is trust. Trust is of course potentially an outcome of the aforementioned factors being present but the perception of trust is important as well.
>
> So corporate reputation depends upon four factors: leadership and fairness; responsibility and trust. When you put these together a corporation that is going to be successful and to have a positive reputation is likely to be driven more by leadership and fairness because they are worth more if the corporation scores well on those measures, rather than by scoring well on responsibility and trust.
>
> But a corporation can still be let down by shortcomings in the areas of responsibility and trust – its overall score can still be reduced. Overall if a corporation is really successful in the marketplace these shortfalls are not always evident. This is part of the dilemma I think. Companies that are very successful, maybe achieved through cutting their costs, maybe by outsourcing, then maybe being tempted to cut wages and conditions or not to improve them and to ignore some of those responsibility issues, they may well continue to be financially very successful and so on, at

least in the short term. But there is something, you know, some concern – a small cancer poten-
tially that could spread and could act in a way to begin to eat away at that success.

Peter's analysis of brand and corporate reputation is very insightful: the observation that the brand can no longer be viewed as separate from the underlying corporation that owns it; and the identification of four key factors that are the critical components of corporate reputation: leadership, fairness, responsibility and trust. All four are closely connected to the theme of business ethics and we look at each of them at various stages of the book.

Consequences of damaged reputation

Individuals

The book does not focus on individual reputation, but the examples used invariably include aspects of individual behaviour. As a general observation, it is more difficult for individuals to regain reputation lost through their actions than it is for organisations to do so, though for both the process of trust-repair can be a long one.

There are many examples that illustrate the truth of Mr Buffett's maxim that reputation takes years to build but only minutes to destroy. In terms of what can happen to individuals, old newspaper copy is full of stories of politicians, celebrities and sports stars whose careers have been tarnished by scandal arising out of any one or a combination of a wide range of potential activities from social misdemeanours to criminality.

In terms of the business world, it is bankers who have been the focus of much of the public opprobrium since the global financial crisis. Perhaps the clearest example of damaged reputation here is provided by the case of Fred Goodwin, who was the CEO of the Royal Bank of Scotland plc (RBS) in the run up to its near collapse in 2008. The bank was only saved from disaster by the injection of approximately £45bn of public funds to provide necessary liquidity by the UK Government. It subsequently reported losses of over £24bn – the largest annual loss in UK corporate history. Formerly Sir Fred Goodwin (he had been knighted in 2004 for services to banking), Mr Goodwin became the target of much anger and criticism in subsequent years. This combined a business narrative around allegations of poor decision-making and extravagance (for example, the purchase of the Dutch Bank ABN Amro in 2007) with a more personal focus on his alleged arrogance and domineering management style.[2] This negative campaign culminated in 2012 when the Queen cancelled and annulled his knighthood on advice from Whitehall, despite Mr Goodwin not being the subject of any criminal allegations or charges.[3]

Another example from the financial world is that of Paul Flowers, the ex-Chairman of the Co-op Bank, who was filmed in November 2013 in the back of a motor car apparently trying to buy illegal drugs. The footage was subsequently sold to the *Mail on Sunday* newspaper and thereafter attracted widespread interest and almost universally negative commentary. Although Paul Flowers had stepped down from his role at the Co-op Bank six months earlier, he had been a powerful figure in the co-operative movement for many years, as well as being a local politician and a Methodist Minister. The newspaper disclosures were confirmed when in 2014 he pleaded guilty to charges of possessing cocaine, methamphetamine and ketamine. The personal reputation of the Reverend Flowers, built up over decades, has been severely damaged by these events. We will look at the example of the Co-op Bank and the Rev. Flowers in detail in Chapter 6 of the book.

How easy might it be for individuals to regain lost reputation? It varies, of course, from case to case. But in the business world the indicators are that it takes time and it may well be difficult to resurrect a career in the same industry sector or at the same level of seniority as previously held.

In the case of Mr Goodwin, some commentators at the time felt that his analytical skills, his abilities as a project manager and experience of running one of the biggest organisations in the world would mean that he would soon be in demand again. It has not turned out that way. In 2010 he was employed as a senior advisor to RMJM, an international firm of architects. He left the position within one year and has not been in employment since.

It is far too early to consider whether the Rev. Flowers will be able to restore his reputation. The case of John Galliano, although very different, might provide some indicators.

The year 2011 saw the sudden and dramatic fall from grace of the British fashion designer John Galliano. Following reports of an anti-Semitic outburst in a Paris bar, the French media obtained a video of a similar rant made by him some months earlier. This was then widely reported in the press. Mr Galliano soon lost his job, despite a brilliant 15-year career at the Christian Dior fashion house, and he was then dropped from his own fashion label. Mr Galliano was subsequently found guilty by a French Court of 'giving public insults on account of race'.[4]

His response was to withdraw himself from the public spotlight and make extensive apologies to all those offended by his comments. He has expressed deep regret and provided the public with an explanation (not an excuse) that his rant was brought about by a mix of drugs and alcohol. He sees an addiction specialist three times a week. In 2013, he took tentative steps towards a comeback in the fashion industry by taking up temporary residency in Oscar de la Renta's studio in New York, but this arrangement did not develop into a permanent position. In May 2014, over three years after the original scandal, it was announced that Mr Galliano had moved from fashion to the beauty arena with his appointment as creative director of L'Etoile, the Russian cosmetics company. This was perhaps not a job with the glamour and reach of a famous French fashion house, but it was a positive step towards restoring his reputation nevertheless. It turned out to be highly significant because in October 2014 it was announced that Mr Galliano is to return to high-end fashion as creative director of French fashion house Maison Martin Margiela.[5]

Corporations

Corporations are also vulnerable to reputational damage, of course. There are a variety of reasons why a corporate reputation or a brand might become tarnished, but two broad categories are crucial. The first is association with a health and safety disaster: death, human tragedy and environmental damage can tarnish corporate reputation very quickly. The second is involvement in fraud, corruption or some other form of financial crime scandal. Both carry the additional threat, depending on the circumstances, of criminal liability and regulatory sanctions.

Set out below are two examples that illustrate what can happen to corporations if they are caught up in a safety failure or a financial crime scandal. They are extreme examples but they show very well how dangerous reputational damage can be to the organisations concerned. The first looks at a recent and notorious disaster event.

Example 1: BP plc

BP's corporate reputation was severely damaged following the disastrous explosion and fire on the Deepwater Horizon offshore oil platform in the Macondo Prospect oil field in the Gulf of Mexico (of which it was the principal developer) in April 2010.[6] The tragedy resulted in the deaths of 11 men working on the Deepwater Horizon platform and in a massive oil spillage, environmental damage and economic harm. It was the worst maritime oil spill in history. BP has set aside over $42bn to 'make things right'.

The reputational damage to BP has manifested itself in many ways. On one level, there is the impact of the tragedy on the company share price, which halved in the months following the tragedy. In fact, BP shares remain depressed and, at the time of writing, the share price has yet to recover to its pre-disaster levels, some four years after the explosion. The BP brand has been damaged also, most notably in its key market of the United States. Trust and respect for BP in the USA have been significantly reduced despite the corporation's efforts to be fair and even generous in its compensation payments to the many local businesses and individuals that have suffered financial loss as a result of the tragedy. The litigation process continues in the USA, in particular the question of whether the courts there will find BP to have been 'grossly negligent'. The reputations of a number of key individuals within the company have also suffered, most notably that of BP's ex-CEO, Tony Hayward, who became almost a 'hate-figure' in the USA, following a number of ill-judged comments and poorly received performances in front of the American media.

The drive for profits is enormous and hugely pressurised in the oil and gas industry. Interestingly, BP's competitors did not seek to make capital out of the Deepwater Horizon tragedy because the risk of disaster is an industry-wide concern. Certainly, BP is not alone in terms of incurring damage to its reputation as the result of a health and safety scandal: Union Carbide (the Bhopal tragedy in India); Exxon (the 'Exxon Valdez' disaster); and Occidental (the fire on the Piper Alpha rig) are other examples from the chemicals and energy sectors.

The second broad area of threat to corporate reputation is involvement in financial crime and malfeasance. Reports implicating an organisation in issues such as fraud or bribery and corruption can be just as corrosive to corporate reputation as death and environmental tragedies – they can tarnish brands and destroy confidence in a business very quickly. There are numerous examples of this over the last 30 years including: Polly Peck, BCCI and Barings Bank in the UK; Enron, WorldCom and Bernard L Madoff Investment Securities LLC in the USA; Parmalat in Italy; Olympus in Japan; and Satyam in India.

I am going to use a different example here to illustrate the reputational risks of being associated with a financial scandal, however, because for me personally this particular chain of events conveys the importance of reputation to a business better than any other case. It concerns a firm of accountants. I am a chartered accountant myself and I worked in the profession for many years – not for the accounting firm concerned in this example I should say. Still, this case has particular resonance for me.

Example 2 below tells the story of what happened to one of the world's leading accountancy firms at the start of the twenty-first century. At that time there were five global accounting firms, today there are only four. And I must say that if anyone had suggested to me in the year 2000 that, less than three years later, one of those five firms would effectively no longer exist I would probably have thought that the person was delusional. This firm had tens of thousands of highly trained professional staff working in offices all around the world and their clients included many of the world's largest and most sophisticated organisations. Yet in short order this same firm's integrity was questioned by a court decision, an extreme event that severely damaged its reputation and caused it to lose many of its clients. In fact, the firm became fatally holed beneath the water line and it lost its core business as a result. So, if anyone suggests that reputational risk is exaggerated somehow or that it is not really all that serious an issue, please refer them to this case. The case concerns Arthur Andersen and this is a summary of what happened.

Example 2: Arthur Andersen (Andersen)

Mr Arthur Andersen founded the eponymous firm in 1913 in Chicago offering accounting, auditing and tax services. The firm quickly became known for an uncompromising adherence to accounting principles. It grew impressively throughout the twentieth century so that in the year 2000 it was the biggest accountancy firm in the world.

However, this success story came to an end in 2002 when Andersen was convicted of one count of obstruction of justice by a court in Houston, Texas.[7] It therefore became the first (and so far the only) accounting firm in history to receive a criminal conviction. On one level, this criminal conviction meant that the firm could no longer provide auditing services to publicly quoted corporations. On another level, it meant that the firm had lost its reputation for integrity and professionalism. Unsurprisingly, thereafter it lost its clients too. How could this have happened to Andersen, a well-respected global professional services firm?

Central to the case was Andersen's relationship with the Enron Corporation ('Enron'), the giant US energy, commodities and services company run by Ken Lay and Jeffrey Skilling based in Houston, Texas. Enron was an important client of Andersen both in terms of fee income and profile. It was a relationship that embroiled Andersen in controversy when Enron collapsed and filed for bankruptcy protection in 2001. The firm had acted as auditors and consultants to Enron for many years. Enron notoriously became bankrupt through corporate fraud.

Much has been made subsequently of the alleged conflicts of interest in Andersen's role as both auditor and consultant to Enron. For example, in 2000 Andersen was paid $25 million for its audit services to Enron and also received slightly more, $27 million a year, for providing Enron with consultancy services. Was it possible for Andersen to conduct a proper audit in these circumstances? Certainly, there were a number of close relationships among individuals working in the finance department at Enron's headquarters in Huston and the professional accountants in Andersen's local Huston office, with a number of secondments and transfers between the two – this network of relationships is highlighted by Bethany McLean and Peter Elkind in their book.[8] Andersen was aware of the risks in the relationship but also was keen to continue with it because Enron was a highly profitable client. So, Andersen tried to manage the risks – unsuccessfully as it turned out.

However, it would be wrong to think that Andersen's client relationships with Enron were extraordinary by the standards of the time. Rather, it was common practice for firms then to provide their audit clients with consulting advice. Indeed, the provision of consulting services was considered to be an essential part of the business models of the big accounting firms – audit fees alone were incapable of generating the required levels of profitability or revenue growth.

It is possible that Andersen might have been able to survive scrutiny of the competence of its audit work in the Enron case. The specific problem facing Andersen – and something that it was unable to deal with – was one of criminal liability. The firm was first accused and then found guilty by a court in Houston in June 2002 of the criminal offence of obstructing justice by shredding documents relating to the police's investigation into the Enron case. Of course, when the verdict was given both the criminal charge and Andersen's by now controversial relationship with Enron were in the public domain and the firm had already lost some business. The court's decision was anticipated, perhaps, but it had the effect of confirming that Andersen had lost its integrity, a core requirement for any professional services firm. Soon after the verdict, Andersen announced that it would stop auditing publicly traded companies, thereby pre-empting an almost certain official ban. Shortly thereafter, it started losing its remaining clients too. After all, why would an organisation pay millions of dollars a year to have Andersen audit its accounts when nobody believed what Andersen was saying anymore?

There is an irony in the ending of this story that is not often mentioned. Andersen appealed against the initial court judgement and the appeal turned out to be successful. In 2005, the Supreme Court overturned the original conviction in a unanimous vote. It found that Anderson had in fact shredded documents in accordance with its own document-shredding policy rather than as part of a scheme to obstruct the authorities. As a result, the firm could claim that it had acted professionally and properly throughout. However, the timing of the appeal hearing was far too late to save Andersen's reputation. The firm's brand had been fatally damaged and it simply could not recover. As a result, the five global accounting firms were reduced to four, a position that remains the same today.

There is one final misconception concerning Andersen. The firm never filed for bankruptcy. After the conviction, the audit, tax and consulting practices were separated and sold to various competitor firms. Andersen remains a business and it continues to operate a training facility for professionals in Illinois.

THE HUMAN FACTOR: PEOPLE, BEHAVIOUR AND CONDUCT RISK

Overview

Introduction

There have been many models developed over the last 20 years to help organisations to manage risk. These include: the governance risk and control models developed in the USA (Sarbanes–Oxley) and in the UK (Turnbull Guidance) around the turn of the last century; the Enterprise Risk Management framework developed by the Committee of Sponsoring Organisations (COSO); the Basel Capital Accords for the banking industry (Basel II and latterly Basel III); and the Three Lines of Defence model. It is important to note that none of these models is or claims to be a fail-safe system. Things can always go wrong, as was demonstrated spectacularly during the global financial crisis. Despite the sophisticated computer risk models that had been developed in financial services firms, the directors and senior managers of many international banks failed to manage the credit, market and operational risks on their books effectively – indeed the computer models may have contributed to the problem.

All these various risk models are vulnerable to technological failure and human factors. Technological failure includes systems glitches and back-office failures. In keeping with the theme of the book, we will concentrate on the second factor here, the various issues with behaviour that I like to refer to collectively as 'people risk'. Every risk management system can be undermined by people in a variety of ways including: human error; poor judgement; unexpected events; 'gaming' of the system; negligence and complacency.

People risk

Clearly, it is not only risk management models that can be affected by 'people risk'. The actions, behaviour and decision-making of people within an organisation, especially those at the top, can have a much broader impact upon the reputation of that organisation, sometimes with significant effect. We have seen that Peter Walsche's work at Millward Brown points clearly towards there being two pieces that are more important than all the others in the jigsaw of factors that combine to make up corporate reputation: leadership and fairness. So, poor decision-making, strategic mis-alignment, the failure to integrate a major acquisition successfully and other mistakes made by senior executives will tarnish reputation and erode value. Similar damage can be caused by actions that appear self-serving and damaging to the interests of stakeholders (for example, the current allegations and investigations into the mis-selling of products and the rigging of interest rate benchmarks that appear to have been carried out by many organisations and individuals in recent years in the financial services industry).

From my own experience, I have always felt that there are two core reasons for the scandals and failures that, from time to time, damage corporate reputation severely: poor decision-making, generally caused by a lack of awareness of emerging issues and the risks associated with them until it is too late; and/or integrity shortfalls brought about by factors such as greed and self-interest. I like to label these underlying causes as 'people risk', which allows an analysis by the four key component parts, as follows:

- incompetence;
- criminal or counter-productive workplace behaviours (including theft, fraud, corruption, collusion, insider trading and conflicts of interest);
- negligence and complacency, generally brought about by a lack of employee engagement; and
- 'custom and practice' – behaviours rooted in the organisation's traditions, developed over time and condoned by management so that they become an established part of corporate culture or else 'perks of the job' but without official recognition in policies and procedures.

We will look at these four aspects of people risk very shortly. But before we do so, it is instructive to consider the current focus being placed on the concept of conduct risk by regulators in the financial services industry around the world and especially in the UK.

The concept of conduct risk

Introduction

The aftermath of the global financial crisis has seen significant changes in the regulation of the financial services industry around the world. While the immediate priority was to strengthen the balance sheets of banks through capital and liquidity reforms, attention has now turned to the behaviour of firms in the sector and how they conduct their business.

The Financial Stability Board (FSB), which operates under the aegis of the G20, looks to develop and promote global financial services policies designed to prevent the likelihood of another financial crisis by, amongst other things, improving the behaviour and risk management within firms. In its Peer Review Report 'Thematic Review on Risk Governance' in 2013, the FSB identified business conduct as a new risk category:

> *One of the key lessons from the crisis was that reputational risk was severely underestimated; hence, there is more focus on business conduct and the suitability of products, e.g. the type of products sold and to whom they are sold. As the crisis showed, consumer products such as residential mortgage loans could become a source of financial instability.*[9]

This is official recognition of the critical role that reputation plays in the maintenance of a functioning financial system because it underpins market and consumer confidence. As we have seen, integrity and trust are essential requirements for confidence and this has led to a focus by regulators on the culture of individual firms and whether or not they are conducting their business in a fair way. So, as part of an attempt to improve the effectiveness of the supervision of national regulators around the world, the FSB has produced guidance on what constitutes a sound risk culture within a firm. It has identified four indicators, which the FSB says should be considered collectively rather than individually because they are mutually self-reinforcing, as follows:

- **Tone at the top**. The directors and senior managers are responsible for setting the financial institution's policies, values and risk culture. Their own behaviour must reflect these. They also need to put systems in place to assess how well policies and values are embedded and monitor progress going forward.
- **Accountability**. Effective risk management requires that employees at all levels understand the values of the institution's risk culture, have the competence to perform their roles and be aware that they will be held accountable for their actions in relation to the firm's risk-taking behaviour.
- **Effective challenge**. A culture promoting effective challenge and an environment of open and constructive engagement should be promoted.
- **Incentives**. Financial and non-financial incentives should support the values and risk culture at all levels of the firm.

Many of the global regulators are now focusing on these ideas, which are collectively being addressed as 'conduct risk'. In particular the SEC in the USA, the Securities and Investments Commission in Australia and the FCA in the UK are putting public trust and consumer and investor protection at the heart of their work.

The FCA in particular has developed its thinking on conduct risk since it was formed in 2013 and we will focus on the ideas and guidance provided by the FCA in this area in the paragraphs below.

Definition

The first thing to note is a surprising lack of clarity around what conduct risk actually means – despite all the 'noise' concerning conduct risk recently, it is difficult to find a clear definition of the phrase in the UK or elsewhere. This point was noted by Thomson Reuters in its Conduct Risk Report of 2013, a survey conducted with compliance and risk officers working in firms around the world: 'The concept of conduct risk is gathering momentum globally but there is still much work to be done and as yet there is no universal definition; 84% of respondents did not have a working firm-specific definition of "conduct risk".'[10]

The Financial Services Authority, the FCA's predecessor as regulator in the UK, had earlier given some guidance in the publication: Retail Conduct Risk Outlook 2011:

> Conduct risk – that is, the risk that firm behaviour will result in poor outcomes for customers.[11]

This serves as a good indicator and guide, although the application needs to be broader than simply a focus on retail conduct risk.

It is interesting to note that the FCA has refrained from following this up and has not issued a broad definition of conduct risk. This is deliberate. It has said that having the right culture – one that puts customers and market integrity at the heart of the firm's business – is an important component of conduct risk. However, the FCA takes the view that, as each firm will have its own conduct risk profile, it is not helpful to put a one-size-fits-all definition and framework in place to assess it.

The FCA has a wide set of strategic objectives: consumer protection for both the retail and the wholesale markets; safeguarding the financial system; and ensuring effective competition. In order to achieve these objectives, it is increasingly prepared to intervene earlier when it deals with regulated firms (for example, at the design stage in the lifecycle of financial products) and also to make judgements on the appropriateness of management decisions.

So, as a working definition, we may say that conduct risk has its roots in fairness to consumers. It is focused on risks to the delivery of fair customer outcomes, in addition to the outcomes themselves. In order to deliver fair outcomes the customer must be placed at the centre of the firm's business model.

The FCA's approach

The idea of treating customers fairly (TCF) has long been one of the principles of business for UK regulated firms, pre-dating the global financial crisis. However, the huge amounts paid out by banks as compensation to customers in recognition that certain financial products, for example payment protection insurance, together with the current allegations surrounding the rigging of interest rate and foreign exchange benchmarks that are being investigated by the authorities in the UK and around the world, indicate that the TCF principle was in fact never fully embedded within those firms.

The FCA is putting increasing onus on firms to define and manage conduct risk explicitly as part of their risk management framework. In order to assist, it identified three main drivers of conduct risk in the FCA Risk Outlook 2013:[12]

- inherent factors, such as information asymmetries, biases and inadequate financial capability;
- structures and behaviours, for example ineffective competition, culture and incentives and also conflicts of interest; and
- environmental factors including economic, regulatory and technological trends and changes.

The FCA Risk Outlook 2013 focuses on how firms are managed and structured. The aim is to ensure that firms treat their customers fairly by having robust systems and controls, adequate skill, care and appropriate judgement in place, rather than through luck, circumstance or where it could be argued that delivering fair customer outcomes is a convenient secondary objective to support the firm's commercial priorities.

Culture is a central theme throughout the report: 'Culture change within firms is essential if we are to restore trust and integrity to the financial sector and the FCA will continue to focus on how firms are managed and structured so that every decision they make is in the best interests of their customers.' It is clear from what the FCA also says in the report that the regulator does not think that this has always been the case in the financial services industry in the past: 'Some firms' cultures, processes and products have been designed to enable them to profit from consumer errors and to exploit their superior access to, or understanding of, information on financial products and services.'

 PEOPLE RISK

Introduction

The FCA is the UK's independent regulator charged with achieving a number of strategic objectives, central to which is protecting the interests of the consumer. Ensuring fairness to the consumer in both the design of financial products and the outcomes experienced by those using those products is the core message. This is reflected in the focus of the FCA's work and in the way that it is approaching the threats posed by conduct risk.

From my experience, however, I can see that one consequence of the way that managers and employees sometimes behave in the workplace is that their actions are harmful not only to the interests of customers, but those of other stakeholders too, such as employees, investors, suppliers and lenders. In addition, of course, egregious behaviour will often result in damage to the organisation itself.

In my view, human factors pose a higher threat to organisations than do process failures. For many years now I have used the phrase 'people risk' to categorise these factors and I still prefer to use it rather than refer to conduct risk, which does not have wide traction outside of the financial services industry. As mentioned above, I find it helpful to divide people risk into four component parts: incompetence; criminality and counter-productive workplace behaviours; lack of engagement, complacency and negligence; and what I term 'custom and practice'. We look at each component part in turn below.

Incompetence

Overview

Competence is one of the essential foundation stones of business success. Technical skill, proficiency and craftsmanship in all of the various departments and functions that combine to make up a modern organisation are fundamental requirements if consistency of performance is to be achieved. We have seen already that consistency of performance is one of the key requirements in order to build up the trust and confidence of stakeholders that forms the basis for corporate reputation. Incompetence is one of the most important reputational risks, therefore.

So, when I work with an organisation I am always keen to understand how it manages the risk of incompetence among its people – what is the extent of its commitment to competence? I have to say that in my experience is not always easy to discern that people are competent in their roles, even in the more senior ranks of an organisation. Sometimes, good technicians do not make effective managers, nor do good managers always make suitable directors. In other cases, individuals may be assigned to roles within an organisation without either the qualifications or the experience to give a reasonable expectation of proficiency and good technical performance.

There are two ways that organisations can demonstrate their commitment to competence. The first is through the quality and rigour of the recruitment process. The second is the priority given to and the amount invested in training and developing programmes for managers and staff at all levels, including directors. This investment needs to continue both in good times and in bad. We will look at each of these areas in some detail later in the book, so I do not wish to say too much about them at this stage.

However, before moving on, we need to consider the key question of competency in the single most important area of any organisation – among those individuals at the top who sit around the boardroom table.

The competency of directors

Are the directors of your organisation competent? This is a provocative question but an important one and one that needs to be answered in the affirmative if an organisation is to have the prospect of sustainable success. There are no objective measures, no tests or examinations that individuals are required to pass before they are eligible to become a director. This may change in the future. For example, the Institute of Directors in the UK runs a number of development programmes designed to equip directors with the all-round skills, knowledge and understanding essential for successfully directing an organisation from a strategic perspective. They lead to recognised qualifications such as the Chartered Director. However, there are currently no requirements for any qualification before becoming a director.

Sometimes surprising things happen right at the top of business. Here are two examples:

- A number of the UK banks that had to be rescued by the government during the global financial crisis were led by CEOs who had no banking qualifications: Fred Goodwin (Royal Bank of Scotland) was a chartered accountant; Andy Hornby (HBOS) was a retailer; Adam Applegarth (Northern Rock) had no formal banking qualifications although he did join Northern Rock straight from university and so had 20 years of experience in the sector. Since the crisis, regulators have taken a more robust approach, looking for evidence of relevant financial experience before giving their approval to those individuals seeking senior positions in banks. It is by no means certain that all of the leaders named above would be approved by the FCA today. Yet, from time to time surprising appointments continue to be made, as shown by the case of Paul Flowers (an ordained Methodist Minister, businessman and local politician) who was made non-executive Chairman of the Co-op Bank with the approval of the Financial Services Authority in 2009, despite having little financial knowledge or experience. We look at the example of the Reverend Flowers and the Co-op Bank in more detail in Chapter 6.
- The role of the chief financial officer (CFO) is, at least in part, to provide the board of directors with expert advice, guidance and assurance concerning the financial affairs of the organisation. The CFO may or may not be a main board director but in every case the baseline requirement is straightforward – above all else, the numbers must be sound. Yet the position of CFO is not always held by individuals with demonstrable evidence of financial expertise as shown by an accountancy qualification. This happens more often in the USA than in the UK. Andy Fastow (Enron Corporation) and Erin Callan (Lehman Bros.) are two examples of individuals without a professional accountancy qualification holding the office of CFO in large organisations. There were unfortunate outcomes for each, though in very different circumstances: Mr Fastow was jailed for his part in the Enron accounting fraud whilst Ms Callan lasted only six months as CFO before resigning after losing the confidence of the Lehman board of directors and the markets.

Controls

Competency is one of the key building blocks of reputation.

There are two areas that all organisations need to focus on here and ensure that they have effective controls in place if the risk of incompetence is to be minimised. The first is at the recruitment stage – the more senior the position, the more important it is to appoint the right people. We look at the appointment process for directors and senior managers in Chapter 5. The second is to ensure that all managers and staff receive an appropriate level of training to enable them to discharge their individual responsibilities effectively. We will look at this whole area in some detail in Chapter 8, in particular by reviewing the options for training and development programmes (for directors and others), because this is one of the most important tools in the ethical toolbox.

Criminality and counter-productive workplace behaviours

Introduction

The threat to corporate reputation of inappropriate or criminal behaviour by managers and staff is serious and so it should be treated by organisations as a high-priority risk. The types of behaviour that can give rise to concern here are wide-ranging, from apparently small-scale or isolated actions such as bad-mouthing the company or being rude and unhelpful to customers, through to covering up errors, manipulating data, theft and other criminal conduct. The problem is that all such behaviour can result in reputational damage to the organisation.

I will concentrate here on criminality for two reasons: first, because of the obvious harmful impact that criminal conduct can have on corporate reputation; and second because of my own extensive experience in investigating financial crime matters. Such criminal actions include: fraud, bribery and corruption, money laundering, tax evasion, collusion, coercion and insider dealing.

Over the years a number of large organisations around the world have been brought down by the criminal actions of senior managers and powerful employees including Barings Bank, BCCI, Enron, WorldCom and Bernard L Madoff Investment Securities. Others, although continuing to operate, have had their reputations tarnished and results damaged by a combination of loss-making transactions, regulatory fines and the payment of compensation resulting from the actions of senior or powerful employees. Examples of organisations damaged in the past by internal fraud scandals are Allied Irish Banks, Parmalat, Societe Generale, Satyam, UBS and Olympus.

Why do people working in business at all levels – directors, managers, employees – commit financial crime? We look at this question below in relation to two types of criminal behaviour: insider dealing and fraud.

Insider dealing

Broadly, insider dealing is the term used when people with access to unpublished, price-sensitive information then proceed to act on the knowledge that this gives them by buying or selling shares, thereby illegally enriching themselves and any fellow collaborators in the scheme. The main motive here is undoubtedly greed, although there is often arrogance too arising from a desire to be seen as a 'player', someone with valuable insights and influence. Conflicts of interest are another unhealthy feature of insider dealing.

To be more technical, insider dealing (or insider trading) occurs when an insider (for example, an officer or employee or the company's broker) trades or attempts to trade in any listed security on the basis of inside information relating to the company or to the listed security. The phrase 'inside information' has three constituent parts: the information is not generally available; it relates to the issuers of the securities or to the securities themselves; and it would, if generally available, be likely to have a significant effect on the price of the securities (for example, when the information concerns a profits warning or a takeover bid).

Insider dealing is considered to be market abuse and manipulation. It is treated very seriously both in the law and in regulations in many jurisdictions. As an example of regulation, the Markets Abuse Directive applies to countries in the EU and is very clear. It seeks to promote clean and efficient markets throughout the EU and it provides for timely disclosure of price sensitive information to market users. The overarching principles of market disclosure in the Directive are: transparency, consistency, integrity and accuracy.

In contrast, the law in this area is often complicated and it varies from jurisdiction to jurisdiction.

In the UK, insider dealing has been a criminal offence since the passing of the Companies Securities (Insider Dealing) Act in 1985 and it carries a maximum prison sentence of seven years and/or an unlimited fine for offenders. It is interesting to note that no insider dealing cases were brought by the authorities in the UK until 2008, a position that changed remarkably during the next six years when a total of 24 convictions were secured. This is a good illustration of the new, more robust attitude of the authorities in the UK towards market abuse and manipulation following the fallout from the global financial crisis.

The authorities in the USA have long taken a robust attitude to insider trading. Perhaps the best example of this is provided by the Galleon hedge fund case,[13] which represents a widespread crackdown on insider trading on Wall Street. The investigation resulted in charges being brought against Raj Rajaratnam, the hedge fund's founder, together with over 50 of his business associates and company insiders, analysts and traders. The core of the allegations was that Mr Rajaratnam was given secret information that enabled him to make significant profits on future trades. There are two unusual and important aspects to this case. The first is the aggressive use of wire-taps by the police (tactics previously associated with actions against drug dealers and organised criminals, not as here against white-collar criminals). The second concerns the seniority and hitherto impeccable reputation of some of the defendants, examples being Anil Kumar and Rajat Guptar, each former senior directors of McKinsey, perhaps the world's most prestigious management consultancy firm. Mr Rajaratnam was found guilty and sentenced to 11 years in prison, the longest term ever for insider trading, a decision affirmed on appeal in 2013. Mr Kumar pleaded guilty and gave evidence for the prosecution. Mr Gupta, despite denying all charges against him, was found guilty of insider trading charges and was sentenced to two years in prison, a judgement that was upheld on appeal in 2014.

Fraud

Fraud against organisations is defined in International Auditing Standard 240 (ISA 240) as follows:

> *An intentional act by one or more individuals among management, those charged with governance, employees or third parties involving the use of deception to obtain an unjust or illegal advantage.*

Fraud can be carried out against organisations either by external parties or by those within the organisation (or through a collusive scheme involving an outsider working with somebody on the inside). For the purposes of this analysis of people risk we will focus on insider or occupational fraud in the section below.

Two years ago I wrote a book on fraud entitled *Managing Fraud Risk*[14] that looks at all aspects of the threat that fraud poses to organisations, including the 'people risk' component. Set out below is a summary of the most important conclusions from the book concerning people risk.

- The biggest risk in any organisation, in terms of losses and reputational damage, lies at the top with the actions of owners, directors and senior managers.
- The Fraud Triangle (based on research by the American criminologist Dr Donald Cressey) points to three factors being present in every fraud case: motive, opportunity and rationalisation.
- So far as motive is concerned, basic greed is often thought to be the main driver of fraudulent behaviour, but the research indicates that the position is more complicated and nuanced in reality. Financial pressure and/or job dissatisfaction are in fact the two main motives for much fraudulent behaviour (although egocentric factors such as ego, arrogance and a sense of entitlement are important too).
- There are two aspects to the opportunity factor. First, the would-be fraudster must work in a suitable position or role within an organisation so that it is possible for him or her to carry out the prospective fraud. The key factor here is seniority that brings with it authority and/or autonomy. Second, the perpetrator must also believe that they can conceal the fraud successfully in order to avoid detection.
- Every fraudster that I have ever met, interviewed or read about has tried to rationalise away their behaviour, for example by: arguing that it is not their fault; providing reasons that 'explain' their

actions; and claiming that they intended to pay the money back in the future. What we see here is a conscious decision by the perpetrator to place his or her needs above the needs of others.

- Another important point when trying to manage fraud risk is to be aware that most fraudsters are first-time offenders. This means that any individual who might be tempted to take advantage of an opportunity and commit fraud in the future is likely never to have been convicted of a crime in the past. Therefore, it is probable that he or she will be fearful of the prospect of being caught, convicted and sent to prison as a result of committing this crime.
- Strong controls can act as a powerful deterrent by increasing the perception of detection in the mind of the individual concerned.

One of the effects of recent difficult economic conditions around the world is that fraud risk has increased in most public and private sector organisations. For example, the public sector in the UK has seen significant redundancies and minimal pay rises since 2010, with the result that the control environment in public sector organisations is likely to have been degraded somewhat, with weaker segregation of duty controls combined with increased motivation to commit fraud. Smarter, more efficient anti-fraud controls are required in all organisations to counter these increased risks. We will look at some examples of practical ways that this can be done in Chapter 7 which examines aspects of compliance.

Controls

Organisations need to have a strong control framework in place to manage and mitigate these various fraud threats and this is discussed further in Chapter 7. For present purposes it is sufficient to say that the framework must combine strong preventative measures with smart detective controls. The purpose of a detective control is always the same, to reduce exposure gap – the length of time between when an organisation starts to have a problem and when it finds out about it. The exposure gap for internal fraud is around two years. An important by-product of having strong prevention is that an organisation will increase its deterrence factor as a result – no potential fraudster wants to get caught and sent to prison. The final piece in the framework is for the organisation to have access to investigative expertise.

The key reference point for these controls is risk. It is important that an organisation assesses its exposure to fraud and other financial crime threats and then designs a control framework that provides it with reasonable assurance that these threats will be managed and mitigated.

Lack of engagement, complacency and negligence

Introduction

Malign intent is one of two very important human factors that can adversely impact upon corporate reputation. The other is negligence – carelessness or a lack of attention to detail. The consequences of this are varied but none of them are good. Sometimes negligence can be irritating or annoying for customers. For example, the sales assistant who cannot be bothered to put in the time to help a customer to find a new pair of shoes that fits both the customer's eye and foot size. Alternatively, consider the manager who fails to take the time to address adequately the reasons for a product defect or a customer complaint. At other times there may be more danger to the organisation arising from negligent behaviour. For example, the risk of poor value for money when a financial controller fails to check the details on an invoice properly before signing it off. Or consider the threats when an account manager rushes through a customer acceptance form without paying attention to all of the anti-money laundering requirements because it is late on a Friday afternoon and he or she wants to start the weekend as soon as possible.

In fact, all such negligent or careless actions reduce value in an organisation. If widespread, they can have a truly corrosive effect. Negligence increases the risk of errors, safety failures, quality defects, absenteeism and control breakdowns. It reduces productivity and profit. In short, it results in dissatisfaction throughout the stakeholder base – dissatisfied investors, suppliers, customers and especially employees. It is indeed a vicious circle.

The root cause of such negligence is poor management – poor management at all levels in an organisation but especially in the middle, at the line manager and team leader level. The main result of this is that management fails to maximise the value of the people working for them.

Criteria of Control Board – 'Guidance on Control' (1995)

I am not an expert in human capital (or talent management as it is sometimes referred to today) but I do understand its importance. This was first brought home to me when looking at the report 'Guidance on Control' produced by the Control Board of the Canadian Institute of Chartered Accountants in 1995.[15] Some years later I became aware of the concept of employee engagement and the work of Gallup, Inc. (Gallup) in this area. Gallup was one of the first companies to put employee engagement research on the map.

Work on employee engagement has served to re-inforce the messages from the Control Board. Their report has come to be known as the CoCo Framework. It places the human element at the centre of internal controls rather than concentrating on systems, processes and documentation. The essence of control under the CoCo Framework is four connected high-level processes: purpose, commitment, capability, and monitoring and learning. The Control Board summarises the framework as follows:

> *A person performs a task, guided by an understanding of its purpose (the objective to be achieved) and supported by capability (information, resources, supplies and skills). The person will need a sense of commitment to perform the task well over time. The person will monitor his or her performance and the external environment to learn about how to do the task better and about changes to be made. The same is true of any team or work group.*

Although it did not use the term in its report, in my view the Control Board highlights the importance of employee engagement in the internal control process and also the need for effective management to make it work.

The concept of employee engagement

The International School of Human Capital Management defines employee engagement as follows:

> *Employee engagement is an outcome-based concept. It is the term which is used to describe the degree to which employees can be ascribed as aligned and committed to their organisation such that they are at their most productive.*

This represents a shift from traditional compliance drivers to commitment drivers in the workplace. Engaged workers feel part of decisions that affect them; they feel valued and trusted and also feel safe to give their opinions. It introduces the concept of stewardship – in other words, a job with trust. Stewards are proactive and resourceful individuals, they provide discretionary excellence.

Gallup and the Employment Engagement Survey Q^{12} and database

Gallup[16] has built on decades of research into human needs and satisfactions by the eponymous Dr George Gallup and Dr Clifton in the USA to develop the Q^{12} instrument designed to measure employee engagement conditions. The research showed that the productivity of each person is the combination of individual talent and workplace conditions, in particular relating to relationships, expectations and recognition and reward. The concepts studied and tested included focusing on employees' strengths rather than on their weaknesses and on the existence of friendship networks and learning and support structures in the workplace.

The final wording and order of the 12-question survey were completed in 1998, since when over 25 million employees have completed the Q^{12} instrument from all around the world, producing an extensive database of information.

Gallup has identified three types of employees through its work, described as:

■ Engaged: employees work with passion and feel a profound connection to their company. They drive innovation and move the organisation forward.
■ Not engaged: employees are essentially 'checked out'. They are sleepwalking through their work-day, putting time – but not energy or passion – into their work.
■ Actively disengaged: employees are not just unhappy at work, they are busy acting out their unhappiness. Every day these workers undermine what their engaged co-workers accomplish.

Using these definitions, Gallup's latest report on the State of the American Workplace in 2013[17] highlights the fact that only 30% of workers are engaged, with a staggering 52% being distracted or otherwise 'asleep' at work and the remaining 18% being actively disengaged. Gallup's research shows that engaged employees are more productive employees so there is a significant competitive advantage to be gained by organisations (and by the US economy as a whole) that are able to increase their percentage of engaged employees. Gallup points firmly to poor management as the biggest barrier to increasing the number of engaged employees.

'Custom and practice'

Introduction

The fourth aspect of people risk is one that I like to describe as 'custom and practice' – certain actions and behaviours that are rooted in tradition and culture, either within an individual organisation (or in a part of that organisation, for example a department or geographical location), or sometimes throughout a particular business sector. These particular behaviours will have been developed over time and are often condoned at some level of management, either explicitly or else implicitly by managers choosing to turn a blind eye to the practices. They are not challenged from within the organisation. The result is that they become embedded customs and are seen as entitlements or 'perks of the job'. They are rarely given official recognition in policies and procedures, however.

The problem with custom and practice issues is that sometimes they can be extremely damaging to reputation. Some customs, certain practices that seem to be standard and non-controversial within an organisation because they have gone on for so long, can appear to be odd, harmful or even scandalous when they are uncovered and the searchlights of public attention are shone upon them. There have been a number of examples of custom and practice activities reported in the media in recent years, including: elected Members of Parliament in the UK using expense allowances claims to supplement their incomes (including a passive approval process by officials, so that these claims were within House of Commons rules); the hiring of students to work as interns during their vacations by organisations often in return for minimal or no pay; and the disregarding of authorisation limits by traders in the pursuit of profit at some international banks (this was a feature in the fraud trials of both Jerome Kerviel, the trader at French bank Societe Generale, and the UBS trader Kweku Adoboli based in the bank's offices in London).

Set out below are two examples of custom and practice in different organisations and with very different results. One is a return to our case study of the infamous Siemens corruption scandal. This is a classic illustration of how existing practices (in this case the systematic use of bribes and corrupt payments to win contracts) became so embedded within the culture of the organisation that it required drastic remedial actions to correct the situation and rebuild its trust and reputation with its stakeholders and with the international business community.

Before we re-visit the case study shortly to see how Siemens was successful in restoring trust, set out below is another example, this time one taken from my own experience. What I discovered during this particular project showed me very clearly just how unhealthy some practices can look when viewed objectively by an outside third party, despite having continued for years within a part of the operations of my client company. Fortunately, in this case we were able to address the issues before they became public and could cause any reputational damage.

Custom and practice example: airline project

A number of years ago, I was part of a team commissioned by a British company to look into the causes of poor profitability from in-flight sales of its airline division. The term 'in-flight sales' refers to the sales made by the cabin crews from the bars carried on the aircraft – the containers wheeled through the cabin periodically holding the stock of perfumes, alcohol, tobacco and gifts that are sold to passengers during each flight. Profit margins on these sales should have been high, somewhere in the 60–70% range. In fact, they were consistently much lower than this, with a number of flights even recording overall losses. Clearly, something was going badly wrong in this part of the business.

The airline operated from bases all around the UK. We found that the management information regarding in-flight sales was poor and the analysis of that information was virtually non-existent. There were a number of possible causes of the problem and we had to construct a number of working hypotheses around what might actually be happening. One of a number of lines of investigation led us to look into the conduct of the cabin crews and the way that they worked, with some surprising findings.

When analysing the results of the in-flight sales from the numerous flights made by the airline all over the world, I noticed an interesting pattern. The profitability of the bars on long-haul flights (to destinations such as Sydney and Los Angeles) was consistently low, with these bars almost always appearing in the bottom quartile of our charts. This seemed counter-intuitive to me: I was expecting that the crews on long-haul flights would have more time to sell products to passengers on these flights than on shorter flights, thereby producing more profits as a result, not less. After discussing these findings with my colleagues on the project team and with management, we decided to raise this anomaly during the various interviews and workshops that we were holding with many of the cabin crew members throughout the course of the project.

One truly surprising factor came out of these discussions and it was something that was disclosed to us entirely voluntarily by the crew members. The airline rosters on long-haul flights were such that the same crew members would work in the cabin of the aircraft the whole way to its destination, after which time they would have three or four days off to relax, all paid for, before working again in the cabin on the return flight to bring the aircraft back to the UK. Crew members told us that at the end of every long-haul flight out of the UK they and their colleagues would routinely take bottles of their favourite alcoholic drinks (for example, whiskey or gin or vodka) off the aircraft in their kit bags for consumption during crew parties at the hotel during their down time.

It was clear from what they were telling us that this had become established custom and practice by crews working for the airline, established over many years. Indeed it was something that was literally being handed down from one generation of cabin crew members to the next and was now firmly regarded as a perk of the job. However, it was all completely unofficial. There was nothing written down authorising this practice anywhere. And it was a practice that was costing the airline a lot of money – I made a quick calculation that put the costs at around £750,000 per annum. To outsiders like me and my colleagues this seemed to be nothing other than theft – and theft on a large scale at that.

We discussed this finding with senior management because it was clearly going to be a difficult issue to raise with the crews and resolve satisfactorily. The great majority of cabin crew members were enthusiastic and dedicated employees. They all seemed to be aware about the practice of taking bottles of alcohol from the aircraft, most of them had done this when working on the long-haul rosters and none of them thought that they were doing anything wrong. Together with management, we formed a plan to try to change the culture and attitudes of the crews by focusing on the cost of this to the company rather than on the question of the legality of the practice. There would be no threats to dismiss anyone at this stage.

By highlighting the costs in discussions with the crews, we succeeded in making an impact and as a result began to change attitudes. The commercial consequences of the practice in terms of costs to the company seemed genuinely to shock the crew members when we told them – they clearly had never thought of the effect of what they were doing in monetary terms. We informed them that going forward the practice of taking alcohol from the bars had to stop. We presented this as part of broader changes to controls over the bars, including the introduction of a revised bonus scheme. In future, crew members would be eligible for bonuses based on two metrics: the value of sales that each individual crew member was able to generate on a flight combined with the efficiency of the crew as a whole as reflected in the profitability of each flight.

This proved to be a successful strategy. It incentivised individual performance on sales while promoting collective control over stock and cash – if items went missing then the bonus of each crew member would be reduced. The cabin crews accepted the new arrangements and they even agreed to our recommendation of spot searches of their kit bags at the end of every flight. Unfortunately, this last control was never implemented because of opposition from a somewhat surprising source – the pilots.

 CASE STUDY

The Siemens corruption case part 2: remedial actions to rebuild trust and reputation

Introduction

In June 2011 the UK Government named a consortium led by the German firm Siemens as its preferred bidder to build rolling stock for the Thameslink rail line. Siemens had beaten competition from Bombardier, which runs the UK's last remaining train factory, thereby triggering a furious row amongst politicians and union leaders – a row that was played out in the media of course – over the failure to safeguard jobs for British workers. The Government's position was simply stated: that the successful bid represented the best value for taxpayers. The award of the contract to Siemens, valued at £1.6bn, was subsequently confirmed in 2013.

What struck me most about the reporting at the time was not so much the question of whether or not the award of this contract to Siemens represented a failure to ensure 'British jobs for British workers' (which is an important issue but one that is impossible to guarantee under existing EU procurement directives). Rather, it was the fact that there was no attempt to discredit either the tender process or the award of the contract to Siemens by references to the widespread bribery and corruption scandal that we scrutinised during the first part of this case study in Chapter 3. We saw then that Siemens was accused of systematic bribery by the authorities in 2006 and, following investigations, it received its record fine from the authorities some two years later. During that period the company was under intense and often hostile public scrutiny and was regarded as something of an international pariah.

Within five years it appears that Siemens has succeeded in re-building trust with the international community and thereby restoring its reputation.[18] How was Siemens able to do this? Set out below in five stages are some of the most important stepping stones that the company took in the transformation process and there is much that other organisations can learn from them. However, one thing to emphasise is that the change process that Siemens initiated was not an easy thing to do – it consumed significant company resources. But it had to be done – it was necessary in order for Siemens to be able to re-build trust.

Stage 1: acknowledgement of the problem and commitment to full investigation

As we have seen, Siemens cooperated fully with the authorities in the USA and Germany during the investigation process. This was acknowledged by the authorities and resulted in a significant reduction in the size of the fines imposed. The cooperation also led to Siemens being re-affirmed as a 'responsible contractor' by the US Defence Logistics Agency, the leading body awarding federal contracts.

In addition, there were three other significant actions that Siemens took to demonstrate its commitment to a full resolution. First, Siemens held its own internal inquiry in addition to the investigations by the authorities. The inquiry was overseen by Debevoise & Plimpton, a New York law firm, and it proved to be a thorough and rigorous investigation. Second, the board appointed Michael Hershman, co-founder of Transparency International, to act as its advisor. This high-profile appointment and affiliation with a leading anti-corruption expert provided visible evidence of the board's determination to bring about change and reform. It proved to be an effective measure too – Mr Hershman provided guidance on the new compliance programme that Siemens rolled out in 2008 (see below). Finally, Peter Loscher announced, as one of his first actions on becoming the new CEO of Siemens, a month-long amnesty for employees to come forward with what they knew about bribery and corruption in the business. This amnesty specifically excluded senior management. It proved to be a success, with some 40 whistle-blowers coming forward with new evidence, some of it relating to senior managers.

Stage 2: independence and change at the top

April 2007 saw the double resignations, within the same week, of the chairman and the CEO, the two men who were in charge at Siemens during the period when a great many of the corrupt payments for contracts around the world were being made. Both denied any wrongdoing, but their departure was significant for two reasons. First of all it provided an important symbol of change – for example, Mr Loscher, the new in-coming CEO was the first non-German and non-Siemens employee to lead the company. Second, it removed even the appearance of any obstruction to discovering the true scale and depth of the corruption because the new CEO was not present in the business when the illegal payments were made and so he was seen to be both objective and independent.

It should also be mentioned that Mr Loscher chose to go outside the company when appointing Peter Solmssen, a US lawyer, as the first ever Compliance Director of Siemens. As a final point here, Siemens acquiesced in demands from the US authorities for an independent 'compliance monitor' to be appointed to report on Siemens' implementation of the new compliance measures. Theo Wegel, a former German finance minister, became the company's first compliance monitor.

Stage 3: the new compliance programme

Siemens rolled out a new set of strict rules and processes on anti-corruption and compliance across its global business in 2008. This programme was designed to confirm for all managers and staff exactly what constitutes 'clean business' and to impose constraints on operating procedures in order to make clean business happen.

Two aspects of the new programme suggest immediately that it represented a significant upgrade for the compliance function throughout the business, in terms of both its credibility and its visibility. First, Mr Solmssen, the new Compliance Director, was given a seat on the managing board. Second, the company hired over 500 full-time compliance officers, thereby increasing the size of the department from 86 (in 2006) to 600. Siemens was committed to building up a compliance function that was appropriate to the size, role and particular situation that it found itself to be in.

Specific compliance tools were developed and enhanced and these were designed to prevent any repeat of the illegal bribes and corrupt payments. The tools focused on three areas: limits of authority, especially concerning the approval process for business projects; due diligence processes on third-party business partners; and gifts and hospitality policies.

There are three dimensions to the Compliance Programme that Siemens unveiled in 2008 – described by the company as: prevent, detect and respond. Although there are three dimensions, in my view the compliance programme actually represents a classic twin-track response. A number of the key 'hardware' components of this programme are set out below (divided into the three constituent parts of the programme) whilst the crucial software components are included under the Stage 4 heading below:

- **Prevent**. Prevention at Siemens involves: embracing the 'tone at the top' principle and extending it to 'tone in the middle' also so that the direct responsibility of managers (especially those with sign-off authority) is emphasised; revised Business Conduct Guidelines; centralisation of the legal and audit functions; and the introduction of compliance helpdesks to promote better communication with employees.
- **Detect**. Detective mechanisms include: an enhanced compliance review programme; case tracking tools and proactive compliance investigations designed to check for possible violations; and a whistle-blower hotline for employees and third parties.
- **Respond**. Siemens' ongoing ability to respond to events is shown through: a rigorous pursuit of compliance violations worldwide, with global case tracking; and a corporate Disciplinary Committee established to ensure that there are consequences for misconduct (this committee looked at over 900 cases involving employees in 2009, resulting in some 200 dismissals).

Stage 4: cultural change

To complement the 'hard' controls and processes put in place above, there were also a number of crucial steps taken to change the culture of the organisation so that managers and staff did not fall back into familiar, cosy and illegal ways of behaviour or patterns of working. The most important of these are set out below:

- Expressing both internally and externally deep regret for past conduct and a determination to do whatever is necessary to prevent any repetition, emphasising the need for cultural change. As an example, Mr Loscher on becoming CEO made the following statement: 'It's completely clear that the management culture failed. Managers broke the law. But this has nothing to do with a lack of rules. Siemens had and still has an outstanding set of rules. The only problem is that they were apparently being violated on an ongoing basis. The management culture was simply not practised consistently and uniformly. This is why my job now is to install a new culture. And I can guarantee you that senior management will practice what it preaches ... to a T.'[19]
- Promoting strong communication (especially with middle management and internationally) and exemplary behaviour (for example, acting as role models) from top management in order to drive the compliance message throughout the business.
- Extending the tone at the top to middle management in terms of engaging in regular communication with employees, encouraging employees to give priority to compliance at all times, explaining and demonstrating best practice in compliance-related matters and anchoring compliance in Siemens' entire value chain.
- Launching a comprehensive programme of training and education on anti-corruption practices for its managers and employees. Siemens was making the commitment to creating awareness throughout the company of the risks of corruption and to giving its employees worldwide a basic knowledge of both international laws and internal guidelines. By the end of 2008 it had succeeded in training more than half of its 400,000-strong global workforce, whether on web-based courses or in a classroom format (that is to say face-to-face training sessions).
- Establishing compliance as an integral part of the incentive pay system for managers. As an example, compliance metrics made up 17% of managers' bonuses in 2009. The aim of this change is to make compliance a common standard throughout the company in the same way as, say, the financials or dealing with customers already are.

Stage 5: consequences

Siemens is now communicating both internally and externally that it has no tolerance of non-compliant behaviour, whether in relation to bribery and corruption or to any other applicable laws and regulations. There need to be consequences for any such violations, therefore, but they must be appropriate to the circumstances of each individual case. As noted above, the Disciplinary Committee looked at over 900 cases in 2009, but not all of these by any means resulted in dismissal. The Committee is there to evaluate allegations of misconduct and then to select the appropriate level of disciplinary sanction, which can range from a verbal warning to dismissal.

Case study: conclusion

Siemens' corporate reputation was badly damaged because of the revelations, uncovered by the 2006–08 investigations, that it had used bribery and corruption on a systematic basis to win contracts and to retain business around the world. We have seen how, on discovery, the company initiated a thorough-going change process that had one overarching aim – to win back the trust of its stakeholders.

Among the many steps taken by Siemens to change its culture and re-build trust, I want to highlight two as being particularly important. First, I think it is significant that the company placed new emphasis on the role of middle management. By engaging with departmental heads and team leaders, the company was able to use them to drive through cultural change. The lesson here is that while tone at the top is important, so too is tone in the middle. Second, the company repositioned the idea of compliance in the organisation, not only by beefing up the number of compliance officers in the department but also by including compliance metrics in the incentive pay system for managers. Both of these actions provided tangible demonstration to everybody of the importance that the business was now giving to compliance.

It is clear from the second part of the case study that the change process that Siemens put in place in order to regain lost trust was not an easy option. It required a significant commitment, not only of time and resources throughout the business but also of will at the top in order to recalibrate the corporate culture around values and integrity. But it was a commitment that was entirely necessary. The main lesson here is a simple one – a healthy reputation is a vital component of corporate success. What we have seen at Siemens is an underlying shift in its business behaviour. Although this process takes time, the Siemens case shows that transformation is possible.

ETHICAL RISK IN THE STAKEHOLDER BASE

Overview

We end this chapter with a short piece on certain aspects of ethical risk that can impact directly on corporate reputation. Successful organisations have always been aware of the importance of ethical risk, but often they handle it in an unstructured, instinctive way that relies on experience and 'gut feel'. As this area of risk has increased, so organisations will need to respond more systematically by including ethics in their formal risk management frameworks in future.

All organisations should be aware of who their key stakeholders are and which are the most important constituents of the stakeholder base – whether it is investors, employees, customers, suppliers, regulators or others. Each stakeholder may have different expectations in terms of both performance and behaviour. Every organisation should take steps to assess its ethical risk with reference to these expectations.

There are two important aspects of this assessment for all organisations: first, the identification of their key stakeholders and what it is about the values of the organisation that are most critical to them; and second, the inclusion in this analysis of risks arising from the personalisation of brands by individuals coupled with the speed of modern technology and communications, which enables those individuals to act effectively (through complaints, negative publicity, disruption or sometimes by some form of attack) if their experience is disappointing. Each of these two aspects of ethical risk is addressed below.

Key stakeholder expectations

Introduction

During my interview with Peter Walshe, the brand expert from Millward Brown, I was particularly struck by his view that it is becoming increasingly difficult to differentiate between corporate reputation and the brands that the corporation owns. One consequence of this is that organisations need to be aware that any negative publicity about their activities or behaviour has the potential to damage the brand. It is not always an obvious relationship, however. This is what Peter had to say on this point during our interview:

> *Things are not always straightforward. So, in a sense it is about how do you fairly balance these things and how then do you also communicate in the right way? Because it's not fair to everybody, the rules are not the same for every brand or corporation. If you are a corporation or a brand which has built its reputation, the DNA of its brand on 'responsibility stuff' (like Ben and Jerry's or the Body Shop) your DNA is absolutely built on sustainability and responsibility. If you then start looking at odds with that in some way you destroy the fabric, the core of your meaningful difference. Therefore you are very vulnerable in terms of responsibility issues if you are not genuinely living up to the promise.*
>
> *Now if your brand is much more leadership driven – more powerful and innovative, something like a Google or an Apple – then those are the things that you are known for and they are what are most important to you. I'm not saying this is an excuse not to take corporate responsibility seriously and so on but it will certainly in the short term play a smaller part in relation to your continued success.*
>
> *Also what's interesting in something like the oil and gas industry is that the people who count if you like are the finance people – the investors and so on. Consumers don't count very much because the money that's made downstream on gas pump prices and all of that stuff is irrelevant to the oil majors – it's really about the upstream stuff. So, the company that is perceived to have the best and most innovative exploration techniques is the one that is considered valuable. Now in a sense that is high risk, so what you saw with something like the BP case or with Exxon when it had previous problems, was that actually and remarkably a lot of these important investors stuck tightly with those companies because they kind of see this as the price of doing this business. So, it's not that they are being unethical I don't think; it's just that their priorities are completely financially driven and so that's where the pressure lies.*

Examples

It is always important that an organisation looks after the interests and expectations of its key stakeholders – to fail to do so is simply poor management and bad business. The media has reported many stories since the global financial crisis showing what can happen to organisations when these ethical risks are not properly managed.

Headline case

As an example, consider the case of Serco Group plc (Serco), the international outsourcing group based in the UK. In 2013 Serco (along with its competitor in the outsourcing sector G4S) was referred to the Serious Fraud Office for over-charging one of its clients by millions of pounds on an electronic tagging contract for the monitoring of offenders when outside of prison – part of the allegation is that charges were made for people who were already dead.[20]

Serco's client on this contract happened to be the UK Government, the same client that provides approximately 25% of the Group's total annual revenues of £5bn. Of course, it is never right to over-charge on any contract but to do so in relation to a contract with its most important customer serves to combine lax controls and unhealthy culture with poor management – there can be no excuse for this, whatever the commercial pressures.

Almost unbelievably, this was not the only allegation of fraud on Government contracts made against Serco in 2013. The police were called in to investigate the management of Serco's prison escorting contract with the Ministry of Justice after Serco had found evidence that prisoners had been recorded as having been delivered ready for court when they were not. Significantly, this was a key performance measure under the terms of the contract. There was no evidence of systematic malpractice outside of the contract team but the Government was understandably very concerned. Justice Secretary Chris Grayling said: 'It has become very clear there has been a culture within parts of Serco that has been totally unacceptable and actions which need to be investigated by the police.'[21]

There were various negative consequences for Serco which included: the resignation of the CEO, millions of pounds being wiped off the share price and the group issuing two profit warnings. But the most important effect was the damage done to relations between Serco and its key client, the UK Government. In order to try to repair this damage, Serco was forced to develop a thorough plan for 'corporate renewal', as it was termed. This seems to have helped the process of re-building trust with the Government during 2014.

Sometimes key stakeholder priorities are not so easy to identify or to keep focusing on, something that I know from personal experience. Set out below is a second and very different example.

Personal experience

Some years ago, I held the office of chairman of a golf club in Hertfordshire, on the northern edge of London. The club was headed by a board of directors and, as chairman, I ran the board. We had to deal with a number of issues that were similar to those faced by many other golf clubs at that time: declining membership numbers (the result of an ageing membership, increased competition from new clubs in the area and pressure on everyone's time, thereby reducing the attraction of playing golf), a reliance on annual subscription fees for the great majority of our income and the escalating costs of maintaining property and equipment alike.

One year an idea was raised at a board meeting to introduce an annual 'bar levy' to be paid by each club member – that is to say, a fixed fee raised in advance from the members at the start of the financial year at the same time as the membership subscriptions fell due, against which would be set the cost of food and drinks purchased by the members in the clubhouse throughout the year. Sums of £100 – £150 for the levy were discussed. All outstanding balances at the end of the year – representing the shortfall of purchases made against the levy – would be forfeited to the club.

I was initially hesitant about this idea. However I listened to the arguments: many clubs in the area were already raising such a levy, it would benefit our cash-flow and a number of the newer board members were strongly in favour of it. Eventually, I decided to support it. In due course the bar levy was approved by the board and subsequently implemented. It did not prove to be universally popular, however – indeed, we probably lost a small number of members because of it. Crucially, in order for the levy to be a commercial success, the club would need to make good on its promise to appropriate all outstanding balances at the end of the year, rather than allowing members to carry the balance forward to the following year.

When it came to the year end, however, the board on reflection was not prepared to do this. We found that a relatively large number of our members, including many of our older members, did indeed have balances remaining on their accounts. Despite having done all we could to inform them of the consequences, the board felt that it would not be fair to those members for them to lose the money in this way. So, we ended up by allowing them to carry the balances forward.

The next year, the board scrapped the levy. We were now focusing on our key stakeholders, the members. We decided that to operate the bar levy in a commercial way would upset too many of them, while to continue to operate it in the way that we had done in the previous year did not make sense from any angle. The decision was clear – the bar levy was not right for our members and, therefore, it was not right for our golf club

Expert's view

The third example comes from Peter Walsche and is taken from our interview for this book. Here, Peter discusses the various issues surrounding the 2013–14 controversy over the arrangements that some corporations have put in place to avoid paying tax. Such schemes are legal (as opposed to tax evasion, which is illegal) but the question increasingly being asked is are they fair? As Peter indicates, each organisation impacted by public criticism on this issue will tend to respond in the way that best reflects its own circumstances and its own stakeholder pressures.

This dilemma applies to the tax issues that we've seen being talked about recently, you know the perception that corporations are just ripping people off and are not paying their fair taxes and so on. There are arguments of course in the opposite direction. The corporations are saying: 'Of course we are paying our taxes ... we are employing lots of people.' Now that's a powerful argument from their point of view: 'We are employing lots of people, keeping economies going.' This plays into the success or leadership part of reputation, which consumers generally recognise as the strongest driver of success of a corporation.

Corporate reputation is a broad concept, it goes beyond just pure responsibility – responsibility is only one aspect and a signpost of it. What has been interesting recently in the UK and in the USA to a degree, is this tax issue, with it being said that corporations have been unfair, that they're not paying their taxes even though actually they are not doing anything illegal. But not following the spirit of the law is the argument. What we have seen is that when the boycotts began to happen (in various ways from a number of different groups) what was really interesting was that the more successful boycott is the one that deals with something tangible, a product that is much more in the public domain where you can be seen to be using or supporting that brand. So the discomfort, if you like, between the effect of people saying:' Oh you shouldn't buy Apple or you shouldn't go on to Google' is minimal compared to the position at Starbucks. There these boycotts had quite an effect on their brand. One of the reasons is that walking along the High Street, there is a Starbucks store, I can be seen going in there and people can see me drinking their coffee and so on. So if you like, that 'shame', that consumer-consciousness is something that's quite tangible. Whereas if I'm buying on Amazon or I'm using Google or I'm buying an Apple machine, I do that in private so it's not so noticeable.

The other thing of course is the competition. You know if somebody is going to boycott Starbucks it's not a big deal for that person because they can walk for about 23 seconds and they are into another coffee shop which, in their view, is probably just as good. So, competition in a sense keeps people honest. The other thing I think that is very interesting is to look at the Starbucks and Costa Coffee situation. Costa Coffee benefitted ... they clearly did benefit (if the figures are true and they seem to be) from any boycott of Starbucks however temporary that might be. The fact is that Costa did not crow about it and did not bring the issue up in their advertising or promotions. They stuck to what their brand was and said: 'Well we don't know about all this, we just offer a great experience.' This was interesting because it is the right way to handle reputation. If you are using reputation as 'I told you – and we're cleaner than the other guys', then you are setting yourself up for a fall potentially. Also, consumers don't like it and certainly not in the UK, you see very little competitive advertising for example compared to the States but even there negativity is really not a great thing to associate your brand with, even if you are in the right.

Importance of stakeholder experience

Introduction

One of the main issues that organisations face today when trying to manage reputational risk is that each individual customer or stakeholder has a potentially powerful platform in social media to leverage his or her discontent and, as always, customers react to events based primarily on their own individual experiences. Sometimes, protest movements (for example, concerning bankers' bonuses or tax avoidance by corporations) do not resonate with large sections of the community because individuals are not affected by the issues. People may read about the largesse of bankers and dislike what they learn, but so long as they are confident that their money is safe in their high street branches they are likely to continue to use the same banks.

When people have a negative experience, however, organisations are increasingly vulnerable because of the speed and reach of mass communications today. Discontent can be mobilised rapidly on social media, which is likely to be quickly picked up by other media outlets too – we will look at how organisations can best respond to this later in the book.

We look in the paragraphs below at an international headline case that has damaged the reputation of a national agency and indeed of a national government, where the case has its origins in the dissatisfaction of one individual stakeholder. Before we do so, Peter Walshe addressed some important issues connected with the stakeholder experience generally during our interview, as follows:

So this is the kind of dilemma. As we see, what increasingly looks like a bit of a wave, a bit of a sea-change … As governments and politicians, pressure groups begin to push these things up the agenda and make noise and waves about them consumers become more aware, listen slowly … then some of these things get associated with disasters. But again peoples' own experience with those brands or corporations is often at odds with all this fuss that is being made and so they kind of go: 'But actually … I'm alright Jack.'

I think this is best illustrated by a bit of research we did some years ago. At the time Nike was under a huge pressure and criticism for the low wages it appeared to be paying at various stages in its supply chain.

So, at that time we were asking people what had they heard about Nike and others, what did they think etc. And people said: 'Yes absolutely disgraceful, they rip their employees off and everything else, it's terrible, shouldn't be allowed.' And then we asked people, subsequent to that and also in a parallel study so that nobody was affected by those comments, to tell us what is really good or bad about the Nike trainers. 'Oh they are fantastic, they are the best in the world; you know they make me run faster, I look great. The only problem with them is that they are just too darn expensive.' So we then asked: 'Ok what could make them cheaper?' And we got the reply: 'Well, I don't know but they have got to get their prices right.' There was a complete disconnect between making them and the price charged at the shop. Although they thought that maybe the brand was

*making too much profit, on the other hand ... really the value equation was pretty strongly in
favour of Nike.*

*These issues are kind of buried or people don't want to feel them, and so therefore they don't –
they are kind of hidden almost from their own psyches. I think we are seeing a bit of a change
with that. Part of that is to do with the speed of communication and the way that people can talk
with each other and therefore can either embarrass each other or highlight and enlighten each
other about some of these issues. So it is easier for that social consciousness to begin to develop
into something that is more meaningful and connected to the world. That applies to environmental issues and so on ... which again, instead of sticking your head in the sand, gradually there is a
feeling: 'Well actually we are all responsible and there is something we can do about it that might
affect my purchasing decisions, the way that I run my life etc. etc.'*

*But brand experience remains the crucial factor. Now, if you then think however good the com-
munications are, however positive the company's advertising messages are, if your last experience is rubbish, bad service whatever it might be, it's going to override all that by a million times.
Also, when we look at this high speed connected electronic world, a bad experience just goes
through like lightening. So experiencing ... how do corporations then ensure that their stakeholders' experience is consistent, is positive, is valuable ... that's an absolute focus today.*

The Edward Snowden factor

We are now living in the age of Edward Snowden,[22] the American computer specialist whose spec-
tacular breach of security at the US National Security Agency (NSA) resulted in the leak of thousands of documents of 'top-secret' classified material by media outlets. Mr Snowden is currently
living in exile in Russia and there is much of the detail of his story that remains untold. So, it is not
appropriate to attempt to construct a case study here. Instead, set out below are some of the main
features of the case. We conclude with a discussion of two important consequences of the Snowden
saga – consequences that all organisations now need to address.

The basic facts of the case are these.

In 2006 Mr Snowden gained a position in information technology at the Central Intelligence
Agency (CIA). He spent some time in Switzerland where his job was to maintain security for the
CIA's computer network and look after computer security for US diplomats based at the Geneva mission. Mr Snowden had access to classified information. It may well have been at this time that he first
became disillusioned with the extent of government spying operations.

Mr Snowden resigned from the CIA in 2009. He was then employed by Dell, the computer firm,
and spent three years working as a contractor at an NSA facility on a US military base in Japan
before being transferred to Hawaii in 2012. His new job was at the NSA's regional cryptology centre
near Honolulu. By this stage it seems that Mr Snowden had convinced himself that the NSA was
invading the privacy of millions of American citizens in a way that violated the US constitution
and that therefore these surveillance programmes were illegal. His new post was to work as an NSA
systems administrator, with access to extensive files of secret material. He apparently formed a plan
to steal top-secret documents in order to obtain evidence of the NSA's alleged illegality and then subsequently to leak the documents to a small number of trusted journalists interested in civil liberty
issues.

In March 2013 Mr Snowden took a new job with the private contractor Booz Allen Hamilton
(Booz). Again he worked as a systems administrator, but his position with Booz granted him access
to lists of machines from all over the world that the NSA programmes had hacked into. He also had

access to files of information from the Government Communications Headquarters (GCHQ), the British intelligence and security agency.

Sometime before 20 May 2013 Mr Snowden managed to access and then to steal thousands of top-secret documents from the NSA's servers.

It remains unclear exactly how Mr Snowden was able to move undetected through the NSA's systems, to steal the documents and to remain undetected thereafter. In terms of the theft, it seems likely that he simply downloaded the NSA documents onto thumbnail drives that he had brought into work with him. Normally, it would be forbidden to most staff to bring their own thumb drives onto the premises, but it appears that Mr Snowden's position as systems administrator made him an exception to this standard security procedure.

On 20 May 2013 Mr Snowden disappeared from his life in Hawaii and secretly flew to Hong Kong. Once there, he met a small number of journalists in June, releasing numerous NSA documents to them, which were published subsequently generating an enormous interest in the story around the world. He then revealed his identity as the source of the leaks in a video published by the *Guardian* newspaper. This triggered a hunt to locate him by the US authorities, which proved to be unsuccessful because he was able to fly into Moscow on 23 June. After much diplomatic manoeuvring, while he apparently remained in transit at the airport, Mr Snowden was granted a one-year temporary asylum by Russian officials on 1 August.

The nature and scale of Mr Snowden's leaks have damaged significantly the reputation of the NSA and also served to undermine trust in the US Government's assurances about its security operations around the world (not least in Germany, after it was disclosed that the mobile phone of the German Chancellor Angela Merkel had also been kept under surveillance by the NSA).

The Snowden saga is unfinished. Mr Snowden remains in Russia at the time of writing in late 2014 and we cannot say what more will be learned about his motives and methods in the years to come. He is certainly a polarising figure, with many people viewing him as either a hero or a traitor.

We will look again briefly at the Snowden case later in the book when we consider the subject of whistle-blowing. It is important to highlight here two significant risks arising out of the case that all organisations need to be aware of. These are as follows:

■ The first concerns the risks associated with those people who have privileged access to an organisation's systems, whether employees or (as in Mr Snowden's case) contractors. I have always believed that the biggest threat in any organisation is represented by the CEO and senior executives. I continue to believe this, but I would now place systems administrators only slightly below them on the risk scale. It is vital that IT specialists and systems administrators are thoroughly vetted before being given access to the systems and that, once access has been granted, their activities are monitored thereafter.

■ Second, this case highlights more than any other the ethical risks facing organisations in the twenty-first century. Why did Mr Snowden leak these documents, at great personal risk to himself? It is not possible yet to be certain about his motives, but nothing that I have read suggests plausibly that money was the primary driver (I am not aware that Mr Snowden has received any payment for his disclosures) or that he was working for another state as a spy. It seems that Mr Snowden was motivated to steal the information and then disclose it to certain carefully selected journalists primarily by his own beliefs, morals and standards. In addition, he may very well have believed that any disclosures of his concerns made internally within the NSA would be ignored. Mr Snowden is not unique in having a combination of strong ethics and high technical skills. But the speed and mass coverage of modern media in the twenty-first century makes this combination a significant risk to organisations today because of the potential for fast and widespread damage to reputation.

 WORKSHOP CONCLUSION

Closing

I say to the team that, before asking them to list out on the flipchart their five key takeaways from today, I want to pull together some of my own thoughts by way of a summary. The first thing to say is that it is important today for all organisations to have in place a system to manage risk that is appropriate to its own circumstances – from everything I have heard it seems that Stronach has such a system in place. However, all these systems are vulnerable to operational risks in two areas: technological failures and human factors (such as errors, poor judgement and malign or self-serving intent). Each can result in significant damage to reputation, which in my view is the most important risk facing all organisations today. Every entity needs to look to its continuing investment in technology, but our main focus is on the human factors – we have already looked at conduct risk and reviewed the main components of people risk.

As an observation, I say to the team that scandals and business failures almost always short-circuit quickly to the actions of directors and senior managers in one of two areas: lack of awareness and/or greed. Sometimes of course it is both. The best antidote is a thorough understanding of risk, especially the principal risks that can threaten an organisation's business model or solvency, coupled with good business ethics at the top of the organisation. So, tone at the top (supplemented by tone in the middle, as we saw in the Siemens case study) is crucial.

Key takeaways

With that, I invite the team to set out their five key takeaways from today's workshop on the flipchart.

I had a suspicion that John Holt, the CEO, might well take the lead here and, without waiting for the discussion to begin, he marches up to the flipchart and notes down the first point – it is one that he clearly wants addressed as a matter of urgency.

✓ **Review the arrangements for the IT systems administration**. At present Stronach's IT system is administered by a third party via an outsourced contract – John just checks with Malcolm Mainwaring, the Group Finance Director, at this point to make sure that his understanding is correct. Malcolm confirms that it is and says that the contract is managed by way of a service-level agreement. John wishes to review this arrangement – his preference is that the IT systems administration is brought back in-house. Clearly, the Edward Snowden case has made a big impression on him. Nobody wants to argue with him on this point and Malcolm simply nods and says that he will look into the feasibility of making the change.

✓ **Improve the board's oversight of risk**. Again it is John who takes the lead here by saying that there should be more time allocated to risk management at board meetings. Malcolm agrees, adding that in his view the board should focus more attention on Stronach's principal risks – for example, those that could threaten its solvency or liquidity. John nods in agreement and makes the additional point that risk needs to be factored in more when considering the Group's strategy, not least in light of the current strategic review process that he is leading. Rachel Gordon, the Chairman, says that she understands the points made and supports them – they will provide greater assurance around the resiliency of the Group. One practical change that she will make is to adjust the board agenda in future to provide more time for discussion and debate on the Group's principal risks.

✓ **Increase the time allocated to risk management in the training and development programmes**. This point comes from David Hurley, the HR Manager. David feels that at present most of Stronach's employees don't really understand risk management at all. If asked, the majority would probably equate it with health and safety risk assessments, as was suggested in the quiz – although important, David says that health and safety is only one aspect of risk that needs to be managed by the Group. He feels strongly that more training is needed and comes up with a slogan that could be used to promote it: 'We are all risk managers at Stronach.' This idea is met with enthusiasm by the team, especially by Rachel, who is once again very supportive. I am impressed at David's contribution here and I can tell that he is pleased at the positive response for his suggestion. I always suspected that he would grow in confidence as the project progressed and this is evidence of him doing exactly that.

✓ **Beef-up the compliance function**. Malcolm is concerned that compliance is currently delegated to an in-house lawyer who has other tasks to perform and little budget to work with. He feels that this is increasingly inappropriate as legal and regulatory risks become ever more complex. John Holt also expresses some concern on this and the two of them agree to work on a briefing paper for the board with a view to increasing the importance of the compliance function at Stronach in the future.

✓ **Take part in the Gallup Q^{12} survey**. This is Rachel's point and it reflects her aim of increasing the passion and drive of employees within the Group. She is aware of Gallup's work on employee engagement and the Q^{12} database and she is concerned that the typical management style within Stronach is not one that obviously demonstrates that all employees are valued. John starts to object but Rachel continues and asks him a question that is taken directly from the Q^{12} instrument: 'John, how many of our people do you think would say that they have received praise for something that they have done at work in the last five days?' John nods his head slowly – he takes the point and replies 'Not too many I guess.' Rachel says that she will make enquiries about Stronach taking part in the Q^{12} survey (or an equivalent) in the future.

Next workshop

I now draw the workshop to a conclusion by thanking everyone for their contributions today. I then move to address the subject of the next workshop. I say that, after looking at reputational risk, we should now focus on the issues of governance, tone at the top and ethical leadership – those issues that the team raised at the last workshop. This is a crucial part of the project and I suggest that, rather than attempting to address all of the issues in one workshop, we should perhaps divide them into two and look at the governance dimension next time and ethical leadership in the succeeding workshop.

This is agreed after a short discussion only, and Rachel undertakes to arrange the next workshop, to be held in approximately four weeks' time.

Reflections

As everyone leaves and I pack away my materials, I reflect on a successful workshop. David Hurley contributed very well today and I particularly like the way that the team started to work together at the end of the session. It was noticeable to me that John Holt and Malcolm Mainwaring were working better together today than in previous workshops – they were certainly thinking along similar lines when putting the key takeaways together. With the CEO and the Group Finance Director working in tandem, I am hopeful that real progress can be made in these areas. Rachel is always committed and enthusiastic in the workshops but I was impressed by her support for David today – I know that he appreciated it.

I am approaching the lift when Malcolm rushes past: 'Great session today Steve, thank you very much.' That is absolutely the best type of feedback and I am just about to say so when he stops in his tracks, turns to me and says: 'Do you fancy a coffee? I can't do anything today unfortunately, but how about after next month's workshop? There is something that I want to tell you.' I have no idea what this is but I reply 'Yes, absolutely – I will look forward to it' and the arrangement is made.

Malcolm remains something of an enigma and I now have to wait for a month to find out what he wants to say to me.

The governance dimension

 EFFECTIVE GOVERNANCE: FOURTH WORKSHOP

Opening

Introduction

I arrive early for this, the fourth workshop to be held as part of Stronach's ethics project, in order to prepare the room and the materials. We are going to review aspects of governance today. Rachel Gordon, the Chairman, called me a few days ago to check that all the preparations were proceeding well and to say how much everyone was looking forward to this session. So, I want to make sure that everything is ready.

After a short time, the four team members start to arrive themselves – they are also early. Everyone seems keen today!

Update

As we are all exchanging greetings and pouring coffee John Holt, the CEO, walks over to me and says that he has a piece of news that I might find interesting. Following the last workshop, he got together with the Group Finance Director, Malcolm Mainwaring, to review the proposals coming out of the Group's strategic review. Apparently, neither John nor Malcolm had been entirely convinced by any of the three proposals on the table for possible acquisitions. Their doubts and concerns had been crystallised by the discussions in the last two workshops – latterly on reputational risk and, before that, on bribery and corruption. They both felt that the proposals in Argentina and Bulgaria carried too much risk given the current circumstances in those two countries whilst the third, the take-over of a British rival, was possible but it does not sit well with the Group's new strategic direction.

I express some surprise and say that I hope I have not said anything to put them off, but John reassures me that in fact the workshops were very helpful. Above all, they have shown the need to factor risk fully into the strategic decision-making process. Looking back, the strategic review they had conducted had been all about brainstorming ideas and looking for opportunities. Strategic risk factors, such as considerations of geo-politics and possible damage to the Group's reputation, had not been taken sufficiently into account. This was now clear to both himself and Malcolm. As a result, they have decided to halt the review and look at other options, something that was put to the board at the last meeting and agreed. Malcolm has joined us and is nodding his head: 'It is the right decision – there will be other opportunities.'

With that, John and Malcolm take their seats and are joined at the table by Rachel and David Hurley, Stronach's HR Manager.

Governance soundings

Question

It is time to get down to business for today. Before looking at corporate governance and the workings of the board in detail, I say that I want to start by exploring some key governance concepts. To do so, I have a question for them, just to get everybody focused on the subject right from the start.

I say to them that the expression 'corporate governance' means different things to different people. I know this because over the last 10 years I have discussed the topic in workshops and on consulting projects with many groups of business people from a variety of sectors and in countries all around the world. There never seems to be complete agreement on this subject. So, I am interested in what corporate governance means here at the Stronach Group – what does it mean to each member of the project team?

The question I put to them is a simple one: What are the two words or phrases that first come into your mind when you hear the phrase 'corporate governance'? I ask the team members to think about this for a moment and then to call out their responses one by one – I will note them down on the flipchart.

Answers

Rachel Gordon is the first to answer and she has chosen 'transparency' and 'accountability' – good words indeed. Malcolm Mainwaring then calls out 'compliance' and 'policies, controls, systems and procedures'. David Hurley, is next to answer and his choice of words are 'integrity' and 'codes, for example codes of conduct'. Malcolm then comes in again and asks whether he is allowed to give an additional answer and, when I say that of course he can, he pauses before saying very deliberately 'box-ticking'. Needless to say, this gives rise to smiles and some laughter around the room. Finally, John Holt answers, but in a rather different way – he clearly has a different perspective. I am pleased to find myself now writing the words 'the oversight of strategy and the management of risk' on the flipchart.

Comments

I thank everyone for their responses. Looking at the words on the flipchart, I say that, taken together, they represent a good summary of the key components of corporate governance. But I do have a number of comments to make.

First of all I say that there is no right or wrong answer to this question. While there are helpful definitions of corporate governance (and we will look at some of these shortly) everyone that I have worked with seems to have a different answer, almost none of which I have ever considered to be either unequivocally right or wrong.

My own answer revolves around two phrases: 'board compliance' and 'board performance'. For me corporate governance is all about how companies are led and run at the top by the board of directors (or by an equivalent body). It has two fundamental components: board compliance – the procedural framework within which the board works; and board performance – leadership, the setting of values, the supervision of management. I emphasise to the team that I am essentially taking the same twin-track approach to corporate governance that I have advocated in previous workshops on different subjects.

I say that I also find the distinction between what is necessary and what is sufficient in order to promote good governance to be helpful here too. Board compliance is necessary for good corporate governance but it will not in itself be sufficient to enable an organisation to achieve its objectives and thereby maximise its value over the long term. In order to do so, the board must also perform.

Looking now at the answers shown on the flipchart, I point out that three of the team (Rachel, Malcolm and David) chose to focus on the board compliance aspects of corporate governance. I understand this. Indeed, the great majority of the people who attend my courses tend to answer this question in exactly the same way. Of course, they are not wrong to do so. An organisation must have in place an effective framework of policies, systems and controls. It must also operate transparently, with integrity and be accountable to its owners if it is to claim with plausibility that it is well governed. Without any one of these components, good corporate governance will prove to be illusive. By themselves these compliance components are insufficient, however.

To achieve good corporate governance in practice, an organisation must add some at least of the key attributes of board performance – where else does leadership or entrepreneurship come from? John's response was pleasing because it highlighted two of the most important indicators of what the board is there to do. First, he pointed to the oversight of strategy: the positioning of the organisation, especially in times of changing markets, is perhaps the single most crucial task facing the board because it will often prove to be the differentiator between success and failure. Second, John identified the management of risk as being a key component of corporate governance. Effective risk management is something that we looked at in the previous workshop when we all agreed that it is an essential factor in the success of a modern business. There are other important aspects of board performance of course, including: the setting of organisational values; the development of business ethics; communicating with investors and with stakeholders; and the supervision of management.

Agenda

It is clear from their subsequent comments that the team both understands and endorses this twin-track approach to corporate governance. This is important because I say to them that the idea of the twin-track is built into the agenda for this workshop, which is broadly four-fold as follows:

- First, we will look at the importance of corporate governance to all organisations through a topical case study that highlights some of the consequences of poor governance processes in areas such as top appointments and succession planning.
- Then I will present an overview of the key aspects of corporate governance including: definitions; board composition; the differing roles of the chairman, the executives and the non-executive directors; and agency risk.
- Next, I will review some of the different governance systems around the world, focusing on those in the US (rules-based governance, established in federal law) and those in the UK (principles-based governance, established on a 'comply or explain' basis).

▪ Finally, we will analyse some of the key requirements for creating an effective and talented board of directors through the medium of the twin-track approach. First, the necessary processes and building blocks that provide assurance of board conformance with all applicable laws, regulations and obligations. Second, we will look at the area of board performance through a review of three modern improvement drivers: personal development programmes for directors; diversity around the boardroom table; and the board evaluation process.

Importance of corporate governance

Before starting the formal presentation, I want to pick up a comment made by Malcolm in the exercise that we have just carried out – namely his reference to box-ticking. Malcolm immediately starts to protest, saying that he only used the term to be provocative. I nod and say that I understand completely, but I also point out that the phrase did indeed have the impact that Malcolm was looking for; all of us either smiled or laughed out loud at the time. This illustrates an important point – corporate governance is still seen by many people as a mechanistic process, literally ticking the box in terms of being seen to comply with the various governance rules and regulations.

While I understand this viewpoint, I have never subscribed to it. I take a simple view here: corporate governance is about what happens right at the top of an organisation and nothing could be more important in determining the success or otherwise of that organisation. So, I tell the team that I am going to demonstrate this by looking at what has happened to two well-known British organisations – each has encountered difficulties recently, partly at least as a result of governance shortfalls. During the next workshop, I will review the problems at one of the most trusted organisations in the country. But today I am going to look at a different kind of enterprise, one that has special associations for me (although perhaps not for everyone in the room), and I ask the project team for their indulgence. I am asking this because my first governance example will be to look at the recent troubles at the football club that I have supported ever since I was a boy.

With that, I begin the presentation with an overview of why good governance matters to all organisations.

WHY GOOD GOVERNANCE MATTERS

Overview

As I have said, the directors and managers who run organisations are often unclear themselves about what exactly corporate governance means – its definition, its purpose and its importance. No doubt this uncertainty is replicated by a far wider audience too. Many people see governance as a dry and dusty subject to do with rules and codes and principles of best practice, something that company secretaries working for big organisations listed on a stock exchange might be concerned about but which does not contribute very much to operational success and has no impact whatsoever on their own lives. The reality is very different.

Often the importance of good governance only becomes clear when hitherto successful organisations run into difficulties. Factors such as leadership and strategy-setting, the mechanisms and structures that determine how directors and managers work together and conduct business and the actions and behaviour of those individuals at the top – all are critical components of success but are rarely scrutinised when performance is good. Scandals and business failures, should they happen, tend to invert this trend, however. Every time that a scandal occurs, the comments and reportage quickly short-circuit to the actions, judgements, decisions and perceived mistakes of the directors and senior managers at the top of the organisation concerned.

Two governance examples

The simple truth is that the quality of governance is of critical importance to the success of all types of organisations and therefore it has an impact on anyone and everyone who has a stake in those entities. This will be evident in two recent examples, both from the UK but with worldwide application: the Co-operative Group (Co-op Group) and Manchester United Football Club (Manchester United). These organisations operate in very different business sectors but each touches the lives of millions of people every day. The Co-op Group has over seven million members in the UK, it employs 90,000 staff and, until recently, it owned and controlled the Co-operative Bank (Co-op Bank). Manchester United is more than a football club, it is a global brand. Although arguable, many people would agree with the claims made on the club's website that it is the world's most popular football team.

Each of these organisations has enjoyed considerable success over a long period of time but this has changed in recent years. A scandal involving the personal conduct of the ex-chairman of its banking subsidiary (in the case of the Co-op Group) and a run of exceptionally poor results on the football field (in the case of Manchester United) have each served to attract negative headlines and to focus attention for the first time on what appear to be significant weaknesses in the governance and decision-making processes of both organisations.

Set out below, in this chapter and the next, is a review and analysis of the circumstances of each case. The analysis seeks to highlight the various governance issues around structure, process and decision-making at the top that I believe are the root causes of the current problems at both the Co-op Group and at Manchester United. Rather than being an irrelevance, corporate governance is of fundamental importance to a proper understanding of these cases, just as it is with so many other examples from all business sectors, regardless of whether the organisation in question is listed on a stock exchange or not.

We will look first at the case of Manchester United and in the next chapter at the recent events that have impacted seriously on the results and reputation of the Co-op Group.

Governance case study one: Manchester United

Introduction

On 22 April 2013 Manchester United[1] defeated Aston Villa 3–0 at Old Trafford to clinch the English Premier League title for the 13th time, which represented the club's 20th domestic championship – both records. The manager of the team was Sir Alex Ferguson who, during an exceptionally long tenure of 26 years in charge at the club, had amassed a total of 38 trophies, including two European Champions League titles, putting him among the most successful football managers of all time. Manchester United went on to win the Premier League title in the 2012–13 season by 11 points, a huge margin. Continued success on the field seemed assured.

Yet, within three weeks, the landscape had changed. Sir Alex announced his retirement and, very quickly, a replacement was appointed. This was David Moyes, hitherto the manager of Everton Football Club (Everton), who started work as manager on 1 July 2013 on an unusually long six-year contract. At first glance, it seemed like a smooth, well-planned handover of power which promised stability and future trophies for Manchester United.

In the event, things have turned out rather differently. Mr Moyes was dismissed on 22 April 2014, exactly one year after the win over Aston Villa, following a most disappointing season both in terms of results and style of play. He was manager for less than 10 months and was replaced until the end of the season by player-coach Ryan Giggs. Manchester United finished the season seventh in the league table and failed to win any of the cup competitions. The team also failed to qualify for the European Champions League, thereby forfeiting significant revenue in the next year. Following brief negotiations, the Dutchman, Louis van Gaal, was appointed manager on 19 May 2014 on a three-year contract.

How could this turn around in the club's fortunes have happened so quickly?

Early concerns

I remember having a sense of foreboding long before a ball was kicked in the 2013–14 football season. My concern was not so much that Sir Alex Ferguson had retired (he was 71 years of age at the time so this was inevitable in the near future) nor that it was Mr Moyes who replaced him (he is an experienced manager, achieving consistently high-placed finishes in the Premier League with Everton, even though no trophies were won during his time there). Rather, I was concerned at the way that Manchester United handled the manager-transition process.

This transition, when it happens, is clearly one of the most critical risks to future success on the field for any football club, yet from what I could gather from media reports, the processes and decision-making behind the transition seemed surprisingly old fashioned. To me they lacked the rigour and professionalism that I expect from a large publicly listed business and certainly from a football club that claims to be one of the best supported and most successful sports teams in the world.

Manchester United has been controlled by the Glazer family – American businessmen, father and sons (the father is now dead) and owners of other sports teams – ever since their controversial takeover of the club, using debt to finance the deal, in 2005. The club's ultimate parent company is listed on the New York Stock Exchange, following an initial public offering of 10% of the shares in 2012. The club has traded successfully since then, announcing record annual revenues of £363m for the year ended 30 June 2013.

So Manchester United is essentially a family-owned enterprise with a small free-float. But it is a large business with a huge fan base all over the world. In 2012 the club claimed that it had 659 million supporters worldwide – as an observation, the recent problems will have led to a lot of disappointed stakeholders!

For me, a number of shortfalls in governance processes contributed significantly to the club's lack of success on the pitch during the season 2013–14. It was always going to be difficult and problematic to replace such a successful manager as Sir Alex Ferguson. However, rather than helping to mitigate the risks associated with this transition, the actions and decision-making at the top seemed instead to magnify them. The outcome was all too predictable.

Set out below are the issues that are of most concern to me. These are personal observations and I divide them between five process shortfalls and two comments on the decision-making and judgement calls made at the top.

Governance shortfalls: process

■ **Poor succession planning at team manager level**. This was a root cause of the club's problems. The owners and directors had a long time to plan for Sir Alex Ferguson's retirement, yet the news seemed to take them by surprise: no timetable had been agreed with Sir Alex; no one within the club was identified as a potential successor; and no external candidate had been lined up. Succession planning seemed non-existent. Significantly, this has since changed with Mr Giggs now working as an assistant to Mr van Gaal.

■ **Poor succession planning at CEO level**. Sir Alex was not the only executive to retire in the summer of 2013. So too did David Gill, the club's chief executive for the past 10 years. Mr Gill's contribution on the corporate side to Manchester United's success was highly significant. He was succeeded by Ed Woodward, the club's vice-chairman, who shadowed Mr Gill for five months before taking over as chief executive in July 2013. So, both Mr Woodward and Mr Moyes started their new jobs at the same time. This collective inexperience was apparent in their approaches in the transfer market over the summer when they failed to sign any of their target players. Losing two leaders such as Sir Alex Ferguson and David Gill at the same time is always likely to produce instability and disruption. But the club's difficulties could have been mitigated or even avoided with better planning and communication. More effort by the owners or the board members to persuade either Sir Alex or Mr Gill to remain in post for a longer period could have secured a smoother transition for the club. To lose one successful manager is unfortunate; to lose two at the same time seems careless.

■ **An old-fashioned appointments process**. The club's appointments process for the crucial position of team manager seems rudimentary at best. Not only were no alternative candidates looked at seriously, there was no interview of the successful candidate either. From the reports, Mr Moyes did not meet the club's owners or directors before being offered the job – by Sir Alex himself at his home over a cup of tea! This is one of the most desirable positions in world football but the appointments process appears parochial. I understand that a committee was established at the club but it is likely that Sir Alex himself played a key role in identifying Mr Moyes as his successor: 'David is a man of great integrity with a strong work ethic. I've admired his work for a long time.' Perhaps he sees a lot of himself in Mr Moyes. However, I read about all this with dismay. To me it resembles distinctly old-fashioned recruitment practices – it smacks of cronyism and seems inappropriate for a large business operating today. The UK Code of Corporate Governance calls for senior appointments to be 'formal, rigorous and transparent'. This is an excellent principle and one that Manchester United would have been wise to adopt.

■ **Wholesale changes at the football club**. Far from a seamless transition, Mr Moyes introduced significant risk into the club by deciding on a full regime change in terms of his assistants. He very quickly made wholesale changes to the experienced group of coaches and backroom staff that Sir Alex had built up, replacing them with his own people from Everton. Such an upheaval seems common practice in the world of football but it is always likely to result in disruption and uncertainty in any organisation.

■ **The old boss never went away**. There is one aspect of football life at Old Trafford that has not changed – strange to say it, but this piece of continuity also causes me concern. Sir Alex Ferguson is no longer the team manager but he is still an important presence at the club. Since retirement he has joined the board and acts as an ambassador for the club. Every organisation faces a dilemma when a successful leader steps down – there is the temptation to find them another position so that their experience and wisdom are not lost. In my view, this is a temptation that should be firmly resisted. Retaining the old boss is at best a distraction and it can be harmful if it undermines in any way the position of the in-coming chief executive. This is especially true if the immediate results achieved by the new regime are less than impressive – exactly the position that Manchester United found itself in.

Governance shortfalls: decision-making

It is always difficult to replace a successful leader. All management decisions involve the use of judgement and ultimately their quality is determined by events and outcomes. There is never any guarantee of success, whatever process is followed. No doubt the owners and directors of Manchester United identified a number of qualities and attributes in Mr Moyes that made him, in their view, the best person for the job. No doubt Sir Alex Ferguson, with his unrivalled experience in football, led the process and the owners and directors were prepared to endorse his judgement. It sounds reasonable but events have shown the decision to be flawed.

Would a more rigorous process have improved the quality of the decision?

There were two areas of concern for me about Mr Moyes' appointment from a business perspective. The first was his track record in terms of experience and pedigree. He did not have experience of running a football club of the stature of Manchester United. I shared the media concerns over his pedigree at the time, in particular his lack of experience of managing teams in European competitions and his lack of success in terms of winning trophies. These were legitimate concerns but perhaps they could be addressed over time. The directors clearly believed that Mr Moyes had the personal character and integrity that they were looking for – by granting him a six-year contract they were giving him time to grow into the job. I could understand this; it seems reasonable (though how he might handle the pressure if results were poor was always unknown of course).

My second area of concern was rather different. Did Mr Moyes have the appropriate appetite for risk to be a successful manager of Manchester United? Sir Alex Ferguson had many qualities – drive and commitment, focus and control, motivational skills. These combined with his expertise in football matters to make him an inspirational leader. However, Sir Alex's standout quality for me was his exceptional feeling for risk on a football field. He always wanted to win and was prepared to take risks to do so, not in a reckless way but with a measured understanding of what was required. His teams won many matches from losing positions, often scoring late on in the game to do so. This was not a coincidence but rather points to attributes such as resilience and courage that have become part of the culture and folklore of Manchester United.

Mr Moyes seemed to me to be more cautious, more circumspect in his approach. His Everton teams played with less speed in attack than United and sometimes seemed prepared to settle for a draw rather than to chase victory and thereby risk defeat. I don't know Mr Moyes personally, of course, but it may be that he is risk averse by nature. The problem is that risk aversion on the football field is simply not the Manchester United way. Each of us has our own individual and inherent appetite for risk. In my view, Mr Moyes would have found this difficult to change, no matter how long he was in charge of the team. I was always concerned that he might not be a good cultural fit for Manchester United.

Conclusion

It is often said that football is a results business. Teams win football matches for a variety of reasons – some to do with skill, some with tactics, some with luck. It may well be that the single most important cause of Manchester United's decline on the football field was the decision of Sir Alex Ferguson to retire. It is never easy to replace such a figure in any business sector. As an example, look at the problems experienced by Tesco plc, one of the world's largest retailers, following the departure of its legendary CEO, Sir Terry Leahy, in 2011 (indeed, there are those who would argue that the seeds of future problems in both organisations were sown during the final years of Sir Alex's and Sir Terry's respective reigns). However, I firmly believe that better processes and succession planning would have made the transition less traumatic than it has turned out to be.

Personally, I feel that another factor may have been complacency. As a team and as a business, Manchester United had been so successful for so long that there may have been an assumption, unconscious perhaps, by the owners and directors that results would continue to be good whoever was in charge. Or to be more precise, that results on the field would continue to be good enough so that the team would continue to challenge for trophies and qualify for the lucrative European competitions in the future, even if the new manager, whoever he was, struggled in his first season to get to grips with the job. This seems plausible. It has been reported that Mr Moyes' compensation for loss of office was reduced by a clause in his contract linking his continued employment as manager with qualification for the Champions League, clearly the minimum requirement at Manchester United.

If there was even a hint of complacency at the club, then it was a significant mistake by those at the top to allow this culture to develop. As in most areas of modern business, competition in the English Premier League is fierce and there is never a guarantee of success. Manchester United began the 2013–14 season as the champion club in England, and by a considerable distance, but the team now looks some way short of the standards being set by its main rivals. The club no longer leads the way and it might be difficult indeed for Manchester United to recover its former ascendency.

I firmly believe that proper process and decision-making at the top are important. My intention in using the Manchester United example is to show the consequences of governance shortfalls. I am not suggesting that better processes would have prevented all of the problems – not at all. But better processes are likely to produce better results – good performance is itself an outcome of proper planning. I believe that earlier consideration of who would succeed Sir Alex Ferguson, more awareness of the risks of allowing two leaders to leave at the same time and a more professional appointments process would have increased the likelihood of a smoother transition.

There is often an element of irony in how business decisions turn out. The owners and directors of Manchester United tried to build on the longevity of Sir Alex Ferguson's reign to promote stability and long-term planning. But a number of essential building blocks required to ensure this were missing.

What has been the result? Since Sir Alex retired, the club has lost many things: one manager (two if Mr Giggs is included), its chief executive officer, its long-established group of coaches and backroom assistants; an important income stream because the team failed to qualify for European competition; and also more football matches than it has done for many years. This sequence of events was not inevitable and there are many reasons why it happened. But one of the root causes of the team's sudden decline lies in the poor planning and decision-making of its owners, directors and senior managers. These decisions matter – to the club's owners and investors of course, but also to the millions of Manchester United fans around the world, me included.

 ## CORPORATE GOVERNANCE OVERVIEW

Definitions

There are many definitions of corporate governance – as we have seen the expression means different things to different people. The one that I find most helpful originates in the UK and is to be found in the UK Corporate Governance Code (the Code).[2] This is appropriate because in 1992 the Committee on the Financial Aspects of Corporate Governance, operating under the chairmanship of Sir Adrian Cadbury, provided for the first time anywhere in the world a written framework for corporate governance. The so-called Cadbury Report included a definition of corporate governance, which it described as 'the system by which organisations are directed and controlled'.[3]

The Cadbury definition is useful even today, but the thinking on governance has moved on since the early 1990s and the latest version of the Code in 2014 reflects this. The importance of corporate governance is described in the very first paragraph:

> *The purpose of corporate governance is to facilitate effective, entrepreneurial and prudent management that can deliver the long-term success of the company.*

Notice the tension in this definition, the juxtaposition of the words entrepreneurial and prudent – this balance is crucial but exactly how to go about driving the enterprise forward while keeping prudent control has often proved difficult to achieve in practice. The job of running a large, modern organisation is not easy or straightforward. The Code then sets out what it considers corporate governance to mean, as follows:

> *Corporate governance is what the board of a company does and how it sets the values of a company and is to be distinguished from the day-to-day operational management of a company by full time executives.*

Board composition, relationships and agency risk

Background

The Code's definition of corporate governance focuses attention on the board of directors. It makes the fundamental point that governing an organisation is different to managing that organisation. This difference applies to all types of businesses regardless of size and to the public sector as well as the private sector. We will look at the composition of the board shortly, but it is helpful first to provide a little more historical context.

The regulation of corporate governance has long been a feature of company law. Indeed, the importance of the shareholders of a business (the owners or investors) being able to hold their directors and managers to account was a key part of the design of the original joint stock companies. Company law has always provided for various aspects of this accountability relationship: companies must hold general meetings each year and provide their shareholders with certain minimum pieces of information, most importantly the annual report and accounts. Proper financial accounting to shareholders is a critical part of good corporate governance. In most countries today this is underpinned by company law and international accounting standards, the correct application of which is verified independently by the external auditors drawn from professional services firms or some other outside body.

The last 25 years has seen a developing interest in corporate governance in many countries around the world. In particular, there have been efforts to improve the governance standards of companies that seek to raise money from outside investors by being listed on a stock exchange. There have been various initiatives to do so, generally in one of two ways: either by drafting tougher laws or by developing codes of best practice. To illustrate this changed governance landscape from personal experience, when I started to investigate the situation surrounding the collapse of Polly Peck in 1990, which was a company listed on the London Stock Exchange at the time, there was not a single code setting out best corporate governance practices anywhere in the world. Today, such codes exist in over 60 countries. These developments have been essentially reactive to a number of corporate scandals and failures, occurring at various times in various countries, generally involving either stupidity or greed at the top and always destroying shareholder value.

There have been three 'waves' that produced significant changes in corporate governance. The first wave was the series of corporate frauds in the UK in the late 1980s and early 1990s (for example, Polly Peck, BCCI and Barlow Clowes) that were the precursors to the Cadbury Report. The second wave concerned the accounting frauds in the USA carried out by senior executives that were uncovered at or around the same time in 2000 and 2001 (for example, Enron, WorldCom and Tyco). These scandals threatened to undermine investor confidence and were directly responsible for the passing of the Sarbanes–Oxley Act 2002 (SOX). The most recent wave has followed the collapse or failure of a number of large organisations in the USA and in Western Europe (such as Lehman Bros. and the Royal Bank of Scotland) during the period 2007–09, that have resulted in recent changes and tightening of laws, codes and regulations in many jurisdictions.

These developments have been driven by investors and their marketplace – the stock exchange. This is particularly true in the UK, with the production of and subsequent amendments to the world's first code of corporate governance and in the USA with the passing of the SOX and subsequent governance-related legislation. We look at each of these later in the chapter.

The key governance players

As we have seen from the definitions, corporate governance is thought of today in more dynamic terms than those envisaged by Sir Adrian Cadbury in 1992 – it is something that facilitates effective, entrepreneurial and prudent management, which can deliver the long-term success of the company. It involves complying with all applicable laws, regulations and rules, but it also involves performance and effectiveness in the relationships between the various governance players: shareholders, directors, managers, company secretariat, the company itself and the company's stakeholders.

Although all stakeholders are important, the key corporate governance relationships and interactions take place between three groups: shareholders, managers and directors. In classic corporate governance theory, it is the shareholders who hold the power in any corporation: they are the owners of the company and have the ability to elect and dismiss directors and to hire and fire managers. No doubt the shareholders were able to exercise effective control in the nineteenth and early twentieth century, especially when many of those owners were also the managers of what were often in essence family-owned businesses. Today, however, the share register of a large publicly listed corporation will typically show thousands of owners at any one time, with the result that the collective power of shareholders has been splintered and diluted.

Composition of the board and committees

The shareholders of a corporation today will appoint professionals to manage their business for them – the executives that comprise an organisation's senior management team. This applies not only to large publicly listed corporations but also many other businesses. One of the reasons why shareholders appoint a board of directors is to oversee and supervise the actions of the managers. The performance of directors is crucial to the success of any business and this will depend on the qualities that they each bring to the role in terms of their skills, experience and attitude.

A prerequisite of business success, therefore, is that the best and most appropriate people are appointed to the board. So, the nominations and appointments process is one of the most important building blocks of success, to be followed by an appraisal process that assesses how every director is performing in his or her roles. We will look at each of these processes later in the chapter.

There are three important components of a modern board of directors, as follows:

- **The chairman**. The chairman is responsible for leading the board and for its effectiveness. Running the board is not confined to chairing board meetings (which includes setting the agenda, the timing and the culture of debate) but has much broader scope, for example facilitating team building, ensuring good information flows and communicating with shareholders. The chairman is therefore the pivotal figure in the governance process. The UK Code envisages the chairman being independent on appointment (that is to say, he or she is expected to join from outside of the organisation) but thereafter will spend a considerable amount of time on the organisation's affairs.

▪ **Executive directors**. Executive representation on the board is almost universal in companies based in the USA or the UK (though less so in some Continental European countries such as Germany, where a supervisory board of non-executives often sits above and separate from the management board). The CEO is of course the most senior manager in the organisation. In many US companies, the CEO will also be the chairman of the board, thereby concentrating power in one individual. The UK prefers a different approach, with the Code recommending that: 'There should be a clear division of responsibilities at the head of the company between the running of the board and the executive responsibility for the running of the company's business. No one individual should have unfettered powers of decision.' In many large US corporations, the CEO is often the only executive to sit on the board. In the UK it is almost always the case that the finance director will also be a board member and sometimes there will be others too (for example, the operations director or the director of human resources).

▪ **Non-executive directors**. Non-executives are individuals who work for organisations on a part-time basis and are paid a fee for so doing commensurate with their responsibility and time commitment. As a result of the corporate scandals and governance changes referred to above, over the last 25 years the role of the non-executive director, especially the independent non-executive director, has grown considerably in importance. Indeed, this is directly reflected in the board composition of modern corporations. The Code states that at least half of the boards of UK companies, excluding the chairman, should comprise independent non-executive directors. In the USA, the number of non-executives will typically far outweigh that of the executives. The main driver of this increased importance has been the desire to reduce the risk of the executives, in particular the CEO, running the business in their own interests rather than in the interests of the shareholders – in other words, a desire to manage what is known as agency risk (see below).

Much of the detailed work of the modern board of directors is delegated to committees, each comprising a small number of board members. Three different board committees are addressed in the Code: the nominations committee, the remuneration committee and the audit committee. The Code stipulates that the audit and remuneration committees should consist of at least three (or, for smaller public companies, two) members, each of which must be an independent non-executive director. Other committees may be formed of course, depending on the individual business needs of each organisation. Each committee should have its own charter.

Agency risk and the role of independent non-executive directors

Executives do not own the business but they work full time in it and so, in economic theory, are referred to as 'agents' – the agents of the owners. Of course, executives and senior managers should act always in the interests of the company for the benefit of the shareholders as a whole. However, as we have seen, the dubious decision-making of certain executives in high-profile business failures and fraud scandals, combined with the very large remuneration packages that they can earn (comprising salary, pension contributions, bonuses and share incentive schemes), makes it sometimes appear that these individuals are acting primarily in their own interests rather than in the interest of the company and of its shareholders.

The technical term for this is agency risk. Much of the work going into the codes of governance and the development of company legislation in the last 25 years has been carried out for the purpose of managing agency risk. To do so, code writers and law makers are increasingly looking to the directors as a whole, and in particular to independent non-executive directors, to strengthen corporate governance frameworks. Non-executives are said to be 'independent' if they have no other connection with the company, its shareholders or its management. The crucial role of independent non-executive directors in modern corporate governance theory is to act as the fulcrum between shareholders and managers. They provide the essential balance between the prime interests of the owners, who provide capital, and those of professional managers, who spend that capital in order to add value to the company. They also provide the owners with greater assurance that the executives are always acting in the best interest of the shareholders and not of themselves. The prime role of non-executives in modern corporate governance structures is therefore to scrutinise and challenge the plans and strategies of the executives.

 ## THE DEVELOPMENT OF CORPORATE GOVERNANCE CODES AND LEGISLATION

Rules-based and principles-based regimes

Introduction

Corporate governance regimes have developed in different ways around the world. History, culture and tradition have played a big part in the way that governance has developed in each country. There is one fundamental difference and that is between those regimes that are based on rules and those that are based on principles, as discussed below.

▪ Some governance systems are based firmly on the law. That is to say, compliance with the system is underpinned by legislation. Codes with legal enforceability are rules and so these are known as 'rules-based' regimes. The most important example of this is the USA where compliance with the SOX, for example, is a legal requirement for listed companies and their directors.

▪ Other systems are based on governance codes of best practice where compliance is voluntary rather than a legal requirement. These are known as 'principles-based' regimes. As we have seen, the first such code emerged in the UK out of the work of the Cadbury Committee in 1992. Here the findings of the Committee were not incorporated into company law as many at the time expected to happen. The Committee took the view that informality would be more powerful than legal rules. Instead, the requirement to comply with the Code was contained within the listing rules for publicly traded companies. The key principle of 'comply or explain' emerged: companies listed on the London Stock Exchange are expected to comply with the Code but, if they choose not to do so, they are required to explain the reasons for such non-compliance in their annual reports and accounts. It is for the market to decide how to react to these disclosures – there are no legal implications, no law has been broken. So, this is a self-regulatory system and is much more flexible than one based on rules. Since Cadbury, many countries around the world have chosen to adopt the principles-based approach.

Whatever type of system is chosen, whether it is rules-based or principles-based, the overriding aim of improved corporate governance is always the same: stronger corporate governance leads to increased investor confidence, which in turn enables access to broader-based and cheaper capital. This aspiration applies at both the individual company level and also for developing nation states.

The US and the UK governance regimes

We now look briefly at the corporate governance regimes in the USA and in the UK. We will use an overview of the SOX and the Code to illustrate the main features of the rules-based systems and the principles-based systems respectively. Both are very important in the development of the modern system of active and informed engagement by the board of directors in the oversight and governance of their corporations. It must be said that neither model, as then existed, was able to prevent the high-profile corporate failures arising out of the global financial crisis of 2007–09.

However, both the USA and the UK governance regimes have been altered in response to the fresh thinking that the crisis has provoked. In the UK, this has resulted in significant changes to its governance code, whilst in the USA recourse was made to further legislation. The widespread calls for more rigour in financial regulation and consumer protection coming out of the crisis led to the passing of another major piece of governance legislation by Congress, this time the Dodd–Frank Wall Street Reform and Consumer Protection Act 2010 (Dodd–Frank Act). Before that, the Fraud Enforcement and Recovery Act had signalled a more aggressive approach by the US authorities against fraud generally and against mortgage fraud in particular.

We look at both systems below, beginning with corporate governance in the USA.

 ## THE US POSITION

The Sarbanes–Oxley Act 2002

Introduction

The Sarbanes–Oxley Act (SOX)[4] was passed by the US Congress in July 2002. It introduced major changes to the regulation of corporate governance and financial practice for all companies listed on one of the US exchanges and therefore regulated by the Securities and Exchange Commission (SEC), wherever situated around the world. The Act is named after Senator Paul Sarbanes and Representative Michael Oxley, who were its main architects.

The law was passed as a direct response to concerns in the investor community following the bankruptcies of Enron in particular in December 2001, but also those of Global Crossing in January in 2002 and WorldCom in July 2002. These were all very large listed US corporations whose collapses were associated with major fraud, conflicts of interest and accounting scandals. How could this happen? The resulting investigations and media publicity highlighted many shortcomings but in particular those concerning financial reporting, internal controls and auditing standards caused dismay to investors.

The SOX sets out to address these shortfalls directly. It imposes new duties and significant penalties for non-compliance on public companies and on their executives, directors, auditors, lawyers and securities analysts. Its primary purpose when passed in 2002 was to bolster confidence in US capital markets.

The SOX is a comprehensive piece of legislation, arranged into 11 'titles' or sections. Compliance with it is of course mandatory. The most important aspects of the Act are summarised below.

Public Company Accounting Oversight Board

The SOX established this independent five-person board, overseen by the SEC and designed specifically to strengthen the assurance provided to investors by the audit process. All accounting firms wishing to audit US listed companies are now required to register with the board. The board has powers to:

- oversee the audit of public companies;
- establish auditing reporting standards and rules; and
- inspect, investigate and enforce compliance on the part of registered public accounting firms and those associated with the firms.

Auditor independence

The independence of the external auditor is a fundamental part of good corporate governance. There was a general perception that the independence of Arthur Andersen from its client Enron had been compromised by longstanding personal relationships and by consulting fees – Andersen was famously paid the same amount in fees each year both to act as consultants to Enron and to act as auditors (about $25 million, in each case). The SOX set out to strengthen auditor independence through the following measures:

- Prohibiting an auditor from undertaking certain specified non-audit services at the same time as performing the audit. These services include: bookkeeping; internal audit; and the design and implementation of financial information systems. Other work, such as tax services, may be carried out for an audit client, providing the audit committee has approved it in advance.
- Introducing an element of auditor rotation by prohibiting an audit partner from being the lead or reviewing auditor for more than five consecutive years.
- Placing a one-year prohibition on an audit firm from performing the audit if one of the company's senior executives had been employed by the same firm and had participated in the audit of the company during the previous year.
- Requiring that audit firms report more fully to the audit committee on contentious matters, for example critical accounting policies, alternative treatments and their implications under US Generally Accepted Accounting Practices.

Independence and responsibility

The SOX gives the audit committee responsibility for appointing, setting the fees and overseeing the work of the external auditors. Also, there is a new requirement that every member of the audit committee should be an independent non-executive director.

The CEO and the CFO are given significant extra personal responsibility under the SOX. They are required to certify personally in financial reports that the reports do not contain material mis-statements, that the financial statements are fairly stated, that they have received all necessary information and that the internal controls have been reviewed for effectiveness within 90 days of the report. As a result, the CEO and CFO have to take ownership of their financial statements in a personal and meaningful way.

Enhanced financial disclosures

Perhaps the most notorious and costly of all the extra requirements on listed companies under the SOX are the Section 404 provisions concerning management's assessment of the internal controls surrounding the financial reporting process. The reason is simple: it was precisely because of poor controls in this area that senior executives of Enron were enabled to mislead investors about the state of health and future prospects of the company.

Section 404 requires companies to publish an internal control report as part of their annual reports concerning the scope and adequacy of the internal control structure and procedures for financial reporting. This internal control report must also assess the effectiveness of such controls and procedures. Also, an external accounting firm must attest to and report on the company's assessment of the effectiveness of the internal control structure and procedures for financial reporting (the so-called Attestation Report).

In addition, companies are required to publish financial statements that reflect all material correcting adjustments and disclose all material off-balance sheet transactions.

The SOX prohibits most personal loans to directors and executives by a corporation.

Significantly, there is also a new requirement for the company to disclose whether or not it has adopted a code of ethics for its senior financial officers and whether its audit committee consists of at least one member who is a financial expert.

Corporate and criminal fraud accountability and penalties

The SOX has very significant deterrence provisions for the would-be white collar criminal built into it, including the following:

- Criminal penalties of fines and/or up to 20 years imprisonment for knowingly altering, destroying, mutilating, concealing or falsifying records with the intention to obstruct, impede or influence either a Federal investigation or a matter of bankruptcy.
- Criminal penalties of fines and/or imprisonment of up to 10 years on any accountant who knowingly and wilfully violates the requirement to maintain all audit or review papers for a period of five years.
- Subjects to fine or imprisonment of up to 25 years any person who knowingly defrauds shareholders of publicly traded companies.
- Provides protection for whistle-blowers by prohibiting a publicly traded company from retaliating against an employee because of any lawful act by the employee to assist in a fraud investigation.
- Provides increased penalties for mail and wire fraud from 5 to 20 years in prison.
- Provides increased penalties for violations of the Employee Retirement Income Security Act 1974 of up to $500,000 and/or 10 years in prison.
- Establishes criminal liability for the failure of corporate officers to certify reports, including a maximum imprisonment of 10 years for knowing that the report does not comply with the Act, or for 20 years for wilfully certifying a statement knowing it does not comply with the Act.

Commentary on the SOX

The SOX has had a tremendous impact on governance standards. It largely achieved its main objective of restoring investor confidence, especially with regard to both the production and auditing of the financial statements. The responsibility on board members for good governance has increased also. Under the SOX, board members are expected to be informed and engaged and their role in the oversight of the financial reporting in particular is now very important.

The SOX has not been without its critics, however. The extra liabilities and penalties on directors for non-conformance are seen by some as a disincentive to entrepreneurship, while the costs on companies of complying with the Act have been high. Compliance costs are particularly burdensome in the area of reporting on the effectiveness of the internal controls over the financial reporting process. One of the ironies of the SOX is that the audit profession has benefitted hugely from this aspect of the Act, certainly in terms of the extra fees that the accounting firms have earned as a result of Section 404 compliance, despite the fact that perceived weaknesses in external auditing was one of its main drivers in the first place.

The SOX and the financial crisis

The provisions of the SOX are specifically designed to address the risk posed to investors by senior executive fraud, accounting irregularities and poor auditing. They are not designed to provide protection against the combination of circumstances that brought about the financial crisis of 2007–09. As the report of the Financial Crisis Inquiry Commission,[5] set up by Congress in 2009 to determine the causes, makes clear this crisis was brought about by a combination of factors including: the relaxation of credit standards in US mortgage lending and the collapse of the subsequent housing bubble; the drying up of credit markets following the panic brought about by the failure of Lehman Brothers; failures in financial regulations and supervision; excessive borrowing and risky investments; and failures of risk management.

The headline finding of the Inquiry is very important:

> We conclude that this financial crisis was avoidable. The crisis was the result of human action and inaction, not of Mother Nature or computer models gone haywire. The captains of finance and the public stewards of our financial system ignored warnings and failed to question, understand and manage evolving risks within a system essential to the wellbeing of the American public.

So, the financial crisis has much to do with poor judgements and decision-making by those at the top of business and by failures of corporate governance. It was not primarily brought about by the malfeasance of corporate executives, as was the case in the headline scandals of the late 1990s. However, although malpractice is not the primary factor, it nevertheless still had a part to play in the actions of the authorities and the thinking of the public following this crisis. For example, the SEC has charged a number of financial institutions (e.g. Citigroup, Goldman Sachs, JP Morgan Securities and Bank of America) with misleading investors and improper pricing in complex mortgage securities transactions relating to the packaging and promotion of collateralised debt obligations. The regulator reached settlements with the firms concerned whereby they agreed to pay penalties of hundreds of millions of dollars and did not admit liability.

More generally, there has been great concern in the USA at what was seen as widespread mis-selling of mortgages to ordinary American citizens. The US Government sought to address this concern directly by passing another piece of legislation, the Fraud Enforcement and Recovery Act 2009.

The Fraud Enforcement and Recovery Act 2009

One of the Government's goals in passing the Fraud Enforcement and Recovery Act 2009 (FERA)[6] is the increased prosecution of fraud at a time when it had just succeeded in passing a trillion-dollar stimulus package for the US economy. So, there was increased risk of fraud against taxpayer funds at that time and calls for better oversight of government contractors. FERA is also an attack on mortgage fraud and related wrongdoing, which was seen as much more prevalent. The Senate Judiciary Committee had revealed that in 2008 there were more than 65,000 suspicious activity reports filed with the Treasury Department alleging mortgage fraud compared with only 4700 in 2001, nearly 13 times as many.

There are three main provisions of the FERA as follows:

- it expands the Department of Justice's authority to prosecute mortgage fraud, commodities fraud and fraud involving the public funds allocated to stimulate the economy under the Troubled Asset Relief Program (TARP) and the Recovery Act;
- it authorises almost $500 million in additional resources for government fraud investigations, prosecutions and civil proceedings; and
- it establishes the Financial Crisis Inquiry Commission to investigate the causes of the financial crisis, as mentioned above.

The Dodd–Frank Wall Street Reform and Consumer Protection Act 2010

Introduction

The main purpose of the Dodd–Frank Act[7] is to make a repeat of the recent financial crisis less likely through regulatory reform of the financial services industry. It makes financial institutions more accountable for their actions and enhances oversight of the industry to detect and prevent systemic risk before it reaches crisis level. The introductory description contained in the Act gives a good idea of its breadth and scope. It describes itself as:

> An Act to promote the financial stability of the United States by improving accountability and transparency in the financial system, to end 'too big to fail', to protect the American taxpayer by ending bailouts, to protect consumers from abusive financial services practices, and for other purposes.

Main features

The Dodd–Frank Act makes a variety of changes specific to the US regulatory framework, including: the creation of a consumer financial protection watchdog for retail financial products and services; the creation of the Financial Stability Oversight Council to monitor and reduce systemic risks; provisions to limit large, complex financial companies and end 'too big to fail' bailouts (including the Volcker rule, which prohibits banks from proprietary trading, owning hedge funds etc); the reallocation of authority among the federal regulators; the regulation of the derivatives market and hedge funds; and the introduction of new requirements and oversight for credit ratings agencies.

There are also a number of important reforms to executive compensation and corporate governance in the Act that are of relevance because they show that the American legislators are trying to influence the behaviour of people at the top of large corporations. In particular, there was a concern that short-term targets and the need always to maximise shareholder value were dominating corporate decision-making, rather than a focus on longer-term sustainability. The scale and structure of many executive incentive schemes in the USA, together with their lack of transparency, seemed designed to encourage greed and risky behaviour. The Dodd–Frank Act tries to address these concerns through a number of measures that give shareholders a 'say on pay' and create greater accountability as follows:

- Shareholders are given the right to a non-binding vote on executive pay and golden parachutes. This gives shareholders the opportunity to voice their disapproval of excessive or misguided incentive schemes and hold their executives accountable.

- The Act gives the SEC the authority to grant shareholders proxy access to nominate directors. This measure is designed to help shift executive focus from short-term profits to long-term growth and stability.
- The listing rules in the USA will be altered so that compensation committees that set the pay levels for executives will in future comprise independent non-executive directors only. This is in line with the best practice principle that no one who works in a publicly listed company should be able to set their own pay. The compensation committees will have the authority to hire compensation consultants in order to strengthen their independence from the executives.
- The Act requires that public companies set policies to take back executive compensation if it was based on inaccurate financial statements.

Conclusion

This section has provided a brief overview of the most important recent developments in US corporate governance. These have been enacted in legislation and are mandatory as a result. We will now look at the alternative system of governance, based around non-binding principles set out in codes of best practice. We will use the system in the UK as our example.

THE UK POSITION

The UK Corporate Governance Code

History

It is the series of corporate scandals in the UK in the early 1990s (for example Polly Peck, BCCI, Maxwell, Guinness, Barlow Clowes) that provides the essential background to the development of the UK's Corporate Governance Code.[8] What was noticeable about these particular scandals was that they were all caused by the actions of directors and senior managers who were directly involved in irregular and/or criminal conduct. Alarmingly for investors, this conduct was not picked up by either the external auditors or by the regulators. As we have seen, a committee under the chairmanship of Sir Adrian Cadbury was set up in 1991 against the background of corporate scandal to improve the running of listed companies in the UK.

The Cadbury Report in 1992 provided for the first time anywhere in the world a written framework for corporate governance. It recommended a principles-based approach. Consequently, self-regulation has become the basis for the governance of companies listed on the London Stock Exchange ever since. UK-listed companies effectively govern themselves, with the crucial reference point being the market. The theory underpinning the comply or explain principle is that if the market does not like what a company is doing in areas of non-compliance as disclosed in the report and accounts, it may decide to 'punish' the company by selling its shares.

The original Cadbury Code has been updated a number of times since 1992. It is regularly reviewed in consultation with companies and investors, most recently in September 2014. The influence of the developing UK Code on corporate governance thinking has been widespread. In the UK it is widely regarded as an indicator of best practice in governance not only for publicly listed companies but also for private companies and for organisations in the public sector. It has also been influential in the development of other governance codes around the world, for example, in the thinking of the King Commission in South Africa.

The post-financial crisis position

The UK Corporate Governance Code (the Code), which replaced the old 'Combined Code' in 2010, was developed in the aftermath of the global financial crisis of 2007–09 and some of its new provisions attempt to address the weaknesses of leadership and judgement shown by the boards of directors of some large companies in the UK at the time. It should be noted that the high profile failures of listed companies in the UK, such as Northern Rock and RBS, during the crisis are not associated with criminality but rather with poor decision-making and with inappropriate boardroom behaviours.

As we have seen, the Code is not a rigid set of rules, nor a 'one-size fits all' template that compels listed companies, regardless of size and business model, to follow it. One of the Code's strengths lies in its flexibility. It consists of Code Principles (Main and Supporting) and more detailed Code Provisions built around five key sections: leadership, effectiveness, accountability, remuneration and relations with shareholders.

Key aspects of UK corporate governance

The key aspects of the UK's corporate governance regime are set out by the Financial Reporting Council (the UK's independent governance regulator) in a paper published in 2010.[9] These are summarised below:

- A single, unitary board, comprising both executive and non-executive directors, collectively responsible for the sustainable success of the company.
- A series of critical checks and balances right at the top of the company including:
    - different individuals holding the key offices of chief executive officer and chairman (the thinking here is simple: the CEO runs the business but the chairman runs the board and thereby provides crucial division of power at the top);
    - balance around the boardroom table (at least 50% of the board, excluding the chairman, should be independent non-executive directors);
    - strong, independent audit and remuneration committees (comprising independent non-executive directors only); and
    - annual evaluation by the board of its own performance (introduced into the Code in 2003, this has moved from being a very contentious provision, resisted by many directors, into an accepted part of the structures needed to improve performance).
- Transparency on the appointment and remuneration of directors.
- Effective rights for shareholders, who are encouraged to engage with the companies in which they invest.
- The fundamental principle of comply or explain on which the Code is based.

The importance of respecting the comply or explain principle

The hallmark of UK corporate governance is the 'comply or explain' principle. As we have seen, this principle allows companies a degree of flexibility in how they put into practice the provisions of the Code. This flexibility has proved to be attractive to corporations around the world. Many companies have chosen to list their shares in London rather than in New York or elsewhere because of it.

The principle of comply or explain is designed to operate in a certain way. The UK Listing Rules require that all listed companies adopt the Main Principles set out in the Code and report to shareholders on how they have done so. These main principles largely address aspects of board behaviour and are the core of the Code – we will look at some of them later at various points in the book. The flexibility in the system is directed towards the extent of compliance with the more detailed

Code Provisions. It is recognised that an alternative to the practice recommended by a particular Code Provision may be justified in the unique circumstances facing an individual company if the alternative provides a better governance solution for that company. So if a board of directors considers that an alternative treatment to the one set out in a Code provision is more appropriate to the circumstances of the company, then the board is free to adopt the alternative. A condition of doing so is that the reasons for the alternative treatment should be explained clearly and carefully to shareholders, so that the market can react on an informed basis.

CREATING AN EFFECTIVE AND TALENTED BOARD

Overview

The board of directors is collectively responsible for the long-term success of the company. It needs to be effective, therefore. The board has a host of responsibilities which include: setting the strategic goals and helping to develop proposals on strategy; reviewing management performance; providing a controls framework that enables risk to be assessed and managed; ensuring that the necessary financial and human resources are in place to meet the corporate objectives; setting company values and standards and overseeing systems designed to ensure compliance with them and with all applicable laws and regulations; succession planning; taking decisions objectively in the interests of the company and its shareholders; and dealing fairly with other stakeholders.

If these board responsibilities are to be discharged effectively, then the dual nature of corporate governance that we discussed at the beginning of the chapter concerning board compliance and board performance in a theoretical context must work in practice also. First of all there must be proper processes around nominations and appointments to provide assurance that the men and women sitting around the boardroom table are the best possible, both as individuals and as a team, to take the organisation forward. Second, there must be measures in place that reflect a genuine commitment by those at the top to assess, develop and improve board performance over time.

Each of these is viewed in turn below primarily through two different lenses. First, I use the Code as the main reference point in terms of governance theory here – my view is that Section B of the Code provides an excellent guide to board effectiveness and we will look at the principles there in some detail. Second, for illustration and insights into how this theory is applied within corporations in practice, I will refer at various times to extracts from my interview with Annabel Parsons, a partner with Heidrick & Struggles (Heidrick), the worldwide executive search firm specialising in chief executive and senior level assignments. Annabel is an organisational psychologist with 15 years' experience of working with businesses and with expertise in executive and non-executive selection, succession planning and in conducting reviews of board performance. She runs the firm's leadership consulting business in the UK.

Board compliance: the key processes

Skills and experience

The modern board should work as a professional, high-performing team. Each member should be appointed on merit with skills and experience that meet the requirements of the organisation concerned as set out in a job description. This applies obviously to the executive directors, but today the same criteria should apply to the appointment of the non-executives too. Gone are the days of the so-called 'country club' boards where non-executive directors were appointed by either the chairman or the CEO, usually through connections of family, friendship or business association. At least in theory that is – from time to time some surprising individuals are appointed as directors even today, as is shown in the Co-op Bank example in Chapter 6.

One highly visible demonstration of this focus on relevant skills and experience is in the financial services industry. One of the causes of the global financial crisis is generally thought to have been the lack of understanding by some directors and senior managers in banks of certain aspects of modern banking practices, for example the failure to appreciate the risk attached to the hundreds of millions of dollars of derivative products sitting as assets in the balance sheets of many financial institutions at the time. Today, there is a significant increase in the due diligence of regulators in the USA and the UK to gain assurance on the technical expertise of the individuals comprising the senior management team of banks and other regulated firms.

Annabel Parsons raised this same point as an observation from her work with companies in regulated sectors and suggested that the likely shortage of generalists on the boards of financial institutions in the future may not be entirely beneficial:

> *The other thing that is interesting in terms of boards and board composition is that – and certainly I have noticed this in regulated businesses – there is a stronger and stronger pull away from the kind of generalist board member. Obviously the regulators are narrowing down the specification as to what qualifies you to be on a regulated board and yet on a number of the boards that I have looked at some of the greatest contributions are from people who actually come from very different backgrounds and industries. So, for example, the person that has been responsible for driving retail strategies in the consumer sector could add tremendous value to the board of an insurer – but that's unlikely to happen now because a much narrower lens is being applied to capability.*

The importance of a balanced board

It is clear in the Code that one of the overarching requirements in terms of the composition of the board and how the directors work together is for balance around the boardroom table. This is explicitly stated in the first of the Code's Main Principles on board effectiveness, B1, as follows:

> *The board and its committees should have the appropriate balance of skills, experience, independence and knowledge of the company to enable them to discharge their respective duties and responsibilities effectively.*

One of my concerns about the current focus of regulators in the financial services sector on technical expertise is that I feel it will, over time, work against the concept of balance. I believe that there is still a place for the generalist on all boards, the person who is not an industry expert but who can ask intelligent and challenging questions from a different perspective to the other directors. Banking is of course a technical industry but there are many different skills needed to run a successful business and not all of them depend upon technical expertise.

Appointments to the board

In terms of process, the Code addresses the need for a proper selection procedure for all directors in the Main Principle B2:

> *There should be a formal, rigorous and transparent procedure for the appointment of new directors to the board.*

The appointments process should be led by a committee (the Code refers to the nominations committee here) which will make recommendations to the board. Implicit in the principle above is that expertise is required in the process, so that external search consultancies (sometimes known as 'head hunters') are almost always used now to draw up a short-list of candidates from which the committee and then the board will ultimately choose. There are still issues around the composition of these short-lists in terms of their diversity (or lack of it) and we will discuss this issue, especially as it relates to gender diversity, below. Indeed, under the Code an explanation must be given if neither an external search consultancy nor open advertising is used in the appointment of a chairman or a non-executive director. So, it should no longer be possible for the chairman to recruit their golfing partner onto the board.

I began the interview with Annabel Parsons by asking her to sketch out the key characteristics that she looks for when conducting an executive search assignment at the CEO level. This is what she told me:

> There tend to be three clusters. The first sounds obvious but actually this is often the place that people have the fewest qualifications and that is the actual experience of running a business and being able to satisfy some of the requirements around the most senior executive role. The second is around the person: so it's around leadership qualities and in that you might put the way that they interact with others, the way that they prioritise, the way that they think so that could be actual ability around strategy and numeracy and that kind of thing. The last area is really content and sector specific so you might want somebody who has got very specific experience of running an upstream oil and gas business for example and there is not very much you can do with the candidate that doesn't have that content. So it tends to be those three areas and trying to strike a balance across all three. The tragedy is of course that sometimes what happens is that one of those three isn't quite in balance and typically that will be the personal areas ... so, it is a combination of fit and personality plus business context.

I then asked her about the mechanics of the selection process. My impression is that today it is a combination of desk-top research, interviews and some form of psychometric testing – am I correct? This is Annabel's reply:

> There was a period in time where CEOs and NEDS for example were very reluctant to be assessed in that way and they really felt that they were too senior. It's interesting that now that we have had so many issues with leadership in businesses that actually what you describe is happening very much more often so it's much more common practice now to put someone through a series of tests. Interestingly, Paul Flowers for example – the chap who used to be at the Co-op – there was a lot of publicity around the idea that he had been assessed for the role of chairman using the Myers–Briggs Type Indicator model. Well, a Myers–Briggs, although it is actually an occupational measure, is not designed as a standalone instrument. In other words it is not enough to have done only that in the selection process.

> Ideally, what you are looking for is a kind of triangulation rather like you would have in navigation. In navigation if you only take one bearing, you might know you are on this line directionally, but you could literally be anywhere along it, which is not helpful. So the idea is that you need to be able to cross-reference with other sources of data. Within the personality space you definitely need to cross-reference with other sorts of data because all of the instruments are looking at slightly different things.

> So you must look at the big qualities of personality and then you look at sub-sections of it such as motivation and drive. You can then get a much more accurate sense of where the individual is

likely to lie on a leadership spectrum. On top of that you have to do structured interviewing and preferably more than one interview. You ought also to be looking at market benchmarks so you need to reference them against the current executive population and you need to be doing referencing in the round. If you do all of that and you have a skills matrix so you are saying these are the skills that are essential, where are the candidates on those scales, you are much more likely to be accurate in your appraisal.

Now that's not to say that you won't have identified an area of risk but you will actually have pinpointed it rather than leaving it as a series of assumptions and question marks. So it should be a very thorough process and in my experience it much more often is these days.

I am sure that Annabel is right and that most businesses today allocate appropriate time and hire in expertise when selecting their top people. This is not always the case, however, as shown by the example of Manchester United above.

The Manchester United example also focused on the importance of succession planning. This is picked up by the Code's Supporting Principle in B2:

The board should satisfy itself that plans are in place for orderly succession for appointments to the board and to senior management, so as to maintain an appropriate balance of skills and experience within the company and on the board and to ensure progressive refreshing of the board.

The activities of the nomination committee are crucial here, with the objective being that the need for change is anticipated by an organisation and planned for rather than being compelled simply to react to events. The focus here should not only be at board level but also at the senior management levels so that the company develops and retains a sufficient pool of top executive talent at all times. Succession planning is often one of the major weaknesses in governance processes, something that was demonstrated by the Manchester United case.

In addition to having a process that provides assurance around people, the Code highlights two other crucial components for the functioning of an effective board: directors must have sufficient time available to enable them to discharge their duties properly; and they must have access to appropriate information.

Time commitment

Embedded within a proper appointments process is the need to ensure that all directors are able to allocate sufficient time to the company in order to discharge their responsibilities effectively. This applies particularly to the role of chairman and also to the non-executive directors (though not to the executives for whom, as full-time employees, time commitment should never be an issue). The Code does not specify what the required time commitment might be as the circumstances of each appointment will be unique.

There is an indicator of time commitment to be found in the financial services industry, however, in the Walker Review.[10] Sir David Walker was commissioned by the UK Government in 2009 to look into the corporate governance practices of UK banks and other financial industry entities (known subsequently by the acronym BOFIs) in the aftermath of the global financial crisis. This is an important report that produced some significant recommendations.

On the matter of time commitment, Sir David stressed the need for the boardroom to become a more challenging environment than it had often been in the past. His view was that this will require a substantially greater time commitment than previously from the chairman and also from the non-executives in order to assess risks and ask tough questions about strategy. The chairman should be expected to commit a 'substantial proportion' of his or her time to the company, which for major banks would be not less than two-thirds of their working schedule. Sir David also recommends that non-executive directors of large banks and other financial institutions should be spending between 30–36 days a year as a minimum in the role. This is a significant time commitment. It might appear excessive for many companies that are not large banks. However, the responsibilities of both the chairman and the non-executives are increasing (for example, the chairman of committees like the audit committee and the remuneration committee where the workloads today are substantial) and sufficient time will be required to discharge them effectively.

Quality of information that the board receives

The Code also focuses on the crucial board requirement for information. The Main Principle in B5 states:

> *The board should be supplied in a timely manner with information in a form and of a quality appropriate to enable it to discharge its duties.*

Under the Code it is the chairman who is responsible for ensuring that directors receive accurate, timely and clear information. Management has an obligation to provide such information, but directors should be proactive and seek clarification or amplification where necessary. In reality, the company secretary will work under the direction of the chairman to ensure good information flows both within the board and its committees and also between senior managers and non-executive directors. Of particular importance are the 'board packs' – the collection of briefing papers that are circulated to directors in advance of a board meeting. It is important that these packs are produced in good time, are comprehensive and contain sufficient scope of information yet, at the same time, are concise and easy to follow.

There is always a potential problem with information asymmetry – the executives and senior managers will always 'know more' in terms of the detail than the non-executives. The management of such information risk can sometimes pose problems. For example, in 2013 the FCA fined Chris Willford, the former Group Finance Director of Bradford and Bingley plc, £30,000 for failing to update the board about its deteriorating financial position during an emergency cash call at the height of the financial crisis in 2008. Mr Willford's delay was only for four days but he was deemed to have failed formally and urgently to escalate the information available to him, thereby breaching Principle 6 of the FCA's Statements of Principle for Approved Persons.[11]

The FCA also takes very seriously the failure of directors to share certain information amongst themselves – for example regarding any such failures as potential conflicts of interest. Full disclosure and transparency helps to foster trust around the boardroom table.

However, for many large organisations, the issue is not so much a shortage of information, but rather too much of it. The lawyers Simmons & Simmons have calculated that the average FTSE 100 board pack is some 288 pages long which, they reckon, would take over nine hours to read! To be effective, information provided to the board needs to be succinct, accurate, timely and clear. Board packs are often put together almost by routine by the company secretariat and it would be advantageous for the board (via the chairman) to become more proactive in this area – perhaps requesting some signposting in the packs or, alternatively, that the information in the packs addresses only those pertinent issues that are relevant to board-level discussion. Without this, information risk can become a serious threat to the efficient and effective running of the board.

Board performance: the key improvement drivers

Introduction

The Code appears on first reading to be simply a framework providing guidance on best practice procedures for corporate governance – a series of principles that a listed company must follow, together with more detailed code provisions where the 'comply or explain' principle allows for some variation in particular circumstances provided that there is disclosure of the reasons for so doing in the annual report.

As we have seen, the Code does indeed provide such a framework, but it goes much further. Embedded within it are three key board performance improvement drivers: the ongoing development of directors; provisions promoting board diversity; and the board evaluation and appraisal process. We will look at each in this section.

Role of the chairman

Actually, there is a fourth promoter of improved board performance contained within the Code and that is embodied in the role of the chairman. The chairman, as described in the Code, is the key governance figure:

> The chairman is responsible for leadership of the board and ensuring its effectiveness on all aspects of its role.

The duties and responsibilities of the chairman are extensive. He or she will chair the board meetings, setting the agenda and ensuring that adequate time is available for discussion of all agenda items, in particular strategic issues. Both around the boardroom table and more broadly, the chairman should promote a culture of openness and debate by facilitating the effective contribution of non-executive directors and by ensuring constructive relations between them and the executives. As we have seen, the chairman is responsible for good information flows. He or she should also ensure that there is effective communication with the shareholders and should regularly review and agree the training and development needs of each director. Finally, the chairman should support the CEO – except that is in wholly exceptional circumstances, where it will be for the chairman to deliver the news that the CEO is to be dismissed.

So, a good piece of practical advice for any organisation that is looking to develop and improve its corporate governance would be, as a first step, to appoint an effective chairman.

Development of directors

The job of a modern director, both executive and non-executive, is a professional one. Part of the personal responsibilities of all professionals is to keep learning and improving their skills over the course of their working lives and always to ensure that they remain up to date with developments in their fields of expertise. This applies absolutely to directors, as is made clear in the Code. Main Principle B4 states that:

> All directors should receive induction on joining the board and should regularly update and refresh their skills and knowledge.

We look at the importance of training and development in detail later in Chapter 8, but there are a number of important points to make at this stage regarding the application of this to directors.

The first is to highlight the importance of the induction and on-boarding process for new directors. This should be an extensive and formal process, for example new non-executive directors need to become familiar with the company as soon as possible and so should have the opportunity to meet senior managers and to visit some of the company's operating units. For publicly-listed companies, all new directors should take every opportunity to meet major shareholders. The second is to say that this commitment to development should be ongoing – in order to be credible, directors need to keep up to date and the company should provide the necessary resources to ensure that the knowledge and capabilities of its directors are developed and updated on an ongoing basis. The final point is that, as we have seen, the Code allocates prime responsibility for the development of directors to the chairman. Indeed the Code envisages that each director should have a personal training and development plan that is regularly reviewed and agreed with the chairman.

Now, all of this is eminently sensible. How is it possible for directors to be able to fulfil their roles on the board and on the board committees without keeping their skills and knowledge up to date? Just to take one example, over the last five years there have been significant developments in aspects of corporate law, in accounting and auditing standards and in risk management theory, all of which members of the audit committee must be aware of if they are to discharge their duties effectively.

Yet, I continue to see resistance to training and development at senior levels in many organisations. There are various reasons for this and pressure on time is certainly one of the most important. But it seems to me that there is sometimes a touch of arrogance or complacency involved too. One director told me of his aversion to the word 'training': 'Dogs are trained, not me.' Cost is another factor, especially in a period of economic downturn. From my lecturing work I see gaps in the awareness and understanding of directors and managers in exactly the areas of the law in which senior people can be held personally liable, for example: competition law and cartels, bribery and corruption and money laundering. It is always important to remember that ignorance is no excuse under the law. Training in business ethics remains haphazard and inconsistent.

We will look at barriers to the training and development of directors and how they can be overcome in Chapter 8. For now, the important message is a simple one: the commitment to competence is one of the key differentiators of a high-performing business. This commitment starts at the top, which means that all directors are supportive of training initiatives and, where appropriate, take part in them too.

Diversity

Diversity around the boardroom table, or the lack of it, has been one of the 'hot topics' of corporate governance for a number of years and it continues to be so. Boards in the USA, in the UK and in Continental Europe have been characterised, until recently at least, as being made up of directors who are overwhelmingly 'male, stale and pale' – in other words they largely comprise middle-aged to elderly white men, all from the same university educated backgrounds, each of whom sits on a number of other boards and has done so for years. Although this is a simplistic portrayal, there is some truth in it. Much of the poor decision-making of the financial crisis is attributed to 'groupthink' arising from homogeneous views around the boardroom table and a lack of vigorous challenge and debate. This lack of visible diversity around the boardroom table has been picked up by politicians, pressure groups and corporate governance specialists alike over the last 10 years or so.

The main focus of concern has centred on one aspect of diversity, that of gender, which has become the subject of intense scrutiny and debate. The proportion of women on the boards of the largest companies in many countries around the world has remained significantly below 50% for decades despite improvements in gender equality in other areas. As a result, politicians in some countries have decided to change the status quo dramatically through legislation. Take Norway, for example, the first country to introduce a gender-quota system by law. In 2003, the percentage of women on the boards of Norway's largest companies was very low (around 6%). The Norwegian Government at the time then passed a law so that, by 2008 at the latest, the boards of all publicly traded and public limited companies must have at least 40% female representation. Companies that fail to comply can, in theory, be shut down. Other countries have followed Norway's example. In France a quota law was passed in 2011 that requires publicly listed companies there to make 40% of the directors women by 2017. At the time of writing, five other European countries have government quotas on female directors in public companies: Belgium, Iceland, Italy, the Netherlands and Spain.

The USA and the UK have chosen, so far, not to go down the quota route, preferring instead to encourage companies to increase the number of female directors on a voluntary basis. In the UK, for example, the Davies' Report: 'Women on Boards',[12] published in 2011, begins with a summary of the position: in 2010 women made up only 12.5% of the members of the corporate boards of FTSE 100 companies, up from 9.4% in 2004. It states that the rate of growth is too slow: 'at the current rate of change it will take over 70 years to achieve gender-balanced boardrooms in the UK'. The report does not recommend quotas but it expects companies to take action voluntarily to alter the gender balance significantly in the short term: FTSE 100 boards should aim for a minimum of 25% female representation by 2015 and there are a series of recommended disclosures to ensure that measures are in place to make this happen, including changes to the Code. The UK Government has indicated that if this target is not achieved, then it will consider bringing in appropriate quota legislation.

The Financial Reporting Council incorporated the relevant recommendations of the Davies' Report into the 2012 edition of the Code. The Supporting Principle to Section B2 on board appointments states that:

> The search for board candidates should be conducted and appointments made on merit, against objective criteria and with due regard for the benefits of diversity on the board, including gender.

There is also now a requirement for the board evaluation process (see below) to consider the company's diversity, including gender. Also, the Code has expanded the disclosure requirements in the annual report concerning the work of the nominations committee. It should now include a description of the board's policy on diversity, including gender, any measurable objectives that it has set for implementing the policy and progress on achieving the objectives.

The subject of gender diversity came up in my interview with Annabel Parsons, initially as part of her observations on the end-result of the executive search process, which is a short-list of candidates provided by the consultancy firm from which the directors will choose the successful individual. This is what she told me:

> Typically it's a short-list so you know you've got two, three, or even four candidates – your investment in terms of the depth of assessment is in that short-list. And then the client makes up their mind about the short-list. I mean obviously you make recommendations, very often you've got three or four very good candidates but they all have differences so you help the client to differentiate between all those strong candidates. I suppose the issue is that when you get to that point it is very much up to the client who they choose. One of the issues that the search environment has been trying to help with in some ways, and in some ways we are still learning to cope with, is the whole idea of diversity within short-lists. Even if you get the 'diversity candidates' through the process to the short-list stage, you still cannot control who the client actually selects. Hence, now the suggestion is that we might have all female short-lists for example in some instances in order that there is no choice but a female candidate.

I then asked Annabel for her thoughts on whether or not this is a helpful development. This is her reply, which she developed into a number of interesting observations on some of the practical issues currently facing women on boards:

> Well, most senior female executives don't want that to happen at all, they want it to be a meritocracy. I think the interesting thing is actually – particularly when you look at the cross over between executive and non-executive roles – that there simply aren't enough women in senior executive roles to populate the non-executive roles, so we do need to tackle this at an executive level.
>
> In terms of non-executives the idea that you would need to have some form of 'NED-qualification' is one of the ideas currently talked about as a route to creating a more diverse population. So in other words it's not about who you know it's the fact that you are qualified. The problem is that it is still, to some large extent, about who you know plus it's a little bit like getting your equity card – until you've been a director sitting on a board, you don't feel fully qualified to be on a board, but you can't get on a board until you've been on one. So it's a somewhat vicious circle in that regard.
>
> We did do a little bit of research on this actually and we found that the only candidates that male non-executive directors felt really comfortable with from a female NED point of view were those who were chartered accountants. In other words, where there was an absolute and universally accepted professional qualification and discipline that qualified them unarguably to be on a board, then they were more likely to be accepted. So having that qualification means that no one is going to question your ability to interpret the numbers and assess business performance, so that gives you a platform.

I then asked her whether she had views or observations about the actual performance of women once they became directors – for example, were female directors able to improve the quality of challenge and scrutiny and boardroom debate. This was Annabel's reply:

> I think there is mixed research on this. One of the aspects of it is that generally the woman at the table is often the only woman there. So, on the one hand there is some research that suggests that the woman is not going to change the culture of the board whilst she remains the single person – that's very difficult to do. On the other hand, since she is not brought into that peer group she is already kind of an outsider and if you think about social psychology that could imply that actually she's got less to lose by challenging. So she's not part of that 'pecking order', she's not part of that social milieu, so in a funny kind of way she's got nothing to lose in challenging it.
>
> Also there's some evidence to suggest that female directors feel they have to prove their worth more than do men, so they're actually quite active board members – where sometimes, you know, we've all seen boards where there is a guy who has missed three of the last six meetings and hasn't read the board papers. There is evidence to suggest that women are terribly keen to prove that they are adding value and therefore they are on the ball, on the numbers, making the challenges. I think also there's ... We simply don't have enough women yet in board positions to have enough critical mass to be able to do much with the numbers statistically but I'm wondering also if the women that get on the boards are absolute survivors.

Personally, I am a strong supporter of diversity generally and I agree absolutely with the opening remark of Lord Davies in his report: 'Corporate boards perform better when they include the best people who come from a range of perspectives and backgrounds.' This will encourage more challenge and scrutiny around the boardroom table, with the prospect of improved decision-making as a result.

In terms of gender diversity, I agree with the voluntary approach taken in the UK – I have never been keen on quotas, to me they seem to be clumsy mechanisms and always run the risk of tokenism. It seems that the aspiration of 25% female representation on FTSE 100 boards by 2015 may well be achieved – the latest Davies Review in 2014[13] (written under the slogan 'Balanced boards mean better business') shows that 20.7% of FTSE 100 board members are women, compared with only 12.5% in 2011. However, the same report shows that of these female directors, only 6.9% are executives. This is an underlying issue that Annabel pointed to in one of the interview extracts above. Clearly, strengthening the position of women in the 'executive talent pipeline' remains a longer term task.

I have two concerns about the current focus on gender diversity. First, gender is only one aspect of diversity – others, especially the ethnicity, nationality, skill sets and age profiles of the directors sitting around the boardroom table, are important too and there is a danger that they can be overlooked. Second, the key to consistently sound decision-making is having directors who are capable of thinking differently, thereby providing a variety of views, perspectives and solutions to business problems, all working under the direction of an effective chairman. So, cognitive diversity, rather than gender diversity, is what I am looking for in a board of directors.

The 2014 version of the Code includes an interesting additional paragraph in the Preface that recognises these two concerns as follows:

> *Essential to the effective functioning of any board is dialogue which is both constructive and challenging. The problems arising from 'groupthink' have been exposed in particular as a result of the financial crisis. One of the ways in which constructive debate can be encouraged is through having sufficient diversity on the board. That includes, but is not limited to, gender and race. Diverse board composition in these respects is not on its own a guarantee. Diversity is as much about differences of approach and experience, and it is very important in ensuring effective engagement with key stakeholders and in order to deliver the business strategy.*

Here we see the Code recognising the importance of diversity on the board but in a suitably all-embracing way. Significantly, race is included for the first time alongside gender but diversity is not limited to these two factors – other aspects, including different experiences and approaches, are important too. In my view, what the Code is advocating here is cognitive diversity.

Board evaluation and appraisal

I first started running workshops for directors and senior managers on corporate governance at the London Stock Exchange in 2005. This was in the aftermath of the Higgs Review into the role and effectiveness of non-executive directors following the widespread concern at the accounting fraud scandals in the USA in 2000 and 2001 (Enron, WorldCom, Tyco etc.). The most controversial issue by far that we discussed during these early workshops was the new requirement in the Code at that time for the board, its committees and the individual directors to be subject to an annual evaluation and appraisal process. The Combined Code as it was then known contained a new Main Principle (which remains unchanged in the latest version of the Code) as follows:

> *The board should undertake a formal and rigorous annual evaluation of its own performance and that of its committees and individual directors.*

It was anticipated that board evaluation would mainly be internal process, although the possibility of using external assessors periodically to advantage was also raised. Almost none of the senior people that I worked with at the time were in favour of board evaluations and some were openly hostile. Various reasons were given: the time and cost involved; a feeling that there was no one who was in a position properly to assess the performance of a director; antipathy towards the idea of third parties being given access to confidential board papers and discussions; a feeling that there was lack of expertise in this area, so that the evaluation reports would be costly but of limited value; and of course there was a certain amount of defensiveness and reluctance to embrace change as embodied in this new initiative.

Today, less than 10 years later, almost all quoted companies in the UK carry out a board appraisal every year, while the great majority of chairmen consider that the process is valuable and has resulted in improved board performance. I would recommend that every organisation, whether listed or not, should put in place some form of periodic board review that is appropriate to its own particular circumstances.

Originally, the focus of the process was very much on internal evaluations – quite a smart move, as an internal review is less threatening than one that is carried out by third parties and so would be easier for directors to accept. The internal process would typically be overseen by the chairman and coordinated by the company secretary. There were (and still are) two key components of an internal board evaluation: first, self-assessment questionnaires that are to be completed by each director on their own individual performance and also on the effectiveness of board and committee meetings; and second, one-on-one interviews conducted by the chairman with each individual director – the chairman is subject to the same process, the idea being that he or she is interviewed by the senior independent director.

This internal focus changed in 2010. The Code was substantially amended in that year as a result of fresh thinking on corporate governance matters following the global financial crisis. Included for the first time in a new Code Provision was a requirement for periodic external review. The Provision stated:

> Evaluation of the board of FTSE 350 companies should be externally facilitated at least once every three years.

The reason for the change was clear: a periodic external review introduces an element of extra rigour and objectivity into the evaluation process. As a result, external evaluations of board performance have become much more of a feature for listed companies in the UK since 2010.

In her role at Heidrick, Annabel Parsons has been commissioned to conduct many board reviews and evaluations, not only in the UK but also around the world (for example, in India, the Middle East and West Africa). Board appraisals are becoming recognised as a key tool to improve board performance and also to show compliance with best practice corporate governance. During our interview I asked Annabel to outline for me some of the techniques that she uses when carrying out these reviews. This was her reply:

> OK. The first thing is that we would probably take a view of the individual members of the board. So, we would look to interview the directors and we would have a set of competencies for a 'standard' NED (and also perhaps for the particular business sector the client is in as well) and we would start to assess them against that. Very often we use 360 degree feedback, so we actually ask all of the board members to give an opinion on each other: the effectiveness of the chairman, the effectiveness of the SID (the senior independent director), the effectiveness of their peers, and what each of them is contributing.

We also carry out a survey on the effectiveness of the board and again we will ask the NEDs to complete that – very often we will ask the executive team to complete it as well so that they start to identify where the issues might lie in terms of that workflow. In addition, we will sometimes use psychometrics actually to look at the personalities around the table, to identify the kind of mix that might be there.

We would also observe the board. We tend to go to at least one board meeting and at least one committee meeting. We always have more than one of us in the room so that we can get a broad view – that way we can actually see the board dynamics in action and we can also see the board process in action. As preparation we will want to see the board papers, the board minutes, look at the connectivity between those and the agenda, whether issues of real substance are given the air time and the focus that they really should have and what the follow through has been like on those actions that were decided upon. So, for example we will follow up looking at the minutes, what has been agreed and who will do it and then we go to the next board meeting to see how well these were followed through on.

Even the decision-making process in the room can be very interesting, whether it is absolutely clear that a decision has been taken. I've been in one meeting where one of the NEDs had actually nipped out to go to the loo and he missed a big vote and when he came back he asked: 'Have I missed anything?' and they all said 'No, nothing important.' He had missed a big vote! I should also say that the reason he nipped to the loo was that the chairman was very ineffective in managing time, there were no breaks, there was no structure to the meeting, and so even simple things can end up having a big impact.

So we then feed all the results back to the chairman – we have a big session with the chairman on his own performance, on the performance of the board as a collective and on the performance of the board as individuals. Sometimes we will do a 'deep dive' on key aspects – the strategy process, risk management or whatever. Typically we give a rounded picture of how well the board is performing. Then we will set out a development plan for the board and we will also give feedback on each individual, typically via the chairman – where necessary each individual director will have a development plan.

What's interesting I think is that a lot of boards have now come to terms with the idea of on-boarding the non-executives. So, the initial few months of a new NED's appointment are seen as very important, with the new NED needing to get to grips with the business, but quite often it stops there. They forget that actually over a period of time the business moves on and the NEDs need to move with that – keeping their knowledge fresh, keeping on building their knowledge, is very important. The company secretary can help here by running a parallel programme alongside the board, so that the NEDs are developing constantly. That is the way to go.

Annabel has set out here the classic components of a board appraisal process involving: interviews of directors; observation of board and committee meetings; surveys to obtain structured views from the non-executives and senior management; and feedback given via liaison with the chairman. The benefits of an external review, in addition to it being objective, lie in the broader perspective of the assessors that enables benchmarking to take place. Typically, the external review will result in a report that would assess the company against a number of measures, for example: board composition and structure; the role and accountability of the board; strategic alignment and engagement with business issues; board processes and practices; board culture and dynamics; and the interaction and relationship with management.

The board performance appraisal, performed annually, is now an established requirement for companies listed on the London Stock Exchange. The concept of regular evaluation of the board and directors is not restricted to large listed companies however – it can be used with benefit by any organisation in any business sector. After all, a feature of modern business life is that all managers and employees are subject to regular performance appraisals – the idea being that if weakness or shortfalls are identified and communicated in constructive feedback, then performance will improve in the future. This principle holds true for those at the top of business also. The appraisal methodology will require adaptation to suit the needs of each individual organisation, of course, but the evaluation process is one of the most important tools available to improve board performance and thereby increasing the chances of long-term business success.

WORKSHOP CONCLUSION

Closing

By way of drawing the workshop to a close, I turn to Rachel Gordon. The pivotal role in corporate governance, especially in the UK model as exemplified by the Code, falls to the chairman. I know from our previous discussions that Rachel is well aware of this and that she takes her governance responsibilities very seriously. I am interested to learn what her plans are to improve governance at the Stronach Group, so I invite her to lead the concluding discussion, with a view to deciding the five key takeaways from the workshop. Rachel is happy to do so.

Key takeaways

Rachel then proceeds to take the other team members through her ideas. Although she is always prepared to listen, it is clear that in the area of corporate governance she has some plans for Stronach already formulated in her mind. Very quickly she notes the following points on the flipchart, building on the twin-track approach of the conformance and performance aspects set out during the workshop.

- ✓ **Introduce a stronger integrity component into the board and senior management appointments process**. Rachel has been thinking since the first workshop of incorporating dilemma-based scenarios into the company's interview process. This might reveal a candidate with surprising attitudes. More importantly, Rachel's idea is that by asking the candidates to articulate their thoughts on a selected scenario, it will give the interview panel a better idea of which one on the short-list is most closely aligned to the values and culture of the Stronach Group.
- ✓ **Improve cognitive diversity at the top**. Rachel has long been a champion of gender diversity but, along with the other members of the team, she was impressed by my comments on cognitive diversity in the presentation. Even after her own appointment as chairman, she feels the current board at Stronach is too homogeneous and that it would benefit from fresh thinking and different perspectives in discussion and debate.
- ✓ **Appoint an external assessor to facilitate the board evaluation process this year**. This is something that Rachel is looking to do in the immediate future. Like the rest of the team she is well aware of the importance of both board process and board behaviour to good corporate governance. She will incorporate this into the selection process of those companies short-listed for the board evaluation work, especially their ideas on how best to assess behaviour, in order to select the external candidate that is best for the Stronach Group.

✓ **Put together personal development plans for each director**. Rachel and David Hurley will work together to develop these. Everyone understands the importance of the board being kept up to date and Malcolm Mainwaring stresses that this is vital today in terms of managing evolving legal and regulatory risk. Rachel feels that they could make more use of board meetings, by scheduling short skill-burst sessions either just before or just after a board meeting. David agrees to think about this and put some proposals together.

✓ **Improve succession planning**. Succession planning is recognised by everyone as an area of weakness for the Stronach Group – it is small comfort to the team to learn that other organisations struggle with this too. Rachel says that the board is currently being refreshed and she hopes to be able to report on the appointment of the new non-executive director shortly. However, more could be done to identify and develop a pipeline of talent internally so that the senior management team is refreshed in a more structured way in the future. David Hurley mentions the idea of putting high performers on management development programmes with institutions such as Cranfield. John Holt is enthusiastic and says that he would like to work with David to develop a proposal on this.

Next workshop

I thank everyone for their contributions today, particularly Rachel for leading the last discussion and pulling everything together in a strong set of takeaways at the end. I say that in my view action in these areas will result in significant improvements to governance at the Stronach Group.

The parameters for the next workshop have already been agreed and these will focus around aspects of ethical leadership and tone at the top. Malcolm asks whether we can include an element of creating a compliance culture in this, and I say that this should be possible. John Holt then alerts us all to the fact that for the next two months or so his workload will be intense – this, with travelling too, means that he may be unavailable for the next workshop. However, he wants to attend the session on ethical leadership very much and he will make every effort to do so.

Rachel agrees to coordinate diaries as she has done previously and will aim to re-assemble the group in approximately four weeks' time for the next workshop.

Reflections

As I leave the boardroom, I feel that this has been a productive session. I have no time to think through what was said at the workshop properly, however, because Malcolm now joins me and proceeds to take me, as agreed, to his favourite coffee shop in Berkeley Square. It turns out that he wants to tell me more about the background to the Group from his perspective of having worked there for many years. Interestingly, he is also keen to give me his views about the previous Chairman and CEO, Duncan Stronach.

This is the gist of what he says to me over our cappuccinos.

> *Rachel Gordon has been a breath of fresh air since she arrived. The ethics project is a good example – I think the workshops are tremendous and Steve, thank you very much for facilitating those. There would be no chance of them happening under the old regime – absolutely none. Duncan did everything his way, no one could control him. And if you weren't an engineer then it could be difficult to get his attention or to get any changes approved by him. I personally got on with him well enough but I found him frustrating sometimes in a business-sense. He was a real chancer you know – in his own way he could be extremely reckless at times. We went into*

India on the back of a hunch, there was minimal due diligence and things could have gone very wrong for us there. Duncan got in over his head, I don't know what he agreed with the people over there because he never discussed any of his projects with me. All I know is that he became very nervous when the rumours started to fly – the denials seemed more like bluster to me. It is a terrible thing to say, but in many ways the car crash was the best thing that could have happened to the Group – there, I have said it now, it's what many of us have been thinking. We now have John and Rachel at the helm and we are all feeling so much more positive as a result. I thought the workshops might be window-dressing at the outset, but they are not, they are helping us to change and to move forward. We need to!

As we part, I thank Malcolm for the coffee and for sharing his thoughts with me – we must do it again, and next time the cappuccinos will be on me.

CHAPTER SIX

Aspects of leadership: ethics, tone at the top and handling a crisis

 ETHICAL LEADERSHIP: FIFTH WORKSHOP

Opening

Introduction

As is becoming my habit, I arrive early for this the fifth workshop of the Stronach ethics project and make my way to the boardroom. I have just started to set up when I am joined by John Holt, the CEO. John seems a little agitated today. He says that he is currently working on a big contract, so his diary is under pressure. This contract requires his attention today and so he might be called out of the workshop before the end. He apologises and says that would be disappointing – he is looking forward to today's session, especially the part on ethical leadership. He is looking for some pointers here – what might he be able to do, as chief executive officer, to set the tone and make a difference? I tell John not to worry, we will be able to work around his time constraints.

As I am considering what to do, the other three members of the team arrive together and immediately head for the coffee. I welcome them and say that John and I have been discussing today's workshop – John has important meetings scheduled and may have to leave early. I have a suggestion. John is interested today in particular in the piece on ethical leadership. So, I suggest that we begin with this and the related topic of tone at the top before reviewing how best to handle a crisis situation, something that Rachel Gordon, the Chairman, has asked about previously.

If we do this, there is one problem. I will not be able to cover the subject of compliance before John is likely to be called away – Malcolm Mainwaring, the Group Finance Director, had requested this in the last workshop. I have another suggestion – rather than trying to rush through all the subjects today, we could have an additional workshop in the near future, slightly shorter than normal, to look specifically at compliance, controls and the related topic of audit. Is this possible? The team consult, more coffee is poured, diaries and iPhones are scrutinised and then Rachel announces that this would work, provided that I can attend one evening next week after work, say 7.30 pm? It is agreed.

Agenda

I quickly set out the agenda for this morning. As already discussed, there are three main areas that I want us to cover in the workshop, as follows:

- We will begin with a review of the concept of ethical leadership by looking at its two component parts: the ethical person and the ethical manager.
- This will lead naturally into a discussion of what the often-used phrase 'tone at the top' actually means in practice. I will provide a number of examples, including a case study of recent events at the Co-op Bank and a much more positive example of ethical leadership from the financial services industry. We will use these to draw out some lessons on what both 'good' and 'bad' might look like in terms of ethical leadership. John gives me a thumbs-up at this.
- For the third component, we will look at the issues presented by an unfolding crisis event, one that arises unexpectedly and develops very quickly. Any organisation, including the Stronach Group, could be confronted by a crisis and it is vital that business leaders understand the ground rules for dealing with it in the best way possible if reputational damage is to be minimised. I say that it is particularly appropriate to cover this subject in this workshop because stakeholders are viewing how a crisis is handled by an organisation as an indicator of the quality of leadership in the enterprise.

Everyone indicates that they are happy with this revised itinerary for today's workshop.

A business dilemma

Before we begin the formal presentation, I have another business dilemma for them. While handing out the sheets describing the dilemma situation, I explain the background. I ask each of them to imagine that they are a chartered accountant who is the finance director of a large organisation – I smile in Malcolm's direction at this point – and find themselves confronted with the following, unexpected discovery:

> *You are attending a dinner at your Institute and are enjoying drinks with a number of your fellow finance directors at the end of the evening. One of them happens to mention to you a mutual acquaintance, Peter Wiggins, who is one of your divisional sales directors. It turns out that this gentleman had gone to school with Peter and was his best friend for a while – small world! The two of them have since lost touch but it is clear from what he is saying that it is the same Peter Wiggins. The finance director then says that he is really impressed that Peter has got on so well in business because he remembers him leaving school at 16 with no academic qualifications and seemingly few prospects.*

You smile, nod, engage in further small talk for a while and then make your excuses and leave. Something is bothering you. Peter Wiggins joined the Group three years ago, since when he has proved himself to be your best salesman, responsible for bringing in numerous new accounts and transforming the performance of his area of the business. As a result of all this success he was promoted to divisional sales director earlier this year. He has also made a very favourable impression on your CEO who has said to you on more than one occasion that he considers Peter to be 'main board material'.

This is all fine and you personally get on well with Peter. However, there is a problem. You joined the company as finance director just before Peter Wiggins was recruited. As a new senior executive, you were asked to familiarise yourself with the company's interview process and so you 'sat in' on the series of final interviews out of which Peter was hired. You remember quite clearly that he claimed on his CV to have a geography degree as well as a number of A levels because you joked with him during the interview about how unusual it was for a geographer to end up in sales! You recall being rather impressed with his reply also. And now this ... What do you do?

As each of them is reading through the dilemma situation, I say that I want them to think through the implications of this situation and that we will return to discuss it at the end of the workshop. I give them some time to read the briefing paper properly before starting the presentation.

 LEADERSHIP

Two examples: theory

Before looking specifically at ethical leadership, there are some important points to make on the broader subject of leading an organisation – what qualities and attributes are needed for success? It is important to say that the two are not disconnected, however. I have always believed that integrity is an essential component of being a leader, whether it is in business or in any other sphere. Having integrity makes a leader believable and therefore worthy of our trust. Without it, trust will be contingent and unlikely to survive a period of poor results or bad news, no matter what other qualities the leader might possess. Here are two examples from leadership experts to support this view.

The first example is from the work of Peter Northouse, Professor Emeritus at Western Michigan University. Professor Northouse defines leadership in his influential textbook *Leadership: Theory and Practice*[1] in the following way:

> *Leadership is a process whereby an individual influences a group of individuals to achieve a common goal.*

Included in the various theories of leadership that he discusses in the book is the traditional 'Trait Approach'. Professor Northouse summarises the five major traits of successful leaders as being: intelligence, self-confidence, determination, integrity and sociability. He points out that the Trait Approach to leadership has its critics today – it has a slightly old-fashioned feel about it because this approach focuses on a number of innate characteristics possessed by 'great' individuals, which largely cannot be taught, in contrast to the more modern 'Skills Approach' to leadership.

Professor Northouse points to the more recent theories around the concept of Authentic Leadership as possibly being a more powerful approach, especially for modern, more sceptical times. According to this theory, the key characteristics for leaders are that they: are genuine in the role above all and are not merely acting; are self-aware and do not try to hide their mistakes; are mission-driven and focused on organisational goals, not on self-interest; lead with conviction – with their hearts as well as with their minds; and they base their actions firmly on their values.

Now, the key point for me here is that the bridge between the Trait Approach and the Authentic Leadership Approach is integrity. Individuals who adhere to a strong set of principles and take responsibility for their actions are exhibiting integrity. Leaders who have integrity inspire confidence in others because they can be trusted to do what they say they are going to do. Integrity leads to trust, the essential x-factor for a leader who is looking for success in his organisation over the long term.

The second example is from the renowned businessman and investor Warren Buffett, the Chairman and CEO of Berkshire Hathaway. In his articles and on his website Mr Buffett refers frequently to integrity – it is one of the key qualities that he looks for in the management teams of businesses that he is considering investing in. Interestingly, one of the ways that he describes integrity is as the ability to say 'no'. My favourite quote of his on the subject is this one:

> *In looking for people to hire, look for three qualities: integrity, intelligence and energy. And if they don't have the first one the other two will kill you.*[2]

Another example: practice

Mr Buffett made this comment in the aftermath of the US accounting scandals of 2000 and 2001. It seems to me that it may have been formulated specifically with Jeff Skilling, the ex-Chief Operating Officer and ex-CEO of the Enron Corporation, in mind, though I cannot be sure of course. Mr Skilling was jailed for his part in the accounting fraud at Enron and his career is often discussed today in almost wholly negative terms. This is too simplistic, however, as was pointed out to me a number of years ago.

I was giving a talk in London that included a piece about the Enron case. I referred to the type of culture that the senior management at Enron created in their organisation and listed some of the problems that I felt this created – it was overly aggressive, self-centred, dog-eat-dog and so on. After a short time, a lady in the audience raised her hand to put forward a different perspective. She said that earlier in her career she had worked as a manager in one of the European divisions of Enron prior to its bankruptcy and had found the culture there to be very different to the one that I was describing – much more positive, inspirational even, based around creativity and risk-taking. She had learned a lot whilst working at Enron and had enjoyed the experience too.

This was a good lesson for me because it illustrates the basic truism that organisations (like people) are rarely entirely good or entirely bad. To be fair, it seems from all that I have read about the case that Mr Skilling did display some excellent leadership qualities at Enron: he was intelligent and energetic; he was creative, a visionary even, and he could be an inspiring figure so that he was able to connect strongly with his followers; and he had both the ideas and the drive to transform Enron's business model. There were also certain more negative features of his leadership style – aggression and arrogance, a relentless and absolute focus on maximising shareholder value and making money as quickly as possible. This aggression and obsession with financial returns led, as Enron found it more difficult to hit its growth targets through its trading activities, to presenting Enron's annual report and accounts in a way that relied on the manipulation of accounting rules to maximise profit. The picture became increasingly artificial. Ultimately Mr Skilling was convicted of fraud.[3]

Summary

I pause here to check with the team and make sure that they agree with my basic point, which is that integrity is the one component of leadership that it is necessary for business leaders to have – it may not in itself be sufficient but it is a necessary condition for long-term success. They all nod their agreement and Malcolm Mainwaring adds a comment of his own: 'Success may come and go but integrity is constant – it is about doing the right thing at all times, in all circumstances, whether or not anyone is watching.'

I am in complete agreement with this – it is a powerful observation and it leads naturally into the main part of the presentation on ethical leadership.

 ## THE COMPONENTS OF ETHICAL LEADERSHIP

Overview

As we have seen, the essence of business ethics is behaviour. Behaviour is determined primarily by the interaction of two factors: character and judgement. So, when addressing ethical leadership, it is most helpful to divide the discussion into its two essential component parts. The first component concerns character and may be termed the ethical person – leaders should live with integrity and lead by example. The second component is to do with judgement. Judgement is the essential requirement for what may be termed the ethical manager – leaders require consistency when making decisions that affect the stakeholders in their organisations, in good times and in bad. I should add that there is also a third component of ethical leadership. This is both being aware of and using what I call the ethical toolbox – the various policies, procedures and controls that are available to provide assurance to directors and senior managers of good business ethics throughout their organisation.

We will look at the first two of these components in the paragraphs below. However, we will return in Chapter 8 to look specifically at the various tools and techniques contained within the modern ethical toolbox.

The ethical person

Introduction

I have mentioned before that there are no saints in business. But this is not the point. Sainthood is not required for ethical leadership and it would be wrong for any of us to pretend that we are paragons of virtue – we are human, we all have flaws, we all make mistakes and the best that any of us can do is to try to improve our behaviour and our performance every day. It is important that character is not confused with flawlessness. What is required from a business leader in terms of ethics is actually quite straightforward – it is about living with integrity and leading by example.

Directors and senior managers need to have good character with strong principles because an integral part of their job is that they are able to embody the purpose, vision and values of the organisation that they lead. In my view, there is no place for actors at the top of business. Equally, saturation news coverage and social media are blurring the divide between the public self and the private self of leaders in every walk of life. For those in the spotlight, there is nowhere to hide anymore and secrets will always come out.

Just ask politicians.

Example from politics

In January 2014, President Francois Hollande of France attended one of the most important press conferences of his life at the Elysee Palace in Paris.[4] After giving a detailed analysis of the economic challenges facing France and his proposals for addressing them, the first question was not about the French economy at all. Inevitably, it was to do with the recent revelations in *Closer* magazine that the President had been allegedly conducting an affair with a French actress – given these allegations, what everybody wanted to know was where this left his companion and official consort Valerie Trierweiler. What did the President have to say? He gave a dignified reply, as follows:

> *Everyone in his personal life can go through difficult periods; this is the case for us. These are painful moments. But I have one principle: private matters should be dealt with privately.*

Was he right to think this? In this instance, it seems that he was. All the indications are that the French press and the French public largely agreed with him. Although embarrassed by the revelations and details that emerged after his subsequent break-up with Ms Trierweiler, President Hollande has not been subjected to either the scale or intensity of media pressure and public outrage that would inevitably have fallen upon a British Prime Minister or an American President in similar circumstances.[5]

In Chapter 4 we looked at the area of ethical risk and the importance of understanding the expectations of key stakeholders. Francois Hollande knows his electorate: the key point here is that, as far as the French are concerned, the alleged affair did not seriously damage his credibility as President. When assessing the likely reaction to character flaws or mistakes that leaders make, context and timing are often crucial. The idea that political leaders in Western democracies today can separate their public and private lives is naïve, however. With the swift dissemination of information afforded by the Internet the private lives of politicians are no longer private at all.

The same is true in the business world also.

Examples from business

Does the personal character of a business leader matter? Is the way that he or she conducts themselves in their private lives relevant to the workplace at all? I know many people who would answer 'no' to both of these questions because they feel strongly that the business environment is separate and that people should be assessed on their abilities to do the job that they are paid to do. I have some sympathy for this argument – religious beliefs, political affiliations, sexual orientation and dietary choices are examples of the personal characteristics of leaders that would be irrelevant in a work context except in all but the most extreme of cases. I only have sympathy up to a point, however, because I do believe that it is very important that business leaders are men and women of good character.

At the most basic level, honesty and integrity can best be re-inforced when a proper example is set. Obeying the law is an essential requirement for a director or senior manager. So too is being aligned to the organisation's core values – a business leader not only has to be able to tell the company's story but he or she must live it too. To be seen to do otherwise will have profoundly negative consequences, inviting either charges of hypocrisy from third-party commentators or deep cynicism from the employees. The leader must be seen to behave in an appropriate way too. For example, racist remarks or sexist jokes made either in public or private will be likely to cause offence and are seen as being completely unacceptable by very many people today.

Set out below are two examples of poor behaviour by business leaders. In each case, the result was the same – a hitherto well-respected and successful CEO lost his job.

Example 1

The first example illustrates the point that business leaders who are shown to have breached trust by acting dishonestly are likely to be in difficulties because they lose credibility and the respect of their stakeholders. This is the case of John (now Lord) Browne, the former CEO of BP plc. In 2007, he resigned his position after he admitted lying in initial witness statements that he submitted to a court about the circumstances in which he had met a former boyfriend during his attempt to obtain an injunction to prevent a British newspaper from exposing details about his private life. The judge in the case was highly critical of his conduct. This case was a personal tragedy for Lord Browne and it illustrates that even the most experienced of people can make poor judgements when in pressure situations.

Speaking to the BBC in 2012, Lord Browne placed the case in the broader context of business intolerance of homosexuality. He told the journalist, Robert Peston, that he had got so used to lying about his sexuality that he did not think through what he was doing when he misled the court. Also, he did not want to upset his mother.[6]

Lord Browne was well used to handling pressure in a business context and he had shown himself to be resilient in the workplace environment. However, in 2007 he had been confronted with threats arising from an aspect of his personal life that he had never felt able to be open and honest about and it seems that he was unable to manage them in an objective and professional way. His judgement in this situation was flawed and it was this that cost him his job. Having admitted that he lied in court documents it was not possible for him to remain as the CEO of what was then the UK's largest company.

Example 2

The second example highlights another area of concern. This is where a business leader allows some aspect of his or her private life to impinge directly upon the workplace in a way that breaks the internal codes and rules of the organisation. There are many possibilities. For instance, it could involve the use of drugs or alcohol on company premises. Another, the subject of the second example below, is where a leader enters into a personal relationship with someone who works in the same organisation – the other party will almost always be in a subordinate position in the company hierarchy, thereby creating risks around conflicts of interest and perceived favouritism.

The case of Harry Stonecipher is instructive here. Mr Stonecipher returned from retirement in 2003 to become the President and CEO of the Boeing Corporation in order to help the company restore its reputation after a procurement scandal involving its then finance director. He was making good progress with this when, in 2005, he was forced to resign by the Boeing board. An investigation, following a tip-off, had uncovered a relationship between him and a female executive at the company that he had not previously disclosed. The executive was clearly in a subordinate position to Mr Stonecipher. Boeing said that he left the company for violating the company's code of conduct which stated that all such relationships with a subordinate colleague within the company had to be disclosed. Mr Stonecipher had himself sponsored the re-drafting of the code of conduct, which introduced this requirement.[7]

There are two important points to make about this case. First of all, it was issues of poor judgement that caused Boeing to press for Mr Stonecipher's resignation rather than the affair itself. Following Boeing's recent reputational damage, the board had little tolerance for any further misdemeanours from senior executives. This leads to the second important point. Boeing was putting down a clear marker that the internal codes and rules matter. Mr Stonecipher had failed to follow the company's new code of conduct that he himself had sponsored. Such failures would now have consequences, no matter who you are within the company.

Difficulty in assessing integrity

When I interviewed Annabel Parsons, the executive search expert at Heidricks, I asked her to what extent questions of integrity and ethics play a part in the assessment and selection process for prospective board members. This is her reply:

> Well I think that it does, certainly. I think a lot of the data is actually based on inference so it's very unusual to have clear indications that somebody lacks integrity, but where you have those indications then the person concerned is a non-starter. In practice, it's more about shades of grey. The other issue is that it is actually very difficult to assess integrity unless there has been some major scandal. Even then I've encountered the situation where somebody was actually the person that sorted out the big ethical issue but they themselves were tarred by the association. So even though they were actually the 'knight on the charger', their reputation was damaged simply because they were in the business. I think there are a good few examples of that actually from the recent issues in financial services.

> The real issue with integrity is that it is easier to prove that you don't have it than that you do and anyone can have it until suddenly they don't. So it's one of those funny sorts of areas where you are looking for omissions almost. After the Enron scandal there was a lot of interest in white collar crime from the psychological point of view. At that stage there was this concept of an entitlement cluster that you could assess for and that became something that everybody wanted to have in their candidate assessments. The trouble is that it's not enough – a set of preferences and inferences is not enough to de-select somebody from the process with any sense of fairness or robustness. So again it tends to be the kind of thing that goes on somewhat behind closed doors.

Conclusion

I firmly believe that the vast majority of directors and senior managers that I have worked with are people who want to do the right thing. Some of them are uncomfortable with using the word ethics, typically preferring to use more everyday words like 'honest' and 'open'. Certainly, many of them are keen to avoid being seen in any way as sanctimonious by their staff or by media commentators. Yet, most are well aware that how they conduct themselves is important, whether within the business or in private.

This may seem like a modern development but actually it was a message that I first heard myself over 30 years ago when I was training to become a chartered accountant. It was made clear to me, along with all of my fellow trainees at Deloitte, that I must not under any circumstances commit any financial misdemeanours, no matter how small or trivial – no bounced cheques, no fines for non-payment of tube fares and certainly no county court judgements for non-payment of debts. Failure to abide by this instruction was likely to result in the loss of my job as I would make myself ineligible to become a practising accountant. The reason was simple. If I was going to present myself as a credible professional accountant, somebody who was capable of looking after the financial affairs of others, then it was imperative that there was no evidence to suggest that I might be incapable of looking after my own financial affairs. To suggest otherwise would bring the accountancy profession into disrepute.

Having a good character and strong values and showing sound judgement and resilience under pressure are all necessary components of being an ethical leader. The case study below provides an example of the reputational damage that can result if these qualities are not present in those at the top, a situation that is particularly dangerous when this absence is combined with flawed decision-making, technical shortfalls and poor trading results in the organisation itself. This is what happened at the Co-op Group in 2013.

Case study two: the Co-operative

Background

The Co-op Group[8] is part of the modern broad co-operative movement, which has grown from a small shop set up by the 'Rochdale Pioneers' in the north of England in 1844 to combat profiteering in the age of the Industrial Revolution in Britain into a worldwide movement. The essence of a co-operative is a group of people acting together to meet the common needs and aspirations of its members, sharing ownership and making decisions democratically. The core principle is therefore one of mutuality – co-operatives are not about making big profits for shareholders but are about creating value for customers.

The Co-op Group is the UK's largest mutual business, with some 4500 outlets, and it looks after 15 million customers every week. It has interests in a remarkably diverse range of business sectors: electrical, food retailing, farming, pharmacies, funeral care, legal services, travel, insurance services and banking. Until the forced restructuring in 2014 (see below), it owned and controlled the Co-op Bank.

Ethical values and principles

The Co-op Group promotes business ethics almost as its unique selling point – one of its stated aims is: 'To be an ethical leader.' It emphasises its social and community-focused principles and highlights its underlying ethical values, which at the time of writing are described on its website in the following terms:

- *Openness – nobody's perfect and we won't hide it when we're not;*
- *Honesty – we are honest about what we do and the way we do it;*
- *Social responsibility – we encourage people to take responsibility for their own community and work together to improve it; and*
- *Caring for others – we regularly fund charities and local community groups from the profits of our business.*

The Co-operative Bank

The Co-op Bank[9] has made use of its co-operative branding to differentiate itself from its competitors in the financial services industry, stating on its website that: 'We are still unique in being the only UK high-street bank to have a customer-led Ethical Policy.' That policy is described as follows:

> *Our unique Ethical Policy covers five key areas: Human Rights, International Development, Ecological Impact, Animal Welfare and Social Enterprise. In line with our customers' ethical concerns, we restrict finance to certain business sectors or activities, while at the same time committing to provide finance to those organisations making a positive community, social and environmental impact.*

Underpinning this, the bank operates an ethical screening policy which, while not perfect, is a market leader in UK retail banking. In its advertising for 'ethical lending' the Co-op Bank stated that it turned down revenue from firms involved in the arms trade, fossil fuel extraction and also from repressive governments. This ethical stance has proved to be popular and one of the by-products has been a fiercely loyal customer base.

Another important series of statements on the website regarding the Co-op Bank's values appears under the heading 'Our Givens' which are stated as being 'the key underpinning foundations of our business'. There are four of them:

> *We champion co-operative values and principles and ethics; We are financially prudent and strong; We share profits with members; and We only do business consistent with our values and principles.*

Personally, I am a little unsure about the expression 'Our Givens' – to me, it smacks of a degree of complacency. No organisation can afford to make assumptions about its culture or about the behaviour of its managers and staff if it wishes to avoid the 'say-do' gap that we discussed earlier in the book and the related charges of hypocrisy. Certainly, these 'givens' seem to be largely absent when reviewing the actual events at the Co-op Bank in 2013 – some of the behaviour and decision-making of the directors and senior managers do not reflect them at all.

Scandal: personal conduct

In November 2013 the *Daily Mail* newspaper published footage on its website of a video showing a man in a motor car engaged in a telephone conversation and then counting out money, which the accompanying article claimed was for the purpose of buying illegal drugs. The man was identified in the article as Paul Flowers.[10] This immediately embroiled the Co-op Bank in a damaging scandal because Paul Flowers had been the non-executive chairman of the bank (and also the deputy chairman of its then holding company, the Co-op Group) from April 2010 to June 2013.

The story was quickly picked up and developed by other media outlets in the UK. An extra damaging angle to the story was soon developed too: that, despite the senior positions that he held (at the Co-op Bank in particular), Paul Flowers had little previous financial or banking experience. He had in fact been a Methodist minister for almost 40 years, had served as a Labour Party councillor in the city of Bradford for 10 years (he was subsequently suspended from both the Methodist Church and the Labour Party) and had been influential in the political wing of the co-operative movement for many years.

The Co-op Bank was a very significant part of the Co-op Group at the time and it continues to be a substantial financial services institution in the UK. Following the merger with the Britannia Building Society in 2009 (see below) it is one of the country's 10 largest lenders and commands significant resources: over 4.5 million customers; assets worth some £50bn; and £36bn of customer deposits. It is subject to regulation by the financial authorities in the UK. How was it possible for the Reverend Flowers, with his background, to be appointed as the chairman of the Co-op Bank?

Subsequent to the media disclosures, the Rev. Flowers was arrested by the police in connection with a 'drugs supply investigation'.

Business shortfalls

Questions about the suitability of the Rev. Flowers for the positions that he held were especially pertinent because this drugs scandal was in fact the second shocking media story concerning both him and the Co-op Group to hit the headlines in 2013.

In previous years the Co-op Group had embarked on an expansion strategy that included the takeover of the supermarket chain Somerfield in 2008. As another part of this strategy the Co-op

Bank then merged with the Britannia Building Society (Britannia) in 2009 – it was effectively a take-over and, as it has turned out, it was ill-advised. By June 2013 the Co-op Bank was close to collapse. It had been forced to pull out of another expansion initiative months earlier, this time a deal to buy over 630 of Lloyds Bank's branches (known as Project Verde), before announcing plans to raise £1.5bn in extra capital to cover shortfalls that it had discovered in its balance sheet.[11] It was against this background that the Rev. Flowers had stepped down as Chairman, also in June 2013.

On 6 November 2013, less than two weeks before being filmed allegedly trying to buy illegal drugs, the Rev. Flowers had testified before a meeting of the House of Commons Treasury Select Committee looking into the circumstances surrounding the failure of Project Verde. He had given a stumbling performance when questioned by MPs on aspects of the Co-op Bank's finances and the circumstances surrounding the bank's capital shortfall. He did not appear to be cognisant of very basic numbers to do with the bank's balance sheet and size. For example, in reply to a question by the Committee Chairman asking what the total assets of the bank were, the Rev. Flowers replied 'just over £3bn'. In fact, the Co-op Bank's Report and Accounts showed this figure to be £47bn – a huge discrepancy that was profoundly unimpressive for everyone to hear. He was accused by the Committee Chairman Andrew Tyrie of not knowing 'very basic' figures about the bank.[12]

Reports of the poor display in front of the Parliamentary Committee given by the bank's ex-Chairman only increased the reputational damage to the bank, occurring as it did at just the time when the extent of the bank's shockingly poor financial performance was also becoming clear. It did not hit the media headlines in quite the same sensational way as did the story concerning the Rev. Flowers' behaviour and his alleged purchase of illegal drugs, but from a business perspective it was equally concerning.

Lessons learned

A number of key questions arise: How was the Rev. Flowers appointed to his roles as Director and Chairman; was there proper scrutiny and challenge of executive plans at the Co-op Bank; and where was the oversight and control from the board of the bank's holding company, the Co-op Group? The reporting and analysis of the various investigations launched as a result of these scandals provides some answers to these questions. Set out below are five areas of weakness in this case from which important governance lessons can be learned.

■ The first and most obvious governance shortfall is in the mismatch between the behaviour of the ex-Chairman of the Co-op Bank and the ethics and values of the bank and the wider Co-op Group, of which he was also Deputy Chairman. Media reports following the publication of the video show that the Rev. Flowers has demonstrated over many years a propensity, from time to time, for extreme risk taking in his private life. In addition to the allegations linking him with illegal drugs arising out of the video, there emerged a number of other significant revelations: the convictions for gross indecency (1981) and for drunk-driving (1990); his resignation from a local council after inappropriate content was found on a work computer that he had handled; indiscrete liaisons with prostitutes; and a history of high-end expense claims.[13] Each of these is a potential red flag, but viewed collectively they indicate that the Rev. Flowers may have been an inappropriate selection for the role of Director and Chairman of a group with such strong ethical values as the Co-op. Accusations of hypocrisy cannot be avoided. It is unclear how much of this information was available in 2008 when the Rev. Flowers was first appointed to the Co-op Group board, though the criminal conviction for gross indecency was known to the regulator (see below). The due diligence carried out on the Rev. Flowers may have been inadequate or perhaps his high profile and influence within the co-operative movement was a factor, enabling his appointment to the board to proceed without robust challenge. But whatever the reasons the result has been damaging to the reputation of the Co-op Group.

■ The second weakness concerns the board appointments process, especially the Co-op's failure to attach sufficient importance to competence and relevant experience at the top. Put simply, the Rev. Flowers did not have the appropriate level of financial skills or experience in the banking industry to be wholly credible in his role as Chairman of a bank. He had worked previously in a bank and had taken the first part of the Banking Institute's exams, but this was over 40 years ago. The decision to appoint him as Chairman is particularly surprising given the well-publicised banking failures during the global financial crisis. When appearing before the MPs, the Rev. Flowers defended his appointment by saying that the Co-op had the practice of appointing a democrat from within its own members and that he was subject to a rigorous selection process as one of four candidates – he was the unanimous choice, a choice subsequently endorsed by the regulator (see below). The interview process included psychometric testing. It appears that his performance in these tests was impressive and gave him the edge in selection over the other candidates. Psychometric tests have a growing role in board appointments; they are based on questionnaires and are designed to assess personality, numeracy and verbal skills. However, they should not be used in isolation and they are not designed to act as a substitute for detailed checks of background and experience. Should they have been allowed to outweigh the Rev. Flowers' lack of financial experience? With the benefit of hindsight his appointment as Chairman of the bank has exposed the Co-op Group to ridicule.

■ The third weakness concerns the skills and experience of the directors on the main board of the Co-op Group. The Co-op Group's Annual Report of 2012 contains a section on corporate governance including a report by the Group's Chairman at the time, Len Wardle. In his report, Mr Wardle states: 'The Board of the Co-operative Group is committed to the highest standards of corporate governance and recognises that good governance helps the business to deliver its strategy, strengthens member confidence and safeguards the long term interests of the Group.' This is a fine statement but is it realistic? The Annual Report shows that there were then 20 directors on the Group board, every one of whom was a non-executive and none of whom was classified as independent. They were all drawn from regional members, selected via the cooperative movement's democratic processes, rather than to meet objective criteria and skills requirements of the job of director. So, in contrast to the typical corporate board comprising professional directors, the Co-op Group board in 2012 included a plasterer, a nurse and a horticulturist. As a result, while it may have been designed to reflect the organisation's values, the composition of the board appears as amateur, old-fashioned and lightweight. It lacks the professionalism, experience and skill-set expected and required of a significant business today if it is to succeed. It seems clear to me that this would place the Co-op Group at a significant disadvantage to its competitors.

■ The sheer size of the Co-op Group board was another weakness. As noted above, it comprised 20 individuals, which is large by most standards and is likely to have been a barrier in itself to the efficient conduct of business. A similar comment can be made towards the Co-op Bank, which had 19 directors on its board in 2012. As a comparison, the average number of directors sitting on boards of the FTSE top 350 companies in the UK is approximately nine. Every organisation needs to consider what is likely to be the most effective size of its board according to its own individual circumstances, but the boards at the Co-op seem unnecessarily large and bureaucratic.

■ The final area of governance weakness to highlight concerns ineffective regulation. The appointment of the Rev. Flowers as Chairman of the Co-op Bank was approved by the Financial Services Authority (FSA), the bank's regulator at the time. This endorsement has since been questioned by MPs. The FSA has defended its decision,[14] however, saying that the Rev. Flowers was subject to a rigorous interview when first becoming a non-executive director of the bank in 2009 and another interview in 2010 when he was to become the bank's Chairman. This second interview was in fact less rigorous than the first and did not include further background checks. The FSA explained that it did not at the time think that the positions of non-executive chairman and non-executive director were very different. Also, the FSA believed that it could compensate for any shortcomings in technical expertise by agreeing with the Co-op Bank to appoint two deputy chairmen who were experienced in financial services, which they proceeded to do (as an aside, it is interesting to note that each of these deputy chairmen later resigned over Project Verde, but the board pressed ahead with the plan regardless). Finally, the FSA felt that the Rev. Flowers' political skills would be useful in running a large and unwieldy board. Despite these arguments, the Chairman of the Treasury Select Committee described the decision to approve the appointment as 'pretty catastrophic'.

Consequences

The events of 2013 have had dramatic consequences for the Co-op Group and its directors (past and present) and they continue to do so. Set out below are some of the most important of these.

First, the outcome of the drugs scandal was that in May 2014 the Rev. Flowers pleaded guilty to charges of possession of cocaine, crystal meth and ketamine. He was fined £400 and ordered to pay £125 in costs. He had earlier apologised for his behaviour, saying that he had been under pressure because of problems at the Co-op Bank and the recent death of his mother.[15]

Second, there have been numerous changes at board and senior management level at the Co-op in the recent past – although the architects of the takeover of Britannia (Neville Richardson and David Anderson) had left in 2011 and 2009 respectively. At the Co-op Bank, Barry Tootell, the former Finance Director who had been promoted to CEO of the bank in 2011, stepped down as CEO in May 2013 as soon as the credit ratings agency Moody's downgraded the bank's debt rating to junk status following the revelation of the £1.5bn black hole in its balance sheet. Before this, James Mack, who was Mr Tootell's replacement as Finance Director in 2011, had left the bank in February 2013 to join another financial services firm. At the Co-op Group, Peter Marks was succeeded as CEO by the retailer Euan Sutherland in April 2013. It was Mr Sutherland who was able to put together a capital action plan to save the Co-op Bank, despite its severely eroded capital base, without recourse to government support. However, as part of the deal, the Group was required to cede control of 70% of the bank to outside institutional investors, including a consortium of Wall Street hedge funds. Despite his successes, Mr Sutherland himself lasted less than a year as CEO before resigning in March 2014. In his resignation letter he said that the governance structure of the Co-op limited the reforms that he wanted to make.[16] Finally, Mr Wardle resigned as Co-op Group Chairman in November 2013 in the immediate aftermath of the Flowers drugs scandal.

Third, the full effects of the Co-op Group's misjudged expansion plans referred to above are now coming through and being reflected in very poor trading results. In particular, the merger with Britannia appears to be a significant strategic error, not least because of continuing write-downs on commercial real-estate loans made by Britannia in the years leading up to the global financial crisis. The Group now faces challenging trading conditions.

In March 2014, the Co-op Bank announced further problems. It had uncovered £400m of unexpected losses relating to a string of misconduct costs that include: provisions against claims for the mis-selling of payment protection insurance (PPI) and interest rate hedging products to customers; technical breaches of the Consumer Credit Act; and a failure to manage properly those customers struggling to make their mortgage repayments.[17] Although virtually all retail banks in the UK are in the process of providing compensation to their customers for the mis-selling of PPI products – PPI is the most expensive consumer scandal in British history – the knowledge that staff at the self-pro-claimed ethical bank were involved in such misconduct still comes as a shock.

In April 2014, the Co-op Group announced losses of £2.5bn for the year 2013 (of which £2.1bn related to the Co-op Bank), marking the worst results in the group's 150-year history. In response, the bank has cut 1000 jobs from its 10,000 strong workforce and has closed 30 of its branches with a further 15 to go in 2014.

Finally, there have been a number of investigations launched into the reasons for the problems at the Co-op Group by various parties: the UK regulators; the Treasury Select Committee; the Kelly Review commissioned to look into the events that led to the announcement of the Co-op Bank's capital action plan to address its £1.5bn capital shortfall; and the review by Lord Paul Myners into the governance of the Co-op Group.

The enforcement investigations by the regulators will take some time to complete. They are important – one key area that they will consider is the role and conduct of the former senior managers of the Co-op Bank. Sir Christopher Kelly's review has been published.[18] He points to systemic failures ranging from shoddy management to IT problems and highlights the take-over of Britannia as one of the root causes of the Co-op Bank's near collapse. He also identifies significant problems in governance:

> Failures in board oversight are inevitable if the criteria used to elect its members do not require those elected to have the necessary skills ... the composition of the Co-operative board and the limited pool from which its members were drawn, made a serious governance failure almost inevitable.

However, it is the Myners Review that is of most relevance in terms of understanding the governance issues at the Co-op and how they might be overcome in the future.

Myners: Report of the Independent Governance Review

In December 2013, Lord Paul Myners, an experienced businessman and former government minis-ter, was appointed as the first independent, non-executive director on the Co-op Group board, with the specific remit of leading a comprehensive, independent review of the Group's governance.[19] Lord Myners produced a progress update in March 2014, following Mr Sutherland's resignation, that was highly critical of the existing governance framework of the Co-op Group (it refers to a 'mas-sive failure of governance') and outlined a number of significant recommendations to address these weaknesses.

The recommendations in the progress report were met with initial resistance from supporters of the Co-op's mutual model and, in frustration, Lord Myners resigned from the board in April 2014. He subsequently published his report in May 2014.

The report's conclusion is highly critical of the Co-op Group's governance:

> The present governance architecture and allocation of responsibilities is not fit for purpose. It places individuals who do not possess the requisite skills and experience into positions where their lack of understanding prevents them from exercising the necessary oversight of the Executive.

Lord Myners places his review in the context of a series of costly strategic mis-judgements by the board that have undermined the Group's competitive position: the board spent too much of its time on the Somerfield and Britannia acquisitions which turned out to be 'breathtakingly value destructive'. He also identifies a significant 'democratic deficit', whereby ordinary members have weak constitutional rights and the core principle of cooperative ownership – 'one member one vote' – has been eroded by a convoluted voting system involving regional block votes. Ordinary members do not have the right to attend the Group's Annual General Meeting or to vote to elect Group board directors. Lord Myners is concerned that the social goals agenda of the Group is insufficiently aligned and connected with the achievement of its strategic and commercial objectives.

There are four core recommendations in the report as follows:

- Reform the Group board. The aim is to create a much smaller board built around a traditional corporate model, including an independent chairman, six to seven independent non-executive directors and two executive directors. One of the important benefits is that the non-executive directors will have the same skills and experience as those on the boards of the Co-op's primary competitors.
- Establish an influential National Membership Council (NMC) of around 50 people, with provision for employee representation. The NMC will engage with the Group board, act as a forum for members and as the guardian of the co-operative values and principles.
- Create a Nominations Committee. The aim here is straightforward – to identify the best possible candidates for the board.
- Extend constitutional rights to the entire membership of the Group. This is based on the principle of one member, one vote.

There are many important and constructive criticisms in the report of shortfalls in the way the Co-op board and the Group have been run in the past. Most interestingly from the point of view of this book is the discussion of cultural weaknesses of the board. Lord Myners identifies four. First, a consistent denial of responsibility – everything was the fault of managers who kept the directors in the dark. This illustrates a lack of understanding of the role of a director and the crucial requirement for challenge and scrutiny of management. Second, corrosive suspicion – there was poor interaction between the board and executives with some board members displaying an arrogant and dismissive attitude towards the managers. Third, procrastination – Lord Myners found a culture of delays in decision-making that was often frustrating and sometimes not conducive to commercial success. Finally, a tendency for board members to hide behind the Co-op's values – this was often used almost as a device to silence opposition and defer consideration of painful choices.

Contrary to Lord Myners' fears and expectations, the recommendations in the report were adopted by the Co-op membership in May 2014.[20]

Conclusion

The Co-op Group case is a good example of the potential harm to results and reputation that can be the outcome of governance shortfalls. As often happens in practice, the focus of attention was directed at the governance practices in the Group only after results had deteriorated. I should say that I do not see the Co-op's problems as indicative of wider issues with the co-operative governance model, which has at its core the concept of the member- or customer-owned businesses, with directors being elected democratically to the board. There are many examples around the world of successful businesses that are run as co-operatives (for example, the UK's John Lewis Partnership and the Folksam insurance company in Sweden). Rather, I see this as a specific failure brought about by the Co-op Group board, in particular through its poor strategic decision-making and an inability to change and adapt its structures to changing circumstances.

The extra dimension in the Co-op case is provided by the conduct of the Rev. Flowers, which gives the case the hallmark of a scandal. His conduct and behaviour was inconsistent with both the values of the business and the position he held as Chairman of the Co-op Bank. Of course, he probably should never have been selected for the role, but the selection process itself had its problems and the root cause was again located in a weak governance framework.

Rather than being irrelevant or providing a useful piece of window dressing for organisations, the Co-op case demonstrates very well that effective corporate governance is actually one of the necessary foundations for long-term business success.

The ethical manager

Overview

Personal character is one essential component of being an ethical leader. The other is managing in an ethical way. In order to be seen as an ethical manager, it is necessary to demonstrate two things above all else: first, a consistency in judgement and decision-making, both in good times and in bad, that is in line with the organisation's values; and second equal treatment of everyone in the organisation, regardless of their position or perceived level of success.

Consistent judgement

The key management decisions in this area are often those taken about people, because it is these which will send the clearest signals about the culture and tone of the organisation: What are the criteria that determine the hiring, promoting, rewarding, and disciplining of individuals? The values of all managers and staff should be aligned to those of the organisation. People should be rewarded and promoted based on a range of measures, including performance in achieving goals around values in addition to hitting financial targets – the so-called 'balanced scorecard' approach that we discuss later in the book. As part of this, managers should avoid setting unachievable goals. This sounds obvious but in practice organisations often set 'heroic' or unrealistic targets for themselves, such as a 20% per annum rise in sales or profits. If employees are set unachievable goals then only one of two things can happen: they will either fail or they will cheat, neither of which is a desirable outcome. In addition, there should be a clear understanding throughout the organisation that there is no tolerance of unethical behaviour.

Treat everyone equally

This last point leads into the second essential characteristic of being an ethical manager, which is being prepared to treat everyone equally in matters of behaviour and integrity. If the values of the organisation or its code of conduct have been violated in some way then the consequences should be the same regardless of whether the individual concerned is a junior accounts clerk, a highly successful salesman or the company's CEO. It is often a hard thing to do in practice to fire a high performing manager, especially if he or she is responsible for generating significant income for the organisation, but these difficult decisions must be taken if the organisation's codes and value statements are to retain their credibility. This can be hard to see in practice and it is something that the business dilemma in this chapter addresses directly.

Summary

To be clear, ethical managers should be prepared to listen. In particular, they should always be willing to listen to bad news and take the time to respond thoughtfully and in line with the organisation's culture. If the bad news concerns a competency issue, then it should be treated differently to an ethical issue. We all make mistakes and, although regrettable, errors do occur in business from time to time. In an open, accountable culture, employees should feel confident that they can inform their line managers of mistakes made without a fear of being punished in some way. So, covering up the error in a culture with strong accountability is likely to be treated differently to making the mistake in the first place – there would no doubt be consequences for those behind the cover-up.

The ethical manager must be prepared from time to time to take difficult decisions. To do so he or she must make a commitment to avoid being self-serving or short-termist or inconsistent and to act always with tough empathy. I myself respect enormously those managers who are able to combine personal modesty with the promotion of their team and the highest professional standards.

Set out below is an example of ethical leadership in action, an example drawn from the banking industry, perhaps the most challenged of all business sectors following the global financial crisis. It demonstrates very well the importance of tone at the top.

Ethical leadership in action: the Westpac banking corporation

Introduction

When first putting ideas together for this book, I knew that I wanted to include a piece on an institution in the financial services sector – after all, the global financial crisis provides much of the context for current perceptions of business. I was looking in particular for a positive story to tell. Much has been written already about the failings of bankers, about their conflation of greed and arrogance with periodic incompetence, while the fact that there is so much potential litigation pending in this area makes a detailed analysis of an individual institution difficult. I tried to interview Antony Jenkins to get his thoughts and insights into the cultural changes that he is introducing at Barclays, but he was too busy to speak to me. Then an opportunity came up from an unexpected quarter.

Included amongst the delegates attending one of my workshops at the London Stock Exchange in 2013 was Chris Bannister, General Manager, Europe and America at Westpac, the Australian banking group.[21] Throughout the day I was impressed by what Chris had to say about Westpac, in particular about the management style there and the culture that underpinned its commercial success. Subsequently, we met up for lunch during which I explained this book project to him and asked him whether it might be possible for me to interview one of the senior executives at the bank with a view to including a piece on Westpac in the book. Chris reacted positively and he followed this up with the appropriate people in Australia, obtaining the necessary approval in due course. As a result, I was put in touch with and subsequently interviewed Peter Hanlon.

Peter Hanlon is an advisor to Gail Kelly, Westpac's CEO. After a career in the military, he joined Westpac in 1990 and worked in a variety of roles in retail and business banking. As part of the senior executive team Peter set up and led the Australian Financial Services division of the bank before moving into his current advisory role on industry and Westpac-specific issues and reputational initiatives.

Background on the Westpac banking corporation (Westpac)

Westpac was founded in 1817 and was the first bank in Australia. Today it employs some 36,000 people in branches and offices throughout Australia, New Zealand and the near-Pacific region as well as having operations in many of the main financial centres of the world including London, New York, Hong Kong and Singapore. Westpac is listed on the Australian Securities Exchange and, at 31 March 2013, it had global assets of A$677.5bn.

Gail Kelly has been the CEO of Westpac since 2008. Under Ms Kelly's leadership, the bank has developed a clear purpose, vision and strategy, described on its website in the following terms:

Westpac Group's portfolio of financial services brands and businesses is focussed on a common purpose – delighting our 11.8 million customers and helping them achieve their financial goals. Westpac's vision is: 'To be one of the world's great companies, helping our customers, communities and people to prosper and grow.'

Our strategy seeks to deliver on this vision by providing superior returns for our shareholders, building deep and enduring customer relationships, being a leader in the community and being a place where the best people want to work.

These are fine words but, as we have seen, they are not untypical of those found in mission statements of many other large corporations. What interested me when I spoke to Peter Hanlon was what he had to say about how Westpac and Ms Kelly in particular have gone about putting these words into practice.

Interview with Peter Hanlon

Peter is located in Australia and I spoke to him via Skype. Our interview lasted for just over 50 minutes. His comments provide a fascinating insight into how a chief executive can develop an existing culture and really make a difference. In my view, Peter's observations of Ms Kelly provide an excellent example of ethical leadership in action. Accordingly, I set out a number of the interview extracts in some detail below and then pick up what seem to me to be the most salient comments at the end.

I began by asking Peter about the global financial crisis and why he thought that, in general, banks in Australia (and also in other jurisdictions like Canada) had come through that period in better shape than those in the USA and the UK. He gave me two broad reasons initially. First of all, he pointed to the quality of the regulation in Australia: 'having a well-regulated market and sensible regulators who had a good arm's length and respectful relationship with the banks was important'. Second, he referred to the reluctance of most banks in Australia, including Westpac, to get involved with sophisticated financial instruments such as collaterised debt obligations and other derivative products. He recalled a meeting in 2006 of Westpac's Credit Committee during which a key decision was taken: 'The view of the meeting – it was a minuted, documented view – was that, well we don't really understand these instruments, we can't see how they would make money and so we are going to steer clear of them.' After that Westpac declined the opportunity to look any further into them. Peter linked this decision to the long-term culture of the bank in terms of doing the right thing:

Certainly in my time in the bank I have seen quite a few examples of the, 'if it doesn't make sense then you probably shouldn't do it' type of example and also that people weren't afraid to speak up against issues like that, against propositions like that. In our trading areas we have had examples where a suspect trade might be happening or something unusual is happening and people are very, very quick to put their hand up and raise the red flag and say 'hey, there is something weird going on here'. So I think it has just been a long term part of the culture of the bank.

I am just saying that our reputation, our license to operate if you like, our social licence to operate is something that is extremely critical and we need to guard that with everything we can. That has certainly been something that I have seen in the bank in my two and a half decades there.

The discussion then moved onto a different area, which turned out to be a third reason why Westpac was able to come through the global financial crisis in good order. This is to do with performance and behaviour over time by the bank's managers and staff that is in line with Westpac's values – this can be contrasted with the well-documented behaviour of traders and others working for financial services firms in the USA and UK that is characterised as greedy, arrogant and self-serving. I asked Peter how Westpac had been able to translate the bank's values into consistent behaviour by their people. In reply, he highlighted two critical areas: the quality of the governance processes and the culture of openness that exists at Westpac.

Peter described the governance processes as: 'onerous but good … I'd say it is onerous but I think it is also necessary and I think as we have seen through the global financial crisis it was I think a key part of how we did so well, touch wood.' Many of the top-level systems and relationships in place at Westpac that he described to me in fact mirror the best governance practices that we discussed in the previous chapter. As an example, he told me:

> So, I think having a good strong independent board, having a good governance relationship and I don't just mean a personal relationship but a governance relationship between the board and between the executive management is critical.

Turning to the openness point, Peter placed this as part of the long-term culture of the bank, beginning with one of the previous CEOs, Bob Joss, and continuing through and being re-inforced by Gail Kelly. He then went on to explain how this principle of openness is reflected in how the bank actually operates:

> Bob Joss brought in a great sense of openness in the employees, in the bank and the relationships between the employees and the most senior levels of management. That improved and continued under David Morgan and I think exponentially has improved under Gail Kelly. What I mean by that is how willing people in the bank are to actually speak up. That might be either through various blogs and other websites we have, or by writing to Gail, or by stopping her in the street.

> Twice a year we have a road show where we go around all of our key offices and key states in Australia – all the states in Australia. It's a big deal, the whole executive team goes out and we spend three-quarters of the day with all of the managers, all of the branch managers and the other types of managers in each state, and in each major office that we have around the world. There will be a presentation, Gail will make a presentation, one or two of the executive team might do that as well and then there is a fairly significant amount of time for an open forum where we just get questions from the floor.

> The thing about these is, if you're a member of the executive team, sitting up the front, you sit on a very uncomfortable stool on the stage, as I have done many a time and you get the 'best' question – well, you have to describe them as either the best questions or the worst questions! They are really good questions if they are asked of somebody else but they are terrible questions if they are asked of you because people are very, very open about asking the toughest possible questions. So it could be something that they've read in the paper, it could be some business decision that we've made that isn't possible etc. etc. So there is a whole range of mechanisms both formal and informal, for feedback, for whistle-blowing if you like, for internal complaint mechanisms, just for people to raise a red flag. And when you get, I would argue, high quality CEOs, like Gail, like David, like Bob, they take those sorts of issues very seriously. So I think the second point about the openness … obviously it depends upon the leader, it certainly depends upon the senior people but most importantly on the leader and the mechanisms that are put in place. There is no point saying 'oh look we are an open organisation, willing to accept criticism or feedback on issues' if we don't then provide mechanisms for 40 odd thousand people to connect directly with the CEO. So we do provide those mechanisms and they work.

I then asked Peter how Westpac go about the process of making their corporate values meaningful throughout the business. I say to him that I know from experience that this requires a lot of work – it is one thing to talk about integrity it is another thing to have a real understanding among managers and staff of what that actually means and to have it embedded in their behaviour. His reply was very powerful and I quote it in full below.

> You have to focus on what I call the 'hard wiring and the soft wiring' or conversely the hard-ware and the software. So the hard wiring in this area is going to be things like: yes you've got to have the value statement, yes you've got to have the code of conduct, yes you've got to have the whistle-blower hotline or as we call it, the concerns hotline. You've got to have these things in place – they are absolutely necessary. So the hard wiring is to have all the mechanisms in place. Also, you have to have in people's performance reviews – we call them scorecards, how you measure performance for a year – you have to have an element of values in there as well. We refer to them as gatekeepers. In other words, unless you get through this gate of values, you won't be assessed to the maximum – if you don't make it through the values gate your assessment will be the lowest score. So all those things are great, and all those things are necessary but they are insufficient.

> To me it is the soft wiring that actually adds the real value on top of that. And the soft wiring is how the leaders behave, it's how open they really are and, you sort of mentioned the phrase of 'they've got to talk the talk but they have to walk the talk' as well. Gail is the best example I've ever seen of that. I'll give you a broad example and then I'll give you a very specific and person-ally embarrassing example.

> So Gail will go out and talk to large groups of employees, or small groups of employees, and she will give them examples of what she means by what poor behaviour looks like and also what good behaviour looks like. Now in getting out there in front of 500 people or 5 people and continually talking about these things, what she's doing is she's opening up the conversation so that people will feel safe to actually provide that feedback. Now if all she did was put out a code of conduct, put a value statement on our website and set up a concerns hotline, if that's all that's happened, then I don't think you would be encouraging people to actually make that move. So we would have the hardware in place but not the software. So, we've hardwired (this is the phrase I've actually used) the organisation but we haven't put the soft wiring in place and the soft wiring is through the behaviour and the silhouettes if you like that the leaders are creating.

> Gail uses that all the time where every single opportunity she is out talking to people, publicly, privately, in front of a small group, about the types of behaviour that we as an organisation expect and the type of behaviour that she wants from people who see things that are wrong. And she will – she goes on and on and on about encouraging this. If she said it once a year in an annual report, then it would be like 'so what?' But she doesn't do that she talks about it all the time. So that's the general example I wanted to give you.

> The other example is where Gail blew me away and embarrassed me a lot I must say, not long after she arrived, and it taught me a lot about communication. Now I used to think I was reason-ably good at communication but she taught me an amazing lesson in one fell swoop.

> And that was not that long after she arrived. We flew together from Sydney to Perth. Now Syd-ney to Perth is about a 5-hour flight – it's a long, long way from one side of Australia to the other and Gail had been in the company for three whole weeks. I was running business banking at the

time and so naturally we sat together and we talked about a lot of issues to do with the bank etc. etc. etc. So it was a very good conversation. We got in about 11 pm at night and first thing next morning we were off doing this forum that I referred to earlier.

On the flight one of the things that Gail had asked me was: 'What's not working well in business banking?' Now I'd been the head of business banking at that stage for probably nine months. I was still in the stage of working through all the issues that I thought we had before deciding how we could go about fixing them. Now I had a good relationship with Gail from the start and I felt very open – she is a very safe type of person to talk to – so I told her all of the big problems that we had. I told her the ways we let customers down and some of the things that we did wrong and so on. Anyway the next morning we had this leaders' forum, this managers' forum and a few other functions to attend and … I hadn't forgotten about the previous evening's conversation exactly but it had gone to the back of my mind.

At lunchtime that day we had a lunch with about 100 business banking customers in a very nice restaurant in Perth, overlooking the river, all that sort of thing, and my job was to stand up and introduce Gail. So I stood up and introduced her. There was a lectern there and a microphone and Gail sort of pushed the lectern to one side and instead of using a lapel mic, she just grabbed a hand held mic and I'm walking off stage as she was coming up and she said: 'No, no, no, you come here as well' – she grabbed me by the arm and dragged me. Instead of standing at the front she went and stood in the middle of everyone and she said: 'Look it's great to be here, it's great to be a part of Westpac, I'm really looking forward to being a part of the bank and helping customers here.' And she then said: 'Now what I thought I would do is just talk to you about what I think is wrong with business banking at Westpac – and I know that I've got this right because Peter Hanlon told me all about this last night!'

Now at that point every single business banker in the room looked at me and wanted to kill me because Gail was about to, and she did, tell all of our customers what was wrong with us. And she just told them all. And of course naturally all the customers said: 'We know, we've got that one, we know that or I haven't heard that one yet.' And of course what it did was it made us fix them even faster than we were planning on fixing them!

And what it taught me about Gail (and I think about communication more generally) is that if Gail is talking to a group of people at a branch or she is in front of a parliamentary committee or she is speaking to an international banking conference she says exactly the same thing – she doesn't have a different message for different audiences.

So to me that was a great example of telling the truth. Because if you think about it, you have a message to give but if you present it in a different way to each different audience there is some sophistry in that, there is some changing of the message to some degree. So her way of operating is to tell the truth and tell it in the same way every time.

I use this as an example, partially because it had a huge impact on me personally but also partially because it has helped to change the culture of the organisation, which at that stage I felt was pretty good anyway. But it has really helped to change it a lot more. And that is because it has become a very, very open organisation where it is incredibly safe to speak up – in fact you are expected to speak up. So if we have one of these leaders' forums – as I said, we have them twice a year – and Gail says 'Ok who has a question?' or 'who's got an issue to raise?' and nobody speaks up then she knows there is a problem. So if people aren't raising issues and problems then she knows something is going wrong!

So, with these two examples Peter gave me a very good picture of how Gail Kelly, the Westpac CEO, 'walks the talk' and what the phrase tone at the top actually means in practice. He then went on to give me a third example, this time illustrating Ms Kelly's approach to customer complaints:

> *The other impressive thing that Gail does – and I'd like to think I used to do a lot of it myself, but since she became my boss I do a lot more of it – is reading customer complaints and then ringing up a customer who has made one and having a chat with them. So Gail does surprise a lot of customers when she rings up and she says: 'Hello its Gail Kelly here and you wrote to me.' Customers are used to someone else intervening and doing all that but Gail would ring them up herself and say 'I just wanted to talk about the complaint you had.' And of course that makes an impression – that sort of news travels very, very fast.*

> *So not only is it safe for our people to speak up but it is also safe for customers to speak up in that they know something is going to happen. And that feeds back through our network, through our branches, through our business banking and so on, with the result that customers think and believe quite rightly that we are an open door organisation and therefore we will not only accept criticism but actually encourage it.*

> *They are just some examples of what I call soft wiring. So the hard wiring is the code of conduct, the value statements, the telephone lines, the blogs all that sort of stuff, that's all the physical mechanism you can put in place. But then you have got to have leadership and a culture and encouragement around these things which is the soft wiring.*

Next, I asked Peter about another issue that is often difficult for business leaders to handle well, which is acknowledging and dealing with criticism and bad news. In reply he gave me another anecdote because, as he so rightly says: 'these examples actually have a huge impact on the organisation'.

> *So we made a decision regarding housing interest rates. Generally when a bank makes a decision about housing interest rates if they drop them it's not enough and if they increase them it's too much. So it's pretty hard to win in this game. Anyway we made a particular decision where we increased rates by more than other banks at the time – things have changed since then. We were extremely unpopular for a period.*

> *Now Gail was the CEO at the time. So she was seen as having ultimate responsibility. I was running, at that stage, the retail and business bank so I was the person with the most direct responsibility. I made the announcement and I got to go on TV and radio and defend the decision – which is always a bit of fun to say the least! Anyway what happened was, on one of our morning TV shows, breakfast shows, which we seem to have copied from you and the USA, one of the commentators there decided to give out Gail's email address and said: 'Look I know Gail Kelly well' (he'd spoken to her once I think) 'and she'd love to get your email if you've got a complaint.' Interestingly, the reaction of our media people inside the bank was: 'Oh my God what are we going to do, they've given out Gail's email address, this is terrible, this is horrible, all of these emails are going to come in and what are we going to do with them?'*

> *Well Gail rang me up ... no, she didn't ring me, at that stage I was round the corner from her, on the same floor and she came round as she does and said: 'Oh, Pete, it looks like you and I are going to be busy.' And she said: 'Let's not email them back, let's call them.' So me, Gail and one of her immediate personal staff, between the three of us we rang 1000 customers. I think it was 1080 people who had sent emails and so we rang them all. Now, in many cases we left messages and we*

followed them up with an email but in quite a few cases and probably about, I don't know 200 or something like that, we actually got to speak to them. I think those 200 people did, not so much if it was me or the other person who did it, but certainly if Gail got them they will probably remember that call for ever, because they had wonderful chats. The interesting thing was that out of the 1080 customers – they were all customers by the way who sent us emails – people could have taken their home loan, their mortgage somewhere else. Not one of them did ... not one of them did.

My next question was about one feature of Peter's examples that struck me forcibly when I was listening to them – the time factor. How is Ms Kelly, as a CEO with no doubt hundreds of other things to do, able to devote the necessary time to do all this?

I think you hit the nail on the head when you talk about and link together time with the comment you made about tone at the top. What it boils down to there is does the person at the top or the people at the top actually think that this is serious or not? So is this issue of ethics, of integrity ... I don't always use words like ethics or integrity, I prefer words like honesty and truthfulness. I mean are these issues that matter? Do you think that if you are untruthful or unethical or dishonest that that is a good way to run a business? If you think that you should behave in the right way then there is no problem about time. Time is not an issue because it's important. If you think it's not as important as some other parts of business then you won't spend the time on it. So the example I used of Gail walking around to my office, there was no debate about 'Gee how are we going to find the time?', it was like 'Let's ring them all back this week!' It happened to be a Tuesday morning and by Friday we had made all those phone calls. It wasn't like 'Oh how am I going to do this? Am I going to be doing it at 10 o'clock at night? I'm so busy the rest of the time.' What it came down to was that this is really important. In other words: 'This is more important than anything else I am doing at the moment.'

The final area that I explored with Peter was the extent to which everybody at Westpac bought into the values that Ms Kelly and her senior management team were promoting. This was what he told me:

I think that you are always going to have some people who believe in it more than others. So my point would be, I don't want to sugar coat it and say that I use Gail as a shining example, which I happen to think she is. Is everybody going to behave as well as she does? And the answer is no actually. But everyone will behave to a minimum standard if you like – some people will behave as good as she does, and some people will go close and some people will do enough if you know what I mean. I don't think you are ever going to achieve a situation where everybody is wonderful. If you've got a leader who is wonderful that's a pretty good start but then what you are going to have is a group of people, all going to be slightly different but they have got to behave, if you like, to a minimum standard. So I think that is the way I would categorise it.

But then the real test, and this is the test that you are familiar with and everybody else is familiar with, is this: Are those people with poor behaviours going to be hired? Are those people with poor behaviours going to be rewarded either financially or through some form of promotion? In the end that's the acid test.

So that's why I think you can have a group of people at the top who are all a little bit different. You want diversity, you are going to have some people who are slaves to honesty, integrity which is a fantastic thing and then you are going to have other people who just think 'Yeah, well that's the way I have to behave' – they'll do the right thing but they may not necessarily believe in it as much as everybody else does.

So the real acid test is where do you draw the line and if someone crosses that line what are you going to do about it? I'm not going to go into any detail for obvious reasons, but there have been people in our organisation who have not been promoted, there are people in our organisation who have had their financial incentives, bonuses, things like that reduced and there have been people who have been fired simply because of the fact that they didn't meet our standards. Now in every case we did the right thing by them and warnings were given, discussions were had and if they still behaved in a way that wasn't up to the standards we expected then the consequences were pretty direct.

That to me is the real test. When I reflect on some of what I have read, particularly about the UK – some of the things that I read about and some of the things that I heard about subsequently, I thought to myself: 'Well if they ever did that here those people would have been sacked long ago.'

There is just a sub-point to that test. I guess my observation is that if someone in a branch, using that as an example, does something wrong, they're gone that day. If they steal some money out of the till, if they transfer some money illegally from a customer's account to their own account, then to use the phrase – their feet don't touch the ground. If that happens to someone at the highest level, part of the executive management, pretty much the same thing would happen – they'd be gone before lunchtime.

Interestingly, one of the things I've observed in other organisations is for high performing middle managers ... they tend to be a little bit different, have a slightly different set of rules. We've seen it in Australia with some cases over the years, probably more so in the world of financial planning than anything, but again what it came down to, you had some sort of middle management or some senior person who was actually a money maker as it were, like a financial planner or something, who broke some code of conduct, who behaved poorly, in such a way that if they were a branch teller or a general manager, they would probably be dismissed, where we've seen examples where they've just been given the benefit of the doubt too many times. And whenever examples have ended up in court in Australia, I can't think of a single one where it's the first time that they have ever done it. In every example it is someone who has done it a number of times. What that means is someone above them has actually made the value judgment that: 'Oh well, you know, they might not be very good at behaviour and culture and so on, but they make good money for us, so we'll hang on to them' – which is just like you know, come on!

So I think that's a real issue. While the obvious test is a senior person, I think a lot of organisations need to look into the middle management levels to see whether or not the speed with which a teller would be dismissed for putting his or her hand in the till literally, whether someone in middle management who is bringing in millions of pounds or millions of dollars every year would actually be treated in the same way. I think that's the real test in an organisation for me.

The key leadership qualities identified

Amongst the many excellent points that Peter makes during the course of this interview I want to focus on five because I think that these demonstrate important aspects of ethical culture and of strong ethical leadership in action. From listening to Peter, these qualities have had real impact in the

Westpac banking group and have been one of the reasons for the bank's success in the recent difficult economic conditions. The points that I would highlight are as follows:

- The first point is that senior managers had the integrity to say 'no'. Derivative banking products became fashionable with many financial institutions attempting to maximise shareholder value in the years leading up to the financial crisis. Westpac's senior executives were honest enough to admit to themselves that they did not fully understand them and did not feel comfortable with them. As a result they did not trade in them either, thereby perhaps reducing short-term profitability but gaining assurance over the long-term management of risk and reputation.
- Second, the culture of openness that Ms Kelly and her predecessors as CEO have consistently fostered throughout the bank is very important. Peter's examples show that it is not always comfortable for senior executives to hear what is really going on inside their business, but it is what they need to hear nevertheless. Westpac's leaders not only encourage this openness but they engage directly themselves and provide mechanisms (hotlines, discussion forums etc.) to enable staff to come forward with their comments. So, good communication including listening to what is happening on the ground is an integral part of good leadership.
- Next, I was struck by the examples Peter gives of Ms Kelly not only 'talking the talk' in terms of the bank's values but also being prepared to 'walk the talk' as well. Peter illustrates this best, in my view, through examples that show that Ms Kelly is committed to communicating with all the bank's stakeholders as often as possible and that she always delivers the same message. There is no equivocation here; she tells it straight, she tells the truth – that, coming from a leader creates a powerful and positive impression. Peter feels that her own candour has been responsible for developing an already open culture within the bank into one where everyone feels that it is safe to speak up.
- The other important thing to note about the culture of openness at the bank is that it not only applies to staff but to the bank's customers also. From Peter's examples it is clear that Ms Kelly is prepared to devote a significant amount of her time, when required, to dealing with customer complaints, on occasion responding directly and in person. She is prepared to tackle the difficult issues herself too, as shown by the example of the 1000-plus emails received, courtesy of the 'friend' who was the breakfast show presenter, following the bank's decision to raise interest rates and how Ms Kelly dealt with them – in person and quickly. The time commitment needed to do this is not an issue for Ms Kelly because this is something that she wants to do – it was important to her. As Peter says, stories like this one can have a huge impact within an organisation, they clearly demonstrate the phrase 'tone at the top' working in practice. In fact over time stories like this become themselves part of the folklore, part of the culture of the organisation.
- The other significant aspect of Westpac's culture that Peter brings out in the interview is to do with discipline and consequences. Individuals at whatever level within the business (and he makes a perceptive comment about high fee-earning middle managers and the temptation, sometimes, to accommodate them if they should break the rules) can be and have been disciplined and even dismissed for not meeting the bank's standards of behaviour. He describes this willingness to take tough action if required as an 'acid test' for an organisation. I agree with him. Good behaviour should be recognised and rewarded. Equally, there must also be consequences for bad behaviour. This integrated approach, combining value-drivers with compliance-drivers, is a critical component in the creation and development of corporate culture.

HANDLING A CRISIS

Background

Introduction

A crisis can befall any organisation at any time. If it happens, a crisis will present the leaders of that organisation with a particular challenge and how successfully that challenge is met will be seen by stakeholders and media commentators alike as a key indicator of the judgement of senior executives. A crisis may very well short-circuit into a test of character, played out in front of a global audience. The CEO will often take the lead in handling a crisis, in which case perceptions of who he or she really is will be formed very quickly and will be magnified by media coverage, with intense scrutiny of the leader's every action – stakeholders and the public will want to know whether these actions live up to the organisation's values.

In this section we will look at how the traditional contingency planning approach of a disaster recovery or a crisis management plan needs to be adapted to the rapid advances of the digital age and ubiquitous social media in the last few years, which have changed the dynamic, putting much more importance on the communications piece of the plan. The emphasis now should be on both speed of response and the emotional intelligence of the individuals leading that response. We will also look at the key role of business leaders in dealing with a crisis and include a number of examples of good practice and not-so-good practice in this area too. But first it is helpful to consider what is meant by the term 'crisis'.

Definitions

The *OED* defines a crisis as: 'a decisive moment, a time of danger or great difficulty'. In the business context, crises typically develop quickly and require a rapid response. They should be distinguished from events that are categorised either as emergencies or as disasters. Emergencies also require a swift response but they are usually smaller in scale (e.g. a car accident or a power outage) and can be dealt with effectively if regular drills and training are in place. An emergency can turn into a disaster if it is left unchecked, however. The OED describes a disaster as: 'a great or sudden misfortune, a complete failure'. So, a disaster is a major event that happens suddenly and causes severe misfortune for a company, city or region and its people. Disasters can be natural, such as fire or floods, or man-made, such as a terrorist attack.

A crisis is an event that develops over time, albeit one that can develop very quickly. In the business context, it is a material threat to an organisation and is likely to lead to a dangerous situation – how management responds will determine exactly how dangerous that situation becomes. A crisis can impact on the organisation in a variety of ways, sometimes overlapping, including: harm to people or property; serious business interruption; significant damage to reputation; and material financial loss. It may be the result of an unexpected disaster event or it may arise out of a failure by management to pick up warning signs in systems or processes over a period of time. Examples that are covered in the book range from: the Tylenol poisoning case in 1982; to the terrorist attacks in the USA on 11 September 2001; to the explosion and fire on the Deepwater Horizon oil rig in the Gulf of Mexico in 2010; and even to the crisis in the processed food industry in the UK in 2013, when certain products that were labelled as 'beef only' were shown in fact to contain traces of horsemeat too.

Management plans

Many organisations have adopted a classic piece of risk management theory in this area by drawing up disaster recovery and/or crisis management plans. As we have seen, a disaster is an extreme event, one that is unlikely to happen but if it does then it will be of extremely high impact. Risk management theory states that this type of high impact, low probability event is best managed in two ways: first, by transferring a proportion of the risk through taking out appropriate insurance and second, by contingency planning. Disaster recovery plans tend to focus on securing the continuity of IT systems, while increasingly crisis management plans need to focus on effective communication.

The advantage of disaster recovery planning was highlighted in the aftermath of the 9/11 attacks. Of all the organisations that lost people on that day, none was hit harder than Cantor Fitzgerald (Cantor), the financial services firm.[22] Cantor lost 658 employees, every single one of those who were working in the firm's offices in the north tower of the World Trade Center at the time of the attack and over two-thirds of Cantor's total workforce in 2001. Cantor also lost its offices and its primary data centre. Although this was an absolute tragedy for all concerned, the organisation itself managed to survive and indeed it is still in business today. Remarkably, Cantor was able to bring its trading markets back online within one week of the attack. It was able to do so through a combination of the indomitable spirit of its remaining people, help from other companies and, crucially, a carefully worked through data recovery plan.

The basic frameworks of crisis management and data recovery plans are similar, although the details will vary. Key ingredients are: the assignment of responsibilities to an appropriate team that will respond to the event on the ground, together with the selection of the leader; the availability of contact details of the crisis management team (and others); engaging in detailed crisis/disaster planning including scenario analysis and a first-hour response checklist; having a media management strategy in place, including selection of a spokesperson and PR agency; having ongoing training; carrying out rehearsals – from desk-top exercises to full-scale simulation; ensuring all data is backed-up and that there is multi-site capacity; and regular reviews, incorporating a periodic vulnerabilities audit.

Proper contingency planning is an essential part of modern crisis management. However, as we will see in Chapter 8, one of the most successful management responses to a crisis (the Johnson & Johnson case) relied less on detailed planning and more on following the company's values as established in its Credo. Set out below is part 1 of the case, which is a brief summary of the events and how Johnson & Johnson dealt with the threats. The corporate credo is discussed in part 2 of the case study in Chapter 8.

Johnson & Johnson – the Tylenol case (part 1)

In many ways, the classic handling of a crisis remains the response of Johnson & Johnson, the US pharmaceuticals, medical devices and consumer health group, to events in the Tylenol case in 1982. At the time Tylenol was the company's most profitable medication. However, someone started tampering with the capsules, putting cyanide poison in them, then re-sealing the packages and depositing them at random on the shelves of pharmacies in the Chicago area. The poisoned capsules were purchased by members of the public and seven people died as a result. Widespread panic followed. The company's market value fell by $1bn as a result.

However, Johnson & Johnson's directors and managers demonstrated excellent crisis management at this time. The chairman charged the response team with two tasks: first to protect the people; and second to save the product. They acted quickly with total openness about what had happened and alerted consumers via the media with the warning not to consume any type of Tylenol product until the extent of the tampering could be determined. They immediately withdrew the product from sale completely, across the whole country, thereby showing that they were prepared to bear the short-term costs in the name of consumer safety – this was not about money or minimising legal liability but about making sure that their products were safe. This established a basis for trust with their customers, who concluded that the company had been the unfortunate victim of a malicious crime. Johnson & Johnson's results recovered quickly.

The following summary of the outcome of the case was written by *Washington Post* journalist Jerry Knight in 1982: 'What Johnson & Johnson executives have done is communicate the message that the company is candid, contrite and compassionate. Serving the public interest has simultaneously saved the company's reputation.'[23]

Johnson & Johnson had a crisis management plan in place and this was important to the successful outcome in this case. The company also had a series of core values (known collectively within Johnson & Johnson as 'Our Credo') that were embedded within the organisation and pointed the way for senior managers to handle this crisis. We will look at this Credo in more detail later in Chapter 8.

The impact of digitisation and social media

Background

Digitisation and social media have, literally, changed the daily lives of people all over the world. Digitisation is the process of converting information (text, graphics, audio and video) into a digital format so that it can be created, viewed, distributed, modified and preserved on computers. Social media is one of the by-products of digitisation. It is the term used to describe platforms that bring people together so that they can create, share or exchange information and ideas in virtual communities and networks.

Consider the impact that digitisation and social media have made. The first email was delivered in 1971. In 1993 CERN (the European Organisation for Nuclear Research) in Switzerland donated the World Wide Web technology developed by the British engineer Tim Berners-Lee to the world. Since then, innovation has developed with incredible speed. Here are some highlights: Google opened as a major Internet search engine and index in 1998; in 1999 Friends Reunited was set up in the UK, the first online social network aimed at relocating old school friends; Apple started selling iPods in 2001; LinkedIn started as a business-oriented social networking site for professionals in 2003; Facebook was founded in 2004 by Mark Zuckerberg, Eduardo Saverin and others at Harvard University; in 2005 YouTube began storing and retrieving videos; and in 2006 Twitter was launched as a social networking and micro-blogging site, enabling members to send and receive 140-character messages called tweets. The impact of these inventions and developments in technology has been felt all around the world: Facebook reached one billion users in 2012, while in 2014 85% of the people in the world had access to the Internet. In 2014, for the first time, more new Internet users came online using a mobile device – a smartphone or tablet – than a personal computer.

These developments have not only affected individuals but have also brought enormous changes to the ways that all organisations are run over the last 20 years. On the one hand, there are significant benefits and opportunities, not least in promoting dialogue and better communication between the organisation and its stakeholders. As an example, thanks to digital media, companies are able to get information into the public domain faster than ever before (e.g. instead of relying on traditional advertising, firms can inform a huge number of people about their exciting new promotion very quickly through email campaigns, social networking sites, websites and Internet advertising). One challenge for many businesses remains how they optimise their use of this new technology of course.

However, together with the benefits of increased speed and greater customer reach also come some new threats: by providing feedback on Facebook or Twitter, or by taking a video or photograph via a mobile phone, customers can now use digital media to take a complaint or other form of negative comment, that previously might well have been resolved privately, and make it very public indeed, viewed by thousands, perhaps millions of people. The phrase used to describe such comments that escalate on this scale is that they 'go viral'. They may well do so if the comment, or picture or video has emotional force. There is nothing more capable of escalating events into a crisis than when people see something on a social media platform that touches them emotionally.

Managing brand damage and reputational risk caused by social media

The media has always represented potential threats to organisations. Today, social media represents an extra dimension, an additional component of reputational risk. There are various reasons for this: the digital world combines speed with ease of access for customers; there is a radical degree of transparency in social media; and we are also witnessing increasingly high customer expectation levels coupled with more stringent ethical standards than in the past. All of these factors mean that poor or unethical performance is likely to receive public scrutiny as never before and that negative sentiment can be mobilised very quickly. All organisations that are customer-facing and rely on consumers as their key stakeholders now need to take greater steps to prove that they are worthy of consumers' trust.

Social media has greater reach and immediacy than the traditional press and there is also a less clear legal and regulatory framework in place. Again, this combination brings with it increased risk. It sometimes appears that comments and opinions given on web forums and blogs are more about 'crowd-checking' and less about fact-checking – that speed is the premium, rather than accuracy. So, it is possible for stories to develop on social media in a less rigorous way than with traditional journalism, with bloggers sometimes being prepared to comment about a developing piece of news without always scrupulously checking the facts with the organisation concerned first – some may be more inclined to publish quickly and correct later if necessary. So, companies need to be able to recognise and react quickly to what can be very rapid changes in the media agenda.

As with any other important area of business, there should be a strong controls framework governing all social media activities within the organisation, with protocols in place setting out the ground rules for managers and employees on their use of social media. We are concerned here with handling negative comment or opinions that appear on social media that might develop into a crisis. Large organisations in particular should make use of PR agencies to help them to manage and protect their corporate reputation.

Five guidelines for managing social media in a crisis

Set out below are five key social media planning guidelines that organisations should put in place internally. Their overall aim is to provide assurance that if an organisation is confronted by a crisis situation it is able to respond in such a way as to prevent the bad news from getting worse in the short term, thereby providing the platform for the recovery of reputation in the future.

- First, monitor the traffic. Organisations should themselves have a presence on various social media venues – indeed, large businesses and big brands really need to have a presence in every social media outpost. As part of normal practice organisations should use social media monitoring software – this not only provides useful feedback but it should act as an early warning mechanism.
- Second, always respond quickly to a developing crisis. There is an expectation and demand for very short response times on social media – 1 hour on Facebook, 15 minutes on Twitter! Even when information asymmetry is at work so that the organisation does not know what the public

knows at the outset of a crisis, it is imperative to avoid a period of silence – there is always advantage in putting out an initial statement, even if it says no more than: 'We are aware that something has happened and are looking into it.' The longer the delay, the harder it will be for the organisation to put its point of view across later with any credibility.

■ Third, make sure that the broad tone of the organisation's response has been agreed in advance as part of the crisis management plan. Liaison with a PR agency can be helpful here, especially for large organisations. Also, as an important practical point, it is particularly important to obtain prior sign off from the legal team, otherwise delays in agreeing wording will be almost inevitable.

■ Fourth, say 'sorry' when the organisation has done wrong and mean it. Be honest and upfront, with full transparency – there should never be any attempt at what might be seen as a cover-up or removal of justified, if negative, comments.

■ Finally, update the debate with accurate and timely information. Often it is helpful to create a crisis 'Frequently Asked Questions' webpage so that all the updated information is available in one place containing, for example: details of what happened; photos and/or videos; specific corrective actions taken; real or potential effects; steps taken to prevent future occurrences; and contact information.

Tesco's handling of the horsemeat crisis in the UK

In January 2013, Irish food inspectors reported that horse DNA had been discovered in frozen beef-burgers sold in several Irish and British supermarkets. This created a frenzy of concern and outraged comment from the public and the media alike because, although horsemeat is not harmful to health and is eaten in many countries, it is widely considered to be a taboo food in other countries including the UK and Ireland. Further testing of samples of processed beef products sold in supermarkets revealed more evidence of adulteration, for example with some beef lasagne products being found to contain up to 100% horsemeat. Not all supermarkets were found to be selling adulterated products, but those that were included Tesco, Iceland, Aldi and Lidl. The most prominent brand named in the scandal was Findus, the Swedish frozen food manufacturer. Although the contamination was shown to be limited to a relatively small number of products, the scandal was not confined to the UK and Ireland. It resulted in the withdrawal of tens of millions of burgers and other processed beef products from supermarket shelves across Europe.

The investigations revealed a major breakdown in the traceability of the food supply chain, which, in the case of some Findus' products, stretched from France to Luxembourg to a Cypriot trader who was supplied from an abattoir in Romania. There are continuing suspicions of food fraud and beef brokerage.[24]

So, the root cause of the problem was shown to lie with the suppliers rather than the retailers. Despite this, however, the scandal impacted negatively upon customer confidence across the food retail industry in the first quarter of 2013 and it threatened to damage the reputation of those super-markets implicated, none more so than Tesco.

Tesco gave a textbook demonstration of how to handle this crisis, in particular in its proactive approach to communication. Tesco published an apology quickly, both on its website and by taking out full-page advertisements in a number of newspapers under the heading: 'We apologise.' Later in January, the company put out a statement on the progress of the investigation into the beef con-tamination. It set out the improvements it had initiated: a re-assessment of its suppliers; an increase in sourcing from the UK and a reduction in the complexity of its supply chains; an increase in unan-nounced audits and in the testing of ingredients. It then responded to the findings that Findus beef lasagne products were found to contain horsemeat by withdrawing from sale all frozen food products from the French company that supplied Findus. Finally, Tesco's CEO at the time, Philip Clarke, posted a 3-minute in-house video on trust, setting out the improvements made in the rigour and checking of the company's food supply chain.

The combination of Tesco's speed of response, its clear and direct messaging and the willingness to take ownership of the key issues was impressive and served to protect the company's reputation. Tesco reported a drop in its sales over the three months ending in May 2013 of which it said that there was 'a small but discernible impact' only on its frozen and chilled convenience food sales as a result of the horsemeat scandal.[25]

The leader's role in a crisis

Overview

Good leadership includes exercising judgement in three key areas: setting strategy and managing risk; hiring, promoting and firing people; and dealing with crises. By its nature, the last of these will be the most visible – demonstrating effective leadership is essential when confronted by a crisis.[26]

The primary role of the business leader in a crisis situation is to reassure people. The leader will present the big picture and be seen to be accountable, while the crisis management team on the ground will give the technical response. It is most often the CEO who is called upon to do this, which seems natural because he or she is seen as the decision-maker. It is not essential, however – the chairman or another senior figure in the organisation could act as the spokesperson. The key point is to select the best person for this role because the decisions taken in crisis situations need to be explained and well communicated to stakeholders, in addition to being taken responsibly. To do so requires situational awareness, not least in making the appropriate emotional connection with those immediately affected and with the wider public.

It is also important that the leader should be visible, especially when trying to handle a crisis that develops out of a disaster event. Disasters most often fall to politicians to deal with rather than business leaders, and in these situations it is frequently the physical presence (or absence) of the leader at the scene of the event, especially in the immediate aftermath of the disaster happening, that is crucial to the public perception of how the disaster is being handled. This enables the leader not only to express concern but also to assess the situation first-hand and to show resilience by speaking credibly about hope for the future.

But leaders have to do more than be visible during a crisis – they will be subject to the most intense scrutiny and they must be able to perform under the particular stresses of the situation. Set out below are two famous examples of crisis situations, with very different performances and outcomes.

Well-received performance under pressure

There were many examples of good leadership shown in New York City both during and after the terrorist attacks on the World Trade Centre on 11 September 2001, not least from members of New York's fire and police departments. For the purposes of this example, I want to highlight just one of these – the performance of the New York Mayor, Rudy Giuliani. Although sometimes seen as a controversial figure, on the day of the attack itself he was able to demonstrate effective leadership under the most extreme pressure.

Mr Giuliani happened to be close to the twin towers at the time of the attack. He spent much of the morning walking the streets, talking to people and no doubt trying to console and comfort them. At the first press conference later that day he said: 'Today is obviously one of the most difficult days in the history of the city ... My heart goes out to all the innocent victims of this horrible and vicious act of terrorism. Our focus now has to be to save as many lives as possible.' One of the first questions that he was asked concerned the number of lives lost in the attacks, to which Mr Giuliani's replied: 'The number of casualties will be more than any of us can bear ultimately.'[27]

Mr Giuliani's ability to find the right words at this time to connect with the people of New York (and America) was impressive. He came across as brave and reassuring, he was very spare with his words but he managed to convey his feelings in a calm way. He was able to maintain poise under pressure – he showed his passion but also that he was in control and was able to remind people that there is hope.

Poorly received performance under pressure

Contrast this with the performance of the then CEO of BP plc, Tony Hayward, when reacting to extraordinary events in 2010. This crisis situation arose out of a tragedy in the Gulf of Mexico when, in April of that year, there was a disastrous explosion and fire on the Deepwater Horizon oil rig, killing 11 workers and causing a massive oil spillage which produced one of the worst environmental disasters in US history.[28] Mr. Hayward became the spokesperson for BP in the aftermath of the tragedy. Unfortunately, with a number of ill-judged comments and poor performances in front of the media, he succeeded only in enraging residents of the Gulf States and US politicians alike, whilst tarnishing BP's reputation in the process.

Two comments from Mr Hayward were particularly inappropriate. First, in an interview with Sky News he said: 'I think the environmental impact of this disaster is likely to be very, very modest.' [29] Not only was this insensitive, it was also inaccurate. One of the features of the crisis was that BP's quantitative estimates of how much oil per day was spewing out of the uncapped well into the Gulf had to be raised time after time. These comments were part of a strategy by Mr Hayward and BP to try to direct blame for the tragedy towards the sub-contractors used on the rig and away from BP itself. This may have been an appropriate litigation strategy, but this message was not well received in the USA and it proved not to be a good reputation strategy.

The second inappropriate comment from Mr Hayward was when he was in the USA in the Gulf region, and he was asked by reporters what he would like to say to the people of Louisiana. This is how he replied: 'The first thing to say is I'm sorry. We're sorry for the massive disruption it's caused to their lives. There's no one who wants this over more than I do. I would like my life back.'[30] This comment (recorded on video and available on YouTube) seemed to many observers to be self-centred and disrespectful to those who had died on the rig and those who had suffered from the environmental damage.

The role of the CEO in these circumstances is to express contrition and to build confidence. Mr Hayward was able to do neither. Rather than giving strength to others, his comments caused outrage.

The importance of emotional intelligence

It is important that someone from an organisation communicates during a crisis, but it is equally important that it is the right person. That individual has to be able to combine authority and responsibility with the ability to connect with stakeholders on an emotional level in order to gain their trust and respect.

One essential aspect of this is to display emotional intelligence. Emotional intelligence is where the head and the heart come together and this is the quality that appears to have been missing in some of Mr Hayward's responses in the aftermath of the Deepwater Horizon tragedy. Mr Hayward is an intelligent man and he was certainly technically competent in his role as CEO of BP, where he combined expertise in geology with in-depth knowledge of the company. When he visited Louisiana, he was accompanied by a team of public relations advisors and PR specialists and there is little doubt that he would have been trained, drilled and schooled in the art of handling the media.

So, was all this simply bad luck, a small number of comments that were taken out of context and exaggerated? Individuals tend to revert to type in high-pressure situations. I have never met Mr Hayward but I have met a number of executives and managers that have worked with him in the past. They all told me the same thing – that it was not a complete surprise to them that he had made these kinds of comments, which might be described as being 'tone-deaf'. Mr Hayward, like all leaders who are potentially going to act as the spokesperson for their organisations in a crisis, should have been subjected to tough questioning during his media training, with his advisors trying to replicate for him the pressure that he would experience in reality from the media and politicians alike. If the performance of the leader is patchy or poor in these simulations, then he or she should not continue in the role of spokesperson.

In November 2010, after he had resigned from BP, Mr Hayward expressed his frustrations by saying to the BBC that: if he had 'a degree in acting from RADA rather than a degree in geology I may have done better' in handling the fallout from the Deepwater Horizon disaster.[31] I think that he was right to identify that sometimes technical proficiency is not sufficient in these circumstances, but in my view suggesting that the ability to act out a part is the answer is to miss the point entirely. The leader's actions must be genuine; the words must come from the heart in order to reassure stakeholders and gain their trust and respect.

 WORKSHOP CONCLUSION

Closing

As things turn out, my timing proves to be almost perfect. No sooner have I finished what I want to say on the subject of handling a crisis situation than there is a knock on the door – it is John Holt's personal assistant, who apologises for disturbing us but she needs to remind John that his next meeting starts in 15 minutes. With that reminder, I suggest that we move quickly to a discussion of the key takeaways from today's workshop.

Key takeaways

John Holt is very keen to complete this exercise before he leaves and he takes the lead in the discussion himself. He is clear about the improvements that he wants to see, from himself as CEO as much as from anyone else – much of what follows could be seen as John's personal action plan, but none of the team has any objections to that. Soon the following points are noted down on the flipchart:

✓ **Commit to consistency in decision-making**. John views this as the essential component of being an ethical leader and he makes a promise to everyone that he will endeavour to be consistent in his decision-making in future, both in good times and in bad.

✓ **Be willing to hear bad news**. John is determined to bring about a more open culture at Stronach – the Westpac example has clearly made a big impression on him. He makes a personal commitment to try and handle bad news better than he may have done in the past. The team all agree about the importance of promoting an open culture if they, as leaders, are to be confident of being told the bad news in the first place. They all want to pick up this theme in more detail in a later workshop.

✓ **Be prepared to say no – sometimes**. John says that he is a positive person, someone who likes to say 'yes'. However, he knows that some proposals and some situations simply carry too much risk. So, he will adopt this maxim – if it is good enough for Warren Buffett then it is good enough for him!

✓ **Review and develop the crisis management plan**. The team admits that Stronach's crisis planning is rudimentary: there is no social media strategy, little in the way of media training has been given to senior managers (John regards this as a priority for himself) and no rehearsals of the plan have ever taken place. This was always one of Rachel's concerns and she agrees to work with the Group's PR people and develop proposals. She will need some assistance – she asks David Hurley and he readily agrees to help.

✓ **Treat everyone equally**. This is another point coming out of the workshop that John feels strongly about. Stronach has developed a staff handbook and has its ethics charter but perhaps in the past it has not always applied the principles therein fairly to all managers and staff. He feels that this was particularly true under his predecessor as CEO – Duncan Stronach always favoured the engineers generally and had a number of particular favourites amongst the managers. John resolves to be different.

Business dilemma

I point to this last item noted down on the flipchart to remind everybody about the dilemma situation that I asked them to think about at the start of the workshop. What would they do in the case of Peter Wiggins, the hypothetical sales director who is very successful but who lied on his CV and application form (and also during the interview) in order to secure the job in the first place?

John Holt is preparing to leave but he stays long enough to provide an excellent answer to this dilemma question. John says that he would have to let Peter Wiggins go, probably by means of a compromise agreement. And he points out that he may very well not have arrived at this conclusion if he had been given this particular dilemma situation before the start of the ethics project – maybe not even if he had been asked to give his opinion at the start of this workshop rather than now at the end of it! He explains what he means by this. As a businessman, he has always been focused on results so he would have been very tempted to retain Peter Wiggins because he is the best salesman that the company has. In fact, John says with a smile directed in David Hurley's direction, he might have been tempted to fire the HR manager because of failure to check references properly during the recruitment process! However, when long-term rather than short-term factors are considered, it is clear that Wiggins has to go – he is a liar and John says that he would not be able to trust him again. Under pressure, how reliable would Wiggins be? How reliable, in reality, are his reported results? After all, there was a time in the early 1990s when the most successful salesman in Barings Bank was a certain Nick Leeson. But his deals turned out to be fictitious – in the end Barings Bank collapsed as a result of Mr Leeson's fraudulent trading!

John looks at me as he says this and I am nodding my head in agreement – I could not agree more with his summary. No one else has anything to add and, with this, John departs.

Next workshop

Arrangements for the next workshop have already been agreed. We will re-convene again next week, this time in the evening at 7.30 pm to discuss the areas of compliance and control.

Reflections

With John having already left, the workshop quickly comes to a close. Malcolm has an appointment with investors in the City and David has to prepare for a round of recruitment interviews this afternoon. Both say that they are looking forward to the next session.

Rachel stays behind; it looks like she wants to talk about something. She begins by saying that she thinks that the ethics project is proving to be a great success and that the workshops are an integral part of that – they produce good discussion and good action points alike. Today was no exception. I agree and say that everyone contributes very well to the discussion. Take David Hurley for example – he has really surprised me with the quality of his contributions at times. Rachel nods and says that she did not really know him well before this project started but she is enjoying working with him.

Rachel then asks me how many more workshops after the one next week do I think will be needed to finish the programme. I say that we will need one more for sure in order to look at the ethics toolbox. Rachel then asks about one of the strong themes coming out of today's workshop, that of openness – is it possible to include an element of speak-up and whistle-blowing as part of the session on the ethics toolbox? I think about this for a moment – it is possible, of course, but I agree with her that this is a crucial component of culture and I would prefer to have a separate workshop on whistle-blowing. It might be an appropriate way in which to conclude the workshop series. Rachel considers this for a moment and then nods – we are agreed.

As I walk out of Stronach's offices into Berkeley Square I consider the remaining subject-matter for the project: compliance and controls; the ethics toolbox; and whistle-blowing procedures. All of these are important if Rachel and her team are going to be successful in embedding good business ethics throughout the Group. There is still much work to do.

CHAPTER SEVEN

Risk, compliance and the controls framework

A THREE-STAGE PROCESS: SIXTH WORKSHOP

Opening

I arrive at the Stronach Group's offices in good time for the scheduled 7.30 pm start for this, the sixth and additional workshop on compliance and the controls framework that was agreed at the conclusion of the last session. The room is ready, coffee and biscuits provided, and the team comes in together only a little time after me – they are clearly keen! Rachel Gordon, the Chairman, asks how long the workshop is likely to last and I assure everyone that it will be 60–90 minutes maximum, so that we will finish by 9.00 pm at the latest. That is acceptable to the team, though I can sense that no one has the appetite for a longer session tonight.

Update

We are all drinking coffee and exchanging small talk when Rachel informs me that the board has made a decision on who will be the Stronach Group's new non-executive director. Somewhat surprisingly (and against her own prediction) the Nominations Committee recommended the female candidate – equally surprisingly, the board agreed with the recommendation and ratified her appointment. The new non-executive is a lady called Lesley Gowing. I have heard of her I think – I ask if she is a big player in the media industry and Rachel nods by way of confirmation. Rachel is clearly delighted and the reactions of her male colleagues are all very positive too. John Holt, the CEO, tells me that the appointment will be announced in the media first thing in the morning.

As we take our places, I say quietly to Rachel that she is making progress, which she acknowledges with the broadest of smiles.

Agenda

I set out the agenda for this evening. After giving the session much thought, I have decided that, rather than simply looking at compliance and controls, I need to include an overview of risk management and internal audit too if maximum benefit is to be gained from this shorter workshop. I make the point that although we are here primarily to examine the crucial question of the effectiveness of compliance and controls in organisations, we cannot do so in isolation. The discussion needs to be 'topped and tailed' so to speak.

Controls exist for many reasons but to me the crucial one from the business perspective has always been to help to manage and mitigate risk. Risk drives controls. So, we need to begin with a review of risk management, particularly because greater attention is now expected from directors and senior managers in this area, especially in the identification and management of the organisation's principal risks. Then, towards the end of the workshop, we will look at the need for the board of directors to have assurance that the controls that it has put in place to manage risk are in fact working in accordance with the way that they were designed. The classic way for directors to obtain such assurance is through the use of an internal audit function, one that exists independently from the operating units and so can report independently to the board, often via the audit committee.

I say that, in terms of our twin-track approach to culture and business ethics, each of these three areas (and certainly compliance and controls) would traditionally fit into the category of ethical hardware. However, I intend to demonstrate that, as elsewhere, there are also software elements that are crucial to the overall effectiveness of compliance and control. Examples include: the active engagement of the board; the creation of a risk-aware culture; the commitment to adapt controls in response to changing risks; and being supportive of the internal audit function through budget, staffing and encouragement to consider all aspects of the organisation in the audit plan.

Everyone seems happy with this outline. Providing there are no questions, I suggest that as we are working to a tight timetable this evening we should begin straightaway. There are no questions, so I begin the presentation.

 RISK MANAGEMENT

Background

History

The management of risk has always been of fundamental importance to all organisations. Yet risk management – the formalised processes used today to identify, assess, prioritise, manage, mitigate, communicate and report on risk – is a relatively new business discipline. As an example, it may well surprise some of the younger readers of this book to learn that there were no 'risk registers' used in any of the clients in my last audit portfolio in 1990. How times have changed!

Risk management, as an idea, developed steadily throughout the twentieth century out of a combination of wars, weather-related disasters, mathematical theories and business imperatives. The advantages of taking a disciplined approach to future uncertainties, based on probabilities rather than on luck or faith, became clear. It was in the 1990s that these ideas gained traction. The title of Chief Risk Officer was first used in 1993 by James Lam at GE Capital to describe a function that involved managing 'all aspects of risk'. Peter Bernstein, in his influential book published in 1996 *Against the Gods: The Remarkable Story of Risk* summarised this changed attitude as follows:

'If everything is a matter of luck, risk management is a meaningless exercise. Invoking luck obscures truth because it separates an event from its cause.'[1] Developments in risk management theory were encouraged and adopted by businesses, driven notably by the insurance and financial services sectors in the USA, so that by the end of the 1990s formalised processes were becoming the norm in many organisations. Risk management was embraced by private sector companies and the public sector alike around the twin goals of prudence and productivity, thereby enabling organisations to avoid unnecessary waste of resources but at the same time providing them with assurance that objectives would be met in a variety of areas from financial planning to health and safety.

Current position

Today risk management is an important part of the day-to-day operations of very many enterprises and for a simple reason – managing risk effectively helps all organisations to perform well in an environment full of uncertainty. In contrast to the mid 1990s, there are now a multitude of institutes, educational courses and books devoted to the subject. Risk management is not the core topic of this book, so we do not need to examine the development of the theory in great detail here. However, in my view an understanding of some of the fundamental principles of risk management is needed in order to run any organisation successfully. We looked at a number of important ideas in Chapter 4 on reputational risk and we build on these here, starting with a definition.

There are many definitions of risk management today. One of the earliest was set out in the first recognised Risk Management Standard published in 1995 following its development by a multi-disciplinary task force of Standards Australia/Standards New Zealand.[2] The Standard has been revised since but the power of the original definition remains and is sufficient for our purposes as follows:

> *Risk management is a process to identify, assess, manage and control potential events or situations, to provide reasonable assurance regarding the achievement of the organisation's objectives.*

The very important principle that risk management provides organisations with 'reasonable assurance' regarding the achievement of objectives, and not with certainty, is set out here. Also, the framework for the management of risk in a business context is established around the achievement of the organisation's objectives. All organisations exist to achieve certain things. These objectives should be articulated by the board and senior management. Risk is anything and everything that could impact on the successful achievement of those business objectives.

Organisations need a structured, disciplined process to manage risk in the twenty-first century because the risk universe is now so complicated and inter-connected. A discussion on risk management in the 1990s would almost certainly have coalesced around two types of risk – financial risks and the important area of health and safety. Today, there are a variety of different risk types that all have to be managed because each could have a significant effect on an organisation. Examples of modern risk types are: reputation, financial, health and safety, technological, environmental, geopolitical, legal and regulatory, credit, operational, competition, liquidity and counter-party, staff-related, political, contractual and physical. In addition, of course there is ethical risk and we saw the importance of this when reviewing the Edward Snowden case in Chapter 4.

As part of the modern risk management structure, the board of directors provides oversight and monitors the organisation's principal risks, while the key tool used by management is the risk register. A risk register is essentially a colour-coded spreadsheet on which risks are identified and assessed for impact and probability (in order to establish the high priority risks), with the controls over them and mitigating actions (if any) being set out. High risk items that are not matched by correspondingly strong controls are typically highlighted on the register by the colour 'red'. These 'red risks' will require an action plan, therefore with an appropriate timetable and responsibilities, that should be set out on the register. This document provides evidence that management has discharged its responsibilities around managing risk.

Risk-aware culture

So, processes like the risk register provide the necessary hardware. By themselves, however, these processes will not be sufficient to create a risk-aware culture – as always there are important software components that must be present if sufficiency is to be achieved. The reason is simple. The culture of an organisation is at least as important as the processes it uses in determining how successful that organisation will be in managing its risks.

As we have seen, the most significant influence on organisational culture is the behaviour and decision-making of the directors and senior managers. It is no different when considering risk. The 'tone at the top' is crucial in creating a risk-aware culture. Important components of this include: a risk awareness training programme; the management of risk being included as part of managers' objectives (particularly important for line managers and team leaders) and performance appraisals; and the communication and reporting of risk issues.

In my view, there is one key issue from a risk perspective when looking at culture and that is the need for the leaders to assess the extent to which there is a 'blame culture' in their organisation. By that I mean does a culture exist in which mistakes and errors of judgement are viewed as career-limiting events? If the answer is essentially 'yes', then the effect within the organisation is likely to be corrosive to transparency, with any issues, shortfalls and problems tending to be swept under the carpet and kept hidden from senior management. This has obvious dangers in areas such as internal fraud. But it is also damaging to effective risk management, which should always embrace the idea of openness. It is crucial that the key risks facing an organisation at any point in time are 'put on the table', are communicated widely and are fully discussed and analysed with a view to managing them successfully in order to achieve stated business objectives. If this is not the case, then risk management is reduced to a box-ticking exercise and trust is forfeited through the absence of transparency.

Risk management models

Introduction

A number of important models exist today to assist organisations to manage risk effectively. These include: the Turnbull Guidance and the SOX model (arising out of the corporate governance developments in the UK and the USA respectively); the Enterprise Risk Management framework, developed by the Committee of Sponsoring Organisations (COSO) in 2004; the Orange Book, developed for the public sector in the UK; the Basel Capital Accords, developed by banking supervisors to provide a common framework for the management of credit, market and operational risks by internationally active banks around the world; the international risk management standard, ISO 31000; and the Three Lines of Defence model.

Risk management in the banking sector seems to have failed spectacularly during the global financial crisis when the risk held on the balance sheets of many financial institutions was found to be significantly under-priced. The new Basel III Framework looks to incorporate many of the lessons learned from the crisis, especially in terms of taking a more robust approach to the liquidity and solvency of banks. However, it should be said that neither the Basel Capital Accords nor any of the other models claim to give certainty in the management of risk, rather their objective is always to provide reasonable assurance. This simply reflects reality. There is never any certainty in business – things can and do go wrong.

What has become apparent is that all of these models are vulnerable to operational risks such as the technological failures that we see from time to time in the banking industry. For example: the computer glitches that prevented many customers of RBS in the UK from accessing their accounts in 2012;[3] and back office shortfalls that have failed to detect failures and breakdowns in anti-money laundering controls at a number of major international banks. However, the key weakness in risk management systems is often a human factor: errors, poor judgement, the slow reaction to unexpected events, attempts to 'game' the system, complacency and negligence. The best safeguard against these human factors is the creation of a risk-aware culture.

Set out below is a brief review of two of these risk management models, the Three Lines of Defence model and the Turnbull Guidance, to draw out some key points in terms of how to apply the theory in practice.

Three Lines of Defence model

As the name suggests, this model aims to provide reasonable assurance by having three separate mechanisms to identify, assess, manage and mitigate risk. The first line of defence is provided by the business operators themselves – the line managers and team leaders. The second line of defence is specialist risk oversight personnel (whether working in the risk or compliance departments or in other critical areas such as health and safety or IT security). The third line of defence is an independent review and challenge process provided by such functions as internal audit. In the model, each of these mechanisms has a reporting line to the board, via the risk committee or the audit committee.

In my opinion, there are two messages embedded within the Three Lines of Defence model that organisations of all sizes and in all sectors would benefit from adopting. The first concerns one of the fundamental principles of modern risk management – namely that risk devolves to the line. It is the departmental heads, the line managers and the team leaders who should take the lead in managing risk in all organisations. If managers and staff at the operational level are encouraged to take responsibility and become the risk owners, then this is a powerful and effective approach to managing risk in the business.

This leads directly onto the second key message, which is that the concept of three lines of defence applies to all organisations, regardless of size. This might seem counter-intuitive because of cost constraints and resource limitations. However, this simply must happen in my view if risk is to be managed effectively in small and medium-sized enterprises. The delegation of risk management to line managers provides the essential basis for this, but this is not sufficient. There must be oversight of risk too, with individuals at various levels given specific responsibility for managing risk in their areas. This will mean that, in small or medium sized businesses, senior managers need to take on this role themselves by being highly visible and hands on in their approach and making sure that their staff know exactly what is expected of them. Without doing so there can be no assurance. Finally, all organisations should have a measure of independent check in all aspects of their business, including the management of risk. If there is no separate internal audit function to do this then alternatives are always possible, for example either through an internal review by management or through the commissioning of the external auditors to conduct a review of the risk management process.

Turnbull Framework (Guidance for Directors)

Nigel Turnbull's Committee published its report in 1999 on 'Internal Control: Guidance for Directors on the Combined Code'. [4] The guidance provides a simple and powerful four-stage framework for risk and controls that is still regarded as best practice in the UK today. A summary of the framework is set out below:

▪ **Stage 1. Identify and assess risks** (looking at aspects such as completeness of risks assessed, the impact and probability of a risk materialising together with time-frames).
▪ **Stage 2. Design appropriate controls over the risks** (controls should be embedded in systems, include both preventative and detective measures and be cost-effective and proportionate).
▪ **Stage 3. Test that the controls are working** (to answer the crucial question: Are the controls operating in practice in accordance with the design?).
▪ **Stage 4. Conclude on the effectiveness of the internal control system** (this should be carried out annually by the board, as stipulated in the framework).

The guidance has been reviewed and updated since 1999, most recently in 2014 when there was a significant amendment to Stage 4 of the guidance, [5] as reflected in changes in the updated UK Code of Corporate Governance of that year. The new Code Provisions on risk management and internal control increase the scrutiny and reporting requirements required from the board. The directors must carry out 'a robust assessment of the principal risks facing the company, including those that would threaten its business model, future performance, solvency or liquidity'. They must also monitor the company's risk management and internal control systems and 'at least annually carry out a review of their effectiveness and report on that review in the annual report'.

These changes illustrate very well the modern focus of risk management.

In particular, the attention by the authorities on the principal risks of an organisation reflects the desire to promote greater resiliency in business following the shocks of the global financial crisis. This means that greater attention must be paid by directors to the solvency, liquidity and going concern of their companies and reporting on how these are being managed to shareholders.

There is also a new focus on areas of high impact risks, often those which may have been 'hidden' or under-estimated in the past. Examples include: losses through fraud, corruption and theft; cyber-crime; brand damage resulting from social media; and problems in the supply chain. As we have seen, the risks posed by cyber-crime, both in terms of the tarnishing of reputation through negative comments on social media, together with the dangers of data theft, hacking and software viruses, have increased significantly in recent years. In order to combat these and other threats, organisations need to have effective controls in place that are capable of responding to changes in risk or to rapidly escalating risks.

COMPLIANCE AND CONTROLS

Overview

Effective and efficient internal controls provide assurance. The importance for improved performance of organisations having internal controls systems in place that are designed to meet individual requirements and work effectively has been recognised for many years and certainly since 1992, when the Committee of Sponsoring Organisations of the Treadway Commission (COSO) produced its seminal report titled: 'Internal Control – Integrated Framework' (the Framework)[6] – see below. More recently, the proliferation of laws and regulations affecting business and the public sector too, especially in highly regulated sectors such as financial services and health care, together with the ever-increasing penalties for rules violations, has seen a dramatic growth in the demand for compliance officers.

The primary responsibility of the compliance officer is to oversee and manage legal and regulatory risk within an organisation. The importance placed on rules in the USA, together with the litigious culture there, means that much of the impetus for the growth of compliance has come from US authorities such as the SEC. This was especially so in the years immediately following the passing of the SOX in response to the high profile bankruptcies at Enron and WorldCom caused by accounting frauds involving the senior management of those companies. However, the demand for compliance officers has certainly spread around the world and has been given added urgency by the fallout from the global financial crisis – for example, the chief compliance officer (CCO) is one of the most sought after and well paid positions in the City of London today. Regulatory risk is now firmly installed as a key risk on the agenda of many boards, not only in the USA but globally.

Compliance and controls are necessary to achieve good business ethics. As we have seen, they are not sufficient in themselves to embed good behaviour, but nevertheless they represent part of the essential hardware, the building blocks that organisations look to for assurance that they will not incur financial and reputational damage because of any breaches of the law or of applicable regulations. We analyse controls below in two ways: first, through a review of the overarching COSO controls framework; and second, through a more in-depth analysis of the controls required to prevent a particular risk from materialising and one that is very relevant to our topic – that of occupational fraud.

But before we consider controls, we need to start with a look at compliance.

Compliance

Definition

Compliance means acting in accordance with the rules that govern the way that all workers (directors, managers and staff) should behave in the workplace. There are two clear dimensions to this. The first is external compliance – behaving in a way that discharges any duty arising from obligations under relevant laws and regulations. The second is internal compliance – behaving in a way that meets the rules as set out in organisational policies, procedures, controls and codes.

Compliance function and compliance officers

Compliance functions are more prevalent in those industry sectors that are more tightly regulated than in others. For example, a recent PwC survey showed that 86% of financial services firms in the USA have a CCO, compared with 54% in less regulated sectors such as retail.[7] Large, complex organisations such as international banks will almost always have a compliance function today. In an international bank the compliance function will exist independently from the banking and operational units. Traditionally, the CCO will have a legal background; he or she will most often be a qualified lawyer and will have reporting lines into the board via the chief operating officer or the CEO.

The CCO and the compliance function are responsible for the organisation of regulatory compliance and the remit is likely to be increasingly demanding. From a high-level perspective, the purpose of the compliance function is to help the organisation protect its reputation and integrity. For example, in the case of a bank this will mean managing the integrity risks related to both its clients (in relation to, say, possible money laundering, terrorist financing or international sanctions listing) and the personal conduct of its staff. At the more detailed level, this will include: keeping up to date with changes in relevant laws and regulations; designing policies, procedures and internal controls to provide reasonable assurance of compliance with relevant laws and regulations; providing training on compliance matters; managing audits and investigations into regulatory and compliance issues; and responding to requests for information from the authorities and from regulatory bodies.

Compliance and the compliance function are evolving as legal and regulatory risk continues to increase in importance in heavily regulated business sectors. Globalisation has had the effect of introducing risk from local regulators too. Established compliance units are operating with larger budgets and increased staffing levels. A recent development is for the compliance department to be staffed by increasingly cross-functional teams encompassing different skill-sets – financial, operational or technological – rather than simply by people with legal (or similar) backgrounds. As the variety of compliance risks becomes ever more complex, so the CCO is assuming a more strategic role, working closely with the CEO and business leaders within the organisation. Another development has been the rise of the role of Chief Ethics and Compliance Officer (CECO) in the USA, which seeks to combine ethics and compliance. Personally, I do not view this as an entirely helpful development because I think that there are important differences between ethics and compliance, as we discussed earlier in the book.

However, in general I believe that these developments in compliance are positive and are an appropriate response to increased risk in the regulated sector. My concern is that there are a large number of small and medium-sized businesses (and some larger ones too no doubt) that continue to operate without a designated compliance officer or a compliance department. Although they may not be in heavily regulated industry sectors, nevertheless the law itself is becoming more complex, with one noticeable trend being the increased possibility of senior officers and directors being held personally liable for the actions of their organisations. The UKBA is a good example of this. Another is provided by anti-competition and anti-trust legislation. All organisations need to assess their exposure to legal and regulatory risks and ensure that appropriate measures are in place to manage and mitigate them.

Compliance framework

A compliance framework is a structured set of guidelines that details an organisation's processes for complying with all relevant laws and regulations. It sets out the regulatory compliance standards that are relevant to the organisation and then describes the business processes and internal controls that the organisation has in place to adhere to those standards. There are many frameworks available (for example, COBIT 5 or the Unified Compliance Framework), but I have worked with a simple and robust four-stage compliance framework in the past that I set out below.

- **Stage 1. Compliance oversight**. Regulatory compliance and reporting should be seen as a natural extension of good governance. Compliance should be firmly established on the board's agenda and so should be aligned to the organisation's business objectives and risk management strategies. Rather than exist in isolation, compliance should be a fully integrated function that sits naturally alongside governance and risk management;
- **Stage 2. Internal controls and behaviour**. We will look at the internal control piece of the framework in detail below. In terms of influencing and embedding good behaviour, the framework includes all of the tools in what we have described as the ethical toolbox and will look

at in detail in Chapter 8 (for example, codes and handbooks, training, hotlines, incentives and discipline).

- **Stage 3. Audit and reporting**. Risk assessment is plugged into this compliance framework here in stage 3, which also includes the important safeguard of an independent monitoring and review process.
- **Stage 4. Managing third parties**. Due diligence is essential if compliance risk is to be managed in today's business environment. As we have seen, it is crucial that the third parties that an organisation chooses to do business with replicate that organisation's own standards as far as possible in the light of modern pieces of legislation such as the UKBA. Another important area here is merger and acquisition activity, which should always be supported by the compliance function conducting a due diligence review.

Internal controls

Overview

Internal control is the term used to describe the various plans, systems, methods and procedures that an organisation uses in order to bring order and efficiency to its operations and to help it meet its declared business objectives. In practice, managers will use controls and procedures to achieve various different but essential aims including to: ensure that the policies of the board are followed; safeguard the assets of the business and prevent and detect fraud, errors, waste, abuse and mismanagement; ensure the completeness and accuracy of records; and of course to ensure compliance with the law and all relevant regulations.

In addition (and in my view as important as any of the other reasons), internal controls help an organisation to manage its risks. Every control should be designed in a way that is proportionate to the risk in question. One of the problems for mature organisations – those companies or public sector bodies that have existed for decades – is that their internal control systems will often predate their adoption of formalised risk management procedures. So individual controls, methods of working and customs and practices may well have evolved without using risk as a reference point at all. Modern control frameworks, like the Integrated Framework that we look at below, adopt a principles-based, risk-focused approach, where the internal control system is closely coupled with the risk management methodology.

Control characteristics

There are many different types of controls that organisations use. Examples are: policies and procedures; authorisation levels; segregation of duties; reconciliations; key performance indicators; physical security and systems access; recruitment and exit processes; internal audit; management review; training and development; ethics charters and codes of conduct; and many others. Some of them serve different purposes and many operate in different ways, so it is helpful to look at a number of key control characteristics.

Internal controls can be categorised into two broad types: preventative controls and detective controls. Each has different characteristics and their major features are as follows:

- **Preventative controls**. The aim of a preventative control is to stop an event from occurring or a risk from materialising in the first place. Robust staff recruitment procedures used by an organisation when hiring new employees are a good example of this. Their overall aim is to ensure that the organisation hires the best available people, but an important by-product of the vetting process is that any undesirable or unsuitable applicants should be prevented from working in the business from the outset.

■ **Detective controls**. Here the objective is different, it is to highlight or flag up or otherwise indicate to management that something has gone wrong – in other words to signal when a risk has crystallised, or when a problem or a fault in the system has occurred. A system of exception reporting, whereby parameters are used to highlight those transactions falling outside of the acceptable criteria, is a good example of a detective control. It is seen in many standard business processes today, for example in credit control where debtors outstanding for more than (say) 90 days are often listed in a separate report for management attention.

Another important distinction to be made when assessing a control is whether the control is manual or is automated. A manual control exists where somebody (an individual) has actually got to do something, where he or she becomes physically involved in the process. For automated controls, however, this is not required because here they are programmed or inherent in the system being used – they are embedded in the system. Automated controls are generally considered to be more efficient and cost-effective than manual controls.

COSO's Internal Control – Integrated Framework – 2013

As a chartered accountant by training and qualification, much of my early career was spent reviewing and testing internal controls and internal controls frameworks. The most important of these was the Integrated Framework produced by COSO in 1992.[8] The Framework was recently updated in 2013 and set out below are its main features. The Framework gives best-practice, principles-based guidance for designing and implementing effective internal controls. It aims to provide a standard against which business and other entities – large or small, in the public or private sector, for profit or not – can assess their control systems and determine how to improve them. The Framework has become the most widely used internal control framework in the USA and has been adopted or adapted by numerous organisations in countries around the world.

The Framework includes an important definition of internal control, as follows:

Internal control is a process, affected by an entity's board of directors, management and other personnel designed to provide reasonable assurance regarding the achievement of objectives relating to operations, reporting and compliance.

The definition is intentionally broad and reflects a number of fundamental concepts. For example: internal control should be able to provide reasonable assurance, but never absolute assurance; and that it is affected by people, so that it is not merely about policy and procedures manuals, systems and forms but about people and the actions they take at every level of an organisation.

Under the Framework, internal control consists of five integrated components. COSO describes each of the five components as follows:

■ **Control environment**. The control environment is the set of standards, processes and structures that provide the basis for carrying out internal control across the organisation. The board of directors and senior management establish the tone at the top regarding the importance of internal control including expected standards of conduct. Management re-inforces expectations at the various levels of the organisation. The control environment comprises the integrity and ethical values of the organisation; the parameters enabling the board of directors to carry out its governance oversight responsibilities; the organisational structure and assignment of authority and responsibility; the process for attracting, developing and retaining competent individuals; and the rigour around performance measures, incentives and rewards to drive accountability for performance. The resulting control environment has a pervasive impact on the overall system of internal control.

- **Risk assessment**. Every entity faces a variety of risks from external and internal sources. Risk assessment involves a dynamic and iterative process for identifying and assessing risks to the achievement of objectives. Risks to the achievement of these objectives from across the entity are considered relative to established risk tolerances. This risk assessment forms the basis for determining how risks will be managed. A precondition to risk assessment is the establishment of objectives, linked at different levels of the entity. Management specifies objectives within categories relating to operations, reporting and compliance with sufficient clarity to be able to identify and analyse risks to those objectives. Management also considers the suitability of the objectives for the entity. Risk management also requires management to consider the impact of possible changes in the control environment and within its own business model that may render internal control ineffective.

- **Control activities**. Control activities are the actions established through policies and procedures that help ensure that management's directives to mitigate risks to the achievement of objectives are carried out. Control activities are performed at all levels of the entity, at various stages within business processes and over the technology environment. They may be preventive or detective in nature and may encompass a range of manual and automated activities such as authorisations and approvals, verifications, reconciliations and business performance reviews. Segregation of duties is typically built into the selection and development of control activities. Where segregation of duties is not practical, management selects and develops alternative control activities.

- **Information and communication**. Information is necessary for the entity to carry out internal control responsibilities to support the achievement of its objectives. Management obtains or generates and uses relevant and quality information from both internal and external sources to support the functioning of other components of internal control. Communication is the continual, iterative process of providing, sharing and obtaining necessary information. Internal communication is the means by which information is disseminated throughout the organisation, flowing up, down and across the entity. It enables personnel to receive a clear message from senior management that control responsibilities must be taken seriously. External communication is twofold: it enables inbound communication of relevant external information and it provides information to external parties in response to requirements and expectations.

- **Monitoring activities**. Ongoing evaluations, separate evaluations or some combination of the two are used to ascertain whether each of the five components of internal control, including controls to affect the principles within each component, is present and functioning. Ongoing evaluations, built into business processes at different levels of the entity, provide timely information. Separate evaluations, conducted periodically, will vary in scope and frequency depending on assessment of risks, effectiveness of ongoing evaluations and other management considerations. Findings are evaluated against criteria established by regulators, recognised standard-setting bodies or management and the board of directors, and deficiencies are communicated to management and the board of directors as appropriate.

The Framework sets out the requirements for an effective system of internal control, one that provides reasonable assurance regarding the achievement of the entity's objectives. In order to do so, each of the five components must be present and functioning. It requires judgement in designing, implementing and conducting internal control and assessing its effectiveness.

The Framework represents the most robust of internal control models. As will be apparent, embedded within it is the same the twin-track approach – the combination of hardware and software – that is discussed and advocated throughout the book.

We now consider a brief analysis of the type of controls needed to manage one particular risk, that of occupational fraud.

Controls in action: anti-fraud measures

Overview: the controls framework

Fraud is a significant risk to all organisations today because it threatens both results and reputation.[9] So, a strong anti-fraud controls framework is needed if this risk is to be managed effectively. There are a number of necessary features to the framework – the hardware as we have described it throughout the book. This includes: strong preventative controls; deterrence features (a by-product of strong prevention); and appropriate detective controls, the purpose of which is to reduce the exposure gap (the length of time between when a fraud happens and when it is discovered). However, as elsewhere, these controls will not, by themselves, be sufficient to provide reasonable assurance that fraud is not happening in an entity. To them must be added the crucial software components comprising: the governance dimension (including the allocation of responsibilities and reporting lines); tone at the top, with the commitment of directors and senior management to a zero tolerance of financial crime being demonstrated though consistent decision-making; awareness-raising training programmes for management and staff; and an understanding of the fraud threats as they apply to each individual organisation.

This last point is crucial. Every organisation needs to assess the risk of fraud in its own operations. This assessment must be informed (that is, it must be put together by those within the organisation who have a good understanding of the threats) and updated periodically. Once risk is understood, then controls can be designed that are appropriate and proportionate to meet those risks.

External and internal fraud

At a basic level, fraud risk divides into two: external fraud, and internal or occupational fraud.

External fraud threats are important today, in particular in connection with organised criminal gangs and cyber-crime. Computer hacking and data theft are growing risks, especially in certain industry sectors such as financial services and retailing. All organisations should have an appropriate information risk management regime in place, together with data security at every level. There are a number of key data security steps: training staff in internal security protocols (in such areas as safe downloads, emails, flash-drives, mobile devices and home working); clear and consistent policies with partners and suppliers (for example on the use of passwords, data encryption, data sharing and systems access); up-to-date security measures (such as malware protection and network security); and monitoring of user privileges and activity. Of most importance is that cyber-crime is not seen as an IT risk but rather as a key operational risk that needs to be managed at a senior level within every organisation.

Although it might appear to be counter-intuitive given the rise of cyber-crime, internal (or occupational fraud) is a bigger threat to organisations. Set out below are the most important anti-fraud controls that organisations can use to manage the risk of internal fraud. Again, we see the mixture of hard controls and soft controls that are available. It is in choosing the right combination and balance between the two that every organisation can provide the best defences to suit its own unique circumstances.

Generic anti-fraud controls

A robust system of internal controls is an essential prerequisite for managing fraud risk. This begins with the broad range of controls that organisations rely on every day. Three of these generic controls are most important in order to prevent, deter and detect fraud: segregation of duties, authorisation limits and safeguards over assets.

Segregation of duties is vital to an organisation's system of checks and balances. The key idea here is that no one person should have absolute autonomy or unfettered powers of decision-making in any area of business. This principle applies to day-to-day business transactions but it is particularly important when considering fraud risk. For example, consider what opportunities there would be if a manager or employee has complete autonomy over the purchasing cycle. Smaller organisations often find it difficult to establish good segregation of duties because of low staff numbers, but it is always possible to compensate by including an independent supervisor in the process or by a hands-on management style from those at the top.

Mechanisms to delegate authority are widely used in organisations to ensure that power is devolved from the top (board of directors) to senior managers and then to other personnel responsible for the day-to-day operations. However, there must be clear authorisation limits in place setting out who within the organisation can spend what amount of money if the risk of fraud is to be minimised. More than that, there must be a controls culture in place so that these limits are always respected and adhered to by managers and staff.

Safeguards and controls over assets break down into two component parts: physical security and computer (or information) security. Both are huge subjects and it is not possible to cover them fully here. Some aspects of the controls needed to manage information security are set out above in the passage on external fraud threats and cyber-crime. Physical security in its broadest sense may be defined as the protection of buildings, equipment, people, hardware and data from circumstances and events that could cause serious loss and damage to an organisation or injury to its personnel. Traditional physical security measures range from the obvious locks on doors to sophisticated buildings security systems with full integration of alarms, CCTV, access control, guarding officers and central monitoring facilities.

Specific anti-fraud prevention controls

Anti-fraud prevention controls aim specifically to minimise the opportunities for managers and staff to commit fraud. There are three that are particularly important: anti-fraud policies, staff vetting procedures and fraud awareness training programmes. Once again, there is a mix here between 'hard controls' (the policy and the staff vetting) and the 'soft control' of the anti-fraud training programme which seeks to raise awareness and influence culture.

- ▪ **Anti-fraud policy**. By publishing an anti-fraud policy statement, signed off by the chairman or the CEO, an organisation is able to set out its attitude to, and position on, fraud in a very direct and straightforward way. The policy should: define fraud; give pointers to staff in terms of what to look for; emphasise the importance of an anti-fraud culture; set out responsibilities;

establish reporting lines; and act as a deterrent by setting out the consequences of engaging in fraud. It should also include a fraud response plan setting out the process that will be followed in the event of a fraud being suspected or discovered. As with the anti-bribery policy that we discussed earlier in the book, the overall aim is to send out a clear message of the organisation's commitment to fighting fraud, along the following lines: 'XYZ Ltd has a zero tolerance of fraud. All allegations of fraud will be thoroughly investigated and, where substantiated, will result in dismissal and/or prosecution.'

▪ **Staff vetting**. Hiring new people is a risky business and I say this with reference to the true meaning of the word risk – new hires present both opportunities and threats to an organisation. When looking at fraud risk the focus is clearly on the threats. Background checks are critical and will include: checking identity; verification of academic and professional qualifications; employment reference checks; and checking international criminal records. One additional check that I always encourage organisations to make (providing it is within the law in their particular jurisdiction) is a credit reference search. The reason is simple – the research shows that some form of financial pressure is the most important motive that drives fraudulent behaviour. Seeking assurance about the financial history of an applicant, especially in the case of an applicant for a senior position, is a smart control because it is designed to match risk.

▪ **Fraud awareness training**. The top fraud prevention and detection resource available to an organisation is in fact that organisation's own people. So it is essential that everyone – managers and staff alike – is trained in what fraud actually is, how fraud damages both the organisation and its employees and how to report any suspicious activities. All fraud awareness training programmes should send a positive message and be non-accusatory. They should emphasise throughout that illegal conduct in any form eventually costs everyone in the organisation through financial loss, low morale and adverse media comments leading to reputational damage. We discuss the power and importance of awareness training programmes more generally in Chapter 8.

Anti-fraud detective controls

Fraud is a hidden scheme. This is an obvious statement to make but it does have one important consequence – it means that fraud is difficult to detect. However, a number of anti-fraud detection controls do exist and it is important that organisations make use of them because they minimise the chance of managers and employees being able to conceal a fraud over long periods of time. Again there are three that are most important: whistle-blowing hotlines, data mining techniques and surprise audits.

▪ **Whistle-blowing hotlines**. Tip-off is the most important way that fraud is detected. So, it follows that a fraud reporting mechanism (sometimes referred to as a whistle-blowing hotline) that makes it as simple and straightforward as possible for staff to pass on their concerns about suspected or actual fraud is amongst the most effective detective controls. We look at the whole issue of hotlines later in Chapter 9 of the book.

▪ **Data mining techniques**. Trying to discover fraud in a modern business is very much like trying to find the proverbial needle in a haystack because of the large data warehouse of information that organisations build up compared with a very small number of fraudulent transactions that are buried somewhere in all the huge volume of information. Data mining provides the means of finding the needle. It is the process of analysing datasets from different perspectives in order to discover new or hidden patterns and relationships and then to summarise this into useful information. Data mining is therefore a proactive technique that is useful in fraud detection because it identifies anomalies, trends and risk indicators within large populations of transactions. Specialist data mining software tools are available that enable auditors or investigators to analyse information most effectively by cutting and pasting the transactions within a population of data according to risk, so that the riskiest items in the population are identified first.

■ **Surprise audits**. A surprise (or spot) audit is one where the audit team arrives unannounced, so that the auditee department or entity has no time to prepare in advance of the visit. Not only can this be an effective way to detect fraud, it also acts as a deterrent – a potential fraudster may well be deterred from proceeding with a scheme if he or she thinks that the internal auditors might turn up at any moment. Interestingly, this is one of the least well utilised anti-fraud controls as the great majority of audits today are planned and scheduled well in advance. This might promote operational efficiency but it does little to help fraud deterrence or detection.

So, organisations should look to identify areas of high fraud risk or concern within their operations and then target specific anti-fraud controls in these areas. This is the essence of taking a risk-based approach to fighting financial crime.

One of the key controls here is the internal audit function, although it is often under-utilised in the fraud arena. We look at internal auditing below.

INTERNAL AUDIT

Overview

Types of audit

Broadly, an audit is an evaluation process. There are many different types of audit today, including quality audits, energy audits and regulatory audits. When I was training to become a chartered accountant at Deloitte, I spent much of my first three years taking part in what are called external audits (sometimes referred to as statutory audits because they are a legal requirement each year for all but the smallest companies in many countries).

An external audit is the independent examination of, and expression of an opinion on, the financial statements of an enterprise. As such, it is an essential part of the governance process, but it is important to understand that external audits have a relatively narrow focus. They concentrate on the financial statements of an organisation (meaning the annual report and accounts) and on whether or not the information contained therein is disclosed in accordance with applicable accounting standards and relevant company law. External auditors do carry out work to review and test controls but they principally examine those controls surrounding the financial reporting process in order to support their audit opinion.

When looking at the systems and internal controls more generally within an organisation, it is the work of the internal auditors that is of more importance.

Internal audit definition

The primary role of internal audit should be to help the board and senior management to protect the assets, reputation and sustainability of the organisation. The Institute of Internal Auditors (IIA)[10] defines an internal audit as:

> *An independent, objective assurance and consulting activity designed to add value and improve an organisation's operations. It helps an organisation accomplish its objectives by bringing a systematic, disciplined approach to evaluate and improve the effectiveness of risk management, control and governance processes.*

Internal auditing is itself a control and it fits into the COSO Framework as part of the monitoring activities of an organisation.

The internal audit function acts as a basic and essential assurance service to directors and senior management. The leaders of any organisation need to know that their policies are being implemented and that the statements they make from time to time to employees, investors and other stakeholders are accurate. There are many ways that they can obtain such assurance: large organisations may well have separate compliance and risk management functions; all but the smallest organisations will have an external audit every year; ongoing management review is crucial, especially in smaller entities; and there will normally be a number of other assurance functions such as quality control, security and insurance. However, in my view it is the internal audit function that provides the most powerful form of assurance because of its combination of independence, objectivity and broad business focus.

Scope of work and advice for the audit committee

The work of internal auditors should be unlimited in its scope. But the IIA's definition points to the three main areas where internal auditing can add value: risk management, control and governance processes. Yet, in my experience of working with many internal audit departments over the years, I do not always see this happening in practice. Internal auditors spend a lot of time on systems and controls, though not always to best effect (see below). They spend less time on reviewing risk management processes. And they spend relatively little time on structured work in the governance piece. I think that this is a mistake and a wasted opportunity, both for an internal audit function wanting to make a difference to the organisation, and for the directors and senior managers looking for assurance throughout their business.

To be effective, the internal audit programme should cover adequately each of the three areas referred to in the IIA's definition and it is important that the audit committee ensures that this happens. My key pieces of advice to the chairman of the audit committee in order to maximise internal audit performance in each of these three areas of work are set out below.

- **Risk management**. Here the point is very simple: internal auditors should review the effectiveness of the risk management processes every year. Specifically, they should ensure that: risk management processes are operating as intended; that they are of sound design; that the responses of management to risks are adequate and effective in reducing those risks to a level acceptable to the board; and that a sound framework of controls is in place to mitigate sufficiently those risks that management wishes to treat. The internal audit report to the audit committee on these issues is fundamental if the board is to obtain assurance on the adequacy of the risk management process.

- **Controls**. The main issue with internal audit work on internal controls is not that insufficient time is spent in this area, but rather that sometimes it is not targeted towards the priority areas that matter most to the organisation. There are two overarching requirements if internal audit reports are to be credible and to add value to an organisation: the first is factual accuracy; and the second is realistic and important recommendations.

This second point was picked up by the experienced businessman Peter Jones during our interview. Peter is the chairman of the audit committees of the United Kingdom Atomic Energy Authority and of the National Nuclear Laboratory. This is what he had to say in the context of a fraud event that happened in one of his enterprises:

And I think another thing which came out of that episode was that the internal audit appraisal programme had perhaps not quite enough emphasis on actual compliance with controls as opposed to systems audit and management recommendations and so forth.

I think there is a risk that internal audit may result in large numbers of pretty insignificant recommendations on improvements which result in some of the key issues, where the controls are not actually operating effectively, being missed or not getting enough profile. There is a need for internal auditors to be fairly self-critical in identifying what is important and what isn't in their recommendations. There is also a need for management when considering internal audit recommendations to be fairly robust, to say sometimes: 'well ok this is perhaps in theory a slight shortcoming but it is not really something which is worthy of a full audit recommendation, it is a management issue, we will take this up but let's not have this on the list of things we have to actually deal with in the next two months'. Certainly we had a raft of outstanding internal audit recommendations which we shouldn't have had. One of the reasons we had a raft of outstanding internal audit recommendations was that there had been too many to start with and I think it is important to get the right balance.

- **Governance processes**. As an observation, I feel that very little internal work is allocated to the governance piece of their remit. This is often a difficult area and when I raised it with Peter Jones he had a query: 'Is it something one can expect an internal audit department to do effectively? I wonder if this isn't something which may be more appropriate to try to do with some external consultancy input and at a relatively senior level as well.' My own view is that internal auditors do have an important role to play in assurance around governance processes in two areas: the adequacy of controls to prevent and detect fraud; and the effectiveness of whistle-blowing arrangements. To be fair, Peter did concede this during our interview. We will look at the whole question of whistle-blowing later in Chapter 9. In terms of assisting in the fight against fraud, internal auditors should always be looking to assess risk and, where the risk of fraud is considered to be high (for example, in the purchasing and procurement cycle), then they should look to carry out pro-active work making use of data mining software where appropriate and always considering the option of surprise audits.

The audit of culture

An interesting recent development in internal auditing has been a focus on culture. This idea was introduced in the UK by the CIIA's new Financial Services Code in July 2013,[11] which provides guidance for internal auditors of financial services firms. Unsurprisingly, given the FCA's focus on conduct risk discussed in Chapter 4, internal auditors in financial services must ensure that their firm is acting with integrity in its dealings with customers and in its interaction with relevant markets. But also included is the new requirement for internal auditors to consider the risk and control culture of the organisation during its work, expressed in the following terms:

> *Internal audit should include within its scope the risk and control culture of the organisation. This should include assessing whether the processes (e.g. appraisal and remuneration), actions (e.g. decision-making) and 'tone at the top' are in line with the values, ethics, risk appetite and policies of the organisation.*

So, in the financial services industry the auditing of culture is now a key feature of the CIIA Code. But there are indicators that this initiative is being picked up by internal auditors in other business sectors too. The CIIA's Governance and Risk Report in 2013[12] noted that ethics and culture was one of the top three areas where Heads of Internal Audit are planning to increase their resources. This presents new challenges for internal auditors in terms of obtaining and assessing evidence to decide whether a cultural change programme is successful – in other words, has a statement of values been translated into action. This will require the use of qualitative testing such as staff surveys and interviews, coupled with techniques such as root cause analysis to identify why issues occur and how these issues can be the drivers of wrong behaviours.

Although it is too early to judge, I think that this new focus on culture will prove to be an important and lasting development. It is another area where internal audit can add value by advising on the processes and controls in cultural change programmes, though the ownership of those programmes must remain with management. In my view, internal audit can be a key player in giving assurance and confidence to directors and senior managers at a time when organisations in all business sectors are under increasing pressure to demonstrate their commitment to improving standards of behaviour.

WORKSHOP CONCLUSION

Closing

My presentation finishes and it is 8.45 pm, so not bad from the point of view of the timing. I say that we ought to move straight into the discussion on the key takeaways from the session. No one has any questions at this stage, so I hand over to them and the flipchart.

Key takeaways

Unsurprisingly perhaps, given the topics under discussion, I had noticed that Malcolm Mainwaring, the Group Finance Director, was the team member who was taking most notes during the presentation. He also takes the lead during the discussion and he is instrumental in drawing together the following five points for subsequent action:

✓ **Internal audit to include specific anti-fraud work in their programmes**. Picking up the last piece of the presentation first, Malcolm is very keen that the internal audit department includes some dedicated time to reviewing how fraud threats are managed throughout the Stronach Group in the future. Being somewhat old-fashioned (as he describes himself) he likes the idea of surprise audits. He has no specific concerns but he is well aware of the amount of money that the Group spends on purchases each year and of the reputational damage that can result from a fraud incident. He undertakes to speak to Ashley Corbett, the Chairman of the Audit Committee and also to the Head of Group Internal Audit, about this.

✓ **Improving the board's contribution to risk management**. Malcolm is aware that the Financial Reporting Council has concerns in this area and has amended the UK Corporate Governance Code in two respects: to require a more robust assessment by the board of the organisation's principal risks – those that could threaten its very survival – with assurance required that the management and mitigation measures in place are satisfactory; and to promote more meaningful reporting to shareholders on the effectiveness of the risk management process. He is determined that the Stronach Group complies with each of these significant new requirements and he asks Rachel Gordon to schedule an additional board meeting to discuss this in the near future. Everyone supports this, in particular John Holt, the CEO.

✓ **Consider the need for a Chief Compliance Officer**. Stronach, as one of the world's leading engineering consultancies, has always complied with all health and safety and environmental regulations. It has done so primarily through having excellent compliance management systems embedded throughout its operations, supplemented by periodic testing and inspections. However, Malcolm feels that the board should consider whether the appointment of a compliance professional, at a senior level, is now appropriate in view of the increasingly complex legal and regulatory landscape. He mentions risks in the supply chain as one example, risks that are likely to increase as the Group looks to expand its operations abroad.

✓ **Put the external audit service out to tender**. This idea comes as something of a surprise because I had not discussed the external audit process during the presentation, other than in passing. It is included as one of today's five takeaways specifically at Malcolm's suggestion. He makes the point that Stronach has engaged the same 'Big Four' audit firm ever since it floated on the London Stock Exchange in 1995 – the contract has simply been renewed each year, with no competitive tender process introduced at any stage. Malcolm is clear that he has no concerns regarding the service provided by the current auditor but he feels that it would be very much in line with current thinking and best practice to put next years' audit out to tender. He feels that this would demonstrate a commitment to independence and value for money that he thinks will be well received by investors. Rachel agrees. She asks that he speaks to Ashley Corbett about this and, providing that Ashley has no objection, she will schedule time for a boardroom discussion in the next board agenda.

✓ **Review the current arrangements for the vetting of managers and staff**. This point is raised by David Hurley, the HR Manager. He says that his concern is the result of a number of points raised throughout this series of workshops, not only in this one. Staff vetting for the Stronach Group is outsourced to an agency via a service level agreement, the terms of which have always been met so that everything seems to be satisfactory, at least in theory. However, he is aware of at least two cases where the checks were not carried out correctly by the agency. He has a sense of unease – is he right to raise the concern here? All the directors assure David that he is. Malcolm says that he will speak to the Head of Internal Audit and see whether the audit team can carry out a targeted review into the effectiveness of the Group's outsourced contract arrangements generally and into the workings of this contract in particular.

Next workshop

It is now 9.00 pm and everybody is clearly keen to go home. I thank them all for their contributions and check to see when the next workshop will be held – the subject is to be what I have termed at various stages during the project as the business ethics toolbox. John Holt just checks what I mean by that – he does not want much time taken up with items like sustainability, caring for the environment and health and safety plans. All of this is central to the Stronach Group's business model and, without wishing to sound in any way complacent he would himself describe the Group's performance in these areas as 'world class'. Everyone concurs with this.

I assure John and the team that I will not be doing this. The focus will be on the behavioural and cultural aspects of business ethics: charters, codes, remuneration structures, incentives schemes and training and development programmes. John is happy with this and so are the other members of the team. David Hurley has a request: he is currently reviewing the ethical training and development programme within the Stronach Group – will it be possible to allocate time specifically to cover this area during the next workshop? I assure him that we can certainly do this – in my view this is one of the most important tools in the business ethics toolbox and this will be time very well spent.

So, it is agreed. We will meet in four weeks' time to discuss the ethical toolbox and Rachel will circulate everyone with the date and time when diaries have been coordinated.

Reflections

Everyone leaves the boardroom quickly. As I am collecting my things, Malcolm puts his head round the door and asks if I am still on for a quick drink this evening. Five minutes later we are heading across Berkeley Square together – it is pouring down with rain so that it feels very good when we get inside the pub.

In amongst the talk about the football, the state of the economy and some political stuff, it is clear that Malcolm wants to ask me a couple of things. First of all, he is anxious to make sure that I don't feel in any way upset or offended that he seemed to hijack the end of the meeting tonight – he had been thinking about the audit process, for example, for some time now and also about how to achieve the right level of board input into the risk management process. It seemed a good opportunity to raise them formally – did I mind? I laugh out loud and say 'No, of course not – I had been expecting you or someone else to do this a lot sooner!'

There is something else. Just before we leave, he raises the subject of the next workshop and the piece on ethical training and development that David Hurley is concerned about. Malcolm wishes to give me some background on this. He reminded me that David had volunteered at one of the first workshops to review the compliance training on the UKBA. Well, Rachel and John have subsequently tasked him with reviewing and upgrading the Group's ethics training too, the project that David had referred to at the end of the workshop this evening. Without wishing to be critical in any way, Malcolm is aware that David has been struggling with this. He thinks that David would appreciate any help that I can give him but he does not want to ask me himself because then it might appear that he is not up to the job. Can I find a way to help David without embarrassing him? My reply is positive – yes I think so, let me think about it and see what I can come up with.

As we leave the pub, it is still raining hard. Malcolm and I shake hands and go our separate ways. Walking to the underground station it occurs to me that there might be a way to help David. I will see if I can contact him in the next couple of days – I have an idea for the next workshop that I think might be very helpful.

CHAPTER EIGHT

The business ethics toolbox

 ## ETHICAL DEVELOPMENT: SEVENTH WORKSHOP

Opening

The team is gathered in the Stronach Group's boardroom in London for this the seventh workshop to be held as part of the ethics project. It is 8.55 am and we are all having coffee prior to the start of today's session. David Hurley, the HR Manager, is looking a little nervous as he gulps down his second cup of coffee in the last 10 minutes. He may well be nervous because I have asked him to do some presenting today.

Following the last evening workshop session which finished at 9.00 pm I shared a drink with Malcolm Mainwaring, the Group Finance Director. He told me that David was struggling with the task of reviewing and refreshing not only the Group's anti-bribery training but also its ethical training programme – he asked me if there was anything that I might be able to do to help David. Having thought about this, I came up with a plan. I called David at work the following day under the pretext of asking him to do me a favour – could he brief me on Stronach's current ethical development programme by way of preparation for the next workshop? This turned out to be a smart tactic because it got David talking and we subsequently arranged to meet up for lunch.

Over lunch David told me all about the current programme. He also made clear to me his frustrations over the lack of budget for this and also the lack of either support or ideas coming from any of his colleagues on ways to improve the training – they were all too busy with other work. I expressed my surprise and asked whether Rachel Gordon, the Group's Chairman, knew about these difficulties? David looked a little embarrassed and said that no, he had not spoken to her about it yet. So, I made a suggestion – why don't we specifically include a piece on the Group's training and development programmes during the next workshop so that at the end of the session we can focus the takeaways around ways to improve it? David jumps at the idea – he likes it very much. However, I tell him that I have one proviso – the most effective way of doing this would be to open the workshop with a short presentation about the Group's current programme. But I need him to take the lead on this – it is not something that I can do. I say that without David's presentation we will not be able to finish the workshop as we have just planned – is he prepared to do this?

Well, it is now 8.59 am, everyone is seated and I check with David, who nods to indicate that he is ready. So, I open the workshop formally by saying that I have a surprise for the team, or at least for most of them. We are going to begin today with a short presentation from David Hurley on the Group's ethical training programme to include anti-bribery training too.

Presentation

With that I hand over to David who speaks very well.

He begins by taking the team back to the summer of 2011 when the UKBA became effective and the first rumours concerning Stronach's dealings in India began to appear on social media. Duncan Stronach, the previous CEO, had always been sceptical about ethics training – he liked to say that certain things could not be taught and that he preferred to rely on the professionalism of his managers in these matters. However, he was persuaded by the Group's lawyers that training on the UKBA was now a legal requirement and it was suggested that an element of business ethics could be included in this also. As a result, David assisted his old boss, the ex-Head of Personnel at the Stronach Group at the time, to produce a piece of face-to-face training on the UKBA. This was subsequently rolled out to all UK staff. David is not sure whether the overseas staff received this training or not. He remembers that a computer-based training module around the theme of business ethics was also produced at this time, although he was not directly involved.

David then proceeds to develop his own ideas – he does so professionally but with enthusiasm and passion too. I am both surprised and impressed. As agreed during the second workshop, David has reviewed the Group's training in both ethics and the UKBA and has to report that nothing has been done since 2011, other than to include these topics in the induction programme for new hires. He has looked at a number of computer-based training models with a view to refreshing and upgrading the training in both areas throughout the Stronach Group. He would like to combine the two if possible. He does not think that a complete re-write is required, although he does want to introduce a different feel and flavour to the training. He thinks that the use of video might help here; enabling what might be seen as dry subjects to be presented in an interesting and therefore an engaging way. Good use should be made of practical examples too and there should be a multiple-choice test at the end of the training to provide assurance that the managers and staff have been paying attention and have learned the key messages.

David then talks about the lack of progress and his own frustrations. One issue is that he has no budget to work with (costs are expected to come out of his HR budget) and so it has been difficult to develop his ideas. Also, although everyone is supportive, in practice no one has the time to discuss content with him in a meaningful way – all the managers are too busy with other projects like this one! Everyone listens to what David is saying and there is some concern and sympathy expressed, particularly by Rachel.

David had done exactly what I wanted him to do. So, I come in myself at this point, thanking David for his presentation and saying that we have the opportunity of picking up these points and developing them during the workshop. With that, I take the team through my proposed agenda for today, which I have put together taking note of David's comments and those of the CEO, John Holt, at the previous workshop.

Agenda

I propose to divide the agenda for today into three parts, as follows:

- First of all, I want to set the broad framework for the ethics toolbox by looking briefly at aspects of corporate responsibility and then at the so-called balanced scorecard approach to pay and remuneration.
- Second, we will review the ethics toolbox itself, paying particular attention here to value statements and codes of conduct.
- Third, we will spend most time today looking at training and development programmes, initially from a general perspective and then focusing specifically on how organisations can best approach the subject of training in business ethics. My aim here is that, by the end of the workshop, the team will be able to develop some of the ideas into key takeaways for application here at the Stronach Group.

Everyone is content with this agenda, so I begin.

CORPORATE SOCIAL RESPONSIBILITY (CSR)

Background

Introduction

Many organisations today, especially large publicly listed corporations, will choose to say something about their position on CSR, or more simply corporate responsibility as it is now often referred to. There is recognition that an organisation's reputation and long-term financial success are difficult to secure without a positive track record on social responsibility, environmental stewardship, safety and business ethics. An organisation's values in these areas will be articulated in various statements of course and, as we have seen, it is vital that these statements are authentic. The real benefit to the organisation comes when these values are embedded in its core business strategy. As we have already discussed, there is danger in any 'say-do' gap in business, but in particular in these areas as they are always likely to engage the emotions of citizens and the attention of the media.

I am no expert in corporate responsibility. However, I have observed its growing importance over the last decade in various ways. For example, I have assisted a number of clients in drafting corporate responsibility statements. One of these is a firm of asset managers that has signed up to the UN's six Principles of Responsible Investment. As an institutional investor, it has a duty to act in the best long-term interests of its beneficiaries. My client believes that this is best done by including environmental, social and corporate governance (ESG) issues in its analysis alongside financial measures because these can affect the performance of its investment portfolio.

I have also viewed corporate responsibility through the lens of the regular workshops on corporate governance that I run at the London Stock Exchange. During these workshops, I invite the delegates to make presentations on various aspects of governance and one of these has always been on CSR. I have noticed a distinct shift in attitudes to this topic since these workshops started in 2005. At that time delegates were reluctant to volunteer to present on their organisation's approach to corporate responsibility and those that did so displayed little real interest in the subject. Listening to these presentations, I formed the view that many organisations were paying lip-service to CSR, involving themselves in ad-hoc activities (donations to charities were often mentioned) almost because it was expected of them, but with no real commitment.

The position today is very different. Not only do delegates want to talk about corporate responsibility, they do so with real passion. I have no sense of lip-service now; rather the presentations convince me that issues such as investing in the local community and being environmentally responsible really do matter to the organisations concerned and are an integral part of their business. They certainly matter to the delegates who speak on these topics at my workshops. As a further observation, I would say that corporate responsibility is an area that particularly engages the younger delegates who attend the workshops – they are emotionally attached to these issues. Many of them take part in community work themselves as volunteers, and their organisation's CSR initiatives clearly build on this spirit – they feel that their organisation makes a difference and they are proud to work for it. We discussed the problems caused by a lack of employee engagement in many areas of business earlier in the book – corporate responsibility stands in marked contrast to that.

Definitions

CSR has its origins in the 1960s and began almost as an ad-hoc damage-control response by organisations to environmental accidents, corruption scandals or accusations of child labour in supply chains. Since then, as business has become more global, the idea and practice of corporate responsibility has evolved into a proactive, coherent global movement.

There are many definitions of CSR. For example, according to the Business Dictionary:

> *CSR is a company's sense of responsibility towards the community and environment (both ecological and social) in which it operates. Companies express this citizenship (1) through their waste and pollution reduction processes, (2) by contributing educational and social programmes and (3) by earning adequate returns on the employed resources.*

This definition combines the economic and social responsibilities of corporations, something that has proved to be controversial in the past. Many have argued that the only responsibility of a business is to produce goods and services that consumers need and want, while making an acceptable profit for the owners and investors. Indeed, the free-market economist Milton Friedman argued in the 1970s that the only social responsibility of business is to maximise its profits for shareholders.[1]

Today, it is fairly widely accepted that businesses do indeed have responsibilities beyond simply making a profit – this was something that we discussed in Chapter 2. The work of Archie Carroll, Professor Emeritus at the University of Georgia, was influential in making this transition. Professor Carroll developed the four-part pyramid model that looks at CSR as a multi-layered concept that can be differentiated into four inter-related aspects: economic, legal, ethical and philanthropic responsibilities.[2] Economic responsibility is primary because, without financial viability, the other factors are irrelevant. However, economics does not exist in isolation and CSR in the model requires the meeting of all four levels consecutively. Professor Carroll's definition of CSR is as follows:

> *Corporate social responsibility encompasses the economic, legal, ethical and philanthropic expectations placed on organisations by society at a given point in time.*

Building on this, more modern definitions tend to highlight the social responsibilities of organisations. Take the European Commission for example, which in 2011 released a new agenda for action on CSR which included a simple and straightforward view of CSR, defined as:

> *The responsibility of enterprises for their impacts on society.* [3]

The Commission aligns CSR firmly with the interests of stakeholders and it encourages that enterprises 'should have in place a process to integrate social, environmental, ethical human rights and consumer concerns into their business operations and core strategy in closer collaboration with their stakeholders'.

The Commission's strategy is to promote the adoption of CSR principles by all enterprises by using the argument that CSR is increasingly important to the competitiveness of enterprises. In this it is building on the principles of the United Nations Global Compact.[4]

The UN Global Compact is a strategic policy initiative for businesses that are committed to aligning their operations and strategies with ten principles in the areas of human rights, labour, the environment and anti-corruption. By doing so, the UN asserts that business, as a primary driver of globalisation, can help ensure that markets, commerce, technology and finance advance in ways that benefit economies and societies everywhere. This initiative is proving to be successful, as shown by the Global Compact's rapid growth. With over 12,000 corporate participants and other stakeholders from over 145 countries, it is the largest voluntary corporate responsibility initiative in the world.

CSR in action

Introduction

As we have seen throughout the book, it is crucial that organisations consider what their stakeholders expect and require before they make decisions that will impact on any or all of the various stakeholder groups. This is a crucial part of risk management today, not only around business risk but also to minimise threats to reputation. Many organisations have responded by seeking to manage and mitigate these risks and a CSR programme is part of the process – it helps to demonstrate that they wish to use their economic power in a responsible way. Whether these initiatives are rooted in enlightened self-interest or altruism may well be arguable but what is unarguable is that such initiatives are happening and on an increasing scale.

A long-running CSR example

As an example of how a re-invigorated commitment to CSR can help to transform perceptions of an organisation, consider the case of Royal Dutch Shell plc (Shell), the Anglo-Dutch multinational oil and gas corporation. During the 1990s it became a focus of attack from environmental campaigners and other critics for its plans to dispose of its ageing oil platform called 'Brent Spa' in the North Sea and for various aspects of its operations in Nigeria.

Shell's response was both significant and innovative for the time. It carried out a market research and stakeholder consultation exercise and as a result virtually re-invented its CSR strategy, which going forward included: revised and updated general business principles which took account of a broad range of ethical issues and committed senior managers to reporting directly on efforts to live up to the new principles; enhanced stakeholder consultation and engagement; and a transformed decision-making process – from the old 'decide, announce, deliver' concept to the new 'dialogue, decide, deliver' framework.

But the most notable change was Shell's introduction of social accounting in its first sustainability report in 1997. This has publicly committed the company to sustainable development and emphasised the 'triple bottom line' accounting of economic, social and environmental performance. Shell's pioneering development of a progressive approach to social auditing and reporting was widely praised.

Despite these initiatives, Shell has continued to attract controversy from time to time. For example, in 2004 the company was found to have overstated its oil reserves, which potentially had serious implications for investors because any mis-statements in this area can mislead the stock market about performance since the level of oil reserves is a strong indicator of future income streams. Confidence in the Shell Group dropped as a result, as did its share price. The Group had to pay fines in the USA and the UK to settle charges that it had mislead investors. Finally, the scandal has had serious repercussions within the Group and led to the departures of the chairman, Sir Phillip Watts, the oil and gas chief, Walter Van de Vijver, and the finance head, Judy Boynton.[5]

Shell's operations in Nigeria have long been the subject of scrutiny and criticism from activist groups, with allegations, always denied by the company, of environmental pollution in the Niger Delta and human rights violations. Shell is now looking to reduce its operations in Nigeria and in 2014 there were reports that it was in the process of finalising the sale of its interests in four Nigerian oil fields.[6]

A modern CSR example

Although I have never done any work for Shell, I have recently worked on various assignments for the board of directors of a Nigerian energy company, one of a number of emerging independent oil and gas corporations in the country that are looking to develop opportunities as international organisations like Shell divest themselves from Nigeria.

When working with this company it was clear to me that CSR is not a separate standalone part of the operations, something that is handled exclusively by a designated CSR department. On the contrary, the commitment to CSR is implicit in everything that this company does. Three of its seven core values are related directly to CSR: safety; environment; and partnership – by 'partnership' the company means making a commitment to create and maintain mutually beneficial relationships with its stakeholders.

In particular, this company recognises the importance of integration with the various different tribes and cultures in Nigeria. It maintains good relations with the communities that host its drilling operations through supporting local businesses, community outreach schemes and improving environment management policies. These are not simply aspirational statements; they are backed up by actions on the ground. The company has supported a number of local healthcare programmes, for example: the 'safe motherhood' programme and the 'eye can see' programme. It also supports the local communities through infrastructure projects including drilling boreholes and completing water projects; and improving facilities in towns by installing electric transformers, installing street lighting, constructing market stalls and renovating town halls.

The company's mission statement is: 'To build and sustain a world-class oil and gas company through innovative partnerships and premium value delivery.' CSR is an integral part of the strategy for delivering on this mission.

Stakeholders

Organisations demonstrate through their commitment to CSR that they are concerned for the interests of their stakeholders – all those parties who are affected by the enterprise and its actions and who have an interest in what the enterprise does and how it performs. As we have seen throughout the book, these stakeholders include many constituencies: shareholders, suppliers, customers, the government, the media, activists and many more. These stakeholders have the power to interfere with an organisation's objectives and activities in a variety of ways, depending on the constituency.

As examples: customers can stop buying products, either by moving to a competitor or through some form of protest or boycott; suppliers can put up their prices; protestors can bring bad publicity; and governments can act to regulate the market in which the organisation operates. Hence, the importance of stakeholders in the modern world – CSR initiatives are an integral part of stakeholder engagement today.

Although the focus of much of the discussion above has been on the various constituents who make up outside stakeholders, it is important to state here that the employees – the internal stakeholders – are crucial too, of course. If relations with the employees should break down, then strike action or some other protest can damage the organisation significantly. As mentioned, my own observations indicate that CSR can be a positive point of motivation for employees, perhaps for the younger employees in the workforce in particular. As always, statements made by the organisation about CSR must be backed up by the actions and commitment of those at the top, so that the hardware and the software elements work together. If this is achieved then there is the prospect of the positive by-product of greater employee engagement through support of an integrated CSR programme.

 ## PAY, BONUSES AND THE BALANCED SCORECARD

Observations

Conscious capitalism

Another and more traditional way that organisations try to engage and stimulate optimal performance from managers and staff is through the incentives provided by the levels of remuneration available in pay packages and bonus awards. Incentives influence behaviour. So, the design of remuneration packages and bonus schemes is an important part of tone at the top, which in my view is all about being able to translate statements about values into consistent behaviour from managers and staff.

The subject of CSR did not come up in my interview with Sandro Boeri for this book – however the related subject of conscious capitalism did come up. Sandro is the founder of Risk Audit Professional Development Ltd, a training company working in the City of London that specialises in working with internal auditors of financial services firms. I have known Sandro for a number of years and I will say more about him in the section below on training and development programmes. In the interview I asked about whether ethical risk is a central part of the risk assessments and processes that he sees at his financial services clients. This was what he told me:

> *I think one of the interesting movements that we are starting to see coming out of the United States is referred to as 'conscious capitalism'. Conscious capitalism is an understanding that to be a successful business in today's world you need to recognise the needs and wants of other stakeholders and not just the shareholder and the employee's bonus account. To do that, you need to really engage with these other stakeholders and understand what they expect of you in terms of behaviour. So when it comes to managing ethical risk in today's world there does need to be a holistic mechanism to recognise these other stakeholders and what is expected of them. Organisations that have got this holistic approach, in my opinion, are more likely to stay out of trouble and quite frankly I believe are more likely to be successful over the longer term. That's very much an aspiration that we have in terms of our own business and its own growth profile.*

Sandro refers here in passing to bankers' bonuses, widely considered to be one of the contributory factors to the global financial crisis because they incentivised inappropriate high risk-taking by executives, traders and other staff. The common factor among these schemes and one that created real problems from my perspective is that they focused on short-term performance measures, a notable feature of bankers' bonuses but a failing that has wider application than in the financial services industry.

Pressure, incentives and short-term targets

Pressure is a major influence on behaviour. For example, as discussed earlier the research of Dr Cressey indicates that the most important reason for fraudulent behaviour in the workplace is some form of financial pressure. In a more general sense, one of the most important causes of poor ethical decision-making within organisations is the pressure that senior management and their workforce are under to hit short-term performance targets. Quarterly reporting is becoming ubiquitous now and it has a lot to answer for!

Problems can arise when directors and senior managers look to grow their organisations and to maximise financial returns, not so much in the long term – this often has little meaning for them – but in the short term. Mr Skilling, the COO and CEO at Enron, is a good example of this. He was so focused on short-term profit maximisation that he made it a condition of him joining Enron in 1991 that Andersen signed-off on the mark-to-market accounting policy that he wanted to use there. His reasoning was simple. The effect of mark-to-market accounting would be generally to accelerate the profits taken on long-term projects – rather than spread them out evenly over the length of the project, which might be 20 years or longer, they could be taken earlier if the value of the project had increased. Of course, this was guaranteed as the Enron managers themselves would determine what figure to attach to 'value'. Mr Skilling's reasoning was that he was a bright man and he wanted to enjoy the benefits of his bright ideas – he was not going to be around at Enron in 20 years' time! Although generally more modest, all employees will have their own targets to meet and, if they are ambitious, they will be desperate to hit them either in order to earn bonuses or, in difficult economic conditions, to better safeguard their jobs.

Lord Browne, the ex-CEO of BP plc, pointed clearly to this is his autobiography *Beyond Business*.[7] Here he says that when he first heard that he was going to be promoted to the role of chief executive he thought in terms of a 10-year plan and what he could achieve for the company during that time. As soon as he was working in the job as CEO, however, he says that his attention became focused on hitting the next quarter's numbers so that the expectations of the market would be satisfied. Rather than a 10-year plan, Lord Browne's vision was quickly changed to 40 quarterly targets.

Incentives can have a major influence on behaviour, depending on their value to the individuals who stand to gain from them. They are thought to have encouraged high risk-taking by traders in financial institutions. Some of the key reforms in the aftermath of the global financial crisis have been designed to modify this by: reducing the percentage of the bonus that can be taken by bankers in cash; spreading the time-period of the bonus out in terms of when it becomes due; and introducing clawback provisions in the event that the bonus was linked to fraud or mis-information.

As we have discussed, a significant part of the poor reputation of the financial services industry currently is caused by perceptions of unethical behaviour, much of it driven by incentives. In the USA one of the key drivers of the sub-prime lending crisis was the lucrative incentive schemes available to mortgage originators such as Countrywide Financial and their salesmen in the form of commissions and fees made on completion of the loan deals. The payment of these incentives was not contingent upon the borrowers, mainly poor families, being able to repay the loans in the future.

One of the consequences was a widespread failure to apply traditional underwriting standards and prudent lending criteria.

In the UK, there has been a public outcry against the widespread practice in recent years of retail banks selling expensive Payment Protection Insurance (PPI) schemes to their customers even when this was not in the customers' best interests. The bankers were driven to do this by the incentives that they could earn and the pressure that they were put under to make the sales targets by their managers. Considerations of business ethics or the banks' obligation to treat customers fairly did not apply, apparently.

The balanced scorecard

Introduction

The balanced scorecard was originated by Dr Robert Kaplan and Dr David Norton in the early 1990s[8] as a performance measurement framework that added strategic non-financial performance measures to traditional financial metrics in order to give directors and senior managers a more 'balanced' view of organisational performance. Today it is used widely in business and industry, the public sector and in non-profit organisations to align business activities to the vision and strategy of the organisation; to improve internal and external communication; and to monitor performance against strategic goals.

There are four perspectives built into the scorecard, the aim of which is to answer four questions, as follows:

- Financial: to succeed financially, how should we look to shareholders?
- Customer: to achieve our vision, how should we appear to customers, how do customers see us?
- Internal business processes: to satisfy our shareholders and customers, what business processes must we excel at?
- Learning and growth: to achieve our vision, how can we continue to improve, create value and innovate?

Balanced scorecard and financial services

The balanced scorecard is a powerful strategic planning and management system that can be used as the basis for assessing the performance of managers and staff and therefore of setting their pay and any bonuses. The key in this application is that it provides for a rounded assessment of performance and is not focused only on one measure of performance – for example, financial performance, or sales made (or even sales booked). Other factors can be built into bonus targets. For example, we saw in the Siemens example earlier in the book that one of the changes introduced by the company in its attempts to re-build trust with the international community following the corruption scandal was to include the meeting of compliance targets in the factors that contributed to the overall assessment of managers' bonuses. Also, Peter Hanlon discussed a 'values gateway' as something the managers at Westpac had to enter through before they became eligible for top bonuses each year.

I asked Sandro Boeri during our interview about the application of the balanced scorecard approach to pay and bonuses in the financial services industry in the UK. Sandro was very positive. This is his reply:

> It is happening, no doubt about it. The balanced scorecard, we saw it as being tested in operational back office functions first. We are now seeing it living and breathing in some organisations in

relation to front office, rain-making type functions which is a real 'hallelujah' moment. I think it is one of the most positive innovations that I have seen in the financial services sector in many a year. I think now it is up to regulators to communicate the use of balanced scorecard with front office, rain-making positions as being emblematic of best market practice.

The balanced scorecard in action

Since my interview with Sandro, details have emerged of the new balanced scorecard approach being introduced at Barclays Bank as part of Mr Jenkins' attempts to transform the bank's brand.[9] Barclays will use a '5Cs' values scorecard, denoting: customer and client, colleague, citizenship, conduct and company. The purpose is to achieve the right aims across the business by references to a series of pledges that include:

- ▪ 'We create a diverse and inclusive environment where colleagues can fulfil their potential.'
- ▪ 'We positively impact the communities in which we operate.'
- ▪ 'We act with integrity in everything we do.' And
- ▪ 'We create sustainable returns above the cost of equity.'

Mr Jenkins has confirmed that every Barclays' employee is now required to complete a mandatory training programme and that the company's values have been integrated into day-to-day operations such as recruitment, performance assessment and reward.

All managing directors across the bank are formally assessed against whether they have 'exhibited the right values and behaviours, as well as producing the business outcomes'. Also, all employees must abide by a new code of conduct.

These are big changes and, as we saw at the start of the book, they are part of Mr Jenkins' transform agenda. Barclays will judge itself against the balanced scorecard in its drive to instil a new set of 'purpose and values' and reposition the brand as the 'go-to' bank for all stakeholders.

The governance dimension

The current focus on recalibrating the design of bonus and remuneration packages away from the achievement of high-risk, short-term performance targets and towards longer-term measures that promote the sustainable success of the organisation is not confined to the trading desks of large financial institutions. Changes to the UK Corporate Governance Code announced in September 2014 include significant alterations to Section D of the Code on the remuneration of executive directors.[10] The aim is to focus companies on aligning rewards (remuneration) with the sustained creation of value.

Earlier changes to the Code on remuneration required companies to put in place arrangements that will enable them to recover or withhold variable pay (that is to say bonuses) when appropriate to do so and to consider appropriate vesting and holding periods for deferred remuneration (share schemes – best practice is now to have a three-year or longer vesting period before which the company shares cannot be cashed in by the executives). This is important because it enables bonuses to be clawed back in the event of malfeasance and it creates a longer term perspective than the old system of paying bonuses in cash or share options that vested in a short period.

Nowhere, however, is the new thinking on remuneration packages better illustrated than in the changes made to the Main Principle at D1 of the Code. The new Code says simply:

> *Executive directors' remuneration should be designed to promote the long term success of the company. Performance-related elements should be transparent, stretching and rigorously applied.*

Contrast this with the paragraph that it replaced, the old Main Principle at D1:

> *Levels of remuneration should be sufficient to attract, retain and motivate directors of the quality required to run the company successfully, but a company should avoid paying more than is necessary for this purpose. A significant proportion of executive directors' remuneration should be structured so as to link rewards to corporate and individual performance.*

The change is striking. It is clear that remuneration policies for senior executives in future will need to be designed, above all, with the long-term success of the company in mind.

THE BUSINESS ETHICS TOOLBOX

Overview

All organisations need to be able to deal with pressure situations and the realities of the workplace environment. As we have seen, the relentless driver of having to succeed and hit short-term targets can lead to actions that are harmful to stakeholders and thereby can increase reputational risk. Directors and senior managers need assurance that the organisation's values translate into behaviour and action. We have seen how the balanced scorecard approach to performance appraisal can, when linked to remuneration, provide some of that assurance. The ethics toolbox builds on this.

The box contains a number of tools and techniques that have been developed over the last 50 years to promote consistency of behaviour and standards of conduct. They are continually being tweaked, refined and improved. There are four main tools in the box: value statements; codes of conduct and ethics charters; confidential reporting lines; and ethical training and development programmes. We will unpack the box and survey each of these tools, but we will consider two in detail: training and development programmes, which are essential in order to raise awareness and influence culture; and reporting lines (often referred to as whistle-blowing hotlines), which I believe are essential in order to enable a culture of openness to become embedded within an organisation thereby providing increased assurance of business ethics.

Value statements

Introduction

Put simply, value statements are expressions of an enterprise's core beliefs. Organisations spend time and effort writing them in order to identify and connect with their stakeholders both internally (mainly with employees) and externally (mainly with customers). They should be seen as guiding principles, positive statements summarising the core mission and aspirations of the entity. These values should be encapsulated and reflected in the way that the people working in the organisation act day to day.

By introducing the vision and values model RICE, developed in the 1990s by the Enron Corporation, in an ironic way at the start of the book, I may have placed value statements in a negative context. I will try and balance this shortly by turning to a more uplifting example, that of Johnson & Johnson. However, directors and managers must be aware of the dangers involved in making claims about the way the organisation acts and treats its stakeholders that are simply not borne out by the reality. Clearly, in the Enron saga the values of respect, integrity, communication and excellence as embodied in the acronym RICE seem, with the benefit of hindsight, to have little connection with the arrogance, deceit and greed that have come to characterise the behaviour of some of the senior managers in that particular company.

Example: poorly embedded values

Enron is not the only example of this 'say-do' gap – there are many other instances where the actions of people, whether senior managers, traders, front-line sales staff or others, are a long way removed from the principles and values promoted by the organisations that they work for. The risk here is both external (of reputational damage) and internal (of cynicism).

Consider the situation of McKinsey & Company (McKinsey), the global management consultancy firm. The firm became embroiled in the Galleon insider dealing scandal that we reviewed in Chapter 4 through the greed and arrogance of two of its former senior executives, Anil Kumar and Rajat Gupta. They were part of a network of insiders who supplied Raj Rajaratnam, the founder of the Galleon family of hedge funds, with information that enabled him to make illegal profits on his share dealings.

The actions of Mr Kumar and Mr Gupta, as reported during the court cases, are far removed from McKinsey's core values. In particular, they stand at some distance from the key McKinsey tenet of client confidentiality. McKinsey states on its website that: 'We are a values-driven organisation. For us this means to always ...' – the website then describes the organisation's five core values in a series of short, pithy and (no doubt it believes) powerful sentences. The third of these five core values of the firm is confidentiality, which was a value sadly lacking in the behaviour of Mr Kumar and Gupta, both McKinsey high-flyers in the Galleon case.

McKinsey describes its core value of confidentiality in the following terms:

> *Keep our client information confidential. We don't reveal sensitive information. We don't promote our own good work. We focus on making our clients successful.* [11]

How does McKinsey's value of confidentiality match up to the reality?

Mr Rajaratnam was found guilty in July 2011 and sentenced to 11 years in prison, subsequently upheld by the Appeals Court.[12] Some of the evidence used by the authorities in the trial was provided by Mr Kumar.

In 2010 Mr Kumar, a former director of McKinsey, pleaded guilty to leaking inside information and passing on tips illegally to Mr Rajaratnam in return for payments of over $1.7 million. He admitted that he gained access to the leaked information while working for McKinsey's clients during the period 2003–09. This behaviour is far removed from the firm's pledge to keep client information confidential. In the event, because of his exceptional cooperation with the authorities in the trials of Mr Rajaratnam and Mr Gupta, Mr Kumar avoided jail and was sentenced to two years' probation.

The case of Mr Gupta is different. He was the prominent Indian business leader of his generation and he enjoyed a most successful business career – he is a former director of Goldman Sachs Group Inc. and Proctor and Gamble Co. In addition, he was managing director of McKinsey from 1994–2003.

He was charged with securities fraud by leaking inside information to Mr Rajaratnam. The allegations did not relate to his time at McKinsey and, in contrast to Mr Kumar, he pleaded not guilty to the charges. However, in 2012 Mr Gupta was found guilty of three counts of securities fraud (and acquitted of two others) and was sentenced to two years in prison, subsequently upheld by the appeals court.

The evidence presented at these trials, showing as it did the clear abuse of client confidentiality, caused consternation amongst the directors and senior managers at McKinsey.[13] Dominic Barton, the Global Managing Director of McKinsey since 2009, has described the case as 'incredibly distressing and embarrassing' and feels the firm will not know for many years to come the possible damage done to its brand as a result.

Example: well embedded values; Johnson & Johnson – the Tylenol case (part 2)

However, I do not wish to appear to be cynical about value statements and the impact that they can have on all stakeholders, both internal and external – not at all. These statements can be very powerful and influential if they become embedded in the organisation so that they are adopted and used to direct the actions of managers and staff at all levels, especially those at the top.

One of the most famous of all value statements is that developed and used by Johnson & Johnson, the US multinational pharmaceuticals, medical devices and consumer health group – we looked at the way that this company handled the Tylenol crisis in the 1980s earlier in the book. The values that guide Johnson & Johnson's decision-making are spelled out in a very simple one-page document called 'Our Credo'.[14] This was drawn up in 1943 by a member of the company's founding family. As the company website states:

> Our Credo is more than just a moral compass. We believe it's a recipe for business success. The fact that Johnson & Johnson is one of only a handful of companies that have flourished through more than a century of change is proof of that.

And success has not always come easily for the company, especially during the crisis concerning the Tylenol poisoning scare of 1982. As we have seen, despite the fatalities and the panic, Johnson & Johnson acted swiftly, openly and in a way that enabled the company to re-build trust with their customers so that results recovered quickly. In Chapter 6 we looked at this as a classic piece of effective crisis-management, which it was.

However, the Tylenol case also illustrates the power of embedded values within an organisation. The Credo was used widely within Johnson & Johnson as a reference point during the crisis. The chairman at the time, James Blake, was quoted as saying: 'After the crisis was over we realised that no meeting had been called to make the first critical decision. Every one of us knew what we had to do. We had the Credo to guide us.'

The Johnson & Johnson Credo has undergone a number of changes since the 1980s. However, it retains its credibility within the business and its core values continue to have widespread respect. The Credo is set out in full below.

> Our Credo
>
> We believe our first responsibility is to the doctors, nurses and patients, to mothers and fathers and all others who use our products and services. In meeting their needs everything we do must be of high quality. We must continually strive to reduce our costs in order to maintain reasonable prices. Customers' orders must be served promptly and accurately. Our suppliers and distributors must have an opportunity to make a fair profit.

We are responsible to our employees, the men and women who work with us throughout the world. Everyone must be considered as an individual. We must respect their dignity and recognise their merit. They must have a sense of security in their jobs. Compensation must be fair and adequate and working conditions clean, orderly and safe. We must be mindful of ways to help our employees fulfil their family responsibilities. Employees must feel free to make suggestions and complaints. There must be equal opportunity for employment, development and advancement for those quali-fied. We must provide competent management and their actions must be just and ethical.

We are responsible to the communities in which we live and work and to the world community as well. We must be good citizens – support good works and charities and bear our fair share of taxes. We must encourage civic improvements and better health and education. We must main-tain in good order the property we are privileged to use, protecting the environment and natural resources.

Our final responsibility is to our stockholders. Business must make a sound profit. We must experiment with new ideas. Research must be carried on, innovative programs developed and mistakes paid for. New equipment must be purchased, new facilities provided and new products launched. Reserves must be created to provide for adverse times. When we operate according to these principles, the stockholders should realise a fair return.

Whose values and do they have traction?

The process by which an organisation's values are articulated varies. For some it is a top-down approach. The Johnson & Johnson Credo was drawn up by a member of the company's founding family and this would still be typical today in family run and owner-managed businesses. For others, the drivers are historical. We saw earlier in the book that the Co-op Group has strong values based on its history and culture, ones which reflect the social and community-focused principles of the co-operative movement worldwide. The values of public sector organisations are centred on service. For example, in the UK the Committee for Standards in Public Life has defined seven principles (some-times referred to as the Nolan Principles[15]): selflessness, integrity, objectivity, accountability, open-ness, honesty and leadership. Many larger businesses are now looking to make this a more inclusive process, with consultation of their managers and staff at all levels though workshops, surveys and questionnaires.

In my view, the key point is not how the values are determined but whether they are authen-tic and have meaning and traction for stakeholders, especially where the managers and staff are concerned. The most direct and powerful way to make values meaningful to everyone is through the actions and decision-making of those at the top, made every day in accordance with the values. It also helps to make sure that the values are displayed prominently and are noticeable in a variety of ways and wherever possible: they should appear on posters on office walls, on screen-savers, on business cards and so on. In order for the message to stick, something thoughtful and snappy tends to have most impact.

Raising core values consistently at the start of every meeting can also be effective, as I discov-ered myself when on assignment in Egypt.

Personal example

I was lucky enough to do some consultancy work for a large Egyptian company in 2010. The com-pany is in the oil and gas business sector. Not surprisingly, one of its core values is safety. It aims to create a working environment where accidents are unlikely to happen and where the health and safety of employees, contractors and the public are not jeopardised. In order to promote this, safety is integrated into all of its decision-making processes. In fact, safety is stated to be the company's top priority, putting it above other key areas such as production, scheduling and cost.

This was interesting to me at the time I was working there because, as an observation, I would not say that there was an obvious safety culture in Egyptian society at that time. For example, being driven to the company's facilities near Alexandria each day was always an interesting experience, with there being evidence on the roadside of motor car accidents on a reasonably regular basis. Given this background, how could the company embed the idea of a safety culture into its workforce, how could it make this idea stick when there was little to support it in everyday life in Egypt?

Well, the company had put in place a very simple mechanism. Before every meeting started, without exception, there was what was described as a 'health and safety moment' where any person present could raise a point about any aspect of safety, either inside or outside the company, whether it was something that they had observed or a concern that they felt. Every single meeting agenda, including the main board agenda, had the identical first line item: 'health and safety'. In my view, this is an excellent example of what can be done by organisations to embed their core values throughout their people – and, as in this case, with third parties too.

Codes of ethics and/or conduct

Introduction

A code of ethics and/or conduct (sometimes referred to as an ethics charter) is an important management tool because it establishes the organisation's expectation of its people in terms of business ethics. It should set out simple and fundamental principles of action that all employees can use as reference points if they ever should get into areas of difficulty or doubt around their own actions. Sometimes these principles are wrapped up in a broader staff handbook, which will set out all the detailed personnel rules and regulations that employees are expected to follow.

My preference is always to keep the core messages of the codes separate from the more detailed staff handbook – these core messages need to be highlighted, rather than run the risk of them being obscured by the detail. It is crucial that everyone understands the principles that must be followed by both the leaders of the organisation and by the employees (and increasingly by service providers also) in everything that they do, day after day in their employment. As part of this, all those coming within the scope of the code will be expected to avoid engaging in any conduct or activity that may give rise to questions as to the organisation's honesty, impartiality or reputation or otherwise cause it embarrassment.

As part of this, it is a fundamental point, to be clearly stated, that the code applies to everyone in the organisation, including directors and senior managers. It follows from this that the board must be prepared to enforce the standards in the code no matter who violates them.

Contents

The code is an important document that should be signed off by the board. Many organisations choose to start their codes with a personal message or statement from the chairman or the CEO. I think that this is excellent practice because it demonstrates clearly the personal commitment of those at the top of the organisation to good business ethics. It also creates impact. These personal statements can be particularly effective when they are made by a new leader who has just been appointed, for example.

The code should address the organisation's ethical standards, which are often summarised in the form of a statement of the fundamental principles that guide its practices. A typical set of these fundamental principles might show how the organisation looks to build trust with its stakeholders by making a commitment to:

- act in accordance with all laws and relevant regulations;
- conduct the organisation's business with integrity;
- behave fairly and honestly; and
- respect others.

In addition to re-affirming core values, the code will typically state the organisation's commitment to promoting working relations that are based on universal principles such as integrity, loyalty and mutual trust.

Key governance policies should be included also. For example: the need for confidentiality around information and data handling; the need to protect the organisation's assets, both tangible (such as what is and what is not acceptable use of the entity's information and communications equipment and systems) and intangible (such as reputation) should be clearly stated; and of course the organisation's policies promoting health and safety and environmental sustainability.

It is important that the code addresses the particular issues that have relevance to the organisation itself. This will often include a number of difficult areas of workplace behaviour, such as the organisation's attitude to alcohol, drugs and substance abuse, gambling in the workplace and sexual relationships at work. As part of this, the code should include reference to corrupt business practices: fraud; bribery and corruption; insider dealing; collusion; coercion; money laundering and terrorist financing. This is where the organisation's zero tolerance of all corrupt business practices should be clearly stated along with a description of the consequences of such corruption – investigation followed by disciplinary action that might lead to dismissal and, in the case of criminality, to prosecution. Some detail is always helpful as guidance in these areas. So, for example (unless stated elsewhere in a separate anti-fraud policy), the organisation should set out clearly what it considers to be fraud and describe how it will deal with evidence to suggest lying, deceit and fabrication of: sickness records, qualifications and references, expense claims and signatures on documents.

Conflicts of interest

Another key area is conflicts of interests. Conflicts arise when the personal, financial or professional activities of a director, senior manager or employee interfere (or could appear to interfere) with their loyalty to the organisation that employs them, such as where they have a personal or economic interest in a transaction. Conflicts can develop in many ways. For example, where an employee has a second job or serves as a director or consultant for another company or holds a financial interest with an existing or potential competitor, customer or supplier. Such a conflict can create problems for an organisation when it: adversely influences a person's judgement, objectivity or loyalty; results in decisions that are not in the best interests of the organisation or its owners; or risks giving the impression that the organisation has acted improperly.

A conflict, when known about, can usually be managed to everyone's satisfaction – it becomes a problem when it remains hidden. So, transparency is crucial. Any affiliations with competitors, customers or suppliers, together with any outside jobs should always be disclosed. Disclosure should also be made in situations involving close relatives and family members, especially when they are known to work for or provide services to competitors, customers or suppliers.

Conflicts of interest can arise from the actions or associations of any individual in the workplace. However, any conflict situations involving directors and senior managers create greater risks because of their position. Accordingly, in those jurisdictions where directors' duties are set out in the law, these will typically include general duties about conflicts of interest and their disclosure. For example, in the UK the Companies Act 2006 sets out directors' duties to: avoid conflicts of interest; not to accept benefits from third parties; and declare any interests that a director may have in a proposed transaction or arrangement.

Conflicts may also be subject to regulation. In the UK the FCA's Principles of Business state that a financial services firm must manage any conflicts of interest between itself and its customers fairly.

Organisations should have a policy in place to deal with all potential conflicts. This policy should require disclosure and written approval for any actual or potential conflict of interest. This is particularly important at director and senior manager level – nothing undermines trust around the boardroom table quicker than the failure to share information, so there should be severe consequences for doing so.

Conflicts of interest should be avoided wherever possible. Real or even potential conflicts can cause damage to profits and reputation – they need to be managed carefully and with transparency.

The affirmation principle

One of the purposes of a code is to assist managers and employees in situations where the 'right' answer may be unclear – it can help to dissuade good people from making wrong choices in moments of weakness or crisis. However, it can only do so if everyone reads the code and understands what is written there. I remain sceptical as to how often this actually happens in practice. In my experience many organisations will address the code formally with each of their employees on one occasion and on one occasion only during their entire working careers with the enterprise. And this is usually the single least appropriate day on which to do so – the day on which the employee joins the organisation. When this happens the directors and managers can have no assurance that their employees truly understand what is expected of them. This can cause practical difficulties for the organisation in any disciplinary process and it would almost certainly attract criticism from an employment tribunal convened in an unfair dismissal case. More importantly, however, it will mean that the power of the message conveyed about core values and principles is dissipated and will have little or no influence with the employees.

This practical issue is being addressed in many organisations today by means of an 'affirmation requirement'. Each year all employees are required to sign a declaration confirming both that they have read the code and that they have understood it. The principle of affirmation is embraced in the USA in particular, but I have to say that a number of my clients in the UK remain resistant to the idea – something confirmed by delegates' comments on my courses also. The underlying issue here is often that the concept of annual sign-off is not part of the existing organisational culture. Many may seek to resist change and will do so here by claiming that the affirmation requirement is merely a routine signature and so is devoid of any meaning – what is the point?

I always advise against taking this attitude for two reasons. First, annual affirmation of the code has clear practical benefits for any entity that is embroiled in a disciplinary situation because the employee will have more difficulty in arguing that he or she was unaware that what they were doing was wrong. Second, and more importantly, it provides an assurance mechanism for directors and senior managers that their people do indeed know what the organisation stands for and are aware of its principles, values and expected standards of behaviour. When added to other measures, such as an ethical training and development programme (see the discussion below), it becomes part of a structured business ethics improvement programme.

I believe that the affirmation requirement is a fundamental piece of ethical hardware and I always recommend it.

Management structure

The affirmation requirement is part of a disciplined approach to the management of business ethics that I fully endorse. There should be a clear management structure in place that facilitates the effective operation of the ethics code and all of the other tools in the toolbox, such as training and development programmes or whistle-blowing hotlines.

This disciplined approach is particularly favoured in the USA. As an example, an increasing number of large organisations there are choosing to appoint an individual with the specific title of ethics officer in either a full-time or a part-time role. One of the responsibilities of the ethics officer is the effective implementation of the code, which will include reporting mechanisms (to the audit committee and/or to the board), together with monitoring and auditing processes to provide the prospect of continuous improvement going forward.

The principle of effective management of business ethics is enshrined in statute in the USA, with a specific section of the SOX referring to it. Here, Section 406 requires all public companies in the USA to disclose whether they have codes of ethics and also to disclose any waivers of those codes for any members of senior management. The code of ethics applies in particular to the CEO and to the company's senior financial officers. Section 406 also sets out a business process to manage the code of ethics: there must be a zero tolerance regime, with the code applying to everyone; periodically, the code must be communicated to everyone in the organisation and evidence must be retained of the employees' both receiving it and reading it; training on the code must be provided, with attendance required; and there must be a management process in place, with the audit committee to monitor the implementation of the code.

I regret to say that there does not appear to be quite the same appetite in the UK for managing business ethics in a robust, disciplined manner. As an example, there is more reluctance in organisations in the UK to give one of their managers the title of Ethics Officer compared with their counterparts in the USA. I have noticed this reticence in discussions with senior business people – almost a feeling that good business ethics, although important, should somehow occur naturally and not require a business process headed up by a named officer. I am surprised. Having someone with the title of Ethics Officer is not a panacea, of course, but it is an indicator that the organisation takes the issue of business ethics seriously and has established responsibility and reporting lines.

Consequences

The final point to make here on codes of conduct and/or ethics is that there must be consequences for those individuals who breach the code, regardless of their position within the organisation. This is the essence of the integrated approach we discussed earlier in the book, which combines values with compliance. The consequences of failing to comply with the code in any of the areas discussed above will normally be dealt with on a case-by-case basis. It is important to set out clearly in the code the principle that any breaches will be treated as a disciplinary offence and may result in dismissal and/or prosecution if deemed to be serious. The application of this principle in practice when the individual concerned is a senior manager or a high-income generating salesman represents what Peter Hanlon described during our interview as the 'acid test' for organisations in this area. I agree with him.

Confidential reporting lines

Some form of confidential reporting mechanism is an essential part of a business ethics programme. We will discuss these reporting lines fully under the heading 'whistle-blowing hotlines' in Chapter 9. It is important of course, that the code of ethics and/or conduct refers to the organisation's whistle-blowing policy if it has one. There may well be other reporting lines, for example around grievances and inappropriate workplace behaviour, which will typically be handled by the human resources function.

There is not much to add here at this stage. However, it is important to say upfront that the fundamental aspect of a whistle-blowing hotline is that the principle of confidentiality is respected. If a reporting line is to provide effective control over the organisation's ethical framework, then it is essential that it is respected and trusted by everyone. The building blocks of this trust are clear: a commitment from the board to protect anyone who makes a disclosure in good faith against any form of retaliation or victimisation; setting up a variety of reporting channels, thereby enabling an employee to by-pass their line manager if needed; guarantees of confidentiality; fair and professional disciplinary and investigation processes; and a proper feedback loop so that the individual making the disclosure is kept informed of progress.

We will return to confidential reporting lines in Chapter 9.

 ## ETHICAL TRAINING AND DEVELOPMENT PROGRAMMES

Framework

Overview

Training and development is a crucial component of modern business. It also provides one of the key software components in our twin-track approach to business ethics because training both raises awareness and influences culture throughout enterprises.

At the organisational level, the commitment to competence is one of the key benchmarks both of culture and success and I am always interested to know whether my clients view the costs of providing their people with appropriate skills and training more as an expense or as an essential investment in talent and in their future. At the individual level, each of us has a responsibility to ensure that we are capable of doing our job and that our skills remain up to date. This is simply not possible to do without undertaking regular training, such is the speed of change in so many areas of modern business. Each of us needs to view such concepts as 'continuous development' and 'lifelong learning' not as aspirations or as impossible dreams because of the time pressures of our work, but rather as an integral part of being a modern business professional.

So, this perspective includes employee training and corporate cultural attitudes related to both individual and organisational self-improvement.

The key point to emphasise here is that organisations should be looking to create a learning environment. Learning is more than the provision of training. It also includes positions like mentors and tutors within the organisation, as well as the ease of communication among workers that allows them readily to seek and obtain help with a problem when needed.

Practical approach

In this section, we develop key principles together with a number of techniques that I have seen work in practice, first around business training generally and then specifically concerning training in business ethics. To do so, I make use of my own experiences (see below), supplemented by the observations of two long-term business associates of mine who have spent many years running specialist training companies: Sandro Boeri, the founder of Risk Audit Professional Development (Risk Audit), a company that specialises in providing training to internal auditors in the financial services sector; and Lis Batteson who until 2010 was Managing Director of Quorum Training (Quorum). Quorum is now a part of the Wilmington Group and provides an extensive range of accounting, finance, tax and management courses to business professionals.

Personal experience

I have had extensive experience in designing and delivering training and development programmes over the last 15 years. This has been technical rather than soft-skills training, covering the broad areas of: corporate governance and business ethics; risk management; financial crime; and compliance and audit. As mentioned at the start of the book, I have run training courses, facilitated workshops, spoken at conferences and delivered lectures to audiences in many parts of the world: in the UK and Continental Europe, in the USA and the Caribbean, in the Middle East and in Asia. It has been my great privilege to do so and I have enjoyed the experiences enormously.

In terms of the programmes themselves, I generally deliver these either on behalf of companies operating in the corporate training market (for example, the London Stock Exchange's Academy, Quorum Training, Risk Audit, Lessons Learned Ltd, Euromoney Training) or for professional associations or trade bodies, such as the Association of Certified Chartered Accountants (ACCA), the Institute of Chartered Accountants in England and Wales (ICAEW), the Gibraltar Association of Compliance Officers (GACO) and the Malta Institute of Accountants (MIA). The format varies but the majority are still public (or open enrolment) courses, delivered face to face in a traditional classroom environment (though of course using PowerPoint slides rather than chalk and blackboard), with a course length of anything from half a day to four days' duration.

More recently, since the global financial crisis, I am increasingly asked to run courses for individual organisations on an in-house basis, where the content is more tailored to the requirements of a particular business. For example, I have run many sessions for internal audit departments and also for companies looking to give their directors timely updates on aspects of compliance or to raise awareness of hot topics in corporate governance.

Finally, it is of course necessary always to keep up to date and to move with the times – the methods of training delivery are changing fast. As a result, over the last three years I have put together a number of webinar sessions, generally around compliance topics such as anti-money laundering and the UKBA, and also helped to develop computer-based training products, more of which below.

We begin this section with some initial observations about the training market and how it has been affected by the global financial crisis, before looking specifically at the area of ethical training and development courses.

The training market: an overview

Introduction

Training is big business today. By 'training' I am referring here to the global corporate market in training, not to either the huge effort that many organisations put into 'on the job' training for their employees or the many government-funded initiatives that are available. While publicly funded training provision aims primarily to raise the qualifications of the workforce, private training services – provided by either an organisation's own in-house training resources or third-party training companies – generally offer training for managers and employees that is business focused. That is to say, these courses aim to improve the functionality, competitiveness and competency of managers and staff, rather than being qualifications based.

While much of this training is in technical areas (for example in IT, accountancy and taxation, the law and compliance), there is also the very significant provision of 'soft skills' training, to large corporations in particular, around such diverse topics as selling skills, motivational techniques and team building. Here there is overlap between training and human resource development services and activities. Examples of soft-skills training include: personal development services (such as assertiveness training); coaching and mentoring; facilitation, business education and management development services (such as leadership training); and what may be termed psychotherapeutic services, such as neurolinguistic programming (designated as NLP).

Size of the market

The global corporate market in the training and development of managers and staff is massive. As an indicator of size, estimates of total spend range from $250bn to $300bn per annum, with some 50% taking place in the USA.

The market has undergone a period of rapid change in the last five years, much of which is intuitive and is the result of two different factors: first, technological developments and second, the state of the economy. Perhaps the most obvious area of change is that e-learning modules and virtual classrooms (typically webinar sessions, which delegates are able to attend remotely from their workstations) are taking an increasingly large share of training hours. This trend is likely to continue, although there remains a demand for traditional, instructor-led and face-to-face classroom sessions – these still account for at least half of all corporate training. The Association for Talent Development estimates that 56% of corporate training spending in the USA is internal, with 44% external.[16]

Bersin's analysis[17] suggests that companies are now looking to reduce the external training component as part of a drive towards bringing down costs. For example, in the UK, not surprisingly, the evidence suggests that the recent sluggish economy has weakened investment in training and development. Deloitte reported in 2013 that training budgets and headcounts had declined overall by some 12% from the levels seen in 2009, with this decline being particularly noticeable in large companies. Compared to 2009, twice as many UK firms are using learning management systems (LMSs) and learning content management systems (LCMSs) and three times as many now use rapid e-learning tools. Informal learning via blogs, social media and online communities has also made an appearance in the UK, though Deloitte reports very limited take up so far.

Consequently, there are now many options both for the provision of training (there are a large number of third-party training providers in the market, many of them small, specialist businesses) and also for the delivery of training available to organisations today. Deloitte reports that for many a blended delivery solution has proved to be an effective recipe. By this they mean: a combination of online learning as a prerequisite to live (or virtual) classroom learning followed by coaching (or online discussion forums) for ongoing support and development.

Training and development: general principles and observations

Commitment to competence

As mentioned, whenever I work with an organisation for the first time, one of the things that I look for is an indicator of its commitment to competence in its managers and staff. When I interviewed Sandro Boeri he talked about the need for effective competence regimes in financial services firms today, so I asked him what he considers the main components of such a regime to be. This is his reply:

> Let's go through the essential characteristics. First of all the organisation itself has to have a very clear stated set of objectives in terms of the skills that it wishes its employees and third party agents to possess. Without that statement you go nowhere. Secondly there needs to be a very strong quality assurance process, I would say either within a learning and development function or within a disseminated structure that shares with the people how you quality assure a training programme. Thirdly there needs to be a framework that tests that the outcomes aligned to each training programme are actually being achieved in terms of the people that have gone through that training programme. And finally – I would say this is the most important piece – there needs to be a consequences framework. If you do not obtain the competency level measured in a sensible fashion there need to be consequences. Now, all my colleagues tell me: 'Sandro, you spend too much time talking the talk about negative consequences, let's talk about positive consequences.' I have no problem with that but without consequences training will always be a Cinderella theme in an organisation.

In my view all organisations, not only financial services firms, need to have these four characteristics as described by Sandro in place if they are to be able to demonstrate a commitment to competence with credibility.

Leadership

As with so much else in business, the tone in terms of an organisation's attitude and commitment to training is set at the top. I firmly believe that, in order for a training and development programme to be successful, the directors and senior managers must support it with both their money and their time. That is to say, they need to allocate a sufficient budget to fund properly the training and development required and they also need to encourage and take part in the programmes themselves.

The leadership participation issue is often a challenge, especially when it becomes difficult to engage directors and senior managers in the training and development process. I put this point to Sandro Boeri during our interview. This is what he had to say:

> In my own experience the word 'training' doesn't fit comfortably with senior management and boards. Maybe I have been scarred by too many experiences but too many senior managers, when you invite them into a training room, will find all sorts of excuses not to be there. If, however you change the word 'training' to something else – we are going to have a debate, we are going to have a brain storming session, we are going to have a facilitated review of practices – then you are more likely to get board-level and senior management engagement.

It's almost as if people who are senior in terms of their title have a fear of being seen to be learning which goes completely against the conventional wisdom which is you are never too old to learn. Life is a learning experience. It's almost as if, in my experience, being subjected to a training programme is a personal admission of weakness. And unfortunately in today's corporate culture, and certainly in the Western world, admitting weakness as a senior manager is not good for one's promotion prospects. Do I sound cynical?

Perhaps Sandro is being a little cynical here, but he is also being realistic. I have certainly noticed myself a similar reluctance to attend at least part of the courses that I run from people at the top. There are probably various reasons for this, depending on the individual. Time is the most obvious one – directors and senior managers are busy people and perhaps they simply cannot find the time for any personal training and development in their full diaries. A certain type of arrogance might be another factor here. Some directors may feel that they are well-qualified and keep themselves up to date, so that they have no need of any further training. Certainly, my experience is similar to Sandro's in that I have found it easier to attract attendance from the top people in an organisation if the word 'training' is excluded from the programme description and more dynamic or high-powered words are used instead. For example, I have had success in attracting senior people to events by describing them as 'skill-burst sessions', a term which conjures up two benefits: the events promise to be dynamic and they also promise to be short. Finally, there may still be a form of defensiveness in play here, with senior people being reluctant to attend courses alongside their subordinates because they are afraid that they will be embarrassed by any lack of knowledge or skill that may become apparent during the training.

Whatever the reasons, it is in my view always a mistake when senior people do not take part in training and development activities. The importance of this point is acknowledged in the UK Corporate Governance Code, which states as one of the Main Principles of the Code in Section B on Board Effectiveness that: 'All directors should receive induction on joining the board and should regularly update and refresh their skills and knowledge.' The associated Code Provision goes on to say: 'The chairman should regularly review and agree with each director their training and development needs.'

In this area, as in many others, the Code sets out best practice that is applicable to all organisations, not only to quoted companies. All directors and senior managers should have a personal training and development plan. They need this in order to discharge their responsibilities as business leaders but also to set the example for their employees – it is simply poor management and poor leadership if an area of training is designated as mandatory and all managers and staff participate in it apart from the CEO. This may sound unlikely but I am not exaggerating – it is something that I have seen happen in practice, to my dismay.

Training costs

The second leadership challenge around training concerns the commitment to fund it. Providing sufficient training for managers and staff has always been a significant cost for those organisations that commit to it, whether it is the expense of establishing and running an in-house development department or the costs associated with external training courses. It has always been expensive to send employees on external courses, not only in terms of the course fees themselves but also the time and expense incurred in travelling to the course venue and the opportunity cost of being away from the office for a day, or sometimes for longer.

Because of the global financial crisis of 2007–09, the issue of training costs has come more sharply into focus. One of the first responses of many organisations to the difficult times that followed the crisis has been to cut back on all non-essential training. A good example of this is provided by the public sector in the UK. Traditionally strong supporters of external training, public sector departments have had their budgets and headcounts reduced significantly in recent years and they have responded by cutting back on their training spend (amongst other measures). So, while the impact of the global financial crisis on the traditional corporate training market has been entirely predictable, there are indicators that this time the effects might be longer lasting than those of previous recessions.

Lis Batteson, the ex-Managing Director of Quorum Training, referred to some unusual aspects of the recent crisis during our interview – she remembers that the impact of it was sudden in her business and she fears that the market will not return to how it was previously. This is what she told me:

> *It wasn't the first time we had seen a recession, we had been through them before. Training is a bit odd and maybe our bit of training is odder than some but finance directors tend to see these things quite quickly and they cut off spending on their own training fairly quickly. So you can find that course numbers go down very swiftly and, certainly this last one was peculiar in that we had probably had our best year ever in 2006/7 and then not long after it started to tail off. It seemed to come on quite suddenly and certainly in the evidence I have heard since then a lot of training companies are now in a real mess. I do wonder whether it will ever go back to the way it was before. I think it won't actually, I think it will be very different.*

I suspect that Lis may be proved to be right in her prediction here. Certainly, in my own experience, I have seen three noticeable changes since 2007:

■ First of all, many more public courses are being cancelled because of a shortage of delegates booking on them. Those courses that are running do so with significantly lower delegate numbers than the equivalent courses held before the downturn, even in 2014.

■ Second, training needs appear to be more short term and contingent. Delegates are booking later in the process, often as late as one week before a course is due to take place, so that there is less appearance of planning and more of reacting to events in today's market.

■ Finally, organisations are looking for alternative solutions to satisfy their training needs. There is increased demand for in-house courses, which are no doubt seen as being both more cost effective and more relevant to the needs of the business. The other trend is for more computer-based training (see below).

The need to cut costs in a recession is understandable of course. The challenge for directors and senior managers is to commit to increasing training budgets once again in the future when the Western economies are restored to growth and businesses are more confident in their future prospects.

Types of training largely unaffected by the global financial crisis

Three areas of business life have continued to engage in training, largely unaffected by the global financial crisis – these are described below. Indeed the third of them as described below has expanded its use of training specifically as a response to the crisis.

The first concerns those areas of an organisation's business where training is a legal requirement and is therefore compulsory. A good example in the UK is the need for ongoing health and safety training. Another example is in connection with the 'adequate procedures' required for compliance with the UKBA that we discussed earlier in the book. Although not a strict legal requirement,

I have run many briefing sessions for enterprises on the UKBA over the last three years, despite those organisations being under increased financial pressure because of the financial crisis.

The second area is around those jobs and positions where training is a requirement for the individual worker and is not optional. Often described as continuing professional development (CPD) this is the means by which people maintain their skills and knowledge related to their professional lives. For example, lawyers, accountants and physicians are all required by their respective regulatory bodies to complete a certain number of hours of CPD every year. One of the parts of my own business that has been largely unaffected by the global crisis has been the lecturing work that I do for the Association of Chartered Certified Accountants (ACCA), whose members have particularly rigorous CPD requirements to meet every year with the ultimate sanction that if they fail to satisfy these requirements they could lose their practising certificates and with it their livelihoods.

The third area concerns the ever-tougher compliance requirements of financial services businesses imposed by the regulators in the UK, the USA and the EU as a response to the scandals and failures both integral to and uncovered by the global financial crisis. One result has been a very significant training effort by some of the world's largest banks aimed at re-inforcing stated codes, values, behaviours and culture. As examples of these initiatives launched by banks, consider the following: Barclays are training their staff of 140,000 people around the world; Deutsche is training 98,000 staff and Goldman Sachs 13,000 of its senior bankers. The training methods vary: Barclays are using workshops led by 1500 'values leaders' from all parts of the group, themselves trained by a faculty of outside experts; whereas Deutsche is relying more on mandatory computer modules to instil an understanding of their compliance and control systems, supplemented with classroom sessions and training in risk culture and awareness.

The cost of all this is significant, but is it money well spent and how effective will the expenditure turn out to be? Of course, training in isolation can only go so far and in order to discourage irresponsibility these initiatives need to be part of a broader business culture and context. The major concern though is that this 'training blitz' is essentially a box-ticking exercise and it will not have a lasting impact. This is a point that Sandro Boeri articulated in our interview when I asked him for comments on the development of training over the last 20 years and where he thought it stood now. This is his reply:

> I think very much the answer to your question, Steve, is hidden in the first line of Risk Audit Professional Development's mission statement which is that 'training is an investment of conscience'. What do I mean by that, why use the word conscience? In the early days of my training business, I would say in the early 2000s, we had the impression that training was very much about interacting with people, sharing material, debating material, and coming to conclusions as to what this meant in terms of governance structures and internal control frameworks. I would say that 9 times out of 10 you would get good feedback from delegates if that interaction had been a positive experience from the delegate's perspective.

> Where we are today is that the tables have turned I think. I would say that probably 8 times out of 10 you would get good feedback from the delegates if you have given them the opportunity to tick boxes, to say they have attended a course and can they have their certificate please. Why? I suspect there is massive pressure from regulators that is creating fear. That fear is very much embodied by the threat of being named, shamed and fined if you do not train your people. So there is now a scramble in my community to actually be seen to be training people. But there is less of a scramble to be seen to be measuring whether that training is fundamentally fit for purpose and effective.

Sandro's concern is that training is being reduced to a box-ticking exercise. As such, it will prove to be ineffective in terms of influencing cultural change. To continue our metaphor that has run throughout the book, training in these circumstances equates to software that is mal-performing.

Computer-based training

There are of course a number of alternatives to traditional face-to-face training that are available to all organisations today and it is for senior managers to decide which is the most appropriate solution for their particular business needs. We have already mentioned webinars and virtual classrooms, which are increasingly seen as an efficient way of delivering short, concentrated learning modules often addressing areas of legal compliance. More broadly, computer-based training (CBT), utilising a learning management system (LMS) so that individual modules are able to be shown directly on an employee's workstation, is increasingly seen as a cost effective and efficient means of imparting knowledge. The employee can then work through the module whenever it is most convenient for him or her, thereby minimising disruption to their work and eliminating completely the time and expense involved in travelling to the venues where traditional external training courses are held. These CBT training modules almost always contain an assessment mechanism towards the end of the piece, usually in the form of a multiple choice test – delegates must achieve a stipulated percentage of correct answers in order to complete the training module successfully.

E-learning training programmes are very popular with large organisations today with an LMS software application taking care of the administration, documentation, tracking, reporting and delivery of the courses. As an alternative to LMS, modern Cloud technology can deliver training content directly to mobile devices such as Blackberries, iPhones and tablets. This is particularly advantageous for a global business with a mobile, international workforce because Cloud technology provides ease for their people in working through training modules and for refreshing knowledge whether working in some of the more remote locations around the world (where desktops are either not available or are limited) or whilst travelling.

There are three significant advantages of e-learning over traditional face-to-face learning: it is more scalable, it ensures consistency throughout the workforce and it is cheaper. LMS will also provide evidence that the employees have worked through the training programme and have succeeded in the subsequent test.

To echo the concerns expressed by Sandro in our interview, however, does e-learning really have impact? An often-mentioned danger with it is that the training modules themselves can be dull and tedious to work through, so that the retention rate for employees is low. In order to counter this, modules are increasingly being designed to be worked through in short sessions, 10–15 minutes maximum, with video dramas or interview-type ('talking heads') content included. As mentioned, with the advent of Cloud technology, these packages can now be delivered directly to the employee's smartphone – the ultimate in training efficiency!

Training in business ethics

Introduction

Today there is a vast amount of business ethics training offered, not only in the USA (which has led the way) and Europe, but in many other countries around the world. This is made clear in a global survey of teaching, training and research in business ethics produced in 2012 and edited by Deon Rossouw and Christoph Stuckleberger.[18] It was not always so, training in business ethics has been a relatively recent development – as an indicator, the pioneering Society of Business Ethics in the USA was established as late as 1980.

Personal experience

I have noticed something similar myself in terms of an accelerated trend in the acceptance of business ethics training in recent years. When I started putting together a series of training courses 15 years ago, much of my focus was on courses that covered various aspects of financial crime, notably anti-fraud and corruption programmes, also anti-money laundering and counter-terrorist financing courses too. This was in the immediate post-Enron and post WorldCom era. Many business people at the time were genuinely shocked by these scandals and by the fact that it was accounting and financial reporting fraud right at the top of these very large US corporations that had brought about their respective bankruptcies. As a result, there was much interest in and demand for courses that addressed the threats of fraud and financial crime.

I was also keen at that time to develop different types of courses, ones that placed Enron and the other scandals of the time in their wider governance context to do with issues of corporate culture, failure of controls over behaviour and poor business ethics. However, I had much less success in attempts to sell these types of courses to the training providers that I was working with during that period. One of these was Lis Batteson when she was Managing Director of Quorum Training. I reminded Lis of this during our interview and asked her why she was always so reluctant to run business ethics courses. This was her reply:

> Well, I think, on a straightforward basis, they are very difficult to sell as public courses. Just thinking about it earlier on before we started, I think it is partly because we were mainly selling into finance directors and I think many finance directors will assume they have an appropriate standard of ethics because they are professionally qualified, they are regulated by professional bodies etc. They won't volunteer probably to send themselves on that kind of training, except for the one or two enlightened ones who may want to get up to speed on the latest legislation etc. but many of them will just think they have read an article on it and will think that's fine. And there is nobody really in a position to send them on an ethics course. They either go themselves, they either volunteer themselves ... we simply don't know. Some companies we know took it very seriously and then they go down the in-house route so I think we thought it was going to be a difficult course to sell as a public course and I think we were largely proved right on that.

And this is true, Lis was indeed proved right. After many discussions I did finally convince her to include my one-day programme on business ethics in Quorum Training's brochure of public courses, but it was never successful in attracting a lot of bookings. The course only ran twice at Quorum Training, each time with small delegate numbers.

The importance of consistency

In contrast, over the last five years or so I have in fact conducted many ethics briefings and training sessions. Almost all of these have been run on an in-house basis, rather than running as public courses. That is to say, I have been commissioned to roll out a dedicated ethics programme for the managers and staff across an organisation. The course content will be referenced throughout to the organisation's own values and principles as expressed in its policies, charters and code of conduct, and will be repeated in each session that is delivered regardless of the seniority or experience of the delegates attending. The result is that every person hears the same message and it is precisely the message that the organisation wishes them to hear.

Consistency of behaviour and judgement is one of the most important aims of these in-house ethics training programmes, therefore, something that Lis pointed out during our interview:

> *Yes, I think that's probably the case with business ethics because you probably want to make sure everybody has heard and gets the same message at the same time. And there is also the element that you don't want people to be told something that you don't know about or that doesn't neces-sarily fit in with what you want to be said. We've often come across that scenario, not necessarily in the business ethics sense but certainly in other subjects where an FD would have sat in on something not appropriate for their level – VAT and subjects like that often – just to make sure that nothing is being said that they don't agree with.*

Can ethics be taught?

As an observation, I think it is fair to say that almost everybody who has attended one of my in-house ethics courses has done so, at the outset at least, with something of a heavy heart, no doubt with the feeling that this will be a dull day full of moralising and platitudes run by a young consultant with little business experience. In the event, they may well find that their preconceptions are shown to be wrong on all counts. I would also say that sometimes I find that delegates come into the classroom with what can only be described as a somewhat resentful attitude – they are busy people, they have more productive things to do with their time and the whole exercise is pointless in any event because 'you can't teach ethics'. This is something that Lis herself has always believed.

I do not happen to agree with her on this point, however. From my perspective, when business ethics training is run on an in-house basis it always succeeds at the very least in raising awareness and sending out a signal of how the organisation itself approaches the subject, what values it stands for and what is and is not acceptable under the organisation's code of conduct or the provisions of the staff handbook. Business ethics is all about how people behave when at work, so when the train-ing begins most delegates become interested quite quickly and this can be developed and built on by means of practical examples.

In my view much of the power and impact of in-house training in business ethics comes from cases and scenarios that are specifically related to the individual business; that are rooted firmly in the organisation's policies and experiences. These scenarios should refer to examples of what has actually happened in the past, either drawn from well-known media headline scandals or from events in the organisation's recent history, so that they are seen to be practical, rather than abstract and theoretical.

Competence in ethics is an acquired reasoning skill. In my experience, managers and employees alike can develop better ethical decision-making skills from working through and discussing together a variety of practical scenarios and dilemmas. Examples of two types of scenario-based training that I have used successfully in ethics training courses are set out at the end of this chapter.

The seven keys to successful business ethics training

In my experience, a blended and varied approach to training in business ethics works best. So, a mix of face-to-face sessions and CBT spread over a number of years may well provide the optimal training solution here.

However, this should always be done within a consistent framework. I know from experience that training in business ethics can produce positive results if the programme is designed thoughtfully. It is never possible to satisfy everyone, of course. Nevertheless I am confident that the great majority of delegates who attend my ethics courses will say at the end of the programme that yes, actually they did learn a lot – a number may even say that they enjoyed the training experience too. How can I be so sure about this? Well, from reviewing and monitoring the feedback forms completed by the delegates at the end of my courses. Feedback is an important feature of the modern training process and one that is not always used to maximum effect.

By reviewing these feedback forms over many years, and also from discussions with delegates and training managers, I have drawn together seven features that I believe hold the key to a successful business ethics training programme. These are set out below.

- **First, a commitment from the top**. Directors and senior managers should set out a clear policy commitment to business ethics training in their organisation. The training programme should always refer to this commitment and to the procedures that underpin it.
- **Then, action is needed to underpin the policy**. This means funding and also participation from those at the top. Personal commitment can be shown most clearly in one of two ways: where the training is face-to-face, every director and senior manager should attend one of the training sessions in person; alternatively, where a CBT format is used, they should take the time to work through the modules, take the tests and let it be known that they have done so. There is one other very important point when CBT is used for ethics training – the inclusion of a short video clip (around two to three minutes in length) featuring a personal message from the chairman or the CEO at the start of the module. In my experience, such a message from the top, emphasising the importance of business ethics, the leader's personal commitment to it and the beneficial outcomes of ethical behaviour for the organisation always carries impact.
- **Third, make training in business ethics mandatory and not optional**. This is sometimes difficult to achieve in practice because of local conditions (for example, I refer in Chapter 9 to the project for a large organisation in Luxembourg, where the culture was such that no training was ever declared to be 'mandatory'). In which case, management must stress the importance of the training, make it as easy to attend as possible and also accessible to all – this is one of the most helpful aspects of CBT. Attendance should be monitored too. However, the point remains that whenever possible, ethics training should be mandatory, with a clear message to this effect coming from the top. As an example, after we had concluded our interview for the book, Peter Walshe of Millward Brown told me that he was very confident that everyone in the WPP Group completed their ethics training every year because the instruction to do so always came from the CEO, Martin Sorrell, personally.
- **Next, ensure that training in business ethics is ongoing and part of a continuous programme**. This process should start when an employee joins the organisation – business ethics should be an integral part of the induction training programme. Thereafter, it should be regularly refreshed and re-inforced – ideally every year but certainly periodically. It should never be viewed as a one-off event – a high-profile presentation that is introduced with a lot of fanfare and promoted by senior management but is then not followed up. If this is the case, it quickly becomes forgotten about in the dynamics of the business. I have seen this happen before. Instead, there should be commitment to an ongoing business ethics training programme, with all managers and staff updating their knowledge and awareness periodically.

- **Point number five is for the training to be evidenced**. Records should be maintained of all ethics training that is carried out. For traditional face-to-face delivery this will mean keeping an attendance register. For all pieces of CBT, there must be an audit trail built into the programme so that the organisation is able to monitor progress and keep track of those employees who have carried out the training satisfactorily and those who have not. An LMS will provide this.
- **Next, the understanding of delegates must be assessed**. This should be done as a matter of course when CBT modules are used, but it can also be used in face-to-face training by the use of quizzes or short examples. Normally when CBT is used the assessment is made by means of multiple-choice questions. A minimum pass mark is assigned – failure to achieve this score will necessitate re-sits until such time as the required pass mark is achieved. One way to introduce extra rigour into this testing process is to compile a large question bank that will enable a randomised selection from the bank for each individual sitting the test – the questions will be different for each re-sit, therefore.
- **Finally, and crucially, the training should be designed to be practical and realistic**. If ethics training is to be effective it must 'come alive' and enable the organisation's managers and staff to relate to it. The best way to do this in my experience is through the use of examples – I would go so far as to say that ethics training should always include a case-based component. One method is to include a small number of headline cases such as the Enron scandal or BP's disastrous blowout of its Macondo oil well and to work through the lessons that can be learned from these examples. Another is to look at the 'business dilemma' type of scenario that we have reviewed from time to time throughout this book. Perhaps the most effective form of scenario training is a series of short cases, each one showing a different type of business problem that managers and staff can relate to. These cases should reflect issues that are relevant to the organisation, perhaps including recent situations that have been dealt with or areas of policy that either have changed or are thought to cause confusion and uncertainty in the workplace. The organisation's policies and code of conduct or staff handbook will always signpost the correct answer to every case.

It is important to say that the type of case-based exercises referred to in the seventh point above can be applied to all forms of business ethics training: in-house courses, public enrolment courses and CBT training. Indeed, they can provide real points of focus and interest in online training modules. Recently I have become involved in designing a number of CBT modules, mainly for the purposes of training and updating knowledge of the UKBA. Working with actors, we have been able to introduce some short video dramas that bring the training messages to life through action and humour, while at the same time conveying the key messages.

Examples of training exercises

I set out below two different types of exercises that I have used successfully with delegates on many training courses. The first is the type of business dilemma exercise that we have looked at throughout the book. The second is different. It is an example of the type of exercise involving a series of short case studies that I refer to above. This sort of work can be beneficial on public courses but I have found it to be particularly effective when delivering in-house courses, where the case studies can be tailored to the particular circumstances, history and culture of the organisation concerned.

Business ethics training example 1: business dilemma

The scenario described below is another classic business dilemma. I have used it during in-house ethics training sessions to good effect because it focuses attention on an aspect of poor behaviour by an individual at the top of the organisation in circumstances where the facts are not entirely clear. Careful thought and judgement therefore need to be applied when thinking about the response, so it is a good case for debate in groups and subsequent discussion in plenary session in the room.

What do you think is the optimum response in the following situation?

You are the finance director of a large manufacturing business. You have put your name down to play in your company's annual golf day. You used to play golf to a good standard (you had a single-figure handicap as a teenager), are highly competitive by nature and have been practising hard recently – you really want to win the event. You learn that one of your two playing partners on the day will be the financial controller, your number two in the finance department, and someone that you know very well. Your other playing partner will be the company's non-executive chairman.

The chairman was appointed from outside the business some 18 months ago to improve the company's image following embarrassing revelations in both the social and print media about the workplace behaviour of a senior executive. The chairman is highly regarded both by other senior managers within the company and by the major investors in the business. You endorse this view – you like and respect him both as an individual and as the chairman. As an example, you think that he did an excellent job in leading the review of the company's code of conduct recently. The new code has been well received by employees, in part because it has brought a more modern approach to some difficult areas of workplace behaviour, for example: the revised drugs and alcohol policy; the new whistle-blowing policy and revamping the approach to sensitive areas such as establishing that personal relationships between employees at different levels within the organisation are inappropriate and, if they should happen, then they must be disclosed. The chairman personally endorsed the new revised code of conduct at the end of the review.

It is now the day of the golf event. You start off by playing very well but you become aware that the chairman does not appear to be quite himself today. He is not playing well and is clearly not enjoying himself. No doubt because of the stress brought on by his poor play the chairman suddenly starts to become very talkative, which is not like him at all. And then, quite out of the blue and following him missing a very short putt on the last green, he starts to boast that, although over 65 years old, he can still teach the younger generation a thing or two. He follows this up by blurting out, in front of both you and the financial controller, that he has been having an affair with the company's in-house lawyer, a lady 30 years his junior, for the last three months. He then storms off to have a shower and no doubt cool off before his speech at the presentation and prize-giving later on in the evening.

What do you do?

Comments

As with all dilemma-based scenarios of this type, there is no unequivocally right or wrong answer to this question. But, as finance director, this situation would indeed give you a problem if it occurred in reality. First of all, you would need to consider whether the chairman's comments are simply braggadocio, a means of deflecting attention from his poor golf, or are they true, in which case do you have to do anything about it? After all, he is doing a good job as chairman and no laws have been broken here. However, you can't simply brush this under the carpet – after all, the financial controller also heard the comments and, if there really is an affair going on, then you know that the details will come out in the end because they always do. Also, you will be aware that by keeping the affair secret, the chairman is in breach of your company's new code of conduct, something that he chose to work on and to endorse personally. What would it do to the credibility of the code if the chairman is able to ignore one of its principles with impunity?

In face-to-face training sessions, I would encourage the delegates to think about the broader implications of this scenario. Perhaps the finance director should raise it with the audit committee? And what are the possible consequences for the chairman? At the end of the debate, I surprise some of the delegates by saying that this scenario is in fact based on a real-life situation involving the American company Boeing and its then President and CEO, Harry Stonecipher – the case that we looked at earlier in the book. In that situation, remember that the saga ended with Mr Stonecipher resigning his positions on the board and leaving the company, despite the fact that he was widely regarded as doing a good job.

Business ethics training example 2: workplace deviancy exercise

Now we turn to the second form of training exercise. In contrast to the last, this one focuses on a series of short cases, any one of which could arise in practice in the workplace – if such an incident does happen in reality then it would need to be handled carefully and appropriately.

In practice, I know that this type of exercise can create much impact and interest in the room. I use a simple technique for maximum effect: divide the delegates into groups, ask them to discuss all of the cases within their groups and to allocate a score to each of them. Each group needs to nominate a team leader and, at the end of the allotted time, each team leader will call out the scores from their own group. The scores need to be integers and not given as a range or as 'half-mark' – in other words, the delegates have to arrive at a decision in each case and are not able to prevaricate or fudge the issue. Meanwhile, I have compiled a grid on the flipchart and I will tabulate the scores from each group on the chart as they are called out. We then review the scores in a plenary session and discuss any anomalies arising, together with the reasons for them.

If done in this way I know from experience that these exercises will succeed in generating a huge amount of engagement, discussion and debate from the delegates. The reason is simple: the scenarios are readily understandable and they are realistic – they can and do occur in many organisations so that the delegates can relate easily to them. Also, in most cases there is no unequivocally right or wrong answer to each of the questions posed which means that some disagreement is almost inevitable. This is particularly so on public courses because the key to answering the cases is always to be found in an organisation's policies, procedures and code of conduct – so, when many different organisations are represented in the same room there is always a lot of discussion.

The same applies to in-house courses in that there will inevitably be a lot of discussion around what precise score should be applied in each scenario. However, what I am looking for above all else from a group of managers and staff from the same organisation is a high degree of consistency in the scoring. This would indicate a good awareness of policies and procedures within the organisation. Sometimes, issues do arise which can then be addressed by reference to the policy. So, I find that these exercises are particularly useful when carried out on an in-house basis and can also help to embed the key messages around behaviour that the organisation wants to communicate to its people.

Although I have used these exercises primarily in classroom-style teaching, it will be apparent that they can be adapted relatively easily to the CBT format too, with multiple choice questions.

Set out below is a typical brief for one of these exercises. I call this particular exercise: 'Workplace Deviancy'. Please read through the exercise and consider how you would grade each of the 10 scenarios, in light of the particular codes and policies in place in your own organisation.

Workplace deviancy – exercise brief

'Workplace deviancy' is the difference between how managers and employees behave at work in reality and how they should behave at work according to their terms and conditions of employment, company policies and procedures, staff code of conduct etc.

Working in groups, you are required to assess the following 10 situations and grade how you think they would be handled in your organisation if they were to arise in practice. The grades are from 1 to 5 in terms of the type of response to the incident, depending on the seriousness of the incident described, where:

- *1 is no concern, so simply tolerate, there is no need for any action;*
- *2 is minor concern, management will be aware but no formal action is required;*
- *3 is a significant concern, which will result in a verbal warning;*
- *4 is serious concern, it will be investigated and, depending on the results, will be followed by a formal written warning; and*
- *5 is very serious indeed, it will be classed as gross misconduct and will result in dismissal and/ or prosecution.*

1. *Two employees, one a director and the other an accounts clerk, have failed to attend any of the mandatory training sessions on the UKBA held during the last 12 months.*
2. *An employee has been signed off sick for six months with a bad back. The organisation has been very supportive but you hear reports that he has been playing golf and squash regularly during this time when he has been off work.*
3. *It has just been demonstrated that a high-flying executive provided false and inflated academic qualifications on his CV and application form when he applied to join the organisation two years ago. Since his recruitment he has been very successful and is now considered to be one of the most highly rated managers in the organisation.*
4. *You receive credible reports from an external source that one of your organisation's most successful salesmen is a habitual user of cocaine and other Category 'A' drugs.*
5. *An executive is found to have family contacts who work for one of your organisation's major suppliers. These contacts have never been disclosed before and the executive was an influential member of the tendering team that awarded the supplier a multi-million pound contract last year.*
6. *You discover, via an internal audit, that the managing director of your main subsidiary company in Eastern Europe has made a series of 'special payments' to agents of two large local companies in order to secure existing contracts and win new business.*
7. *You learn that one of your top salesmen attended a corporate hospitality event thrown by a potential new supplier at the Wimbledon tennis tournament on Men's Singles Final Day last year. He failed to disclose anything about this entertainment in your organisation's Gifts and Hospitality Register, despite attending training on the UKBA.*
8. *A senior manager in your Corporate Finance department had her company laptop stolen from her car whilst stopping to buy a newspaper on her way home from work last week. Enquiries revealed that she had left the laptop on the passenger seat of her car when she went into the shop.*

9. *The managing director and the finance director of one of your subsidiary companies have been shown to have inflated sales figures last year in order to hit their targets.*

10. *A number of longstanding members of staff, including the financial controller and two research analysts, have never complied with your organisation's 'clear desk policy' and regularly leave company documents and customer information on their desks when they leave work to go home in the evening.*

Comments

As will be seen, there is no absolute right or wrong answer to any of these scenarios, with the exception of case number nine which, on the facts as stated, amounts to fraudulent manipulation of figures in order to hit targets – fraud is likely to be classed as gross misconduct in most organisations, so that the grade here should be either 4 (if waiting for the results of an investigation) or 5. However, the signpost showing the delegates the way to the answer will always be the same – the organisation's policies and codes, which will point the way to the action required in each case, thereby ensuring consistent decision-making that is in line with the values of the enterprise.

 ## WORKSHOP CONCLUSION

Closing

As I finish the presentation, I am interested to note how the dynamics of this particular workshop are a little different from the others. I have observed how David Hurley, the HR Manager, is the most engaged of the team and, sure enough, when I suggest that, provided there are no questions, the team now need to draw together the key takeaways from today's session, it is David who takes the lead.

Key takeaways

David says that, having given a lot of thought to the subject matter of this workshop, he has a number of ideas on how the Group's training and development might be improved that he would like to suggest as takeaways. The team is quite happy to listen to what he has to say, though Rachel Gordon, the Chairman, says that there is one action point for her coming out of the workshop. So, the first takeaway is hers, with David then taking over, as follows:

- ✓ **Draw up a personal development plan for each director**. Rachel wants to bring the Stronach Group in line with best practices and she is aware that, as Chairman, she is responsible for overseeing the development of the board. She commits to discussing training and development needs with each director individually as part of setting each of them objectives for the coming year.
- ✓ **Adopt the seven-point business ethics training plan**. David likes the seven-point plan that I recommended during the presentation as providing the basis for a successful ethical training and development programme. He recommends that Stronach should use it in future and everyone agrees with this.
- ✓ **Make use of video scenarios in the CBT ethics module**. David is impressed with the use of video in a number of the examples of CBT modules that he has been reviewing. He is persuasive

when he argues that short video clips, using actors and professional camera work, embedded in the modules can be highly effective – he believes that they can be used to highlight the key messages in the training that need to be re-inforced better than any other computer-based method. Also, if some humour can be incorporated in the clips then this will also add to the interest of the training. Malcolm Mainwaring, the Group Finance Director, is predictably concerned about the potential costs of this but David feels that they will not be prohibitive and points to the spiralling use of YouTube videos. David agrees to put costings together for Malcolm to review.

✓ **Begin the ethics training programme with a personal video statement by the chairman**. David then builds on the video theme with a connected point. He feels strongly that a personal statement either from John Holt, the CEO, or from Rachel will send out a powerful message about just how important those at the top consider this training to be. It will be impactful because people will see that it comes from the heart – good business ethics is one of their own core values. Both John and Rachel support this, they think it is an excellent idea – after some discussion, it is decided that Rachel will be the one to deliver the statement.

✓ **Take advantage of Cloud technology**. John Holt now comes in with a point of his own. He is interested in the opportunities provided by Cloud computing, in particular the idea of being able to stream training modules directly to employees' smartphones. David supports this strongly and says that, as an example, they could use it to provide a cost-effective solution to a gap that currently exists in the Group's anti-bribery training – the overseas workforce have not yet received it. David talks enthusiastically on this subject, about the efficiency of employees working abroad being able to log into a CBT anti-bribery module whilst they are at the airport waiting to catch their flights back to the UK. This is not fanciful, it is possible and he has seen a demonstration of the technology. John is clearly very interested in this idea and David agrees to show him the demonstration.

Next workshop

We are now out of time for the session – John and Rachel need to be elsewhere and it is clear that Malcolm has to leave quickly too. The subject matter for the next workshop, scheduled to be the last in the series, has already been agreed. It will be around confidential reporting, whistle-blowing hotlines and the creation of an open culture. As always, Rachel will see that the diaries are coordinated and we will meet again in approximately four weeks' time.

Reflections

John and Rachel have left. Malcolm smiles and gives me a big thumbs-up gesture as he walks out of the boardroom – he clearly thinks that the workshop has been successful and so do I. But the person who has enjoyed it the most is still sitting at the table. David Hurley is genuinely delighted with the outcome of today's session. He thanks me profusely for engineering things so that he was able to put his case – I point out to him that while that might be true, he still had to make the case and he managed to do so very effectively indeed. With that, David stands up, we shake hands and he too leaves the room.

Five minutes later, I am walking out of Stronach's offices into Berkeley Square. The weather is beautiful and I think that this somehow is very appropriate – it is not every day that I witness a young manager finding the confidence to be able to articulate his ideas as well as David Hurley did today. Enthusiasm and good research make a powerful combination and David used them both to succeed today – well done to him!

CHAPTER NINE

Whistle-blowing: encouraging a culture of openness

CREATING AN OPEN CULTURE: EIGHTH WORKSHOP

Opening

It is just before 9.00 am and the team has gathered in the boardroom of the Stronach Group for this, the eighth and final workshop in the series on the ethics project. We are just about to start. Unusually, Rachel had called me a couple of days ago to tell me a little about how whistle-blowing is handled at Stronach – the general topic for discussion at today's workshop. She seemed a little concerned, embarrassed almost.

This is what she told me.

Update

Like many organisations today, the Stronach Group does indeed have a whistle-blowing hotline in place. It was introduced five years ago, together with a whistle-blowing policy and a piece of training for managers and staff. However, nothing has been done since that time to update the policy or to re-visit the training. Rachel is concerned that the hotline is not operating effectively – there are no metrics in place, the internal audit function has apparently never looked at the workings of the hotline and the board receives no regular reports. She feels that Stronach is simply going through the motions here, that this is a tick-box exercise and she does not like it.

She has spoken with Malcolm Mainwaring, the Group Finance Director, about her concerns – he has been with the Group much longer than her. Malcolm told her that he remembers hearing something about a couple of calls that came through on the hotline a few years ago, around the same time as the rumours about Stronach's dealings in India began to circulate. But he was not informed of any of the details at the time – what issues were raised in the calls, what measures were taken to investigate or how they had been resolved. Apparently, in those days Duncan Stronach used to deal with any matters like this personally.

Rachel knows very well that the hotline and the procedures surrounding it need to be improved but she is unclear on what precisely to do and what is the best way to go about it. She asks whether I could use this workshop to give them some specific advice on the subject. I reply positively and say that I will come to the workshop prepared to do exactly that.

Reassurance

I decide to begin the session by giving the team some reassurance. I say that Rachel has briefed me on the situation at the Stronach Group regarding whistle-blowing and that, in all honesty, I am not too surprised by what she told me. From time to time I hear similar concerns from directors and managers on courses when discussing this particular topic, not least from the chairs of audit committees. I have seen experienced chairmen who become a little uneasy when this topic is raised and who will readily agree that more could and perhaps should be done in their organisations to develop a confidential reporting process that fulfils its purpose – namely, as an effective governance control.

I give the team my own view. For me, an effective confidential reporting process is one of the most important governance controls for organisations today if they want to manage the high-impact risks that we have discussed in earlier workshops and thereby minimise the chance of reputational damage. Take fraud risk, for example. I give them my killer statistic – three times as many frauds are discovered by a tip-off than by any other method. Also, almost all of the high profile bribery and corruption scandals of recent years have been uncovered by whistle-blowers. This makes an impression. I then say that the principle of confidential reporting has wider application than financial crime – an effective whistle-blowing process is the most likely way that organisations will uncover practices that are unsafe, or that involve the systematic cover-up of errors or that constitute any form of illegal behaviour in the workplace.

So, I am always a little disappointed to learn about a reporting process that is not operating effectively – to me this represents a missed opportunity for the organisation concerned. Organisations sometimes convince themselves either that they do not need a hotline or else that they can somehow operate one without putting in the necessary effort, thereby paying lip-service only. In other words, they have the hardware in place (the hotline facility, perhaps a policy also) but the software (the commitment and guarantees from the top) is missing. The result is predictable – the control will not work effectively or at all. This situation is not uncommon.

Before continuing, I pause for effect. I then ask them directly about their own commitment to making the whistle-blowing process work throughout the Stronach Group – are they prepared to do what is needed to establish an open culture that encourages people with concerns about harmful or illegal practices to report them internally? There are two prerequisites for this, two guarantees that must come from the top: first that confidentiality will be respected in all cases of disclosures made in good faith; and second, that all disclosures made will be properly investigated. Is Stronach prepared to do this?

The team is unanimous in voicing their immediate agreement – yes, this is what they want to do.

With that I reassure them once again, this time to say that these improvements are realistic, they can be made. With a combination of time, commitment and effort from the top and following some best practice principles concerning whistle-blowing, it will be possible for them to develop their hotline into an effective control. I will take them through how they might achieve this during the workshop.

Agenda

The agenda follows naturally from this introduction. I will divide the time into five segments so that we look at the following areas:

- First of all, I will provide an introduction of and background to the subject of whistle-blowing. We will review definitions and explanations of what whistle-blowing is all about and how attitudes to it have developed over the last 50 years.
- Second, we will review a number of the issues and controversies that continue to surround the subject of whistle-blowing. We will look at some famous cases and examine the two main reasons why people continue to be reluctant to come forward with their disclosures, especially a reluctance to use internal reporting mechanisms. These reasons are a fear of reprisals and scepticism that any effective action will be taken by the organisation to address the issues following the disclosure.
- Next, we will look at the various legal approaches to whistle-blowing around the world, with particular attention paid to the different positions taken in the USA and in the UK.
- Fourth, I will put whistle-blowing into its day-to-day business operational context using examples from my own experience together with the observations of two colleagues who work in this area. These examples will highlight a number of issues that can arise in practice when putting in place whistle-blowing hotlines.
- Finally, I will take the team through a practical action plan for installing a whistle-blowing hotline and making it effective. I will personalise this section and badge it as my 'Top 10 Tips' for success because I have seen evidence that this is an approach that actually does work in practice. I say to the team that this is exactly the approach that I will be recommending that the Stronach Group follows, with the important caveat that the team makes any adjustments required so that, in their opinion, it best fits the individual circumstances of their own business.

Everyone agrees with my proposed agenda, there are no questions. So, with that, I start the presentation.

 ## INTRODUCTION AND BACKGROUND TO WHISTLE-BLOWING

Definitions

Whistle-blowing

The subject of whistle-blowing is addressed in many pieces of legislation and in numerous reports, so there are various definitions available. One of the most up to date is set out in the report of the UK's Whistle-blowing Commission in 2013[1] and I like it because it is at once a powerful and straightforward explanation of the word whistle-blowing. It is as follows:

> *Whistle-blowing is the raising of a concern, either within the workplace or externally, about a danger, risk, malpractice or wrongdoing which affects others.*

Hotlines and other communication mechanisms

However, there is another word that we need to consider when discussing whistle-blowing, because organisations that put a whistle-blowing policy in place almost always attach to it the word 'hotline'.

Now, a hotline may very well be used for confidential reporting purposes but it is not the only mechanism. The Online Directory defines a hotline as follows:

> *A hotline is a direct and immediate telephone linkup, especially between heads of government, as for use in a crisis; a telephone line that gives quick and direct access to a source of information or help.*

This is a useful definition because most people associate the term 'whistle-blowing hotline' primarily with a telephone facility, a number that they can call to report a concern. Indeed, the provision of a dedicated telephone number is a central feature of almost all hotlines. However, a hotline is often not required – indeed, it may well be considered to be inappropriate for small organisations. This does not mean that small organisations do not benefit from a culture of openness – not at all. Openness can be achieved without a hotline. The phrase 'speak up procedure' is more appropriate to match the circumstances of many small organisations than is a whistle-blowing hotline.

So, I encourage people to think of the concept of the 'hotline' in a broader context for whistle-blowing purposes. It is most powerful when it is used as an umbrella term such that it includes other reporting mechanisms as well such as: a website, with a web-based reporting system; reporting by surface mail to a specified address; and the traditional oral reporting within the organisation, either to a line manager (or to another designated officer) or, in certain circumstance, to the boss.

This umbrella concept is important. It helps to avoid situations of misconception when, for example, directors and managers say to me that whistle-blowing is not something that they need to concern themselves with because their business is too small. If they thought in terms of the broad umbrella concept rather than a hotline, then they would see that whistle-blowing applies to all organisations regardless of size. Those with responsibility at the top always need to know when something is going wrong inside their operation and this principle applies regardless of the size of the organisation. So, those leading small and medium-sized businesses should be looking to demonstrate to their workers that they are approachable at all times and are prepared to listen, even when the news is bad. Fundamentally, whistle-blowing is about having a culture of openness in the workplace.

We will discuss how to make these reporting mechanisms as effective as possible later in the chapter.

Core principles

A number of important principles are embedded in these definitions. There are four that I like to highlight at the outset when discussing whistle-blowing.

The first principle is that a whistle-blower is a person who raises a concern that affects other people, not himself or herself directly. Blowing the whistle is therefore something quite different from making a complaint. When someone complains they are saying that they personally have been treated poorly, that they have a personal grievance. This could be a breach of their employment rights or the result of inappropriate workplace behaviour such as bullying, sexual harassment, discrimination and so on. Organisations should have a different and separate set of grievance procedures. This fundamental point of difference should be made clear to all employees through the staff handbook (setting out both the grievance procedure and the separate whistle-blowing policy), training programmes and the existence of separate reporting mechanisms for each.

The second principle is that whistle-blowing is about things that happen inside the workplace. It does not follow, however, that it always has to be the result of disclosures made by those inside the workplace. The majority of whistle-blowing disclosures are made by employees or managers within an organisation of course, but other stakeholders should be encouraged to come forward if they have a concern – for example, customers, suppliers, patients and so on. This inclusion of an external perspective is a feature of the most progressive hotlines today.

The third principle relates to whistle-blowing disclosures. They can be made either internally to those in positions of authority or trust within the organisation or they can be made externally, for example to the police, to regulators, to politicians or to the media. This is a crucial area. Every organisation, whether in the public sector or in the private sector, should be looking to ensure that all disclosures are internal, at least in the first instance. To succeed in this objective, organisations will need to work hard to establish awareness of and trust in the whistle-blowing process. We will look at this area in some detail later, not only the measures that organisations should be taking to embed the principle of confidential reporting within their business but also the reasons why whistle-blowers take their concerns outside and what protections are available to them when they choose so to do. Broadly, for legal protection to exist, external disclosures should only be made where they are in the public interest.

There is one other important principle to mention here and it is one that is implicit in the definition of a hotline – in order for a hotline to work effectively, it must be manned 24 hours a day, 7 days a week. It is vital that if somebody calls the designated telephone number they are able to speak to a person straight away and the person who answers the call has been trained in how to respond to the whistle-blower and how to gather information. Aligned with this (and something that we will discuss in full later in the chapter) is that all reports must be handled confidentially.

Background

History

The concept of 'blowing the whistle' has existed for centuries. For example, when Sir Robert Peel established police forces in the UK for the first time in the middle of the nineteenth century, the early police officers developed the practice of blowing their whistles when they noticed a crime – the noise of the whistle would alert other law enforcement officers and the general public of danger. Also, whistles are used by referees in many sports to command attention and alert the players to a suspension of play, most commonly for foul play.

US initiatives

But it is in the USA that most of the developments and impetus behind modern whistle-blowing have occurred. Here, US laws reflected the importance of reporting concerns at an early stage too. There are various strands in the development of the US position. In 1863 the original False Claims Act in the USA provided protection for whistle-blowers. During the Civil War the authorities were keen to combat waste and fraud by military suppliers. The False Claims Act encouraged people with concerns to come forward by protecting them from wrongful dismissal and by promising them a percentage of monies recovered or damages won by the government. In the 1960s the term whistle-blower started to be used to distinguish those people with concerns about an organisation from informants who provided information for the FBI against the Mafia. Some credit the civic activist Ralph Nader with legitimising the word in the early 1970s as a means of moving away from pejorative terms such as 'grass', 'snitch' or 'rat'.

Whatever the exact origins, whistle-blowing has become since the 1970s a common means of describing the reporting of concerns in public sector bodies in the USA to do with public safety, health, fraud and abuse of office. In order to facilitate such reporting, whistle-blowing hotlines were developed and have been used in government agencies in the USA for decades. More recently they have been seen as an important potential tool for helping to prevent and detect corporate wrongdoing in the private sector also.

Governance developments

Whistle-blowing hotlines are now widely regarded as a feature of governance best practice. The SOX requires audit committees to establish procedures for the confidential and/or anonymous submission by employees of concerns regarding questionable accounting or auditing practices.

In the UK, the Corporate Governance Code requires audit committees to 'review arrangements by which staff of the company may in confidence raise concerns about possible improprieties in matters of financial reporting or other matters', while 'speak up' mechanisms are one of the adequate procedures referred to as providing a possible defence against charges brought against a commercial organisation for failing to prevent bribery under the Section 7 corporate offence in the UKBA. In February 2013, Public Concern at Work established the Whistle-blowing Commission to review the effectiveness of whistle-blowing in the UK and to make suggestions for improvement. The Commission reported in November 2013 with 25 recommendations and the inclusion of a draft Code of Practice for whistle-blowing arrangements.[2]

Personal view

I fully support the efforts of the authorities to promote whistle-blowing. In my view it is a crucial component of good governance today, whether in the public or private sectors. The reason is simple: whistle-blowing can uncover and highlight organisational failures that may culminate in very serious harm across many parts of society better than any other mechanism. These failures can be of various types and include: criminal activity (for example, fraud or bribery and corruption); health and safety shortfalls; environmental damage; negligence (in a school or hospital or care home for example); and the mis-selling of financial products (such as insurance policies or pensions or interest rate hedges).

ISSUES AND CONTROVERSIES

Examples of whistle-blowing cases

Introduction

There are many examples of whistle-blowing disclosures over the last 20 years or so. These support my contention that the reporting of concerns by those who work in the business day to day is one of the most important ways that serious issues in organisations are uncovered as a first step in the process of correcting them. The very fact that these cases are all in the public domain, however, points to some of the key issues and controversies that still surround the subject of whistle-blowing. We will examine these later in the chapter.

Set out below are brief summaries of a small number of the most important and eye-catching of these cases, grouped by location, which demonstrate that whistle-blowing disclosures have uncovered harmful practices in many parts of the world.

Examples from the USA

As we have seen, the USA has been at the forefront of developments in thinking around whistle-blowing.

- There was seen to be almost a heroic quality about those responsible for blowing the whistle on the scandals at the turn of the last century concerning the accounting frauds at Enron and WorldCom and also the failures of the US intelligence agencies prior to the terrorist attacks on 11 September 2001. *Time* magazine famously made the three whistle-blowers concerned its 'persons of the year' in 2002.[3] They were all women and they all displayed courage in setting aside personal risks in order to blow the whistle on what were catastrophic failures at their respective organisations. These whistle-blowers were: Cynthia Cooper, the Head of Internal Audit at WorldCom, who uncovered the accounting fraud carried out by some of the most senior executives in her company; Sherron Watkins, the Enron executive who wrote to Chairman and CEO, Ken Ley, with her concerns about what she described as the accounting tricks that the company was using to boost its share price; and Colleen Rowley, Special Agent for the FBI, who wrote to the Director of the FBI in 2002 setting out the mishandling of the intelligence that her office had gathered prior to the 9/11 attacks and who later gave evidence on this before the Senate.
- More recently (and more controversially), in 2012 the Internal Revenue Service awarded Bradley Birkenfeld, a former banker at UBS, a reward of $104 million for revealing a tax evasion scheme relating to secret bank accounts in Switzerland and elsewhere that cost the US government billions of dollars in lost tax revenues. The information supplied by Mr Birkenfeld led to UBS entering into a deferred prosecution agreement and paying a fine of $780 million to settle with the Department of Justice. As a result of the investigation, the US government has collected some $5 billion in back-taxes. Mr Birkenfeld himself received a 40-month prison sentence after pleading guilty to one charge of helping a billionaire property developer to evade tax.[4]

Examples from the UK

- In the UK the emphasis has been more on high-profile cases rather than individuals making the disclosures. Here, various organisational failures made headline news because they resulted in tragedies that could have been prevented had whistle-blowers been listened to when they first came forward internally within their respective organisations. A good example is provided by the disaster involving the ferry 'The Herald of Free Enterprise', which capsized and sank off the coast of Belgium in 1987. A total of 193 people died in the tragedy, which was caused by the ferry sailing with its bow doors open. How could this possibly have happened? Well, there had been warnings. At the subsequent inquiry it was found that on five separate occasions staff had raised concerns about this serious safety risk but that their warnings had been lost somewhere in layers of middle management and bureaucracy.[5] Other health and safety cases include the poor standards of care at the Mid Staffordshire NHS Foundation Trust and the poor safeguarding procedures surrounding the tragic death of 'Baby Peter' in August 2007. What all these cases have in common is a failure by management to listen to reports of what was really happening on the ground in the organisations concerned.

An example from Europe

- Perhaps the most famous case of whistle-blowing on Continental Europe concerns disclosures of wrongdoing at the European Commission. In 1998 Paul van Buitenen, an assistant auditor in the European Commission in Brussels, went public with details of cronyism in appointments, of corrupt dealings with contractors and of abuse of power in the Commission. The result was that in March 1999 the entire team of 20 commissioners resigned in a symbolic gesture of commitment to reform. Mr van Buitenen says that he was treated poorly by his employers subsequent to his disclosures, however. Initially suspended, he claims to have been vilified by his former friends before being moved to a lower position in Luxembourg on half of his previous initial salary. He resigned in 2002.[6]

An example from Japan

■ In October 2011 Michael Woodford hit the headlines by becoming the first CEO of a global corporation to blow the whistle on his own company. He was dismissed from his post at Olympus, the Japanese manufacturer of cameras and medical imaging equipment, after he had persistently raised questions with his fellow directors in Tokyo about a number of significant and dubious payments made by the company in the past. Mr Woodford was unable to obtain satisfactory answers, with the result that he decided to go public with his concerns. Following the subsequent inquiries and investigations into the accounting irregularities, the main board directors resigned and the share price plunged. Mr Woodford has since settled his claim for unfair dismissal with Olympus.[7]

Key issues arising: why report externally?

The problem

Many people will be familiar with some, perhaps with most, of the examples set out above because, in each case, the disclosure was made to an external party and thereafter was in the public domain. This is an obvious point to make perhaps, but it is important nevertheless because each of the organisations caught up in the scandals became the subject of intense public scrutiny and severe (and often well-deserved) criticism. Each of these organisations incurred significant reputational damage as a result – in the cases of Enron and WorldCom they both went bankrupt. In these situations it would have been a better outcome for everyone impacted by the disclosures and for the organisations themselves if first of all the reports had been made internally and, second, where this had been done, if the disclosures had been investigated professionally and acted upon.

I interviewed Cathy James for the purposes of this book. Cathy is the Director of Public Concern at Work (PCaW), the independent charity set up in the UK in 1993 that aims to protect society by encouraging workplace whistle-blowing. During the course of my interview with Cathy, I asked her to outline what in her opinion are the main reasons why managers and staff sometimes feel so dissatisfied with the internal whistle-blowing mechanisms that they decide to report to an outside agency. This was her reply:

> *There are two reasons.*
>
> *One is they've raised it, nothing's happened, they've had no feedback. It feels like it has gone into a big black hole. They may have been told it was being dealt with but there has been no visible action taken as a result. So the sense that nothing will be done really means that people want to take the next step, think about what their next options might be.*

Or, of course, the more obvious reason is that they actually feel something is going wrong with their working lives because they've questioned it. Perhaps a promotion they thought might come their way hasn't happened or it's a big piece of work they expected to be involved in, but they are suddenly side-lined, or worse, they are demoted or they're disciplined or informal reprisals start to happen or formal reprisals or actual dismissal. Any one of those could be a trigger for someone taking advice from us at PCaW.

We have done a piece of research actually into our advice line, which we are about to publish which has got a very strong message for corporates. Because the average whistle-blower, from the 1000-odd cases on our advice line has worked for a company for less than two years, has seen something happening for six months or so, raises it internally once, maybe twice, but only the very tenacious raise it more often, doesn't generally want to go outside. Because they quite rightly understand that this will affect their job, the more senior they are the more quickly they are out of the door, the more junior they are the more likely they are to be ignored.

Now I'm not suggesting this research is a snapshot of the British workplace, because it is not. We at PCaW are seeing a very select group of people who have faced challenges in relation to raising concerns. Those that don't face those challenges probably wouldn't call us for advice. I really don't want to be giving that impression, because one of the things we want to do is to publicise the good work, to say that whistle-blowing hotlines can work, to help organisations do better and to find ways where that does work better. But this is the pattern that we are seeing.

Also what is quite interesting is that if an employee goes to a regulator, this lessens the risk of dismissal. It doesn't lessen the risk of reprisal, so informal reprisal may still go on, but it does lessen the chances of dismissal. I wonder if that's perhaps because the law and that external oversight makes organisations think 'hold on a minute, if we do that are we going to be in trouble'. It doesn't lessen the challenge to the individual I don't think but it does give them perhaps a little bit more strength in terms of their position – perhaps.

To summarise, Cathy identifies here the two key issues that drive whistle-blowers to report their concerns externally. The first is a fear of retribution – or, in many cases, the actuality of retribution in some form by managers and/or colleagues for blowing the whistle. The second is an absence of feedback to the whistle-blower once a disclosure has been made, leading to the belief that no action has been taken and nothing will be done to address the reported concern.

Whistle-blowing controversies

Overview

It is important to recognise that the idea of blowing the whistle at work continues to attract controversy. It can be a cultural thing, a mistrust of the whole idea of whistle-blowing hotlines. I have seen this myself in some of the smaller jurisdictions that I have worked in, such as Gibraltar and Trinidad and Tobago. Here, with small, tight-knit communities and close family connections, where everyone seems to know everyone else, the concept of a confidential reporting hotline struggles to gain any traction – the culture is such that it is simply not going to be trusted.

But it is not only small nations that have difficulties with embracing the concept of whistle-blowing. When Ernst & Young carried out a survey in 2007 on attitudes of staff to whistle-blowing in multinational companies, they noted a much less positive response from employees of multinationals based in countries in Continental Europe than from those in the UK and the USA.

Personal experience

Once again, this is something that I have noticed myself. In 2009 and 2010 I was part of a team running an anti-fraud and corruption training programme for executives and staff of a large bank based on the continent. The bank had, in 2009, issued a new, enhanced whistle-blowing policy covering the actions of its employees both internally and also in their dealings with all the third-party individuals and organisations that made up the various parties involved in its extensive lending operations. A major part of the training programme was to raise awareness of the whistle-blowing policy and how it was designed to work in practice. The employees that worked with us were generally very positive about the programme and understood very well the need for the bank's operations to be free from any suggestion of fraud or corruption.

Nevertheless, there were two issues that we came up against consistently during the training programme that suggested to us that the whistle-blowing hotline might not be as effective in practice as the senior management of the bank were hoping for. First, many employees seemed to have a problem with the idea of reporting their suspicions – as opposed to their belief, with proof – of any fraud or other corrupt practices that they became aware of, as they were required to do under the new policy. Suspicion is some way short of proof and there was concern that people and projects could be unfairly disadvantaged as a result. Second, many employees indicated during the course that they would be more likely to report concerns about the actions of third parties than they would be to report concerns about the conduct of their colleagues. There was resistance to the idea that some employees might be involved in any form of fraud or corruption and also genuine concerns that their own reputation and standing within the bank would be damaged if knowledge that they had made such a report ever became public. This was indicative of a positive culture of trust and loyalty but I had a real sense that people working for this bank were extremely uncomfortable with the idea of filing a report about the actions of a co-worker.

Recent controversies

The attitude of society to whistle-blowers has been tested in the USA and the UK recently by a series of massive leaks of classified information about the actions of the US military and of the security services of both countries. The activities of Julian Assange, who burst into public consciousness in 2010 when his WikiLeaks site released vast archives of government files, of the US Army Private Bradley (now Chelsea) Manning who was sentenced to 35 years in prison for leaking that material to WikiLeaks[8] and more recently of Edward Snowden, a contractor working as systems administrator for the NSA in one of its facilities in Hawaii who disclosed top secret intelligence data on American and British surveillance programmes to several Western media outlets in 2013,[9] have polarised opinion. These individuals are regarded either as heroes (for exposing what democratically elected governments are actually prepared to do in the name of security and for raising important questions about surveillance in a free society) or as villains – traitors even – for potentially compromising security, aiding terrorists and putting people's lives in danger.

This is in many ways a classic moral dilemma, rather than a business dilemma. Putting it at its most neutral, the disclosures of Messrs. Manning and Snowden, facilitated by Mr Assange and others in various media outlets, have increased scepticism of government at a time when the trust of citizens in their elected politicians is already at very low ebb.

Scepticism and fear in the workplace

Introduction

It is the negative attitude towards whistle-blowing that I have observed in some of the people who attend my courses and in some of my clients in the UK – not all by any means – that is of most concern to me. My own view could not be more different – as I have said before, I think whistle-blowing is both powerful and progressive. The reason why I think this is quite simple: whistle-blowing is a critical early warning system that can alert organisations to a wide variety of illegal, dangerous or corrupt practices that might be happening within the business. It should benefit everyone.

In my experience, there are two main reasons why not everyone agrees with me on this. The first reflects attitudes that are sometimes prevalent at the top of an organisation and then tend to permeate downwards from there: scepticism over whether whistle-blowing procedures actually produce positive results, often combined with a passive approach to managing those procedures, almost as if installing a hotline ticks the box and that is sufficient. Lip-service is the result. The second is a fear of potential whistle-blowers that they will suffer some form of harm if they come forward with a disclosure, despite assurances to the contrary. Perhaps this is in part a consequence of a lip-service culture, but this fear is real, it is unfortunately backed up by statistics and it can act as a significant roadblock to whistle-blowing in any organisation. If employees do not trust management assurances of confidentiality and protection from harm for all good faith whistle-blowers, then they are simply not going to come forward with their disclosures.

Scepticism

When I encounter scepticism about the effectiveness of whistle-blowing, I like to start exploring the reasons for this attitude with the directors and managers concerned by telling them a short story. It is a hypothetical story but one that reflects the views that some business leaders have about whistle-blowing and it often resonates with my audience:

> I visit the finance director of an old client and he tells me that two years ago the organisation decided to take my advice and install a whistle-blowing hotline. The costs were not insignificant in terms of the time spent planning the initiative, writing the new policy, installing the line and making everyone aware of it. Nevertheless, the directors thought that it was a worthwhile investment because they felt that they were putting in place a really strong anti-fraud and corruption control that would bring tangible benefits to the organisation. However, the finance director tells me that he and his colleagues now feel more than a little disappointed. He says that the hotline has now been in operation for over two years and in all that time the organisation has only received two calls on the line – and one of those was a wrong number!

As I mentioned, this is a hypothetical story, it has never actually happened to me. Should it ever happen in the future, I would like to think that my response would be to ask the finance director what he thought was really going on here, what did the low levels of reporting say to him about his own organisation. Did the fact there had been so few calls on the hotline indicate that the organisation had no problems with fraud, corruption or other criminal acts? Or was the reason for the small number of calls more to do with their employees not knowing about the hotline or (more likely still) not trusting it?

These are questions that all organisations need to ask if they have a hotline in place but they receive very few reports. Should the answers to these questions be unclear, my strong recommendation would be to commission an internal audit review into the workings of the hotline, perhaps to include a staff 'awareness and attitudes' survey. Fundamentally, this is an issue about the effectiveness and efficiency of the whistle-blowing hotline as a key governance control. It is entirely appropriate that internal audit should carry out work in this area and report back to the board, via the audit committee, with recommendations for improvement.

Fear and mistrust

The other negative attitude that I have seen regarding hotlines is fear, leading to mistrust. In particular, staff are reluctant to report concerns they might have about colleagues because of a number of related factors: fear that their identity as a whistle-blower might be revealed with negative consequences for their own career or reputation; fear that they do not have sufficient evidence to 'prove' fraud, so that the colleague they suspect might be unfairly treated or dismissed as a result of their disclosure; or a basic fear and dislike of the idea of 'telling tales' on colleagues which they feel will inevitably result in trouble, either for themselves or for others.

Crucially, the whistle-blowing mechanism should allow for confidential reporting to someone who is not the employee's line manager. The theory suggests that if an organisation has a good whistle-blowing policy in place that embodies this principle, then it is likely that any concerns that an employee might have will be raised with his or her employer in the first instance, rather than going outside to the public authorities. The UK's Committee on Standards in Public Life explains the main principles clearly:

> The essence of a whistle-blowing system is that staff should be able to by-pass the direct management line because that may well be the area about which their concerns arise and that they should be able to go outside the organisation if they feel the overall management is engaged in an improper course.

 ## THE LAW AS IT APPLIES TO WHISTLE-BLOWING

Overview

The need for protection

Blowing the whistle carries professional and personal risk. The decision to step forward and report a concern is always a difficult thing to do and will involve countless hours of personal stress and hard work at the very least for the individuals concerned. As we have seen, the two most formidable barriers that would-be whistle-blowers face are: the fear of retaliation and the sense that their disclosure will not make a difference.

It is therefore vital that employees have sufficient protection under the law and reliable avenues to report wrongdoing. At a time when headline scandals are not rare and when the role of whistle-blowers in exposing these scandals is increasingly well known, it might be thought that most countries around the world would by now have enacted comprehensive laws to protect the rights of individuals to blow the whistle on wrongful conduct.

Somewhat surprisingly, this is simply not the case.

Variations in the law

In many countries employees still face the threat of being fired, demoted, intimidated or harassed if they come forward with their concerns because there is no comprehensive and clear legislation in place to protect them. There are signs that the global picture is improving – the Organisation for Economic Cooperation and Development (OECD) carried out a study on whistle-blower protection in 2012 which reported that 'legal protection for whistle-blowers grew from 44% to 66% in OECD countries between 2000 and 2009'.[10] The same report gives examples of countries with comprehensive and dedicated legislation to protect public sector whistle-blowers: Australia, Canada, Ghana, Japan, South Korea, New Zealand, Romania, South Africa, the UK and the USA. It highlights the position of the UK as unusual because in this country there is a single disclosure regime for the protection of whistle-blowers in both the public and the private sectors. The World Law Group produced a report in 2012 providing a global guide to whistle-blowing programmes.[11] Countries analysed that still did not have specific whistle-blower protection laws in place at that time included Argentina, Chile, India, Israel, Switzerland, Thailand and Turkey.

The obvious but very important point to make here is that the law varies from country too country. Individuals need to understand the specific legal conditions that apply in their country. So do organisations, in particular multinational corporations that have operations around the world. This presents them with many challenges; not least around the difficulties of drawing up policies that can be consistently applied yet still manage to reflect not only the law but the different culture and history of the various individual countries in the group.

Different approaches

We look briefly below at the law as it applies to whistle-blowing in three different parts of the world: first in the European Union (EU) as a whole; then specifically in the UK; and finally in the USA.

The EU

A counter-intuitive picture

In 2013 Transparency International (TI), the global civil society organisation leading the fight against corruption, produced a report called 'Whistle-blowing in Europe', which looked at the legal protections available for whistle-blowers in each of the 27 countries that make up the EU.[12] Its findings are surprisingly counter-intuitive. Although the EU aspires to lead the world in human rights, individual liberties and justice, most of the EU countries lag behind international standards insofar as whistle-blowing is concerned.

Take basic human rights for example. The report states that: 'Most whistle-blower laws in the EU do not live up to the EU's Charter of Fundamental Rights, three provisions of which form the basis of whistle-blower protection: freedom of expression, protection from unjustified dismissal and a right to effective remedies.'

The report's main conclusion is shocking. Only four countries in the EU have existing legal frameworks for whistle-blower protection that are considered to be advanced: Luxembourg, Romania, Slovenia and the UK. Of the remainder, 16 countries (including France, Germany and Italy) have partial legal protections for employees who come forward to report wrongdoing. The remaining seven countries (Bulgaria, Finland, Greece, Lithuania, Portugal, Slovakia and Spain) have either very limited or no legal frameworks to protect whistle-blowers.

The UK: The Public Interest Disclosure Act (PIDA)

Introduction

The PIDA[13] was the first comprehensive whistle-blower law to be passed in the EU. Once the PIDA became law in July 1999, it was quickly established as an international benchmark and it inspired whistle-blower laws in many other countries including Australia, Ireland, Japan and South Korea. Amended as part of the Enterprise and Regulatory Reform Act 2013 to enhance whistle-blower protection, the PIDA is still widely considered to be the strongest such law in Europe and among the best in the world.

Overview of the PIDA

The PIDA was introduced to protect 'workers' making disclosures of malpractice by their employers or third parties, providing they reasonably believe it to be in the public interest to do so, and to allow them to claim compensation at an employment tribunal for any victimisation following such disclosure. The Act makes it unlawful for an employer to dismiss or subject a worker to a detriment for having made a 'protected disclosure' of information. The definition of workers is very broad and covers nearly all employees in the public, private and non-profit sectors, including contractors, agency staff and trainees.

The PIDA applies to workers blowing the whistle on a wide variety of wrongdoing: crime, civil offences (including negligence, breach of contract etc.), miscarriage of justice, danger to health and safety or the environment and the cover-up of any of these. It applies whether or not the information is confidential (so-called 'gagging' clauses in contracts of employment are deemed null and void if the disclosure is in the interests of the public), though breaches of the Official Secrets Act are not covered. The PIDA extends to malpractice occurring in the UK and any other country or territory. Employment law restrictions on minimum length of service and age do not apply.

Key aspects of the PIDA

Three aspects of the PIDA are particularly important:

- First, it introduces a stepped 'protected disclosure' regime. The Act encourages workers to blow the whistle internally to their employers by putting a low bar in place in terms of considering such internal disclosures to be protected. Disclosure to the employer is the first tier of the regime. Here, a disclosure in good faith made to the employer will be protected if the whistle-blower has a reasonable belief or a genuine suspicion that the malpractice has occurred, is occurring or is likely to occur. The second tier of disclosure is to a 'prescribed person', normally a regulatory body, and here there is the extra requirement that, in order to be protected, the information or allegation made by the whistle-blower is believed to be substantially true. The third tier of the regime looks at wider disclosure (for example, to the police, to politicians, to the media etc.) and here protection is only given when a number of detailed conditions are satisfied. These include a requirement that the worker does not make the disclosure for purposes of personal gain and a requirement that it is reasonable to make the disclosure in the circumstances.
- Second, the reverse burden of proof. The PIDA requires employers to prove that any action taken against a worker was not motivated by the fact that that worker was a whistle-blower. This burden of proof reversal has since become a critical international standard.

▪ Third, whistle-blowers are entitled to full compensation under the PIDA. Where the whistle-blower is victimised in breach of the Act, he or she can bring a claim to an employment tribunal for compensation. Awards are uncapped and are based on the losses suffered. Also, where an employee is sacked they may apply for an interim order to keep their job. In addition to actual financial losses, employees who have been retaliated against can also claim compensation for aggravated damages and injury to their feelings.

Comments

There is no doubt that the PIDA is a significant piece of legislation providing important legal protection for workers if they seek to blow the whistle.

It has also had significant implications for all employers. There are no requirements that organisations have to comply with the Act. Indeed, one of the striking features of the PIDA is that it does not compel employers to do anything at all. Lord Nolan praised the Act for 'so skilfully achieving the essential but delicate balance between the public interest and the interest of the employers'.

The PIDA does increase the risk for employers if whistle-blowing disclosures are not handled appropriately, however. As a result, it has been responsible for some important changes. One aspect of this was that it initiated a traditional procedural response – many organisations set up formal procedures to encourage, manage and control whistle-blowing for the first time after the Act became law in 1999.

Another aspect of change was at the cultural level. Cathy James had some interesting things to say about this during our interview:

> The Public Interest Disclosure Act doesn't require people to do anything, it doesn't have an obligation for any organisation to have a whistle-blowing policy, it does not require regulators to do anything either. But what it does is to give a route to compensation for the individual and where there is a stick organisations start to change their behaviour. That is where the cultural mechanism of the law I think is really important. It won't save people because what it is doing is looking back at when the damage has been done, but it will signal that society wants whistle-blowers to be protected.

The USA

Introduction

The USA has numerous specific whistle-blower protection laws and provisions in place at both the federal and state level covering a wide variety of topics. There also exists, particularly at federal level, legislation that seeks to encourage whistle-blowers to come forward by providing monetary awards for those whose claims are successful and result in recoveries for the authorities.

The key pieces of legislation

The key federal whistle-blower statutes in the USA include the following:

▪ **The Whistle-blower Protection Act 1989 (WPA).** The WPA protects federal government employees in the USA from retaliatory action for voluntarily disclosing information about dishonest or illegal activities occurring at a government organisation. The law prohibits a federal agency from taking action, or threatening to take action against an employee or applicant for disclosing information that he or she believes violated a law, compliance rules or other regulation. The disclosed information could include reports of mismanagement, wrongdoing, the waste of funds, an abuse of authority and/or a potential risk to public health or safety. The US Office of Special Counsel has special jurisdiction over allegations of federal whistle-blower retaliation and investigates federal whistle-blower complaints. In 2009 the Whistle-blower Protection Enhancement Act was brought in to strengthen the legislation.

■ **The False Claims Act**. This Act prohibits the submission of 'knowing' false claims to obtain federal funds. Whistle-blowers with evidence of fraud against government contracts and programmes may bring an action, known as a *qui tam* case, on behalf of the government in order to recover the stolen funds. In compensation for the risk and effort of filing a *qui tam* case the citizen whistle-blower may be awarded a portion of the funds recovered, typically between 15 and 25%.

■ **Sarbanes–Oxley Act 2002 (SOX)**. The SOX applies to publicly traded companies listed on a US stock exchange and requires them to enact whistle-blowing programmes. Specifically, it requires the audit committees of these companies to establish procedures for: the confidential and/or anonymous submission by employees of concerns regarding questionable accounting or auditing; and the receipt, retention and treatment of complaints received relating to accounting, internal accounting controls or auditing matters. Companies subject to the SOX that fail to meet these requirements may potentially face enforcement action from the Securities and Exchange Commission (SEC) and/or civil penalties.

■ **Dodd–Frank Wall Street Reform and Consumer Protection Act 2010 (Dodd–Frank)**. Dodd–Frank significantly increases the regulation of financial institutions in the USA with the goals of restoring public confidence in the financial system and avoiding future financial crises. It establishes an entirely new category of whistle-blower – those that give the SEC 'original information'. Under this programme, whistle-blowers are eligible to receive cash awards of 10 to 30% of the sanctions collected by the SEC arising from original information that they reported.

Comments: the use of incentives

The use of incentives to encourage reporting is one notable difference in approach between the authorities in the USA and those in the UK to whistle-blowers. The US approach recognises that blowing the whistle is often a tough and difficult choice to make, so the authorities are prepared to offer incentives to encourage bona fide whistle-blowers to come forward with their concerns. The UK continues to reject this approach. This was illustrated most recently in 2013 when the Whistle-blowing Commission, having discussed the American model, decided not to recommend the introduction of financial rewards or incentives. The Commission concluded that such rewards are not a substitute for legal protection. It did recognise, however, that other forms of reward or acknowledgement for whistle-blowers might be appropriate, such as recognition in the workplace through employment promotion.

 WHISTLE-BLOWING IN ACTION

Introduction

We have discussed confidential reporting largely in terms of the formalisation of process (the whistle-blowing hotline) in response to developing legislation and best practices around the world. But as with all aspects of business ethics the process, the control, the hardware as I have termed it through-out the book is not sufficient on its own to provide reasonable assurance. It must be combined with the appropriate culture and tone at the top. In the case of whistle-blowing, this short-circuits to directors and senior managers being committed to developing an open culture, where confidential disclosure is promoted, encouraged, acted upon and, in some way, recognised and rewarded.

I pull these ideas together in the 10 steps to an effective whistle-blowing process set out in the next section, but before we look at this, I want to illustrate how disclosures actually come about in practice because they are not always the result of a perfect process. To do so I will tap into real-life experience. As part of the research for this book I spoke to Louise, the Ethics Officer in the UK subsidiary company of a large international business. Louise did not want to be identified in the book, but she did give me some good insights into how hotlines work in practice and some of the challenges involved. But before we look at these, I want to say a little about my own experiences in this area.

Personal experience

Anonymous tip-offs

I had direct experience of whistle-blowing disclosures myself during the 1990s and early years of this century, when I was working as a forensic accountant. The disclosures were in many ways more rudimentary back then, with fewer formal hotlines in place. Instead, one typical means of commu-nication was via an anonymous letter, often pushed under the chairman's door after work. I inves-tigated a number of such anonymous disclosures, none was straightforward and the fact that the identity of the whistle-blower was unknown was often an obstacle to progress. The importance of securing confidential, as opposed to anonymous, disclosures is discussed below because this is a crucial element in making the whistle-blowing process as effective as possible.

Face-to-face disclosure

Another method of tip-off that I became familiar with was face-to-face disclosure. Again, as we will see, this idea of workers simply telling someone (normally their line manager) about their concerns remains a very important component of whistle-blowing and one that is sometimes overlooked in the debate about hotlines. One such disclosure made a particular impression on me because it came about in unusual circumstances and was totally unexpected. It was made by a manager who I had previously investigated following an anonymous tip-off made by someone about certain of his own activities! However unexpected, the case shows very well how important whistle-blowing can be in the detection of internal fraud and illegal practices.

Example

These are my recollections of that meeting.

> It is May 2000 and I am sitting in a conference room in the London head office of one of the largest companies in the UK. It has been a difficult meeting, one of those high pressure situa-tions that come with the job from time to time. Sitting alongside me is the company's director of human resources. Opposite us on the other side of the table is one of the company's area manag-ers – or to be more precise, one of the company's ex-area managers as the director of human resources has just fired him. Before he did that I spent 30 minutes going through the results

of my investigation into the ex-manager's activities following an anonymous tip-off alleging various forms of misconduct: complaints of sexual harassment and inappropriate workplace behaviour; the submitting of inflated expense claims; the use of company property for private purposes; and alcohol misuse. Working with the company's internal auditors, I found evidence to substantiate most of these allegations – not all of them, but sufficient for these purposes. The man is no longer with the company.

My method throughout the interview has been pure text book. I have simply presented each piece of evidence that we found to the ex-manager during the 30 minutes of discussion, going through each component part in a calm, methodical, non-judgemental manner. After some initial objections, he has listened to what I have had to say and remained silent, by and large. At the end of my review, the director of human resources has told him that in his opinion all this added up to a track record of unacceptable behaviour that constitutes gross misconduct. A deal is quickly done, much to my frustration because I feel that we have more than enough evidence to justify a straight dismissal without the need for any deal. The ex-manager agrees to leave the company without recourse to any tribunal or legal process, in return for which he is to receive a sum of around £40,000 by way of a 'compromise agreement' together with a 'clean' reference.

The formal meeting is now over and I begin to clear away my papers. I start to become aware that the ex-manager is staring straight at me; he seems to be concentrating hard. Clearly he has some-thing on his mind. He then begins to speak – he is not angry any more but speaks in a very flat, matter of fact tone of voice: 'Steve, I have to tell you that I don't think that I've done anything terrible here and yet I've just lost my job. It's clear from everything that you have said that you think I've behaved very badly. Maybe I have. But all this talk about fraud and abuse – well, you don't know the half of it, old son. If you want to get serious about what goes on in this company I can tell you that you have been looking in the wrong place and at the wrong man. You should take a look at Mr "X" and what he and his gang have been up to in Northampton. Some of that stuff will make your eyes water. Then come back and talk to me about fraud and abuse.'

Now, the name Mr 'X' meant nothing to me at the time, I had never heard him mentioned before. However, I distinctly remember that there was just something about the way that the ex-manager came out with this, the way that he was looking at me at the time that made the hairs on the back of my neck stand up. Immediately, I had a very strong gut feeling that there was real substance to the ex-manager's allegation, that it was not simply a malicious reaction to his sacking.

Subsequent actions and conclusion

And so it transpired. Subsequently, I headed up a team that carried out an in-depth review into the activities of Mr 'X' and his department – an investigation that was to last for almost two years in total. Mr 'X' turned out to be the head of the group's property team and we uncovered evidence that he had been receiving backhanders from suppliers in return for awarding those suppliers both additional contracts (on favourable terms) and repeat business. The outcome of the investigation was that Mr 'X' and two of his team were dismissed and that my client was able to recover from the insurers almost all of the £4.8 million that we calculated had been lost originally as a result of the fraud.

It is impossible to say how much longer Mr 'X' would have been able to continue his corrupt activities undetected. He was not under any suspicion at the time so it is likely that the tip-off served to reduce that time significantly.

The ethics officer

Introduction

I spoke to Louise in late 2013 whilst writing this book. She is the in-house lawyer and Ethics Officer of the UK subsidiary of a large global operation. Their whistle-blowing policy was developed as part of a broader initiative around business ethics. The UKBA had also provided a catalyst as the company wanted to be able to prove that they had adequate procedures in place against the new offence under the Act of failing to prevent bribery.

Louise developed the whistle-blowing policy herself, which was then signed off by the board before being rolled out in the training programme. This happened in 2011, so the policy had been in place for two years when our discussion took place.

Discussion extracts

I asked Louise what the reaction of the staff had been to the training sessions in business ethics, and this is her reply:

> *I think it was very mixed and it tended to be the people who didn't like it who were obviously most vocal in the course of our training sessions. I think people were concerned about the creation of a feeling of discomfort between individuals ... that people might be sneaking behind their back, making complaints on the whistle-blowing hotline – you know, your neighbour sitting next to you makes a complaint on the whistle-blowing hotline.*

> *I think there was also concern as to the reporting route in that in our policy we have it that if someone wants to blow the whistle they need to report it to the ethics officer, or the HR manager, or the MD and I think there was concern that the line manager should be involved somewhere along the line in the process I remember there was also talk about if someone had a concern about something shouldn't they go and chat with their line manager first. If their line manager was involved shouldn't they go and confront their line manager first. So, there was quite a lot of lengthy and sometimes quite heated debate on how to approach it.*

> *We did try and say to these people that reporting to the ethics officer or HR manager or MD is the safest route. If, say your line manager was indeed involved, and then you go and talk to them about it you could get yourself implicated in the whole process. So it's a much cleaner route if you follow the reporting procedure as set out in the policy.*

Picking up her point about the various different reporting routes for whistle-blowing disclosures being built into the policy, I then asked Louise if this had been successful in allaying employees' fears about using the hotline. This was her reply:

> *In all honesty I don't think it does entirely work. I think for it to be entirely successful ... I mean we have an ethics hotline, a phone number and we also have an ethics email address, neither of which has ever been used and I think there are concerns over confidentiality. I think one option we did look into was having an external body hosting a confidential email service. We are not really big enough to do that or bear the cost of that. I think for it to be a truly successful reporting line it really needs to do that confidentially.*

> *The issues that have come up have not been reported by the email line or the hotline. They have been either reported to a line manager who has then spoken to me about it or an individual has*

spoken to me directly. So I guess it is working to that extent but there have not been a tremendous number of reports. Whether you would expect more I don't know. Whether there are things out there that aren't being reported – I can't say.

There is an important point here – in two years, neither the hotline number nor the ethics email address had ever been used. So, I asked Louise two questions about why she thought this was the case – first, was it because of a lack of awareness of the policy and second, was it because, although people knew about it, they did not trust the assurances of confidentiality built into the policy?

This was her reply to my first question:

I don't think that they were aware last year. I think that obviously we publicised all of our policies and required people to acknowledge that they had read them, but I don't think that all of them actually did, I think some ticked the box at the bottom without reading them. We have recently rolled out an online assessment so they are required to answer questions at the end of the train-ing module, so whether going through that they are more aware of the policies ... I would like to think that they are, time will tell.

And obviously they have now been trained in the policies. We have the physical training courses where we talk about whistle-blowing policies. There is a tick to say they have read them and now they have this online course. I worry that it still mainly hasn't sunk in so we will have to see. But what more you can do I'm not sure. I mean this is a process; the annual assessment is a process which we will repeat every year. People are already complaining that this is far too much but if it is not being driven home should we be doing it more despite the complaints, do we do something every quarter, every six months, how do you drive it home, that I'm not entirely sure about.

Louise answered my second question as follows:

I think it's this whole area of confidentiality, it is very tricky. We do allow anonymous reporting. We also say that if you do report anonymously there may be very little we can do about it as we can't get all the details we need from you. Also you may not be protected by the policy if we don't know who you are. But then obviously if they do report confidentially we may have to speak to others in the business, to ascertain exactly what happened so inevitably more people are going to have to be involved and I think that concerns people. So how you get round that; as I said, perhaps it would put people's minds more at rest if they were reporting to a service provider, so using someone who is more independent and they don't know, but inevitably at some point people in the organisation will need to get involved.

I think that some people are worried about losing their jobs to be honest. I think one of the inci-dences where someone made a report, it was about a contractor who wasn't particularly senior and I don't think there was a concern there. Whereas, compare that with a report concerning someone who is more senior in the organisation – and there was an incidence of that as well – and that puts the reporter in a very awkward position because they are reporting against someone very high up in the organisation, with more influence.

Comments

The company that Louise works for has introduced new policies and this is a good illustration of the basic point with new processes of the period of time that it can take for these to become accepted by all managers and staff. There is often resistance to any organisational change. Nevertheless, her comments do show that whistle-blowing remains controversial in certain respects, with a fear of reprisals remaining a formidable obstacle to assurance around compliance. Louise remains optimistic about the future, however – the processes in her organisation are improving and she remains hopeful that there will be increasing compliance and commitment to them over time.

 ## THE 10 STEPS

How to implement an effective whistle-blowing process

Set out below is a summary of the key components of successful whistle-blowing programmes that I have witnessed from my own experience. Taken together, I believe that they constitute an effective framework for confidential reporting. They comprise a good practical guide for directors and senior managers, both those looking for advice on how to set up a new hotline and those looking for a benchmark against which to measure the effectiveness of an existing policy and hotline.

I call these the 10 steps to an effective whistle-blowing process. Each step is described below.

Step 1: establish the baseline

A whistle-blower is a person who raises a concern about wrongdoing in terms of either an illegal act or a dangerous activity within an organisation that they have become aware of through their work. Whistle-blowing should be clearly differentiated from a personal complaint or grievance therefore. It is important that the two have separate reporting mechanisms. Every organisation should have a separate and distinct grievance procedure in place. Normally the reporting line for grievances is to someone in the HR department, and these procedures afford employees the prospect of redress if their employment rights have been infringed or if they have been subjected to inappropriate workplace behaviour such as bullying, discrimination, sexual harassment and so on.

Step 2: review the whistle-blowing policy

Organisations that wish to promote effective whistle-blowing need a policy around which to work. This will include a working definition together with the mechanics of how the policy will work in practice. But there are perhaps two key points that need to be addressed and emphasised in the whistle-blowing policy document, as follows:

▪ The first is that the policy should place whistle-blowing in its proper context as a positive measure that will assist in enabling workers to conduct business honestly and with integrity at all times. A good number of employees are likely to have some negative feelings both about the word whistle-blowing and also about the concept of blowing the whistle on others – no one likes to think of themselves as a 'snitch'. It is important, therefore, that there is a consistently positive message coming from the top of the organisation. The policy should emphasise this point. Whistle-blowing is a key element in safeguarding the organisation's integrity: it applies to illegal and corrupt practices, to health and safety failures, to environmental damage, to negligence etc. It is aimed at enhancing transparency and underpinning the organisation's system for combating all illegal activities that might damage its operations and reputation. The policy should be suitably drafted and signed off by the board.

■ The second point is equally important – the policy needs to address workers' concerns and provide them with reassurance. Directors and senior managers must ensure that the policy covers a number of critical areas concerning whistle-blowing: that workers can raise any matters of genuine concern without fear of reprisals; that they can do so on a confidential basis, which means that their identity will be protected if they so wish; that all reports will be taken seriously and the matters raised will be investigated appropriately; and that they will be given feedback periodically on the progress of the investigation. All of these points need to be clearly stated in the policy.

Step 3: scope of the policy

The policy should of course apply to all managers and employees within the organisation. Best practice suggests that the scope could be extended with advantage to include anyone performing services for or on behalf of the organisation (for example, to agents, brokers, consultants, contractors, etc.) and also to other stakeholders (in particular to customers and suppliers). This inclusive approach, where adopted, has been shown to work well in the area of fraud detection. Of course, if it is to be effective then the policy needs to be communicated both within the organisation and outside of it.

Step 4: reporting obligations

The policy should address the question of what is expected of managers and employees should they become concerned about something that they observe is happening in the workplace. Generally, concerns should be reported to nominated officers (see below) as soon as possible – speed of disclosure is important and the policy might provide for a very prompt response time such as 'within 24 hours'. There are two other important points to make here:

■ First, in my opinion whistle-blowing is most effective when managers and employees are required to report a concern (as defined in the policy) to a nominated officer. In other words, blowing the whistle becomes a duty rather than a voluntary act and this duty should be set out clearly in the whistle-blowing policy. Not everyone agrees with this stance, for example many public sector bodies in the UK are concerned that making disclosure of concerns a duty of workers will lead to related problems such as over-reporting and scapegoating.
■ The second point is that this requirement or duty should be to report not only actual incidents but also suspicions. In my experience, the reporting of suspicions is a concept that many people working within organisations feel less than comfortable with. Managers and staff are often reluctant to report their true suspicions without first obtaining 'proof', so organisations need to make it clear that they value any concerns reported in good faith, even when the employee is uncertain. In reality it is often extremely difficult to obtain proof in such areas as fraud and corruption, even for trained investigators. The duty of the employee should be to report their suspicions, which can then be properly investigated by the people with the required training and experience to do so.

It is also worth repeating here that it should always be possible to raise concerns both orally by calling a dedicated telephone number (as is implied by the term 'hotline') or in writing using a web-based portal or by speaking directly to one of the individuals nominated for these purposes in the policy.

Step 5: reporting lines

It is very important that the organisation establishes a number of alternative reporting channels in order to facilitate disclosure. The most traditional route for such a disclosure would be to the employee's line manager. Many experienced professionals in this area, especially those working in the public sector, would say that it is important that the line manager is one of the reporting options available to a whistle-blower. I am not so sure myself. In my experience, workers do not always feel comfortable discussing concerns with their direct line managers in situations of possible illegality or negligence – and sometimes it is the line manager who is the source of the problem. The line manager could be retained as an option but for me, personally, I would much prefer to see the reporting line going elsewhere, to someone in the organisation who is in a senior and trusted position – for example, the ethics officer, or the head of internal audit or the company secretary. As an alternative (and certainly in extreme cases) the organisation's chairman or the CEO could be contacted. Also, it is important to recognise that some workers are likely to be uncomfortable with the prospect of talking to anyone internally in the first instance. So, it is always helpful to have an external point of contact also, in addition to the various internal reporting lines. As an example, in the UK many organisations take out support packages with Public Concern at Work, the whistle-blowing charity. If any of the managers or staff in such an organisation is unsure whether or how to raise a concern or alternatively they want some confidential advice, then they can contact PCaW either by telephone or by email.

Step 6: confidentiality and/or anonymity

Ideally, whistle-blowing hotlines should aim to accommodate both confidential and anonymous reporting. There is an important difference between the two, however, and the policy should make this clear. A fundamental aspect of effective whistle-blowing is that people are confident that they can raise concerns on a confidential basis – in other words that their identity, while known to the ethics officer and those investigating the report, for example, will not be made public elsewhere.

This is a totally different concept to anonymous reporting, whereby the whistle-blower simply reports a concern, either on the hotline or in writing, but withholds all details of his or her identity. It is much more difficult to follow up and investigate anonymous tip-offs simply because there is no possibility of obtaining additional information after the initial report has been made. The whistle-blowing policy should make it clear that, while anonymous reporting is catered for, the organisation cannot guarantee to investigate all anonymous allegations. Proper investigation may prove impossible if the investigator cannot obtain sufficient information or ascertain whether the disclosure was made in good faith.

It is always preferable for whistle-blowers to reveal their identity because only then is the organisation in a position to take measures to preserve and protect their confidentiality. Finally on this point, the policy should state that all whistle-blowers will be expected themselves to keep the fact that they have raised a concern confidential, together with the nature of the concern and the identity of those involved.

Step 7: protection for 'good faith' whistle-blowers

All organisations seeking to have an effective whistle-blowing mechanism in place must emphasise that anyone who reports incidents in good faith under the policy will be protected from dismissal or any form of disciplinary action, retaliation or victimisation. Also, no manager or member of staff should be able to use their position to prevent a whistle-blowing disclosure from taking place. The phrase 'good faith whistle-blower' should be taken to mean in this context that the employee concerned reasonably believes the transmitted information to be true. It is to be contrasted with disclosures that are made maliciously, in bad faith or with a view to gain personally from the disclosure. This can sometimes happen in practice and it is important to realise that whistle-blowing is not a panacea – it is a mechanism that can be abused by 'bad faith' whistle-blowers to settle personal scores or to gain an advantage in an improper way. It should be stated in the policy that the organisation offers no protection to bad faith whistle-blowers, who may be subject to disciplinary action subsequently.

Step 8: raising awareness

It is an obvious thing to say but, in order to be effective, people need to know that the whistle-blowing hotline exists. Sometimes organisations do very little to publicise this control and to raise awareness of it. This is a mistake that can be avoided relatively easily with a few simple processes. In addition to receiving copies of the policy, employees should learn about the hotline as part of their initial induction training programme, and thereafter there should be periodic reminders on notice boards and on screensavers and so on. There should also be specific training sessions aimed at showing how the mechanics of the process work in practice and also to answer any questions or concerns that employees might have.

It is important that senior managers are seen to take part fully in the whistle-blowing training process as this will serve not only to raise awareness but also to emphasise its importance. Senior managers should be looking to be proactive here. In my experience I have always found it to be very helpful when a member of the top management team speaks directly to the other delegates taking part in the training about the importance of the whistle-blowing process. When the training is a conventional, face-to-face session, this can be done easily by means of a short presentation at the start of the day. When the training is computer-based, the same effect can be achieved by inserting a short (two or three minute) video presentation, featuring the chairman or the CEO speaking directly into the camera about the importance of this training module.

Publicity of the hotline should be extended outside the organisation also if maximum benefit from the control is to be achieved.

Step 9: the investigation process

It is of fundamental importance that if whistle-blowing is to remain credible within an organisation, all disclosures made are followed up quickly and are properly investigated. There are two crucial aspects to this: first, the investigation process itself and second, how the whistle-blower is treated as the investigation progresses.

- ▪ In terms of the process, all organisations should follow the best practice principles of any investigation when they handle a whistle-blowing disclosure – namely that they should be committed to investigating the matter fully, fairly, quickly and confidentially. The length, nature and scope of the investigation will depend on the subject matter of the disclosure. It may be possible to resolve the concerns raised by some form of internal review. Alternatively, if the allegation is one of serious fraud, corruption or other illegality then a full investigation might be required, perhaps to be carried out by third-party forensic accountants, for example. The individual with responsibility for receiving whistle-blowing reports (for example, the ethics officer) will normally make the decision on the format of the investigation and will arrange, coordinate and oversee the investigation process. Exceptionally, there might be matters that cannot be dealt with through internal channels. In these cases, external authorities will need to be notified and become involved either during or after the investigation. Finally, it is important to make clear that, as an integral part of an effective investigation process, the basic rights of any individual implicated in a whistle-blowing disclosure will always be respected. These include the right to receive a fair hearing.

- It is very important that in cases where the identity of the whistle-blower is known that he or she is kept informed of progress and is not simply ignored once they have been interviewed and all the information concerning the disclosure has been obtained. This is crucial, because without any feedback thereafter the whistle-blower may well assume that nothing is happening, that the organisation is not really committed to stamping out harmful or illegal practices (despite what the policy might say or the messages included in the training), become disillusioned and feel that the only recourse left is to report his or her concerns externally, to the authorities or the regulator or the media. So, although investigations often take a long time to complete properly and it might sometimes appear to be a waste of time to contact the whistle-blower if nothing much has happened (as there will be nothing much to say), it is always important to keep the whistle-blower informed and abreast of progress, even if it is only to say that the investigation is still ongoing.

Step 10: reporting results

The person who oversees the whistle-blowing process (for example, the ethics officer) should be responsible for reporting on the progress of individual investigations to the audit committee or to another nominated body. Also, the organisation should ensure that internal reports are produced periodically on the outcomes from the whistle-blowing process and are publicised internally. Of course, any such report will need to be general in nature and should not refer in any detail to specific cases, but managers and employees alike will be interested to read these reports. The benefit to the organisation from doing this is potentially significant – as always, confidence in the process is likely to be increased through transparency.

 ## WORKSHOP CONCLUSION

Closing

By way of concluding on the 10 steps, I say that the concept of the whistle-blowing hotline is another classic example of the twin-track approach that we have discussed throughout the ethics project. There are various hardware elements, for example the policy itself, the mechanics of the hotline and/or the web-based portal and the reporting procedures to a number of nominated individuals. These are all necessary but they are not sufficient for assurance without the crucial software of training, management commitment and consistent decision-making that embed the hardware components into organisational culture and make them stick.

I have a request to make of the team. As this is the last workshop, I ask the team if it would be acceptable for me to write up the key takeaways on the flipchart today myself, rather than simply being an observer as in the other workshops. Everyone is amused at this and Rachel Gordon, the Chairman, says that she will need to check first to make sure that she will be able to decipher my handwriting! But the request is quickly acceded to.

I have some suggestions to make – I am going to encourage them to look at the current weaknesses of their whistle-blowing process as an opportunity. In order to do this I say that we need to focus on the software elements – they can benchmark their existing hardware of policies and procedures against the relevant elements in the 10-step plan.

So, now leading the discussion, I find myself writing the following five points on the flipchart:

Key takeaways

✓ **Re-brand the reporting line**. I say that we have seen how controversial the word 'whistle-blowing' can sometimes be, even with less prejudice today than in the past. As a suggestion, I remind everybody of the way that guidance notes for the UKBA referred to confidential reporting mechanisms. Rachel quickly nods her head: 'Yes, the phrase used there was speak-up.' So, could Stronach make use of the same phrase? Rachel likes this idea and thinks that this simple change will send important signals. She also thinks that it will be helpful in encouraging a more open culture in future. The other team members are enthusiastic too – it seems that this recommendation is agreed.

✓ **Communicate the new speak-up programme**. The board should kick-start this whole process by reviewing and then issuing the new policy to everybody, accompanied by appropriate messaging. This means ongoing publicity on notice boards, screensavers and so forth and also in training programmes. David Hurley, the HR Manager, is quick to say that he will include 'speak up' in his re-vamped ethics training modules and also in induction training.

✓ **Consider incentivising or rewarding whistle-blowers**. This will send the clearest signal to employees that the new speak-up programme is valued by directors and managers. It might be the difference between their people coming forward with concerns and deciding not to do so. It will also help to promote trust in the programme, providing always that those at the top take decisions consistently in line with the policy. One possible outcome may well be more disclosures and these will need to be properly investigated of course (see below). I remind the team that incentives do not have to take the form of cash; they could be promotions or recognition in some other way. The team is clearly interested in this idea but it is a more controversial recommendation for them. No decision is reached, simply a commitment to consider it further in the future.

✓ **Direct internal audit to review the effectiveness of the new programme**. A regular review of the programme, once it is established, will help to provide the board with assurance that it is operating as intended. Everyone agrees with this and Malcolm Mainwaring, the Group Finance Director, agrees to speak to the head of internal audit and the chairman of the audit committee about this in the near future

✓ **Commit to a proper investigation of all disclosures**. As we have seen, people who blow the whistle (or who are thinking about blowing the whistle) need to have a sense that their disclosures will mean something and that their organisation will take action as a result – if not, they may decide to take their disclosures to an external third party. Important components needed to instil confidence here are: a professional investigation process; keeping the whistle-blower informed of progress periodically during the investigation; reporting the results of each investigation to senior management; and appropriate communication of the corrective actions taken in response to the disclosures received. The team support this proposal.

Next workshop

With the last of the takeaway points noted down, the room falls quiet for a moment. There is no next workshop to arrange because this is the final one in the series. The Group's CEO, John Holt, then speaks and directs thanks and some kind words towards myself, both on behalf of the team and from him personally – he admits that he had been more than a little sceptical about the value of the ethics project when Rachel had first proposed it to him, but he is very pleased with the way that it has all turned out. Malcolm and David echo the words of thanks and I am invited back for lunch in the near future.

Rachel and I now shake hands, John, Malcolm and David all having left the boardroom. Rachel is looking through her diary – she is trying to find a convenient date when we can get together for a de-briefing session. She suggests a date in approximately four weeks' time – we both smile. Given the rhythms of the project over the last 10 months or so, this should certainly be possible. I will get back to her.

Reflections

And so the project is complete.

As I walk out of the Stronach Group's headquarters onto Berkeley Square for one last time, I reflect on what an excellent project it has turned out to be. Having the participation and support of Rachel and John, Chairman and CEO respectively, throughout the whole process was an added bonus and a clear example to me of tone at the top in action. Malcolm and David both contributed very well to the project too. Malcolm was a real surprise to me, I had mis-judged him when we first met, while it was a pleasure to watch David grow in confidence and performance as the project progressed.

I feel a quiet sense of satisfaction as I make my way across the Square – all in all, it is a job well done. I can't help smiling as I wonder what I am going to do with all my free time now. Just then I notice my BlackBerry flashing at me. I have a message from Veronica, how interesting – I have not spoken to her in ages. The message is quite brief: How am I; something new has come up; she wants to talk, what is my availability like for later in the week?

Now, what is this all about I wonder?

Epilogue

 ANOTHER SURPRISE

It is 8.30 in the morning and I am sitting in the chairman's office on the top floor of an office block with excellent views over Berkeley Square in central London. I am drinking coffee and listening as Rachel Gordon tells me what she wants to cover in our meeting today. I also have a strong feeling of déjà vu, and when I mention this to Rachel we both laugh.

This is the first time that Rachel and I have met since the Stronach Group ethics project ended almost six months ago now. We have both been busy and I have been travelling abroad so it is very good to see her. However, this not a social call – when Rachel rang me two days ago she said that she has something that she wants to talk through with me.

She has given me no hint so far as to what it might be, although she does have some news concerning David Hurley. Rachel and John Holt, the CEO, had been impressed with David's performance both as part of the team working on the ethics project and subsequently when implementing a number of the recommendations coming out of the project. Consequently, David has been promoted – he is now Director of Personnel. It is not a main board position but it carries a significant salary rise and it is a fair reflection of his ability, hard work and commitment. I am genuinely delighted and say so – I must try to see David when the meeting with Rachel finishes so that I can congratulate him in person.

Although I have not seen Rachel since the project ended we have kept in touch by email. I have also exchanged a number of emails with Malcolm Mainwaring, the Group Finance Director. So I do know that good progress has been made at the Stronach Group in implementing some at least of the 40 plus key takeaways coming out of the ethics project. From what I can gather some important building blocks are now in place thereby providing solid foundations for the application of the twin-track approach that I advocated throughout the project. For example:

- The new non-executive director, Lesley Gowing, has made a positive contribution so far, with the result that John and Malcolm are facing more scrutiny and challenge of their plans and strategies than previously, not only from Lesley but from the other non-executives too.
- Rachel appointed a consultancy to carry out a board performance review, which has been completed. It was generally well received, with all the directors taking part. The results are expected shortly.
- John has led a review of the Group's risk management processes, with the board now focusing on the principal risks and other areas of concern identified during the project (crisis management, due diligence, cyber security and compliance with the UKBA) all being worked on.
- Malcolm has just appointed a compliance officer and she will start work next month.
- David has made good progress on his training and development agenda, with a new ethics module now designed and ready for roll-out. The module contains a presentation from Rachel and

a number of video sketches to highlight the key points. It also makes use of Cloud technology so that, for the first time, the overseas staff will be included in the training – they will be able to access and work through the module on their mobile phones.

▪ The whistle-blowing policy and supporting procedures have been reviewed and re-designed to bring them into line with my 10-step plan as outlined in the final workshop.

No doubt there have been other developments too, but I don't think that Rachel has asked me to meet her simply to go through any of these. She is now starting to get to the point because she asks me how my diary is looking over the next few months. I reply that have some lecturing assignments but otherwise I do have some time available – what does she have in mind?

Rather than answer directly, she asks what my reaction would be if I heard a board of directors described in the following way: 'charming people; they seem to get on well together; experienced and knowledgeable; little challenge or scrutiny; perfunctory board appraisals; an absence of diversity'. I am frowning now, this description sounds very familiar. Then I remember: 'I would say that you are describing the Stronach Group board. That was exactly how I remember you described the board to me during our first meeting here.' Rachel smiles and then adds: 'Well, the old Stronach board anyway – we are very different now! But you are right, well remembered!'

She then tells me that Stronach is about to make a strategic acquisition – in fact John is with the Group's city advisors preparing to make the announcement as we speak. Rachel goes on to say that I am not unfamiliar with the target company. Do I remember the various options for a strategic acquisition that the Stronach Group was considering when the ethics project first began? Well, the third of the options on the table then was the chance to acquire a rival engineering group in the UK. At the time, John was not enthusiastic because of the flat UK economy and the fact that the Stronach board had recently decided to change the strategic balance of the Group so that in future more of its work would come from contracts overseas. Well, circumstances have changed. Although the intention to have a higher proportion of business overseas in the future still remains, the UK economy is now picking up whilst the Eurozone remains stalled. The opportunity to acquire the rival has recently re-surfaced and this time John wants to go ahead – after some thorough questioning, the board agreed and ratified the decision.

Rachel says that the directors and senior managers are all agreed that the new company will be an excellent fit for the Stronach Group operationally. There is a concern about the cultural fit, however. She then smiles and says that the description of the board of directors that she had given me earlier relates in fact to her impression of the board of the target company. She feels that it is actually similar in many ways to how the old Stronach Group board used to be before all the changes of the last 18 months – the board and its performance have been transformed during that time.

So, John and Rachel have been thinking about this and are in agreement. They have a proposal for me. How would I like to facilitate another project, similar to the ethics project, but this time working with a team from the new company and reporting back to her and John on progress? They have in mind the same outline for the new project in terms of template and timescale to last time, but of course it will be up to me and the new project team to agree the details. What do I think?

I am smiling now – I can only conclude that Rachel and the Stronach Group continue to be full of surprises. I have no difficulty in accepting the offer: 'Yes, great, thank you. When do we start?'

Notes

PROLOGUE

1. There have been many books and articles written about the Enron scandal. In my view, one of the most comprehensive and authoritative accounts is provided by: McLean, B. and Elkind, P., *The Smartest Guys in the Room: the Amazing Rise and Scandalous Fall of Enron* (Portfolio 2003). There is also an insightful documentary film based on the book: 'Enron: The Smartest Guys in the Room' (2005) directed by Alex Gibney.
2. Enron: 'Annual Report 1999: Our Values' (2000).
3. YouTube: Enron – Vision and Values 1998 (VHS DUB).
4. www.edelman.com/2012-edelman-trust-barometer.
5. www.barclays.com/content/dam/Transform/antony-jenkins-speech.pdf.

CHAPTER 1

1. Collinsworth, E., *The Tao of Improving Your Likability: The Personal Guide to Effective Etiquette in Today's Global Business World* (Xiron Books Co., Ltd 2012).
2. Based on research conducted by the Association of Certified Fraud Examiners. See Giles, S., *Managing Fraud Risk: A Practical Guide for Directors and Managers* (John Wiley & Sons Ltd 2012) pp. 70–71.
3. See the work of Gallup, Inc. (www.gallup.com) on employee engagement, in particular the Q^{12} indicator. For example, *State of the American Workforce: Employee Engagement Insights for U.S. Business Leaders* (Gallup Inc. 2013).
4. Based on the research of Dr Donald Cressey, Richard Hollinger, John Clark and others. See Giles, S., *Managing Fraud Risk: A Practical Guide for Directors and Managers* (John Wiley & Sons Ltd 2012) pp. 71–78.

CHAPTER 2

1. It was Peter Hanlon, senior executive at the Westpac banking group in Australia, who introduced me to the idea of ethical hardware and ethical software during our interview for this book – see Chapter 6 for detailed extracts from this interview.
2. www.fca.org.uk.
3. www.icaew.com/media/instilling-integrity-in-organisations.pdf.
4. Milton Friedman's article: 'The Social Responsibility of Business is to Increase its Profits' was published in *The New York Times Magazine* in September 1970. *Delivering Good Governance in Local Government: Framework* (CIPFA 2007).

5. www.legislation.gov.uk/ukpga/2006.

6. Trevino, L. and Nelson, K., *Managing Business Ethics: Straight Talk About How To Do It Right* (John Wiley & Sons Ltd 2011).

7. Ibid. p. 17.

8. Ibid. p. 19.

9. Much has been written about the Edward Snowden case. For a good summary of events and insights into Mr Snowden's actions see Harding, L., *The Snowden Files: The Inside Story of the World's Most Wanted Man* (Guardian Books 2014).

10. www.ibe.org.uk.

11. YouTube: Enron – Vision and Values 1998 (VHS DUB).

12. www.fca.org.uk/about/what/regulating/principles-for-business.

13. www.ge.com/files_citizenship/pdf/TheSpirit&TheLetter.pdf.

14. Dietz, G. and Gillespie, N., *The Recovery of Trust: Case Studies of Organisational Failures and Trust Repair* (Institute of Business Ethics 2012).

15. See Smith, C. and Quirk, M., 'From Grace to Disgrace: the Rise and Fall of Arthur Andersen' (*Journal of Business Ethics Education* 1 (1): 2004) pp. 91–130 for a comprehensive summary of the Andersen/Enron case.

16. For a good summary of the JP Morgan legal settlement position at the time, see the BBC article at www.bbc.co.uk/news/business-25009683.

17. Foot, P., 'The Problem of Abortion and the Doctrine of the Double Effect' (*Oxford Review* 5: 1967), pp. 5–15.

18. Thomson, J., 'Killing, Letting Die and the Trolley Problem' (*The Monist* 59 (2): 1976) pp. 204–214.

CHAPTER 3

1. See report headed 'Nearly a year on, one in four worry that Bribery Act is affecting UK competitiveness' at www.ey.com>Home>Newsroom>Newsreleases (cached).

2. www.bbc.co.uk/news/world-europe-25637710.

3. www.bbc.co.uk/news/world-asia-china-29892732: there were many articles covering the anti-corruption drive of authorities in China during 2014 – this is a later article by the BBC that provides a good summary.

4. www.bbc.co.uk/news/world-europe-25635858.

5. www.bbc.co.uk/news/world-asia-india-25663763.

6. Transparency International (www.transparency.org).

7. Corruption Perceptions Index (www.transparency.org/research/cpi/overview).

8. The Galleon case attracted widespread media interest, especially in the USA. See the *New York Times* commentary and archival information at http://topics.nytimes.com/top/reference/timestopics/people/r/raj_rajaratnam/index.html for a good summary of the case.

9. www.bbc.co.uk/news/business-25490876.

10. Foreign Corrupt Practices Act (www.justice.gov/criminal/fraud/fcpa).

11. A copy of the United Nations Convention Against Corruption may be accessed on the website of the United Nations Office on Drugs and Crime (www.unodc.org/documents/treaties/UNCAC/.../08-50026_E.pdf).

12. www.siemens.com.

13. Many articles and reports have been written about the Siemens scandal. For comprehensive and insightful coverage, refer to the following article: Schubert, S. and Miller, C., 'At Siemens Bribery Was Just a Line Item' (*The New York Times* 20 December 2008).

14. For details of the case against Siemens and details of the settlement reached with the US Securities and Exchange Commission see www.sec.gov/spotlight/fcpa/fcpa-cases.shtml.

15. www.nytimes.com/2008/12/16/business/worldbusiness/16siemens.html.

16. Schubert, S. and Miller, C., 'At Siemens Bribery Was Just a Line Item' (*The New York Times* 20 December 2008).

17. Ibid.

18. Ibid.

19. Web.worldbank.org/News

20. Mr Loscher's interview was 'Our Management Culture Failed' (*Der Spiegel Magazine* December 12 2007).

21. www.justice.gov/archive/opa/pr/2008/December/08-opa-1112.html.

22. The Bribery Act 2010 (www.legislation.gov.uk/ukpga/2010/23/contents).

23. www.bbc.co.uk/news/uk-england-london-15689869.

24. www.justice.gov.uk/downloads/legislation/bribery-act-2010-guidance.pdf.

25. www.justice.gov.uk/.../legislation/bribery-act-2010-quick-start-guide.pdf.

26. www.sfo.gov.uk>Our-views>Director's-speeches>Speeches 2013.

CHAPTER 4

1. refspace.com/quotes/Warren_Buffet/Q1057.

2. Much has been written about Mr Goodwin's tenure as CEO of RBS. See the following for a comprehensive account: Martin, I., *Making It Happen: Fred Goodwin, RBS and the Men Who Blew up the British Economy* (Simon & Schuster UK Ltd 2013).

3. www.bbc.co.uk/news/uk-politics-16821650.

4. www.bbc.co.uk/news/world-europe-14833259.

5. www.bbc.co.uk/news/business-29506035.

6. There has been extensive media coverage of the BP oil spill and deaths arising from the Macondo well blow-out, as well as a report from the US National Commission investigating the tragedy. See the in-depth archive at the *Financial Times* for a good summary: www.ft.com/indepth/bp-oil-spill.

7. See Smith, C. and Quirk, M., 'From Grace to Disgrace: the Rise and Fall of Arthur Andersen' (*Journal of Business Ethics Education* 1 (1): 2004) pp. 91–130 for a comprehensive summary of the Andersen/Enron case.

8. McLean, B. and Elkind, P., *The Smartest Guys in the Room: The Amazing Rise and Scandalous Fall of Enron* (Portfolio 2003).

9. www.financialstabilityboard.org/wp-content/uploads/r_130212.pdf.

10. Thomson Reuters Accelus: Conduct Risk Report 2013 (accelus.thomsonreuters.com).

11. www.fca.org.uk/your-fca/documents/fsa-rcro-2011.

12. www.fca.org.uk/your-fca/documents/fca-risk-outlook-2013.

13. The Galleon case attracted widespread media interest, especially in the USA. See the *New York Times* commentary and archival information at http://topics.nytimes.com/top/reference/timestopics/people/r/raj_rajaratnam/index.html for a good summary of the case.

14. Giles, S., *Managing Fraud Risk: A Practical Guide for Directors and Managers* (John Wiley & Sons Ltd. 2012) pp. 65–86.

15. The Guidance on Control can be accessed in the paper 'Two Sides of the Same Coin' at portal. publicpolicy.utoronto.ca/.../OversightRiskControlCCAF.

16. Gallup Inc. (www.gallup.com).

17. Gallup Inc. *State of the American Workforce: Employee Engagement Insights for U.S. Business Leaders* (2013).
18. There have been many articles and reports on the change process at Siemens. See the following for insightful coverage: Dietz, G. and Gillespie, N., *The Recovery of Trust: Case Studies of Organisational Failures and Trust Repair* (Institute of Business Ethics 2012) pp. 8–11.
19. Mr Loscher's interview was 'Our Management Culture Failed' (*Der Spiegel* Magazine December 12 2007).
20. www.bbc.co.uk/news/uk-24289650.
21. www.bbc.co.uk/news/uk-england-23868222.
22. For a good summary of the Snowden case (so far) see: Harding, L., *The Snowden Files: The Inside Story of the World's Most Wanted Man* (Guardian Books 2014).

CHAPTER 5

1. Manchester United (www.manutd.com).
2. The UK Corporate Governance Code is produced by the Financial Reporting Council. The latest version is dated September 2014. The Code can be accessed at www.frc.org.uk.
3. Report of the Committee on the Financial Aspects of Corporate Governance (Gee 1992).
4. See www.soxlaw.com for a comprehensive guide to the Sarbanes–Oxley Act.
5. National Commission on the Causes of the Financial and Economic Crisis in the United States: *The Financial Crisis Inquiry Report* (US Government Edition, January 2011).
6. The Fraud Enforcement and Recovery Act 2009: https://www.congress.gov/111/crpt/srpt10/CRPT-111srpt10.pdf.
7. The Dodd–Frank Wall Street Reform and Consumer Protection Act 2010: www.sec.gov/about/laws/wallstreetreform-cpa.pdf.
8. Financial Reporting Council: 'The UK Corporate Governance Code' (September 2014).
9. Financial Reporting Council: 'The UK Approach to Corporate Governance' (October 2010).
10. Walker, D. 'A review of corporate governance in UK banks and other financial industry entities. Final recommendations' (26 November 2009). A copy of the report may be accessed at: webarchive.nationalarchives.gov.uk/+/.../walker_review_261109.pdf.
11. https://www.fca.org.uk/static/documents/final.../christopher-willford.pdf.
12. Lord Davies of Abersoch 'Women on boards' (February 2011). A copy of the report may be accessed at: https://www.gov.uk/government/.../11-745-women-on-boards.pdf.
13. Lord Davies of Abersoch 'Women on boards: Davies Review Annual Report' (March 2014). A copy of the report may be accessed at: https://www.gov.uk/government/.../bis-women-on-boards-2014.pdf.

CHAPTER 6

1. Northouse, P., *Leadership: Theory and Practice* (Sage 2010).
2. www.businessinsider.com/warren-buffett-hiring-strategy-2014-10.
3. McLean, B. and Elkind, P., *The Smartest Guys in the Room: The Amazing Rise and Scandalous Fall of Enron* (United States of America: Portfolio 2003).
4. www.bbc.co.uk/news/world-europe-25736136.
5. www.bbc.co.uk/news/world-europe-25959740.
6. www.bbc.co.uk/news/business-18258538.

7. The case of Mr Stonecipher and Boeing attracted much media attention in the USA at the time. See the *Washington Post* article on March 8 2005 for a good summary of the case.

8. The Co-operative (www.co-operative.coop).

9. The Co-operative Bank (www.co-operativebank.co.uk).

10. The original article was posted online on 16 November 2013 and appeared in the *Mail on Sunday* newspaper the following day under the headline: 'Crystal meth shame of bank chief: Counting off £20 notes to buy hard drugs, this is the man who ran the Co-op Bank ... three days after telling MPs how it lost £700m (Nick Craven for the *Mail on Sunday* and Ross Slater).

11. www.bbc.co.uk/news/business-22949431.

12. www.bbc.co.uk/news/business-24999781.

13. There was widespread reporting in the UK media of the Rev. Flowers and his background. For a measured summary see www.bbc.co.uk/news/uk-25046413.

14. www.bbc.co.uk/news/business-25637998.

15. www.bbc.co.uk/news/uk-27305701.

16. www.bbc.co.uk/news/business-26525590.

17. www.bbc.co.uk/news/business-26711702.

18. Kelly, C., 'Failings in management and governance: report of the independent review into the events leading to the Co-operative Bank's capital shortfall' (30 April 2014).

19. Myners, P., 'The Co-operative Group: Report of the Independent Governance Review' (7 May 2014).

20. www.bbc.com/news/business-27450295.

21. The Westpac Banking Corporation (www.westpac.com.au).

22. www.bbc.co.uk/news/business-14857354.

23. Knight, J., 'Tylenol's Maker Shows How to Respond to a Crisis' (*Washington Post* 11 October 1982).

24. There was widespread coverage of the horsemeat scandal in the UK media at the time. For a balanced and comprehensive account, see www.bbc.co.uk/news/uk-21335872.

25. www.bbc.co.uk/news/business-22778145.

26. See Jordan-Meier, J., *The Four Stages of Highly Effective Crisis Management: How to Manage the Media in the Digital Age* (CRC Press 2011). Also see the Crisis Intelligence Blog by Melissa Agnes (agnesday.com/blog).

27. Powell, M., 'In 9/11 Chaos, Giuliani Forged a Lasting Image' (*The New York Times* 21 September 2011).

28. There has been extensive media coverage of the BP oil spill and deaths arising from the Macondo well blow-out, as well as a report from the US National Commission investigating the tragedy. See the in-depth archive at the *Financial Times* for a good summary: www.ft.com/indepth/bp-oil-spill.

29. News.sky.com/story/780332/bp-chief-oil-spill-very-modest.

30. www.bbc.co.uk/news/business-11709027 and www.youtube.com.

31. www.bbc.co.uk/news/business-11709027.

CHAPTER 7

1. Bernstein, P., *Against the Gods: The Remarkable Story of Risk* (John Wiley & Sons Ltd 1998).

2. Joint Australia/New Zealand Standards Board, 'Risk Management Standard' (1995).

3. www.bbc.co.uk/news/business-18575932.

4. Financial Reporting Council, 'Guidance for Directors on the Combined Code' (1999, revised 2005, revised again 2014).
5. Financial Reporting Council, 'Guidance on Risk Management, Internal Control and Related Financial and Business Reporting' (September 2014).
6. Committee of Sponsoring Organisations of the Treadway Commission, 'Internal Control – Integrated Framework' (1992).
7. PwC: 'State of Compliance Survey' (2014).
8. Committee of Sponsoring Organisations of the Treadway Commission, 'Internal Control – Integrated Framework' (May 2013).
9. See Giles, S., *Managing Fraud Risk: A Practical Guide for Directors and Managers* (John Wiley & Sons Ltd 2012) for a comprehensive approach to the fraud problem.
10. The Institute of Internal Auditors (www.theiia.org).
11. Chartered Institute of Internal Auditors: 'Financial services code: effective internal audit in the financial services sector' (July 2013).
12. Chartered Institute of Internal Auditors: 'Governance and Risk Report 2013: Internal audit's perspective on the management of risk'.

CHAPTER 8

1. Milton Friedman's article: 'The Social Responsibility of Business is to Increase its Profits' was published in *The New York Times Magazine* in September 1970.
2. Carroll, A., 'The Pyramid of Corporate Social Responsibility: toward the moral management of organizational stakeholders' (*Business Horizons* 34 (4): 1991) pp. 39–48.
3. europa.eu/rapid/press-release_MEMO-11-730_en.htm.
4. United Nations Global Compact (https://www.unglobalcompact.org).
5. See Crane, A. and Matten, D., *Business Ethics: Managing Corporate Citizenship and Sustainability in the Age of Globalisation* (Oxford University Press 2007) pp. 209–213 for a summary of the Shell case.
6. Macalister, T., 'Shell poised to sell four oilfields and a pipeline in Nigeria' (*The Guardian* 27 August 2014).
7. Browne, J., *Beyond Business* (Weidenfield & Nicolson 2010).
8. Kaplan, R. and Norton, D., 'The Balanced Scorecard – Measures that Drive Performance' (*Harvard Business Review* January–February 1992).
9. Brownsell, A., 'Barclays reveals '5Cs' values scorecard in drive for brand transformation' (*Marketing Magazine* February 2014).
10. Financial Reporting Council: 'The UK Corporate Governance Code' (September 2014).
11. McKinsey & Company: 'Our Values' (www.mckinsey.com).
12. The Galleon case attracted widespread media interest, especially in the USA. See the *New York Times* commentary and archival information at http://topics.nytimes.com/top/reference/timestopics/people/r/raj_rajaratnam/index.html for a good summary of the case.
13. Hill, A., 'Inside McKinsey' (*FT Magazine* 25 November 2011).
14. Johnson & Johnson: 'Our Credo Values' (www.jnj.com).
15. Committee on Standards in Public Life: 'Second Report – Local Public Spending Bodies' (Cm 3270-1 May 1996).

16. ASTD: '2012 State of the Industry Report'.
17. Bersin by Deloitte: 'The Corporate Learning Factbook 2013'.
18. Rossouw, D. and Stuckleburger, C, (eds), *Global Survey of Business Ethics: In Training, Teaching and Research* (Globethics Publications 2012).

CHAPTER 9

1. The Whistle-blowing Commission: 'Report on the effectiveness of existing arrangements for workplace whistle-blowing in the UK' (*Public Concern at Work* – November 2013).
2. Ibid.
3. 'Persons of the Year 2002' (*TIME* Magazine 2002).
4. www.bbc.co.uk/news/world-us-canada-19564884.
5. News.bbc.co.uk/onthisday/hi/dates/stories/October/8/.../2626265.stm.
6. van Buitenen, P., '*Blowing the Whistle: One Man's Fight against Fraud in the European Commission*' (Politico's Publishing 2000).
7. Woodford, M., '*Exposure: Inside the Olympus Scandal – How I Went from CEO to Whistleblower*' (Penguin Group 2012).
8. www.bbc.co.uk/news/world-us-canada-23784288.
9. Much has been written about the Edward Snowden case. For a good summary of events and insights into Mr Snowden's actions see Harding, L., *The Snowden Files: The Inside Story of the World's Most Wanted Man* (Guardian Books 2014).
10. G20 Anti-Corruption Action Plan: 'Protection of Whistleblowers – Study on Whistleblower Protection Frameworks, Compendium of Best Practices and Guiding Principles for Legislation' (OECD 2012).
11. 'Global Guide to Whistle-blowing Programmes' (World Law Group 2012).
12. 'Whistle-blowing in Europe: Legal Protection for Whistleblowers in the EU' (Transparency International 2013).
13. The Public Interest Disclosure Act 1998 (www.parliament.uk/briefing-papers/sn00248.pdf).

Index